The
Limits of
Democratization
Climate, Intelligence, and
Resource Distribution

The Limits of Democratization

Climate, Intelligence, and Resource Distribution

Tatu Vanhanen

Washington Summit Publishers
Augusta, Georgia

A National Policy Institute Book
2009

Washington Summit Publishers
P. O. Box 3514
Augusta, GA 30914-3514
Books@WSPublishers.com

Library of Congress Cataloging-in-Publication Data

Vanhanen, Tatu.
  The limits of democratization : climate, intelligence, and resource distribution / Tatu Vanhanen.
      p. cm.
  "A National Policy Institute Book."
  Includes bibliographical references and index.
    ISBN 978-1-59368-032-9 (library binding) -- ISBN 978-1-59368-031-2 (perfect binding)
  1. Democratization. 2. Democracy. I. Title.

JC421.V275 2009
321.8--dc22
                              2008054091

Printed in the United States of America
Typeset in Sabon LT Std font by L. R. Andrews, Inc.

For Anni

My companion and beloved of life

CONTENTS

Appendix 1

Appendix 2

Appendix 3

Appendix 4

List of Illustrations

Figures

Tables

Preface

The problem of this study concerns the persistence of great global differences in the nature of political systems from the perspective of democracy. Many countries have democratized since the 19th century, but the quality of democracy varies significantly, and several countries have remained below the minimum threshold criteria for democracy. Therefore it is reasonable to ask about causal factors of democratization as well as its limits. Can we expect all countries to become democratized and to achieve an approximately similar quality of democracy, or are there some ultimate constraining factors which limit the spread of democracy and maintain significant differences in its quality? These are the central research questions of this study.

In my previous comparative studies of democratization (Vanhanen 1984, 1990, 1997, 2003), I used an evolutionary resource distribution theory of democratization to explain variation in the level of democratization. According to that theory, the distribution of important intellectual and economic power resources is expected to lead to democratization and to support the survival of democracy, whereas the concentration of the same resources in the hands of the few is expected to lead to hegemonic and autocratic systems. However, in my previous studies, I did not attempt to explain why the degree of resource distribution varies so greatly from country to country. Now I come to the problem of the limits of democratization. I try to show that resource distribution is partly dependent on some ultimate causal factors which are not under conscious human control, and therefore, it is not reasonable to expect that the great global differences in the nature of political systems and the quality of democracy will disappear.

In this analysis, I am going to use as my theoretical starting point Montesquieu's idea that climatic conditions affect human nature, and through it, social and political institutions and differences in human conditions. Because differences in climatic conditions have existed from time immemorial and preceded the emergence of our species and all later differences in human conditions, it is justified to regard climate as an ultimate independent factor. The problem is how it could affect resource distribution in human societies and democratization. What are the intervening mechanisms?

I have, in fact, already explored this problem briefly in my 1971 report *Dependence of Power on Resources: A Comparative Study of 114 States in the 1960s.* I referred to Montesquieu's assumption "that temperature, humidity, and some other aspects of physical environment influence human nature as well as social and political institutions" and that "colder climates are favorable for liberty and warmer unfavorable" (Vanhanen 1971: p. 29). The results of empirical analysis indicated that the average annual temperature is negatively related to most political and social variables, as hypothesized, but correlations were weak. The average annual temperature did not explain more than 8 percent of the variation in the "votes 1960–69" variable and 14 percent of the variation in the "index votes 1960–69" variable. It explained more of the variation in social variables used to measure the degree of resource distribution: for example, 27 percent of the variation in the "per capita income" variable and 42 percent of the variation in the "literates" variable.

I came to the conclusion that because only approximately 10 percent of the variation in the nature of political systems is dependent on such an unchangeable environmental factor as temperature, nations "are not deterministically condemned by some unchangeable environmental factors to certain types of political systems, although environmental factors, at least temperature, have some indirect influence" (p. 133). Because of the observed weak correlations, I did not pay attention to the possible impact of climate on democratization in my later studies.

Now I return to this problem because I have found that the direct relationship between temperature and democratization is clearly stronger than my 1971 study indicated, and because the evolved differences in mental abilities of individuals and populations seem to provide an intervening mechanism which strengthens the impact of climatic differences on resource distribution and democratization. Richard Lynn (2006) has explained how race differences in intelligence evolved during the last 100,000 years, when people became adapted to varying climatic conditions outside Africa. People in cold climatic conditions evolved to become somewhat more intelligent than people living in the original tropical Africa, and thus in turn helped people to survive in new and more difficult environmental conditions outside Africa. Later on, these group differences in average intelligence affected contemporary social conditions in such a way that the distribution of intellectual and economic power resources tends to correlate positively with the average intelligence of a nation. Consequently, the average national intelligence (see Lynn and Vanhanen 2002, 2006) is assumed to function as a crucial intervening mechanism between climatic conditions and the variation in resource distribution.

My intention is to explore to what extent it is possible to explain the variation in resource distribution by differences in average national intelligence and in climatic conditions measured by the annual mean temperature. If national intelligence and mean temperature are able to explain a significant part of the variation in resource distribution, it would be reasonable to argue that they constitute the ultimate constraints of democratization and make it highly improbable that we could ever establish and maintain equally democratic systems in all parts of the world. My purpose is to explore to what extent empirical evidence supports these arguments about the ultimate limits of democratization. The study begins with the formulation of theoretical arguments and basic hypotheses, after which empirical variables intended to measure hypothetical concepts will be defined, and hypotheses tested by empirical evidence.

Part I deals with this argument and the evidence for it.

Chapter 1 focuses on theoretical argumentation. The purpose of the chapter is to show why it is reasonable to assume a causal relationship between global climatic (and geographical) differences and human mental abilities (intelligence) and why the evolved human diversity is assumed to have an impact on human conditions, especially on the distribution of intellectual and economic power resources, and through them, on the level of democratization. Finally, three hypotheses are derived from theoretical arguments.

In Chapter 2, operationally defined substitutes for hypothetical concepts are introduced. Empirical variables will be used to measure the level or index of democratization (ID), the degree of resource distribution (index of power resources or IPR), the average national intelligence (national IQ), and the annual mean temperature of countries (MT). The hypothesized causal relations between these variables are discussed. It is assumed that the causal path extends from MT through national IQ and IPR to ID.

In Chapter 3, the research hypotheses are tested on empirical evidence obtained for a group of 172 contemporary countries. The results of correlation analysis show to what extent empirical evidence supports or contradicts the hypotheses. The relative importance of single explanatory factors and the causal path from climatic conditions to the level of democratization is explored on the basis of multiple correlation and multiple regression analyses. The purpose is to find out to what extent the causal path extends from MT through national IQ to IPR and ID. First, climate is hypothesized to affect differences in national IQs. Second, it is expected that national IQ explains a significant part of the variation in IPR, which is assumed to explain a major part of the variation in the level of democratization (ID).

In Chapter 4, regression analysis is used to test the first research hypothesis, on the impact of MT on national IQ at the level of single countries. The purpose is to see how well the average relationship between MT and national IQ predicts the actual values of national IQ in single countries and which countries deviate most from the regression line.

In Chapter 5, regression analysis is used to test the first and second hypotheses, on the impact of MT and national IQ on the distribution of power resources (IPR) at the level of single countries. The purpose is to see how well the average relationships between MT and IPR and between national IQ and IPR predict the actual values of IPR for single countries, and which countries deviate most clearly from the regression lines.

In Chapter 6, regression analysis is used to test the third hypothesis, on the impact of IPR on the level of democratization (ID-2006) at the level of single countries. It is interesting to see in which countries the level of democratization is approximately in balance with the degree of resource distribution and which countries deviate clearly from the hypothesized relationship. Attention is focused on the most deviant countries because they contradict the hypothesis. Each deviant country will be briefly discussed to find out what particular factors might explain its deviating position.

In Chapter 7, direct relationships between the two ultimate explanatory factors—mean temperature (MT) and national IQ—and the level of democratization (ID-2006) will be analyzed at the level of single countries. The purpose is to see to what extent their relationships with ID-2006 overlap with the relationship between IPR and ID-2006. The purpose of these analyses is to show that the causal roots of democratization can be traced not only to the degree of resource distribution (IPR) but also to national IQ and MT, which constitute the two ultimate constraining factors of democratization.

In Chapter 8, I will compare the quality of democracy at different levels of national IQ. For this purpose, the 172 countries of this study are classified into seven national IQ categories. The hypothesis is that the quality of democracy rises with the level of national IQ no matter what variable is used to measure the quality of democracy. The hypothesis is tested by using 13 different variables which measure, at least to some extent, the quality of democracy from different perspectives. The purpose is to show that there is a persistent positive correlation between the level of national IQ and the quality of democracy, although many countries may deviate from this average pattern at all levels of national IQ.

Part II deals with descriptive reviews by country and the conclusions reached by this study.

In Chapters 9–16, differences in the quality of democracy between the seven national IQ categories will be described at the level of single countries and explanations given. These data are consolidated and charted in chapter 17

In Chapter 18, the results of empirical analyses are summarized and conclusions on the limits of democratization are discussed. A central conclusion is that it is probably never possible to achieve the same level and quality of democracy in all countries of the world because of the impact of the two ultimate constraining factors (MT and national IQ), which are outside conscious human control. We should learn to accept the fact that because of the evolved human diversity, we are bound to live in a world of many types of differences and inequalities. Four appendices complement the eighteen chapters with detailed data on variables.

Acknowledgments

This book is based on the foundation of my previous studies of democratization since the 1970s. I am grateful to many colleagues and researchers who helped me by their critique, comments, and advice during the past decades. I had an opportunity to introduce the idea of this new research project at the 2004 APSA Annual Meeting in Chicago, Panel 45, in which I presented my paper "Climate and Democracy." I want to thank the discussant Karen L. Remmer for her highly critical comments and especially a participant Zheng-Xu Wang for his more positive attitude, which encouraged me to continue this project. Another paper, "Limits of Democratization," I presented on this research project at the 2007 APSA Annual Meeting in Chicago, APLS Roundtable on Biopolicy. I thank particularly the panel's chair Donald Tannenbaum for his comments.

Finally, I want to express my gratitude to the publisher, Louis R. Andrews, who kindly accepted the manuscript for publication and whose help was crucial in the publication of this book and I am grateful to the copy editor Sarah Forman for the significant improvement of the texts.

PART I

The Argument and the Evidence

CHAPTER 1

Theoretical Arguments

Political systems vary greatly from the perspective of democracy. They range from stabilized democracies, in which people can elect and remove their rulers by free and honest elections, to autocracies, in which people do not have any legal opportunities to elect or dismiss their rulers. In democracies, people are relatively free to express their opinions, to establish associations to pursue their ideological or economic interests, and to select their way of life. In autocracies, freedoms are more strictly limited; people are not allowed to establish independent political or other interest organizations, and in extreme cases they are suppressed, jailed, and even killed arbitrarily. So democracy matters. In autocracies, many people dream of freedom and democracy and they are willing to struggle for political rights and liberties, but the fact is that all nations have not been able to establish democratic political systems; in many countries the established democratic institutions have more or less failed, or the quality of democracy has remained much less than expected. Why? That is the problem. First of all, why do countries differ so greatly in the degree and quality of democracy? And second, where do the ultimate causal roots of this differentiation lie, and hence of the limits of democratization?

Philosophers and social scientists have provided various answers to the first question since the days of Aristotle. Some of these answers have been reviewed in my previous studies (see Vanhanen 1979, 1984,

1990, 1997, 2003). My own explanation is based on the evolutionary resource distribution theory of democratization, according to which the variation in the level of democratization is causally related to the differences in resource distribution within societies. Such an explanation is derived from a Darwinian interpretation of politics, according to which politics is a forum where the general struggle for existence and scarce resources takes place. In this struggle, we have evolved to resort to all available resources. Consequently, it is reasonable to hypothesize that political power tends to become distributed among the many in societies in which important power resources are widely distributed, and that it tends to become concentrated in the hands of the few in societies in which relevant power resources are highly concentrated. This regularity is assumed to explain the variation of political systems from democracies to autocracies. In my latest study (Vanhanen 2003), the index of power resources (IPR) explained 72 percent of the global variation in the Index of Democratization (ID–2001) in a group of 170 contemporary countries. This finding represents a quite satisfactory level of explanation.

Thus my answer to the first question is that countries differ in their degree of democratization because there is significant variation in the extent to which important economic, intellectual, and other power resources are distributed among the many or concentrated in the hands of the few. The Darwinian interpretation of politics formulated in the same book explains why this must be so. I do not have anything to add to the explanation given in my previous studies, but it should be noted that I have not explained why power resources are much more widely distributed in some countries than in others. In short, my explanation of democratization does not answer the second question concerning the roots of differences in the degree of resource distribution: Where do the ultimate roots of differences in resource distribution lie and thence in the level of democratization? That is the principal question I try to tackle in this study.

I think that we should seek an answer to the second question from among the factors which clearly preceded contemporary social conditions and political systems. What might such factors be? It is evident that differences in geographical and climatic conditions preceded the emergence of contemporary societies, social structures, and political institutions. Therefore, it is justified to assume that some causal paths lead from differences in geographical and climatic conditions. But how?

Montesquieu's idea

Montesquieu (1748, 1989) was the first to pay serious attention to the impact of climate on human nature, and thence on political and other human conditions. He argued that many variations in human conditions can be traced to great differences in geographical and climatic conditions in the world. He assumed that temperature influences the human body and the mind and passions of people, and that consequently there are many differences in people's mores, manners, and characteristics between hot and cold climates. He assumed that such differences in human nature are reflected in social and political institutions. Montesquieu, for example, argued that people are more vigorous, self-confident, and courageous in cold climates than in hot climates and that people in cold countries also tend to be freer than in hot countries. This argument implies a connection between the level of democracy and differences in climatic conditions.

It may be that Montesquieu exaggerated the effects of climate on human nature. Differences in human characteristics between cold and hot climates may not be so extreme as Montesquieu assumed, since all human populations belong to the same species, and since genetic differences between populations are relatively small, although there are measurable genetic differences between geographical populations (see Cavalli-Sforza et al. 1996; Wells 2003). The existence of genetic differences between populations implies that populations may differ not only in their physical features but also in their mental abilities and behavioral characteristics (cf. Rushton 1995, 2003; Jensen 1998; Lynn 2006). Thus Montesquieu's basic idea is still valid; he urges us to seek the roots of differences in human conditions in climatic and related geographical factors, although, of course, many more proximate environmental and social factors may also influence human conditions.

Contemporary research has disclosed the existence of some genetic differences between geographical populations. To some extent, such differences seem to be related to temperature—to the hot and cold climates—as Montesquieu assumed. My basic idea is that human populations have adapted to varying climatic and other environmental conditions through evolution by natural selection and, as a consequence, have evolved differently to some extent. The observable human diversity concerns both morphological characteristics and mental abilities, and probably also some behavioral dispositions. Climate is the most conspicuous environmental factor that varies greatly in different geographical parts of the world. It is plausible to assume that because the survival of people in different climatic conditions required to some extent different mental abilities, people in more difficult climatic conditions evolved to have somewhat more complex mental abilities than people in less difficult climatic conditions.

It should be noted that I do not assume, nor did Montesquieu, that there is a direct causal relationship between temperature and human social and political institutions. There are intervening mechanisms which mediate the impact of temperature on social and political institutions. Montesquieu indicated the existence of such mechanisms, arguing that temperature and other climatic conditions affect human nature, and thence social and political institutions. I assume that differences in the average cognitive abilities of populations constitute the most important intervening mechanism between climatic conditions (temperature) and resource distribution. So my theoretical argument is that the great variation in the level of democratization can be traced causally first to the variation in the distribution of important power resources, further to the variation in the average mental abilities of nations, and finally to the variation in climatic conditions. It is possible to test this theoretical argumentation by empirical evidence if we find suitable operationally defined measures of democracy, resource distribution, average mental abilities of nations, and climatic conditions.

Because I assume that the impact of climate on the degree of resource distribution and democratization takes place through the mental abilities of nations, we have to start by exploring how to measure differences in the average mental abilities of nations and how to explain the emergence of those differences.

Mental abilities of nations measured by national IQ

People have always been conscious that individuals differ from each other in many respects, not only in morphological characteristics, health, and physical strength, but also in personal characteristics, skills, and mental abilities. It has been difficult to agree, however, on the causes of such differences and to measure them, especially differences in mental abilities, including intelligence. From the perspective of this study, intelligence is the most important aspect of mental abilities. Intelligence can be assumed to be causally related to resource distribution in such a way that economic and intellectual power resources tend to become more widely distributed in countries in which the average intelligence of the population is high than in countries in which it is low.

Intelligence has been measured by intelligence tests since 1905. The results of measurements are quantified by the intelligence quotient (IQ). Measurements are based on the idea that intelligence is largely a single entity. Charles Spearman showed in the beginning of the 20th century that all cognitive abilities are positively intercorrelated. He invented the statistical method of factor analysis to show that the efficiency of performance on all cognitive tasks is partly determined by a common factor, which he designated g for "general intelligence." There are a number of specific abilities in addition to g, but all are related to that single general factor. We cannot measure g directly, but the scores obtained from intelligence tests and expressed as IQs are approximate measures of g (Lynn and Vanhanen 2002, pp. 20–21, 2006, pp. 29–31; cf. Jensen 1998, pp. 73–91; Lynn 2006).

Ever since the publication of Charles Spearman's seminal writings on intelligence, "the almost universally accepted assumption among many psychologists, educators, and even popular writers has been that there does indeed exist a single general factor of intelligence" and that there are individual differences in intelligence (Carroll 2003, p. 5). It has also become generally accepted that individual differences in IQ scores are substantially due to genetic differences. Robert Plomin notes that the "case for substantial genetic influence on g is stronger than for any other human characteristic." According to him, all "the data converge on the conclusion that the heritability of 'g' is about 50%; that is, genes account for about half of the variance in 'g' scores" (Plomin 2003, pp. 107–108).

Arthur R. Jensen says about the heritability of intelligence: "The broad heritability of IQ is about 0.40 to 0.50 when measured in children, about 0.60 to 0.70 in adolescents and young adults, and approaches 0.80 in later maturity" (Jensen 1998, p. 169). Jensen emphasizes that "the heritability of g increases throughout development and the importance of shared environmental factors that make family members similar decreases" (Plomin 2003, p. 109; cf. Jensen 1998, pp. 169–197). J. Philippe Rushton (2003, p. 167) argues that the general factor g is a product of human evolution and that "massive evidence indicates that g is related to the size and functioning of the brain."

Richard Lynn (2006, pp. 3–4) notes that there "is a widespread consensus that intelligence is a unitary construct that determines the efficiency of problem solving, learning, and remembering." He refers to Linda S. Gottfredson's definition of intelligence published in the *Wall Street Journal* in 1997:

> Intelligence is a very general mental capacity which, among other things, involves the ability to reason, plan, solve problems, think abstractly, comprehend complex ideas, learn quickly and learn from experience. It is not merely book learning, a narrow academic skill, or test taking smarts. Rather, it reflects a broader and deeper capability for comprehending our surroundings—"catching on," "making sense" of things, or "figuring out" what to do (Gottfredson 1997, p. 13).

Of course, there are researchers who deny the existence of intelligence differences, or at least the idea that such differences and especially the existence of intelligence differences between racial groups are substantially due to genetic differences (for the debate about intelligence differences, see, for example, Gould 1981; Rose et al. 1984; Herrnstein and Murray 1994; Jacoby and Glauberman 1995; Nyborg 2003b; Rindermann 2007).

Richard Lynn and Tatu Vanhanen have in their recent books *IQ and the Wealth of Nations* (2002) and *IQ and Global Inequality* (2006) measured differences in the average mental abilities of nations by national IQ. In this study, my intention is to use those data on national IQ to indicate differences in the average mental abilities of nations. National IQ is assumed to function as an intervening mechanism between climatic conditions (principally temperature) and the degree of resource distribution.

The impact of climate on human diversity and intelligence

It is reasonable to argue that human diversity at the level of populations emerged as a consequence of the adaptation of human populations to greatly varying climatic conditions during the evolutionary history of our species. The fact is that contemporary human populations live in greatly varying climatic conditions and that there are evolved genetic differences between geographical populations (see

Ritter 1981; Jones 1992a; Cavalli-Sforza et al. 1996, Oppenheimer 2003; Wells 2003; Wade 2006). Because various morphological differences between human populations are based on their genetic differences, it is justified to assume that there are also evolved differences in the mental abilities of populations, including differences in the average intelligence between geographical populations, racial groups, and nations. It is highly improbable that mental abilities of all human populations have remained the same, although populations as a consequence of evolution by natural selection differ genetically from each other in many other respects.

Jensen was the first to pay scientifically grounded attention to intelligence differences between "whites" and "blacks" in the United States in his 1969 article "How Much Can We Boost I.Q. and Scholastic Achievement?" (Nyborg 2003a, pp. xiv–xv). He argued that this difference and other intelligence differences between racial groups are substantially due to genetic differences (g) between populations. Jensen (1998: 419–530) emphasizes that races should not be regarded as discrete, mutually exclusive categories. According to his definition, races are "breeding populations that differ from one another in gene frequencies and that vary in a number of intercorrelated visible features that are highly heritable." Lynn presents a similar definition of race:

> a race is a breeding population that is to some degree genetically different from neighboring populations as a result of geographical isolation, cultural factors, and endogamy, and which shows observable patterns of genotypic frequency differences for a number of intercorrelated, genetically determined characteristics, compared with other breeding populations. (Lynn 2006, p. 7)

In this study, I use the term "race" in the same sense. Rushton (1995) emphasizes that racial differences extend to many types of behavioral differences between the three main racial groups, Negroids, Caucasoids, and Mongoloids. Despite extensive evidence, some researchers still believe that there cannot be any differences between populations in their intelligence. Anthony Giddens (1995, p. 442) argues that differences "in average IQ scores between blacks and whites are almost certainly the results of social and cultural influences, not of differences in genetic inheritance." Steve Olson (2002, pp. 62–63) claims: "People are too genetically similar to have developed the kinds of intelligence differences cited by hereditarians" (see also Jared Diamond 1998, pp. 18–22;

Brody 2003). Jensen notes that given "the variation in allele frequencies between populations for virtually every known polymorphic gene, it is exceedingly improbable that populations do not differ in the alleles that affect the structural and functional basis of heritable behavioral traits" (Jensen 1998, p. 433). I agree with this argument. There are enough evolved allele differences to provide material basis for intelligence differences both between individuals and between populations.

Richard Lynn (1991a, 1991b, 1997, 2003, 2006) has extensively studied geographical variation in intelligence. He argues that differences in IQ "must have developed together with differences in skin color, morphology and resistance to diseases as adaptations to the environment in which the races evolved" (Lynn 2003, p. 141). Climatic differences have had crucial significance. According to his explanation, *Homo sapiens* (modern humans) appeared about 150,000 years ago in equatorial Africa. They began to migrate into other regions of the world approximately 100,000 years ago, and they had colonized most of the globe by around 30,000 years ago.

Lynn argues that when people migrated from tropical and subtropical Africa into North Africa, Asia, Europe, and America, they faced the problem of survival during the winter and spring in temperate and cold climates. They had to learn to hunt large animals for food, to keep themselves warm, to build shelters, and to make fires and clothing. Temperate and cold climates exerted selection pressure for higher intelligence: "The colder the winters the stronger this selection pressure would have been and the higher the intelligence that evolved." This explains the broad association between the coldness of winter temperatures and the intelligence of the races (Lynn 2006, pp. 205–209).

Lynn describes the evolution of racial groups—Africans, Bushmen, South Asians and North Africans, Southeast Asians, Pacific Islanders, Australian Aborigines, Europeans, East Asians, Arctic peoples, and Native Americans—and explains how race differences in intelligence evolved during the last 100,000 years when human populations became adapted to different climatic and other environmental conditions. The last ice age began about 28,000 years ago and lasted until around 10,000 years ago. It made survival more difficult and exerted further selection pressure for enhanced intelligence. He estimates that this selection pressure was sufficient to raise the IQ of the South Asians and North Africans to the present-day level of about 84. The Native Americans' IQ is only slightly higher (86). They migrated into America before the onset of the last ice age. Climatic conditions were more severe in Europe and even more severe in North East Asia, and consequently the IQs of the Europeans rose to 99 and the IQs of East Asians up to the present-day level of 105 (Lynn 2006, pp. 223–244; see also Lynn 2007).

It should be noted that researchers are not quite sure when modern humans migrated out of Africa. Stephen Oppenheimer (2003) estimates that the successful migration out of Africa took place approximately 80,000 years ago. Spencer Wells (2003) argues that it occurred only 50,000 years ago. Nicholas Wade (2006) also assumes that the successful migration out of Africa took place approximately 50,000 years ago. He estimates that the departing group was very small, perhaps just 150 people. This disagreement about the time of out of Africa migration does not affect Lynn's argumentation, for he assumes that the most important differences in intelligence between racial groups evolved during the last 50,000 years.

J. Philippe Rushton (1995, 2000) presents similar arguments about the evolution of racial differentiation as a consequence of migrations and adaptation to different climatic conditions. The first split took place about 100,000 years ago between groups that remained in Africa and those who left. The next major split took place about 40,000 years ago when the group that had left Africa divided once again, into the ancestors of today's Whites and Orientals. The Caucasoid and Mongoloid peoples "were subjected to pressures for improved intelligence to deal with the problems of survival in the cold northern latitudes" (Rushton 1995, p. 228).

Rushton explains that obtaining food and keeping warm was much more difficult in the cold northern latitudes than in tropical Africa. Peoples in tropical and subtropical latitudes were largely gatherers, whereas in the cold climatic conditions they had to hunt and fish. For hunting and fishing purposes they had to learn to manufacture a variety of tools from stone, wood, and bones. They needed also a variety of sophisticated cutting and skinning tools. They had to solve the problems of making fires, clothes, and shelters in order to keep warm. Clothing and shelters were unnecessary in sub-Saharan Africa.

These differences in climatic conditions explain why natural selection improved general intelligence in the northern latitudes. Rushton shows that evolved differences between major racial groups are not limited to intelligence. There are also several morphological and behavioral differences. The brain size of Caucasoids and Mongoloids is larger than that of Negroids (cf. Lynn 2006, pp. 205–222). There are also race differences in r–K strategies, which differences are reflected in some biological and behavioral characteristics.

Jensen (1998) refers to climate as the most important causal factor behind racial differences in mental abilities. He notes that racial differences are a product of the evolutionary process working on the human genome, which consists of about 100,000 polymorphic genes. The extent of genetic distance "between separated populations provides an approximate measure of the amount of time since their separation and of the geographical distance between them" (p. 424). He continues that the "environmental forces that contributed to the differentiation of major populations and their gene pools through natural selection were mainly climatic" (p. 435). Extreme seasonal changes and the cold climate of the northern regions demanded more complex mental abilities than the hot climate of the sub-Saharan Africa. In the cold northern climate people needed "the ingenuity and skills for constructing more permanent and sturdy dwellings and designing substantial clothing to protect against the elements."

This selection pressure markedly intensified during the last glaciation, which occurred approximately 30,000 to 10,000 years ago. During this long period, "the north Eurasian winters were far more severe than they have ever been for over 10,000 years" (p. 436). Climate also influenced the evolution of brain size differences between the major races. They are related to IQ differences. Jensen comes to the conclusion: "It is exceedingly improbable that racial populations, which are known to differ, on average, in a host of genetically conditioned physical characteristics, would not differ in any of the brain characteristics associated with cognitive abilities, when half of all segregating genes in the human genome are involved with the brain" (p. 445; see also Itzkoff 2000).

Cavalli-Sforza et al. (1996) have analyzed the genetic history of world populations by calculating genetic distances between geographical populations on the basis of gene frequencies. Their interest is limited to aboriginal populations, which are defined as those already living in the area of study in A.D. 1492. According to their findings, there are clear geographical differences in gene frequencies. The first split took place between Africans and non-Africans, with the exception of Berbers in North Africa, who join the Caucasoid cluster. Consequently, the greatest genetic difference within the human species is between Africans and non-Africans.

Later on, the peoples that migrated out of Africa became separated into several clusters. One partition separates Caucasoids from all Asian, Oceanian, and Amerindian populations, and another partition separates New Guineans and Australians from all other non-African populations. They found nine major clusters: Africans (sub-Saharan), Caucasoids (European), Caucasoids (extra-European), Northern Mongoloids (excluding Arctic populations), Northeast Asian Arctic populations, Southern Mongoloids (mainland and insular Southeast Asia), New Guineans plus Australians, inhabitants of minor Pacific islands, and Amerinds. There are clear genetic distances between all of these clusters, although, of course, all "population clusters overlap when single genes are considered, and in almost all populations, all alleles are present but in different frequencies."

Cavalli-Sforza (1996) note that the cluster formed by Caucasoids, northern Mongoloids, and Amerinds is reasonably compact in all analyses, whereas there are uncertainties concerning the similarities between Southeast Asians and Australians plus New Guineans (pp. 29, 73–83). It should be noted that their main purpose was to calculate differences in gene frequencies between population clusters, not to explain differences in human characteristics, including mental abilities. However, they pay attention to correlations between gene frequencies and climate and latitude. They found that some individually tested genes were correlated with distance from the equator, indicating a climatic effect. So their results to some extent support the assumption about the impact of climate on human diversity. As an example they refer to skin color, on which climate acts in many ways, and they assume that, as a consequence of the migration of farmers from the Middle East to Northern Europe, the white skin color of Northern Europeans evolved in the last 5,000 years from a light-brown color characteristic of Caucasoids from West Asia and North Africa (pp. 142–145).

Steve Olson (2002) describes in detail the human migration from Africa to other parts of the world and the divergence of modern humans, but he pays only little attention to the impact of climatic differences. He argues that the climate was an important factor that contributed to the cultural efflorescence of Stone Age Europe. The summers were warm, but the winters were brutal. He admits that such a climate "must have posed severe challenges to modern humans, whose long limbs are more adapted to the warmth of the tropics." These challenges intensified during the height of the Ice Age, between about 20,000 and 16,000 years ago, when the weather became even colder, and "glaciers pushed south until they were within a hundred miles of modern-day Stonehenge, Amsterdam, and Moscow." He assumes that Europeans responded to these challenges by retreating into the warmer areas around the Pyrenees and the Balkans and north of the Black Sea (Olson 2002, pp. 161–162). According to Olson, the cold northern climate had an impact on the culture of Europeans, but not any impact on their mental abilities.

However, he admits that there is a relationship between skin color and climate. Dark skin is a great advantage in equatorial regions because it is less susceptible to damage by the sun's ultraviolet rays. Because dark skin can be a liability in parts of the world where sunlight is less intense, the skin color, through beneficial mutations, became lighter among the people in the north (pp. 40–41). Otherwise, Olson believes, people remained similar in all parts of the world despite enormous differences in climatic and other environmental conditions. He emphasizes that there cannot be any group differences in genetic capabilities of people, particularly not in IQ scores; the mental abilities of peoples have not changed since they migrated from Africa (Olson 2002, pp. 60–63). It is a really strange argument that there cannot be any differences in the mental abilities and intelligence of populations, although it is an established fact that there are genetic differences between populations which affect their other characteristics.

Stephen Oppenheimer (2003) provides an excellent description on the peopling of the world in his book Out of Eden, but he does not say anything about the impact of climatic conditions on the mental abilities of populations, although he pays attention to evolved physical differences between racial groups and connects some of these differences to climate. The racial terms used by him are Africans, Negritos, Caucasoids, Australoids, Melanesians, Southern Mongoloids, and Northern Mongoloids. Spencer Wells (2003) avoids saying anything about the impact of climatic differences on human mental abilities.

W.W. Howells (1992) analyzes the dispersion of modern humans and pays attention to many physical differences and genetic distances between Caucasoids, Negroids, Mongoloids, and Australoids, but he does not say anything on the impact of climatic differences on the mental abilities of geographical populations (see also Jones 1992a). Steve Jones (1992b) argues that most physical differences between geographical populations are connected with climate. He notes, for example, that most "tropical peoples have slim bodies and long limbs, whereas those from colder climates are more compact" (p. 284). His analysis is limited to the impact of climate on physical differences between tropical peoples and those from colder climates.

Philip M. Parker's book *Physioeconomics* (2000) is highly interesting from the perspective of this study. He refers to Montesquieu and argues that the closer a country is to the equator, the more likely it will have lower than average consumption per capita. Montesquieu "correctly predicted the higher levels of economic development of temperate countries (e.g. northern Europe) than warmer countries (southern Europe), versus hotter countries (India and Africa)" (p. 25). Parker notes that when "a single exogenous variable, in this case a country's absolute latitude, explains up to 70 percent of the cross-country variances in income per capita, some explanation is required" (pp. 2–3). He explains this equatorial paradox by certain physics-based physiological mechanisms.

His basic argument is that man is a species of tropical mammal and that there is "a limited degree to which human anatomic physiological mechanisms can adjust to nontropical conditions" (p. 116). Man can maintain body temperature in hot climates without difficulty, whereas he has to have artificial means of insulation in cold climates. Consequently, in cold climates people had to invent various means (including shelters and warm clothes) to create a "comfortable" or "tropical" environment: "The farther the environment deviates from our tropically evolved set point, the laws of physics require that the more compensation be made to a thermally comfortable zone" (pp. 120–121). Thus inventions and technologies were driven by the need to maintain physiologically comfortable body temperature.

Such an adaptation was most important for those living farthest from the tropics with the greatest seasonal variation. The body strives for homeostasis or comfort, which is defined as the maintenance of a body's constant state, within narrow limits (pp. 122–132). According to Parker's interpretation, this body's striving for homeostasis explains why most technological inventions have been made in the northern latitudes and why the level of economic development correlates with latitude. Parker does not pay any attention to climate's impact on the diversification of human mental abilities, but his findings do not contradict the hypothesis that differences in national IQs are causally related to differences in climatic conditions, principally in temperature (cf. Kanazawa 2007).

Nearly all researchers agree that there are significant evolved genetic differences between geographical populations or major racial groups and that these differences are related to climatic conditions, but it has been much more difficult to agree on the significance and nature of human diversity. Some researchers tend to limit the effects of genetic diversity to physical characteristics, especially to skin color, whereas some others emphasize that there are also differences in the average mental abilities of populations and that these differences are partly based on genetic differences between populations. Olson (2002) emphasizes the genetic unity of the human species and limits the impact of climate on skin color. He denies the existence of any significant differences in the mental abilities of populations. Cavalli-Sforza et al. (1996) measure genetic distances between populations, but they do not present any assumptions about the impact of genetic differences on mental abilities or behavioral traits of populations. Oppenheimer (2003) recognizes the impact of genetic differences on physical characteristics of major racial groups. Parker (2000) emphasizes the crucial importance of climatic differences and notes the strong connection between latitude and the level of economic development. Lynn, Jensen, and Rushton argue that human adaptation to varying climatic conditions led to the enhancement of intelligence and other mental abilities in the regions of cold climate. Their arguments about the impact of climate on intelligence are in harmony with Montesquieu's idea.

I think that the adaptation of a "tropical animal" to colder environmental conditions caused strong selection pressure for enhanced intelligence.

Hypotheses to be tested

Montesquieu's idea about the impact of climate on human nature and through human nature on social and political institutions and conditions leads me to argue that it is possible to trace the roots of democratization to climatic conditions, principally to differences in annual mean temperature. The problem is how to connect differences in climatic and geographical circumstances to differences in human conditions. What are the intervening mechanisms? I think that there are two intervening mechanisms in the causal path from climate to democracy: differences in the average intelligence of populations and differences in the degree of resource distribution within societies. The survival in cold climates presupposed more intelligence and other mental abilities than the survival in tropical climates. As a consequence, the average intelligence of populations is expected to vary in such a way that populations adapted to survive in cold climates tend to be somewhat more intelligent than populations adapted to life in tropical climates. The national IQ variable is intended to measure national differences in average intelligence (Lynn and Vanhanen 2002, 2006). Further, because all people tend to use all of their abilities, including intelligence, in the continual struggle for scarce resources, it is plausible to assume that important resources become more widely distributed in countries where the population's average intelligence is relatively high than in countries where it is low. In this way my theoretical argumentation connects differences in climatic conditions to differences in resource distribution via one crucial intervening variable measuring differences in the average mental abilities of nations.

Thus my theoretical argument is that differences in the level of democratization can be causally traced first to the variation in the distribution of important power resources, further to the variation in the average mental abilities of nations, and finally to the variation in climatic conditions. There are four variables: the level of democratization (ID), the index of power resources (IPR), the variation of mental abilities of nations (national IQ), and the variation in climatic conditions (annual mean temperature, MT). It is possible to test the theoretical argument on the causal path from climate to democracy by empirical evidence on these four variables.

It is justified to assume that temporal sequence determines the causal relationships between these four variables. The cause must precede the effect (see Manheim and Rich 1986, p. 22). It is obvious that differences in climatic and other geographical conditions have temporally preceded the characteristics of the three other variables and that differences in national IQs have preceded contemporary social and political conditions measured by IPR and ID. It is also justified to assume that in the relationship between resource distribution (IPR) and the level of democratization (ID) IPR is a more independent variable than ID, although their relationship may be partly interactive. The assumption about the causal priority of resource distribution is based on the fact that it is much more difficult to change most of the conditions measured by IPR than to change a country's political institutions. Differences in resource distribution have nearly always preceded significant changes in political systems (cf. Vanhanen 2003, pp. 101–102). Briefly stated, the relation of cause and effect can be assumed to extend from MT to national IQ and further from national IQ to IPR and from IPR to ID. MT is the independent factor in its relation to IQ, IPR, and ID, which are dependent variables in this relationship. National IQ is the independent variable in its relation to IPR and ID, whereas in its relation to MT it is a dependent variable. IPR is the independent variable in its relation to ID, but in its relation to national IQ and MT it is a dependent variable. Finally, ID is the dependent variable in its relation to the other three variables.

This kind of causal argumentation leads to the following three hypotheses about the causal roots of differences in resource distribution (IPR) and in the level of democratization (ID):

1. The higher the annual mean temperature (MT) of a country, the lower the values of national IQ, the Index of Power Resources (IPR), and the Index of Democratization (ID).

2. The higher the average intelligence of a nation (national IQ), the more widely power resources (IPR) are distributed and the higher the level of democratization (ID) in a country.

3. The higher the degree of resource distribution (IPR), the higher the level of democratization in a country.

The third hypothesis has already been tested several times by empirical evidence in my previous studies (Vanhanen 1984, 1990, 1997, 2003). In this study, I extend the causal analysis by attempting to explore to what extent differences in the distribution of power resources (IPR), and through it in the level of democratization (ID), can be traced to differences in average mental abilities of nations (national IQ) and ultimately to differences in climatic and other geographical conditions. I assume that the ultimate limits of democratization are in those factors which are nearly completely outside conscious human control, and that, therefore it will never be possible to achieve the same level and quality of democracy throughout the world.

CHAPTER 2

Empirical Variables

Before we start to test the hypotheses formulated in Chapter 1, it is necessary to define the four variables which are intended to measure the variation in climatic conditions (mean temperature), mental abilities of populations (national IQ), degree of resource distribution (IPR), and level of democratization (ID). It is also necessary to discuss the availability and quality of data on these variables. Let us start from the measures of climate, which is assumed to be the ultimate causal factor.

Annual mean temperature (MT)

People have observed the great variation in climatic conditions since time immemorial. Climatic conditions vary not only by temperature but also by other atmospheric variables, including relative humidity, sunshine duration, amount of precipitation (rain), wind, and air pressure. My attention is focused on a country's annual mean temperature because it is assumed that the evolved differences in mental abilities of populations are principally due to selection pressures in cold climatic conditions.

What kind of data are available on annual mean temperatures? The thermometer invented by Galileo in 1593 made it possible to measure temperature differences. Systematic temperature measurements have been carried out in some places since the 17th century and more extensively since the 19th century (see *Encyclopedia International*,

Vol. 11, 1964, p. 569). The International Meteorological Organization (IMO) was established in 1878 to coordinate the collection of meteorological data from different parts of the world. It was replaced by the World Meteorological Organization (WMO) in 1951. The WMO is a United Nations specialized agency that facilitates worldwide cooperation in the establishment of meteorological observation stations, collects climatological data, and ensures the uniform publication of observations and statistics (see Banks et al. 2007, pp. 1612–14). The WMO has published "climatological normals" for 1931–1960 and 1961–1990. "Climatological normals" are defined as "period averages computed for a uniform and relatively long periods comprising at least three consecutive ten-year periods" (WMO No. 847, Foreword).

I collected data on mean temperatures from the World Meteorological Organization's Climatological Normals (CLINO) for 1961–1990 (WMO No. 847). This publication provides statistical data from nearly 4,000 stations in more than 130 countries. In addition to mean temperature, this source provides data on 12 other climatological elements, but data on all the elements are not available for each station. Mean temperature is given in degrees Celsius (°C) and tenths. All data concern single observation stations by regions, and within regions by countries. The tables contain monthly and annual normals of the elements. Usually they represent 30-year averages of the monthly and annual values obtained during the period. The annual normals are the mean of the monthly normals. So in the case of each station, the data on mean temperature contain 30-year (1961–1990) averages for each of the 12 months and the mean of the 12 monthly normals. The number of stations varies greatly from country to country, from one station in several countries to 303 stations in the United States and 703 stations in New Zealand. The data on mean temperature are available from 125 countries (WMO No. 847, pp. ix–xiii).

The problem is how to calculate the mean temperature for a country on the basis of data concerning single observation stations. As far as I know, such calculations have not been done or published, although many sources include general information about climates by countries. *Philip's Encyclopedic World Atlas* (2000), for example, describes the climatic characteristics of each country and provides information about average monthly temperatures and the amount of precipitation. Data on average monthly temperatures usually concern the capital city or some other cities. The CIA's *World Factbook* (2000) briefly describes the climate of each country with terms such as tropical, hot, humid, temperate, cold, subarctic, and informs also about seasonal variations. The *Europa World Year Book* (2003) provides information about the climate of each country in general terms but also gives data on average monthly temperatures, usually the monthly maximum and minimum temperatures in the capital city.

Because temperature may vary considerably from season to season and in different parts of a country, especially in mountainous countries and geographically large countries, it is problematic to speak of the mean temperature of a country. Therefore, the World Meteorological Organization has never calculated "mean temperatures" for countries. Because it would not be possible to test the hypotheses of this study without an operationalized measure of climatic conditions, I decided to solve the problem by calculating the mean of the annual normals of all the observation stations of a country. So the annual mean temperature of Finland, for example, is the mean of annual normals of 12 observation stations, and that for Japan is the mean of 158 observation stations. The annual mean temperatures calculated for countries in this way are artificial, but I assume that they satisfactorily measure relative temperature differences between countries. The data are most reliable for countries in which temperature is approximately the same in all parts of the country. The annual mean temperatures are much more problematic and artificial for countries which contain highly different climatic zones. However, if observation stations cover all types of climatic zones, the mean of all stations represents some kind of average temperature of the country.

Because the World Meteorological Organization's Climatological Normals (CLINO) for the period 1961–1990 (WMO No. 847) does not provide data on mean temperature from all countries in this study, I had to complement the available data with data from other sources. For more than 20 countries, data on mean temperatures are from WMO's Climatological Normals (CLINO) for the period 1931–1960 (1971). *World Weather Records 1971–1980* (1991–94), published by the U.S. Department of Commerce, National Oceanic and Atmospheric Administration, provides data on several other countries. All data on annual mean temperatures (AMT), number of stations, and periods of observation are presented and documented in Appendix 1.

The Climatic Research Unit, Tyndall Centre for Climate Change Research, University of East Anglia, has produced an alternative dataset on the annual mean temperatures (TYN CY 1.0). In their dataset, the annual mean temperatures are averages of the period 1961–1990. The observations from meteorological stations are assimilated onto a 0.5° latitude by 0.5° longitude grid covering the land surface of the earth. The gridded data of this dataset are transformed into country averages by allowing each 0.5° grid box to a single country. Then they calculated the mean of the constituent grid-boxes of each country. If more than one country had land within a grid-box, the box was usually allocated to the country with the single largest stake within that grid-box (Mitchell et al. 2001, 2003).

The TYN CY 1.1 (2003) dataset covers all 172 countries examined in this study except Taiwan and East Timor. Taiwan's MT is from WMO No. 847. In the case of East Timor, it is assumed that annual mean temperature is the same as for Indonesia. In the cases of Canada and Russia, I found it necessary to deviate slightly from the TYN CY 1.1 dataset. Because many of Canada's 229 and Russia's 174 meteorological stations are in the extremely thinly populated northern regions of these countries, the annual mean temperatures in Canada (-5.4) and in Russia (-5.1) are exceptionally low. From the perspective of this study, I think that it is more realistic to calculate the mean temperatures for these countries by excluding the meteorological stations that are situated in the thinly populated northern regions of these countries. Using data given in WMO No. 847, I excluded 39 northern stations in Canada and 77 Siberian stations in Russia. The mean temperature is 3.9 for Canada on the basis of the remaining 190 stations and 3.6 for Russia on the basis of the remaining 97 meteorological stations. The TYN CY 1.1 data for the 172 countries in this study (with corrections in the cases of Canada, Russia, and Taiwan) are presented in Appendix 1.

We can see from Appendix 1 that in most cases the TYN CY 1.1 data on mean temperatures and the alternative data calculated by me differ only slightly if at all. There are, however, several cases in which differences are more than 3 degrees Celsius (°C). Most of these countries are mountainous. The mean temperatures based on grids are lower than mean temperatures based on observation stations. Tajikistan is the most extreme case; the mean temperature based on one observation station is 14.7, whereas the mean temperature based on grids is only 2.0. The correlation between the two datasets is 0.965, which means that their covariation is 93 percent. Because the two datasets differ, to some extent, from each other I decided to combine them by calculating the means of the measures, the combined mean temperature (MT). So I have three highly intercorrelated measures of annual mean temperature: AMT, TYN CY 1.1, and MT (see Appendix 1). Of these three measures, only the combined annual mean temperature (MT) will be used in statistical analyses.

It is possible that the variation in temperature is not the only aspect of climatic conditions which has affected the differentiation of the mental abilities of human populations, but because it seems to be the most relevant characteristic of climatic differences, the measurement is restricted to this variable. Besides, there may be other geographical factors that have affected the evolution of human mental abilities, but because I do not have any theoretical grounds to define them and to indicate their effects, other geographical factors are excluded from this analysis. It is plausible to assume that the data on annual mean temperatures presented in Appendix 1 are hard data. Their validity and reliability can be assumed to be high, although there may be some errors in single cases, especially in those in which the regional variation of temperature is high.

National IQ

National IQ is another variable needed in this study. It is intended to measure the average intelligence of nations. According to my theoretical argumentation, differences in the average national intelligence constitute the principal intervening mechanism between climate and the degree of resource distribution. As indicated above, it is assumed that differences in national intelligence emerged as a consequence of people's adaptation to varying climatic and other geographical conditions. Unfortunately it is much more difficult to measure differences in the average national intelligence than differences in temperature. The measurement of temperature is based on values given by thermometer. It is the generally accepted indicator of temperature and produces the same values independently of its users. We do not have a similar generally accepted instrument to measure intelligence. However, there is one instrument—the intelligence quotient (IQ)—which has been used to measure individual differences in general intelligence, but it is not

yet a generally accepted instrument for this purpose. Many researchers argue that it is not possible to measure intelligence reliably, and
especially, to measure differences in the average intelligence of populations. Consequently, this instrument is still hotly disputed, although it
has been used since the beginning of the 20th century (see Jensen 1998;
Rindermann 2007).

In Chapter 1, I already referred to some definitions of intelligence
and to intelligence tests. According to one definition, intelligence determines the efficiency of problem solving, learning, remembering, and the
performance of various tasks. Another definition emphasizes that intelligence means the ability to understand complex ideas, to adapt effectively
to the environment, and to overcome obstacles. Further, intelligence is
said to be a very general mental capacity which involves the ability to
reason, plan, solve problems, think abstractly, learn quickly, and learn
from experience (Lynn and Vanhanen 2002, pp. 19–20; cf. Jensen 1998,
pp. 45–57; Nyborg 2003b). The complexity of these definitions indicates
that it has not been possible to define intelligence as simply, if at all, as
temperature. Because of the difficulties in defining intelligence satisfactorily, Jensen prefers to use the term "mental ability" (Jensen 1998, pp.
52–53). Rosalind Arden (2003, p. 540) notes that a clear definition is
often the end point of science, not the starting point, and she continues:
"a reasonable battery of IQ-type tests will yield, with stolid reliability and with remarkable accuracy, a ranking order that shows where
each person stands relative to others in the population under study."
She emphasizes that the relative nature of IQ scores is important. In
our coauthored books (Lynn and Vanhanen 2002, 2006), we have used
national IQ to indicate where each nation stands relative to others.

Another contested problem of intelligence concerns the extent to
which differences in intelligence are heritable. The relative significance
of genetic and environmental factors has been investigated since the
1930s. A consensus has emerged that genetic factors constitute a significant determinant of intelligence. "The magnitude of the contribution of
genetic factors is measured by the heritability, which consists of the pro-
portion of phenotypic (measured) variance that can be accounted for
by the genetic differences among individuals. Heritability is measured
on a scale from 0 to 1.0, and is also expressed as percentages" (Lynn
and Vanhanen 2002, pp. 23–24). Heritability estimates range from 0.4
to 0.8, and many researchers have come to the conclusion that genetics

plays a bigger role than environment in creating IQ differences among individuals (see Jensen 1998, pp. 169–182; Lynn and Vanhanen, 2002, pp. 23–25, 2006, pp. 226–229). The hypothesis about the causal link between climate and intelligence is based on the idea that intelligence has a high heritability as a consequence of evolution by natural selection.

The subject of the evolution of race differences in intelligence was raised in Chapter 1. The first studies on race differences in intelligence were carried out on black and white conscripted men in the United States during the World War I. A 17 IQ point difference in favor of whites was found. Several hundred studies have confirmed this conclusion. In the late 1970s, Lynn decided to examine race differences from a worldwide perspective. His review showed that the Caucasoid peoples of Europe, the United States, Australia, and New Zealand obtain average IQs around 100; there was a little evidence that Oriental or Mongoloid peoples, mainly Chinese and Japanese, tend to score a little higher; Negroid peoples invariably obtain low average IQs, not only in the United States but also in Britain, the Caribbean, and in Africa; American Indians in the United States score about midway between blacks and whites; and Australian Aborigines obtain average IQs of around 62 (Lynn 2008, pp. 47–50).

In the 1980s, Lynn produced updated worldwide literature surveys of the intelligence of the major races. He related racial differences in intelligence to the geographical and climatic environments in which they had evolved and found clear relationships. Median IQs of racial groups are higher in the geographical locations with cold and temperate climates than in temperate-tropical and tropical climates (Lynn 1997, pp. 261–262; 2003, 2006; cf. Lynn 1991a, 1991b; Herrnstein and Murray 1994, pp. 269–315; D'Souza 1995; Rushton 1995; Jensen 1998, pp. 350–417).

In this study, I use data on national IQs calculated and estimated in our second book (Lynn and Vanhanen 2006) to measure average national differences in intelligence. Lynn collected data on intelligence tests made in 113 nations and calculated the mean IQs of populations for these 113 countries. In these calculations, the mean IQ in Britain was set at 100 with a standard deviation of 15. The mean IQs of other nations were calculated in relation to this standard. The methods to calculate national intelligence levels are explained and the sources of all data on national intelligence tests used in these calculations are documented in the book (Lynn and Vanhanen 2006, Appendix 1). The calculated national IQs vary in the group of 113 nations from Equatorial Guinea's 59 to Hong Kong's and Singapore's 108.

The reliability of calculated national IQs was tested by correlating two extreme values of national IQs in the group of 71 countries and subcategories within countries for which there are two or more scores. The correlation between the two extreme IQs is 0.92, which indicates that different intelligence tests in the same country have produced highly similar results. In other words, the reliability of national IQs is high (Lynn and Vanhanen 2006, pp. 61–62).

What about the validity of national IQs? Because many researchers have argued that no valid comparisons can be made between IQs obtained from different nations, it was useful to measure the validity of national IQs by several methods. It was possible to test the validity of national IQs by correlating national IQs with various measures of educational attainment in mathematics and science. Data on the scores of educational attainment cover 27–40 countries, and correlations vary from 0.79 to 0.89 (see Lynn and Vanhanen 2006, pp. 62–70; cf. Lynn and Vanhanen 2002, pp. 64–71). They indicate a strong correspondence between national IQs and national differences in school attainment. The fact that national IQs are more or less in harmony with educational attainments in mathematics and science across cultural borderlines contradicts the argument that intelligence tests were biased to favor the white Americans and Europeans. The connection between educational attainments and national IQs has been discussed and analyzed extensively in Heiner Rindermann's (2007) article on international cognitive ability and achievement comparisons and in numerous peer commentaries on his article published in the *European Journal of Personality.*

National IQs were estimated for the 79 countries with populations of more than 40,000 from which Lynn had not been able to find IQ data. It was assumed that unknown national IQs would be closely similar to those in neighboring countries whose IQs are known. The fact is that the IQs of neighboring countries are usually quite similar. In Western Europe, for example, the IQ is 98 in France, 99 in Belgium and Germany, 100 in Britain and the Netherlands, and 101 in Switzerland. The similarity of IQs in neighboring countries makes it justified to estimate unknown IQs on the basis of neighboring countries. Where there are two or more appropriate neighboring countries, the IQs of these countries were averaged to obtain an estimated IQ for the country whose IQ is unknown. Table 4.3 in the book (Lynn and Vanhanen 2006: 56–62) shows the comparison countries and their IQs in each case. For example, to estimate an IQ for Algeria, we averaged the IQs of Morocco (84) and Egypt (81), which gives an IQ of 83. In the case of Burkina Faso, we averaged the IQs of Ghana (71), Nigeria (69), and Sierra Leone (64), which gives an IQ of 68 for Burkina Faso (Lynn and Vanhanen 2006, pp. 53–55; cf. Lynn and Vanhanen 2002, pp. 73–80).

The national IQs calculated on the basis of national intelligence tests (113 nations) and estimated for 79 countries are presented in Table 4.3 and in Appendix 1 in our book (Lynn and Vanhanen 2006, pp. 55–61, 295–313). I am going to use these data, which cover the countries of this study. However, because East Timor was not included in our study and because Serbia and Montenegro constituted the combined state of Serbia and Montenegro, I had to estimate national IQs for these new states. I think it reasonable to use Indonesia's national IQ (87) for East Timor and Serbia and Montenegro's national IQ (89) for both Montenegro and Serbia. Data on national IQs are certainly not as reliable as data on mean temperatures, but they are the only available data on differences in average mental abilities of nations. I assume that they measure satisfactorily relative differences in average national intelligence.

The Index of Power Resources (IPR)

It has been observed at least since the days of Aristotle that important economic and other resources are unequally distributed within societies and that the distribution of such resources has an impact on political structures from the perspective of democracy. Aristotle related different forms of government to differences in economic and social structures. He noted that the most obvious division of the city is into two parts, the poor and the rich, and he explained, for example, that "a democracy is a state where the freemen and the poor, being the majority, are invested with the power of the state. An oligarchy is a state where the rich and those of noble families, being few, possess it" (*The Politics of Aristotle* 1952, Book IV, 112). The existence of significant differences in resource distribution within all societies is a fact of life, but we do not have a generally accepted thermometer to measure such differences. Social scientists have investigated social stratification and inequalities extensively, but they have usually focused on some specific aspects of inequalities; they have not attempted to measure the overall degree of inequality in resource distribution (see, for example, Bendix and Lipset 1967; Grusky 1994).

In my comparative studies of democratization (Vanhanen 1984, 1990, 1997, 2003), I attempted to measure differences in the degree of resource distribution between countries because my Darwinian interpretation of politics led me to the idea that the distribution of political power in a country must depend on the distribution of resources used as sanctions in the struggle for power. I have focused on economic and intellectual power resources, which are everywhere utilized as important sources of power.

Indicators of resource distribution in the 2003 study

In my latest study, *Democratization: A Comparative Analysis of 170 Countries* (2003), I used five variables to measure, at least indirectly, the relative distribution of some economic and intellectual power resources. The variables are defined in greater detail and data on them are presented in the book (Vanhanen 2003, pp. 89–100, Appendices 2, 3, 4, and 5).

1. Students (students in universities per 100,000 inhabitants). The absolute number of students per 100,000 inhabitants is transformed into percentages by using 4,000 students per 100,000 inhabitants to represent the level of 100 percent, which is the upper limit for this percentage.

2. Literates (the percentage of literates from the adult population, usually from the population 15 years of age and over).

3. Family farms (FF). The area of family-size farms (owned by the cultivator or in ownerlike possession) as a percentage of the total area of holdings or of the cultivated area.

4. The degree of decentralization of mainly nonagricultural economic power resources (DD).

5. Real GDP per capita (PPP US$). This variable was transformed into percentages by using 25,000 dollars per capita to represent the level of 100 percent (GDP%), which is the upper limit for this variable.

Empirical data on students are relatively reliable, but are not without serious errors. The definitions of "universities" may differ significantly from country to country; for some countries data are available only for all institutions of higher education, or the reported data are defective. Data are principally from UNESCO's *Statistical Yearbook 1999*, but because it does not contain data on all countries, missing data for more than 30 countries were complemented from other sources. This variable was used to measure the distribution of intellectual power resources from the perspective of intellectual elite. According to my assumption, the higher the number of students per 100,000 inhabitants, the more widely intellectual power resources are distributed.

Data on literates can be regarded as highly reliable, although data given in original sources are estimates in many cases. Nearly all data are from UNDP's *Human Development Report 2000*, and they concern the year 1998. Similar data are available from the World Bank's *World Development Report 2002*, UNESCO's *Statistical Yearbook 1999*, and from several other international yearbooks. In most cases, data given in different sources differ only slightly from each other, but in some cases data differ significantly. In such cases, I calculated the mean of adult literacy rate given in different sources. This variable is used to measure the distribution of intellectual power resources from the perspective of the total adult population. I assume that the higher the adult literacy rate, the more widely basic intellectual resources are distributed in a society.

Data on family farms are calculated and estimated by the author. The U.N. Food and Agricultural Organization (FAO)'s reports on the 1960, 1970, 1980, and 1990 world censuses of agriculture, the Land Tenure Center's *Land Concentration in the Third World: Statistics on Number and Area of Farms Classified by Size of Farms* (1979), and J. W. Bruce's *Country Profiles of Land Tenure: Africa, 1996* (1998) were used as the principal sources of data, but data were collected also from many other sources. This variable is intended to measure the relative distribution of economic power resources based on the ownership or control of agricultural land. The higher the percentage of family farms, the more widely economic power resources based on the ownership or control of agricultural land are distributed within the agricultural population. The term "family farm" refers to farms that provide employment for not more than four people, including family members. This criterion is used to separate large private and collective farms cultivated mainly by hired workers from family farms. This criterion is not based on any fixed size of farms. Because the quality of agricultural land and agricultural technologies varies greatly in the world, it was necessary to define hectare or other criteria of "family farms" separately for each country.

The definition of "family farms" has been most problematic for sub-Saharan African countries because of their communal land tenure systems. I decided to include 50 percent of the land under de facto community-based land tenure systems under the category of family farms. The selection of 50 percent criterion is arbitrary, but I assumed it is reasonable. African farmers are economically and socially less independent than individual owner-cultivators, but they are on the other hand more independent than the peasants of socialist collective farms or workers and tenants of large private farms and haciendas. I think that the values of the family farms variable reflect relative differences between countries in the distribution of power resources based on land-ownership (see Vanhanen 1997, pp. 47–51; 2003: 91–93, Appendix 3). Data on family farms cannot seen to be as reliable as data on students and literates. The margin of error may rise to 10–20 percentage points in some cases.

The degree of decentralization (DD) is the most problematic of my measures of resource distribution. This variable is intended to measure the relative distribution of mainly nonagricultural economic power resources among individuals and various sections of the population. It is based on the assumption that extreme poverty as well as the concentration of economic resources in the hands of the few constrain the decentralization of economic power resources in a society. Consequently, data on the percentage of people below the poverty line and data on the distribution of income or consumption were used as criteria in estimating the degree of decentralization of economic power resources (DD) for single countries. It is justified to argue that people below the poverty line have very scarce resources to participate in national or even local politics. They have to focus on the day-to-day struggle for survival.

The nature of the economic system was also taken into account in several cases, especially those in which economic power resources are highly concentrated in the hands of the few. Statistical data on the population below the poverty line and on the distribution of income or consumption were available principally from the World Bank's *World*

Development Reports and the UNDP's *Human Development Reports* (for this variable, see Vanhanen 2003, pp. 93–98, 257–264). Since the estimated values of the DD variable are based on empirical data on constraining variables, the scope of subjective judgments remained quite limited in nearly all cases. However, the margin of error may rise to 10–20 percentage points, and in some cases even higher. I assume that the higher the value of DD, the more widely the ownership and control of mainly nonagricultural economic power resources are decentralized in a society.

Real GDP per capita (or some other measure of per capita income) is the most common indicator of the level of economic development, but I used this variable to measure, at least indirectly, the distribution of economic power resources. It is usually plausible to assume that the more widely distributed the significant economic power resources are, the higher the level of economic development. There are more interest groups in economically highly developed than in less developed countries, and the ownership and control of the means of production tend to be more widely distributed. Therefore my argument is that it is justified to regard per capita income not only as an indicator of the level of economic development but also as an indicator of resource distribution.

There are different indicators of per capita income: GNP per capita, GDP per capita, GNP per capita measured at PPP (purchasing power parity) dollars, and GDP measured at PPP dollars. One problem with GNP and GDP measures is that they overstate real income differences between developed and developing countries for the reason that many economic activities in developing countries are not taken into account in GNP and GDP. The PPP exchange rate tries to take into account the currency's real domestic purchasing power (see Nafziger 1997, pp. 21–26; Gardner 1998: 22–26; the UNDP's *Human Development Report 1999*: 254). I selected Real GDP per capita to measure indirectly the relative distribution of socioeconomic power resources from the perspective of the total economy. Nearly all data on GDP per capita (PPP US$) in 1998 are from the UNDP's *Human Development Report 2000*. The reliability and validity of these data can be regarded as high, although they are in many cases based on estimates (see Vanhanen 2003, pp. 96–98, 165–169). I assume that the higher the level of Real GDP per capita (PPP dollars), the more widely socioeconomic power resources are distributed.

Because these five explanatory variables are intended to measure the degree of resource distribution from different perspectives, it is reasonable to assume that a combination of them would be a theoretically more valid substitute for the hypothetical concept of "resource distribution" than any of them separately. Consequently, I decided to combine them into an index of power resources. For this purpose, students and literates were first combined into a sectional index of intellectual power resources (IR) by calculating the mean of the two percentages. Family farms (FF) and the degree of decentralization of economic power resources (DD) were combined into a sectional index of economic power resources (ER) by weighting the values of FF and DD by percentages of agricultural (AP) and nonagricultural populations (NAP), respectively, and then by adding the weighted values of FF and DD. After these operations, there are three explanatory variables: IR, ER, and GDP% (real GDP per capita).

Finally, I used three different ways to combine the explanatory variables into a composite index. First, IR and ER were combined into an index of power resources (IPR) by multiplying the values of IR and ER and dividing the product by 100. Second, IR, ER, and GDP% were combined into an extended index of power resources (IPR-2) by multiplying the values of the three variables and dividing the product by 10,000. The third way was to calculate the mean of the five explanatory variables (Vanhanen 2003, pp. 98–100).

The values of IPR for the 170 countries are given in Table 7.3 in my 2003 book (pp. 141–144). The values of IPR vary from zero (North Korea) to 68.8 (Iceland). Because IR and ER are multiplied, IPR's value drops to zero if the value of either variable is zero. The values of the mean are always higher than zero because it represents the arithmetic mean of the five variables. In the case of North Korea, the value of the mean is 26.0. Note that IPR is not a complete operational substitute for the hypothetical concept of "resource distribution." It does not take into account all important power resources, it principally measures the distribution of some universally used economic and intellectual power resources. Many kinds of locally important power resources are excluded as well as the means of violence, which may have a crucial impact on power distribution in some circumstances. However, I think that IPR satisfactorily indicates the relative differences in the degree of resource distribution between countries.

Indicators of resource distribution in this study

For this study, I have updated and recalculated the values of students, literates, family farms, and DD variables. Real GDP per capita (PPP dollars) is excluded from this analysis. It should be noted that data on Students are now based on tertiary gross enrollment ratios (percent of relevant age group), not on the number of students per 100,000 inhabitants. Most data on tertiary enrollment ratio are from the World Bank's *World Development Indicators* for 2006 and 2004. Most data on adult literacy are from the UNDP's *Human Development Report 2006*. The updated data on tertiary enrollment ratio, literacy, and IR (index of intellectual power resources) are presented and documented in Appendix 2.

The results of FAO's *World Census of Agriculture 2000* made it possible to update data on family farms in approximately 60 cases. Besides, other sources were used to update data on family farms and to correct previous estimations in many other cases. The updated data on family farms are presented and documented in Appendix 3.

Data on DD (the degree of decentralization of economic power resources) have also been extensively updated and corrected. In 161 cases, the value of DD is principally calculated on the basis of empirical or estimated data on the percentage of population below poverty line and on the richest 10 percent's share of income or consumption. These data are principally from the World Bank's *World Development Indicators 2006*, the UNDP's *Human Development Report 2006*, and the CIA's *World Factbook 2007* and they are presented and documented in Appendix 4.

Data on "population below poverty line" in Appendix 4 are arithmetic means of data given in two or three sources and in some cases only in one. Data on population below the poverty line vary depending on the criterion of "poverty line." There are data on population below the national poverty line and the international poverty line. Besides, in the case of the international poverty line, there are data on population below $1 a day and $2 a day, and, in the cases of OECD countries, Central and Eastern Europe and the CIS, below 50 percent of median income, below $11 a day and $4 a day. If all these data were available, I calculated the mean of data given in *World Development Indicators 2006*, and the mean of data given in the *Human Development Report 2006*, after which I calculated the mean of these two means and data given in the

World Factbook 2007. This final mean is given in Appendix 4 in the first column (population below poverty line). If data are not available on all measures of population below the poverty line, the mean in Appendix 4 represents the mean of the available data, which in some cases is based on the data given in only one source. My argument is that the mean of different measures of poverty may be a better measure of population below the poverty line than data based on only one criterion of poverty.

Data on "richest 10% minus 10%" in Appendix 4 are arithmetic means of data on this variable given in two or three sources. In some cases data on this variable were available only from one source, usually the *World Factbook 2007*. Note that the values of the richest 10 percent given in Appendix 4 are not original percentages. Ten scores are subtracted from each percentage; the rest indicate how much the share of the richest 10 percent deviates from an equal distribution of income or consumption. "Population below poverty line" indicates the share of the extremely poor people who have hardly any resources to take part in national politics, and "richest 10% minus 10%" indicates the degree to which economic resources are concentrated in the hands of the richest 10 percent of the population. Together they indicate relative differences between countries in the degree of decentralization of economic power resources.

Data on these two variables were complied from other sources, as indicated in Appendix 4, but unfortunately it was not possible to find statistical data from all countries. Data on both variables cover 123 countries; data on one or both variables were estimated on the basis of neighboring countries for 38 countries.

A problem arises as to how to combine the two percentages, which measure the concentration and decentralization of economic power resources from two different perspectives. They are combined by adding the two percentages. Their sum indicates the degree of concentration of economic power resources, and the inverse of this sum (inverse total %) given in Appendix 4 indicates the degree of decentralization of economic power resources (DD). In most cases, "inverse total %" is used to indicate the degree of decentralization of economic power resources (DD), but in some cases I found it necessary to modify the value of DD by taking into account the nature of a country's economic system.

First, the value of DD was completely estimated for nine oil producing countries (Bahrain, Brunei, Iraq, Kuwait, Libya, Oman, Qatar, Saudi Arabia, and the United Arab Emirates) as well as for Cuba and North Korea. Data on "population below poverty line" and "richest 10%" were not available from those countries. Because crucial economic power resources are highly concentrated in the hands of the government or private corporations in all these countries, I estimated the value of DD to be relatively low in all these countries. The estimated DD values vary from 5 (North Korea) to 25 (Iraq, Kuwait, and Libya).

Second, the DD value based on "inverse total %" was reduced by 20 scores in the cases of Algeria, Azerbaijan, Burma, Egypt, Iran, Jordan, Morocco, Singapore, Syria, and Tunisia. Economic power resources are highly concentrated in the hands of the government and/ or private corporations in all these countries.

Third, the DD value was reduced by 20 scores in the cases of contemporary (China, Laos, and Vietnam) and some former socialist countries (Belarus, Kazakhstan, Kyrgyzstan, Russia, and Uzbekistan). Despite economic reforms, one-party governments still control crucial economic resources in all socialist countries, and despite market reforms, socialist economic structures have to some extent survived, especially in Belarus, Kazakhstan, Kyrgyzstan, Russia, and Uzbekistan.

Fourth, the DD value was raised to 5 scores in seven countries for which "inverse total %" is less than 5 (Central African Republic, Haiti, Mali, Namibia, Sierra Leone, Swaziland, and Zambia). It is reasonable to assume that economic power resources are to some extent decentralized even in these poor countries.

Data on family farms and DD are combined into an index of economic power resources (ER) in the same way as in my 2003 book by the formula ER = (FF * AP) + (DD * NAP), in which formula AP = the percentage of agricultural population and NAP = the percentage of nonagricultural population. Data on agricultural population are principally from the CIA's *World Factbook 2007*, and are presented in Appendix 3. Most data on AP are from 2000–2005; the calculated values of ER are given in Appendix 2.

The value of IPR is calculated in the same way as in my previous study by the formula IPR = (IR * ER)/100. IPR will be used as the principal operational substitute for the hypothetical concept of "resource distribution." However, the arithmetic mean of the four basic variables can be used as an alternative index of resource distribution. The IPR and mean differ in one important aspect: IPR gets high values only if the values of both its components (IR and ER) are high; a low value of either component decreases the value of IPR near zero. In the case of the mean, a low value of any of the four basic variables does not decrease the value of the mean to zero if the values of other variables are moderate or high. Data on the IPR and mean for 172 countries are given in Appendix 2.

The Index of Democratization (ID)

The degree of democratization is the ultimate dependent variable in this study, whose purpose is to see to what extent the roots of democratization can be traced to climatic differences through the two intervening variables described above. Political philosophers and researchers since Plato and Aristotle have paid attention to the variation of political systems from the perspective of democracy, but until the 1950s they were content to classify political systems without attempts to measure the degree of democracy or autocracy. Since the 1950s, social scientists have developed various operational measures of democracy and autocracy (see, for example, Schmidt 2000; Vanhanen 2003, pp. 49–53; Tilly 2007; Berg-Schlosser 2004, 2005; Keman 2004; Lipset and Lakin 2004; van Beek 2005; Inglehart and Welzel 2005; Somit and Peterson 2005; Lindberg 2006; Bogaards 2000a, 2000b; Welzel 2007).

Freedom House's Comparative Survey of Freedom and the Polity project, initiated by Ted Robert Gurr in the 1970s, have produced the two best known measures of democracy, although they are not intended to measure the degree of democratization directly. They are quite different. Freedom House's survey rates political rights and civil liberties separately on a seven-category scale, 1 representing the most free and 7 the least free. The ratings are based on responses to the checklists and the judgments of the survey team and cover the year 1972–73. The polity project measures democracy by an additive 10-point scale derived from coding of the competitiveness of political participation (1–3), the competitiveness of executive recruitment (1–2), the openness of executive recruitment (1), and constraints on the chief executive (1–4). They measure autocracy by a similar 10-point-scale, which measures the lack of regulated political competitiveness (1–2), regulation of political participation (1–2), the lack of competitiveness of executive recruitment

(2), the lack of openness of executive recruitment (1), and the lack of constraints on the chief executive (1–3). Their data cover the period since 1800 (Vanhanen 2003, pp. 51–52; cf. Gurr et al. 1990; Jaggers and Gurr 1995; Marshall and Jaggers 2003; Karatnycky et al. 2003). Both of these measures of democracy are based more on the judgments of survey teams than on statistical data on political phenomena.

I have used a different method to measure political systems from the perspective of democracy. Like Robert A. Dahl (1971), I have focused on two crucial dimensions of democracy—competition and participation—since my first comparative study (Vanhanen 1971). My basic argument is that these two dimensions represent the most crucial aspects of democracy. There cannot be democracy without legally allowed competition for the highest positions of power, and it would not be appropriate to speak of democracy without extensive popular participation in elections. So both of these dimensions are necessary for democracy. The legal opportunity to compete for the control of political institutions through elections indicates that people and their groups are free to organize themselves and to oppose those in the government. Indirectly, it also indicates the existence of political rights and liberties. The degree of participation indicates the extent of "the people" taking part in politics. My argument is that as the political system is more democratized, the higher the degrees of competition and participation rise.

As stated above, I use two simple political variables—competition and participation—to measure the two crucial dimensions of democracy. The value of the competition variable is calculated by subtracting the percentage of votes won by the largest party or the percentage of the seats in parliament won by the largest party from 100. The value of the participation variable is the percentage of the total population who voted in the election. The impact of referendums is added to the participation variable in such a way that each national referendum adds the degree of participation by 5 points and each state referendum by 1 point for the year when the referendum took place. The impact of referendums is limited to 30 points for a year, because it should not rise higher than the degree of electoral participation, and the combined score of electoral participation and referendums is limited to 70. The same 70 percent upper limit is used in the case of competition.

My measures of democracy are principally based on statistical data on competition and participation, but interpretations are needed of several points in the calculation of the values of the competition and participation variables. First it is necessary to decide what governmental institutions are taken into account. The values of these variables can be calculated on the basis of parliamentary or executive (presidential) elections, or both. The selection of the governmental institution depends on the assumed importance of the two institutions. Depending on how power is divided between them, we can speak of parliamentary and presidential (or executive) forms of government. Sometimes their powers are so well balanced that both of them should be taken into account. Therefore I distinguished three institutional power arrangements at the national level: (1) parliamentary dominance, (2) executive dominance, and (3) concurrent powers. In the first case, the values of competition and participation are calculated on the basis of parliamentary elections; in the case of "executive dominance," they are calculated on the basis of presidential or other executive elections (or the lack of elections); and in the case of "concurrent powers," both elections are taken into account.

Because the two basic measures of democracy are assumed to indicate two different dimensions of democratization, it is reasonable to combine them into an index of democratization. There would be many different ways to combine the two variables, depending on how we weight the importance of competition and participation. My argument is that they represent equally important dimensions of democratization. Besides, I think that both are necessary for democracy. Therefore, I have given an equal weight for both of them and combined them into an index of democratization (ID) by multiplying the two percentages and by dividing the product by 100. This means that the lack of competition will reduce the value of ID to zero when the value of participation is high, and vice versa.

An alternative way to combine them would be to calculate the mean of the two percentages, but I rejected this method because it would produce a moderate value of ID for a country in which the value of competition or participation is high, but the value of the other variable is zero or near zero. My argument is that a country with a high degree of competition cannot be regarded as a democracy if the degree of participation is zero or near zero, and vice versa. The method of multiplication cancels the misleading information provided by competition or participation in such cases by producing a low ID value for such countries. The two basic measures of democracy and their composite index are defined and described in greater detail in my previous book (Vanhanen 2003, pp. 53–67).

Empirical data on the two basic political variables for the years 1999–2001 are given and documented by countries in Appendix 1 of my 2003 book (Vanhanen 2003, pp. 190–232). In this study these measures of democracy are extended to cover the years 2002–2006. Data on political variables are given and documented in *FSD1289 Measures of Democracy 1810–2006* (Finnish Social Science Data Archive 2007).

To some extent, it is possible to test the validity of the index of democratization (ID) as a measure of democracy by correlating its scores with the values of alternative datasets, the Freedom House's combined ratings of political rights and civil liberties, and the Polity project's democracy and autocracy scales. For the year 1988, ID's correlation with Freedom House's measures was -0.778 and with the Polity measures 0.830. For the year 1998, corresponding correlations are -0.811 and 0.861. These strong correlations indicate that in most cases results correspond with each other, although the three alternative measures of democracy are quite different. There are, however, several cases in which the results more or less clearly differ from each other (Vanhanen 2003, pp. 68–77). I think that the validity of my measure of democracy (ID) is relatively high (cf. Bogaards 2007a, 2007b)

In 2006, I invented a gender modified version of ID. A problem with existing measures of democracy is that they are gender-blind. They do not take into account the sexual dimension of democracy, in other words, the fact that women's representation in national decision-making bodies varies greatly. Traditionally women have been seriously under-represented in all national decision-making bodies, including parliaments and governments, and they are still completely excluded from some parliaments (cf. Ballington and Karam 2005).

The new gender-weighted index of democratization (GID) is intended to correct that oversight in Vanhanen's index of democratization (ID). GID is based on the idea that, at the same level of ID, a country with a high level of women's representation is more democratic than a country with a low level of women's representation in national decision-making bodies. In this index, women's percentage share of seats in parliament (W) is used to indicate differences in women's representation. Data on women's percentage share of seats in parliament have been published in the Inter-Parliamentary Union's

Chronicle of Parliamentary Elections since 1969, but data were lacking from many countries up to the first years of the 1990s. Therefore, the calculation of GID values is limited to the period 1995–2006 in my dataset. All data on women's representation in parliaments are from the Inter-Parliamentary Union's *Chronicle of Parliamentary Elections* (1969–2006) and, in the case of Taiwan, from IDEA's *Global Database of Quotas for Women* (2006). IDEA's database provides detailed information about women's representation and about constitutional and party quotas for women. Available data on women's representation in parliaments are given in a dataset *FSD2183 Women's Representation in National Parliaments 1970–2006*.

GID is a combination of ID and W (women's representation in parliament). The gender-weighted index of democratization is calculated by the formula: $GID = ID \times [1 + (W/100)]$. In this formula, W = women's percentage share of seats in parliament. The formula is such that the calculated GID value will always be higher than ID if the values of both ID and W are higher than zero. The W value raises the GID value up to full sexual equality in representation (50–50%). In the extreme case, when the value of W has risen to 50 percent or higher, the GID value will become 50 percent higher than the ID value. However, the absolute increase in GID depends not only on W but also on ID. At a low level of ID, the increase in GID remains small even when women's representation is high. At a high level of ID, a high level of women's representation (W) raises the absolute value of GID much more than at a low level of ID, even when the percentage increases are the same.

The dataset FSD2140 gender-weighted index of democratization 1995–2006 covers 184 independent countries of the period 1995–2006. The group includes all countries that were already independent in 1995 and whose population was at least 40,000 inhabitants in 2000. The dataset provides values for ID, W, and GID for each country and for each year from 1995 to 2006. GID can be used as an alternative version of ID in this study.

Research hypotheses and units of observation

The definition of the four variables intended to measure annual mean temperature, differences in the average intelligence of nations, the distribution of intellectual and economic power resources, and the level of democratization makes it possible to transform the original hypotheses formulated in Chapter 1 into testable research hypotheses.

1. The higher the annual mean temperature (MT), the more the values of national IQ, IPR, and the index of democratization (ID) tend to decrease.

2. The higher the national IQ, the more the degree of resource distribution (the IPR and the mean) and the level of democratization (ID) tend to rise.

3. The higher the degree of resource distribution (IPR), the more the level of democratization (ID) tends to rise.

All hypotheses presuppose linear relationships between variables. The first hypothesis here predicts negative correlations between variables, and the second and third predict positive correlations. The hypotheses can be tested by empirical evidence on variables. Correlations should be relatively strong; weak or opposite correlations would falsify hypotheses.

Since these hypotheses are universal, intended to cover all contemporary countries of the world, it is reasonable to test them in a group of countries which covers practically all countries of the world. Of course, it would be possible to test the hypotheses also by a representative sample of countries, but I prefer a total population of countries because data on the four variables are available from nearly all countries of the world. The test based on the total population of countries can be assumed to produce more reliable results than the tests based on more limited samples of countries.

Empirical data on mean temperature (MT), national IQ, and ID and GID variables would be available from nearly all countries of the world, whereas my data on IPR are available only from 172 countries whose population was more than 200,000 inhabitants in 2000. Therefore I decided to restrict this analysis to this group of 172 countries. They are independent countries, except Taiwan, which is regarded to be a province of China. The population criterion of 200,000 inhabitants excludes the smallest countries, but it is justified to assume that their exclusion does not bias the results to any significant extent. The group of excluded small countries includes, in addition to some dwarf states, Antigua and Barbuda, Dominica, Grenada, Kiribati, the Marshall Islands, Micronesia, Nauru, St. Kitts and Nevis, St. Lucia, St. Vincent and the Grenadines, Sao Tome and Principe, Seychelles, Tonga, Tuvalu, Vanuatu, and Samoa (Western).

CHAPTER 3

Hypotheses Tested

In this chapter, the three research hypotheses will be tested by empirical evidence on the four variables introduced and defined in Chapter 2. Because data on all variables are at the interval or ratio level, it is possible to test the hypotheses by correlation and regression analyses. The hypothesized correlations should be relatively strong; zero or opposite correlations would falsify hypotheses. Multiple regression analysis will be used to illustrate the relative significance of each explanatory variable.

Correlation analysis

In the following sections, the three research hypotheses on the relationships between variables are tested by empirical evidence on mean temperature, national IQ, measures of resource distribution, and measures of democratization. There are two indices of resource distribution: the index of power resources (IPR) and the mean, that is, the arithmetic mean of the four basic explanatory variables [mean temperature (MT), national IQ, IPR, and the index of democratization (ID)]. There are also two measures of democratization: ID and GID. The original ID will be used as the principal measure of democratization. Freedom House's combined ratings of political rights and civil liberties (FH-2005) provide an alternative measure of democracy (*Freedom in the World* 2006). Of the three alternative measures of mean temperature (AMT, TYN CY 1.1, and MT), which are extremely highly intercorrelated, only MT (mean temperature) is used in this analysis. All correlations are calculated in the total group of 172 countries. Let us start from the intercorrelations of the four explanatory variables (Table 3.1).

Table 3.1. The intercorrelations of MT, national IQ, and the two alternative indices of resource distribution (the IPR and the mean) in the group of 172 countries

Variable	MT Mean	National IQ	IPR	Mean
MT (mean temperature)	1.000	-0.659	-0.695	-0.683
National IQ		1.000	0.754	0.795
IPR			1.000	0.963
Mean				1.000

The two measures of resource distribution are extremely strongly intercorrelated (0.963). They measure the degree of resource distribution from slightly different perspectives. In the following statistical analyses, I will use the new version of IPR (see Chapter 2) as my principal measure of resource distribution.

According to the first hypothesis, the values of national IQ and the IPR (and the mean) are expected to be lower, the higher the annual mean temperature. The results of correlation analysis support this hypothesis. All correlations are clearly negative as hypothesized. MT explains statistically 43 percent of the variation in national IQ ($r2$), which indicates that the contemporary variation in national IQ is still significantly related to differences in climatic conditions as measured by annual mean temperature. It is justified to regard MT as the causal factor in this relationship for the reason that differences in climatic conditions certainly preceded the emergence of differences in national IQs. On the other hand, the fact that more than half of the variation in national IQ remains unexplained indicates that the relationship between MT and national IQ is imperfect and that there are other factors affecting national IQ. It is plausible to assume that many population migrations after the last Ice Age have weakened this correlation. The examination of the results of regression analysis of national IQ on MT at the level of single countries will help to determine what kind of countries differ most clearly from the average relationship between MT and national IQ.

The correlations between MT and the two measures of resource distribution are also clearly negative as hypothesized and slightly stronger than the correlation between MT and national IQ. MT explains statistically 48 percent of the variation in the IPR and 47 percent of the variation in the mean. The hypothesized negative relationship between MT and measures of resource distribution is clear, but correlations do not indicate to what extent the impact of MT on resource distribution is direct and to what extent it takes place through national IQ. Multiple regression analysis helps to solve this problem. In any case, it is clear that MT and national IQ are independent factors in their relationship to the measures of resource distribution for the reason that differences in MT certainly preceded all contemporary differences in the degree of resource distribution and that evolved differences in national IQs also most probably preceded contemporary differences in the measures of resource distribution.

According to the second hypothesis, national IQ should be positively correlated with the IPR and the mean. The results of correlation analysis support this hypothesis strongly. National IQ explains statistically 57 percent of the variation in the IPR and 63 percent of the variation in the mean. According to my theoretical argumentation, this relationship is causal. Important power resources tend to become more widely distributed in countries for which national IQ is high than in countries for which national IQ is low. Intelligence is a factor which increases the ability of people to invent new things and technologies, to produce more effectively, to work in different trades, and to establish organizations to further their various interests. However, approximately 40 percent of the variation in the degree of resource distribution seems to be due to other factors. Resource distribution is constrained by the level of national IQ, but it is not completely determined by it. It would be interesting to find out by what means it has been possible to raise the degree of resource distribution higher than the average relationship between national IQ and the IPR presupposes, and what types of factors have lowered the level of resource distribution more than expected. We shall return to these questions on the connection of regression analysis of the IPR to national IQ.

MT and national IQ explain a substantial part of variation in the IPR and the mean, but Table 3.1 does not show to what extent they are able to explain variation in different components of the IPR (and the mean). Are all components approximately as strongly correlated with MT and national IQ, or are there significant differences between them? To what extent are the components of the IPR intercorrelated? The correlations given in Table 3.2 provide answers to these questions.

Table 3.2 shows that all components of the IPR (and the mean)

Table 3.2. *The intercorrelations of MT, national IQ, and the components of the IPR in the group of 172 countries*

Variable	MT	National IQ	Tertiary	Literacy	IR	Family Farms	DD	ER
MT	1.000	-0.659	-0.681	-0.558	-0.680	-0.311	-0.565	-0.546
National IQ		1.000	0.766	0.733	0.818	0.275	0.701	0.562
Tertiary			1.000	0.682	0.928	0.308	0.714	0.613
Literacy				1.000	0.905	0.103	0.568	0.364
IR					1.000	0.231	0.704	0.541
Family Farms						1.000	0.432	0.670
DD							1.000	0.891
ER								1.000

are negatively correlated with MT as hypothesized, but there are significant differences in the strength of correlations. Tertiary education is most strongly (-0.681) and FF most weakly (-0.311) correlated with MT. The combination of tertiary and literacy variables (IR) is clearly more strongly correlated with MT than the combination of FF and DD (ER).

Nearly all components of the IPR are more strongly correlated with national IQ than with MT. The highest correlation is between national IQ and tertiary and the weakest correlation between national IQ and FF. National IQ explains 59 percent of the variation in tertiary, but only 8 percent of the variation in FF. IR is much more strongly correlated with national IQ (0.818) than ER (0.562).

The intercorrelations of the four basic explanatory variables imply that they measure different aspects of resource distribution. Most correlations are only moderate. Tertiary is strongly correlated with DD but only slightly with FF, while its correlation with literacy is relatively strong (0.682). They measure the distribution of intellectual power resources from clearly different perspectives. Literacy is moderately correlated with DD (0.568), but its correlation with FF is near zero (0.103). Family farms is only slightly correlated with the three other explanatory variables and seems to be nearly independent from them. The major reason for these weak relationships can be traced to the fact that the share of Family Farms is relatively high in sub-Saharan African countries and in some other poor countries, for which the values of the three other explanatory variables tend to be low. The correlation between IR and ER is only moderate (0.541), which indicates that the index of intellectual power resources (IR) and the index of economic power resources (ER) represent clearly different dimensions of resource distribution and that their combination (IPR) may be a better measure of resource distribution than either of its two components.

The index of democratization (ID) and the gender-weighted index of democratization (GID) are used to measure national differences in the extent of democratization. Data on these variables are from the years 2002, 2003, 2004, 2005, and 2006. Furthermore, I use the combined scores of the Freedom House's ratings of political rights and civil liberties as an alternative measure of democracy. Data on the FH variable concern the year 2005. All measures of ID and GID are extremely strongly intercorrelated over the period 2002–2006. The intercorrelations of IDs vary from 0.917 to 0.981 and the intercorrelations of GIDs from 0.927

to 0.983. FH-2005 is not as strongly correlated with IDs and GIDs. Correlations vary from -0.792 to -0.819, and the covariation from 63 to 67 percent, which leaves a lot of room for differences in measurements. Table 3.3 illustrates the strength of correlations between IDs and GIDs over the period 2002–2006.

Table 3.3. Correlations between ID and GID measures over the period 2002–2006 in the group of 172 countries

Variable	ID-2002	ID-2003	ID-2004	ID-2005	ID-2006
GID-2002	0.990	0.976	0.960	0.941	0.919
GID-2003	0.969	0.990	0.969	0.939	0.917
GID-2004	0.957	0.972	0.990	0.961	0.939
GID-2005	0.936	0.938	0.955	0.990	0.955
GID-2006	0.908	0.912	0.930	0.951	0.989

Table 3.3 shows that IDs and GIDs over the period of five years are extremely strongly intercorrelated. The covariation between IDs and GIDs vary from 82 to 98 percent, which means that it would not much matter which one is used to indicate the level of democratization.

According to the first hypothesis, the measures of democratization should be negatively correlated with MT, and according to the second and third hypotheses, they should be positively correlated with national IQ and the measures of resource distribution. The correlations between these variables indicate (Table 3.4) to what extent it is possible to explain national differences in the level of democratization by the four explanatory variables.

Table 3.4 shows that MT explains 26–32 percent of the variation in ID and GID variables, but only 13 percent of the variation in FH-2005. Thus the causal roots of democratization can be partly traced to differences in climatic conditions, although on the basis of these correlations it is not possible to know whether this relationship is direct or mediated by some intervening variables (national IQ and IPR).

National IQ is more strongly related to the measures of democratization. It explains 33–41 percent of the variation in ID and GID variables. In the case of FH-2005, the explained part of variation is no more than 20 percent; in other words, FH-2005 is only weakly correlated with national IQ, whereas my measures of democracy are moderately correlated with

Table 3.4. Correlations between explanatory variables and the measures of democratization in 2002–2006 in the group of 172 countries

Variable	MT	National IQ	IPR	Mean
ID-2002	-0.528	0.616	0.830	0.780
ID-2003	-0.552	0.638	0.847	0.801
ID-2004	-0.515	0.619	0.833	0.793
ID-2005	-0.510	0.597	0.824	0.771
ID-2006	-0.523	0.575	0.813	0.758
GID-2002	-0.552	0.624	0.845	0.788
GID-2003	-0.569	0.636	0.856	0.803
GID-2004	-0.539	0.622	0.845	0.799
GID-2005	-0.533	0.600	0.834	0.775
GID-2006	-0.537	0.580	0.819	0.759
FH-2005	0.356	-0.450	-0.702	-0.626

it. The causal roots of differences in the level of democratization can be traced to differences in national IQs, but this relationship does not need to be independent of intervening factors. It is possible that the impact of national IQ on the level of democratization takes place through the measures of resource distribution (the IPR and the mean).

According to the third hypothesis, the measures of democratization should be positively correlated with the measures of resource distribution. The results of correlation analysis support this hypothesis very strongly. The IPR explains 66–73 percent and the mean 57–64 percent of the variation in ID and GID measures of democratization. IPR based on the multiplication of IR and ER clearly seems to be a better explanatory variable than the mean, which is the arithmetic mean of the four basic explanatory variables. Therefore, in later statistical analyses, I shall use the IPR as the principal indicator of resource distribution. It is interesting to note that the strength of correlations varies only slightly over the years. The highest correlations are for the year 2003. The correlations with GID are slightly higher than with ID, but I shall use ID as the principal dependent variable in later analyses because the original ID is a less complicated measure of democratization than GID. In the case of FH-2005, the explained part of variation is much lower than in the cases of ID and GID.

The very high level of explanation implies that the variation in the level of democratization is principally due to the variation in the level of resource distribution within countries, although approximately 30 percent of the variation remains unexplained. Later in this book, the examination of the results of regression analysis of ID-2006 on IPR at the level of single countries will disclose factors which are related to some large deviations from the regression line. I want to emphasize that a part of the unexplained variation in ID is probably due to various accidental factors, which always play a role in politics (cf. Taleb 2007).

The correlations between the components of IPR (and Mean) and the measures of democratization presented in Table 3.5 complement the results given in Table 3.4 by indicating to what extent the different components of IPR can explain the variation in the measures of democratization.

Table 3.5. Correlations between the components of the IPR (and the mean) and the measures of democratization in the group of 172 Countries

Variable	Tertiary	Literacy	IR	Family Farms	DD	ER
ID-2002	0.709	0.522	0.677	0.397	0.770	0.762
ID-2003	0.724	0.550	0.701	0.401	0.787	0.769
ID-2004	0.698	0.541	0.681	0.421	0.781	0.771
ID-2005	0.675	0.507	0.650	0.426	0.768	0.774
ID-2006	0.657	0.480	0.626	0.450	0.746	0.780
GID-2002	0.726	0.523	0.688	0.398	0.775	0.763
GID-2003	0.738	0.549	0.708	0.397	0.786	0.766
GID-2004	0.719	0.541	0.693	0.418	0.779	0.767
GID-2005	0.695	0.506	0.662	0.415	0.765	0.768
GID-2006	0.676	0.482	0.638	0.436	0.743	0.768
FH-2004	-0.543	-0.381	-0.509	-0.325	-0.669	-0.680

The pattern of correlations is in most points similar to that in Table 3.4. GID values are slightly more strongly correlated with explanatory variables than ID values, and all correlations between FH-2005 and explanatory variables are clearly lower than in the cases of ID and GID. The fact that all correlations between measures of democratization and single explanatory variables are weaker than correlations between measures of democratization and the IPR implies that the IPR is a more powerful explanatory variable than any of its components.

The differences between single explanatory variables are similar to those in Table 3.2. The Tertiary and DD variables are more strongly correlated with the measures of democratization than the literacy and FF variables. Family farms does not explain more than 16 to 20 percent of the variation in the ID measures of democratization, whereas in the case of DD the explained part of variation rises to 55–62 percent. The index of economic power resources (ER) clearly explains more of the variation in the measures of democratization than the index of intellectual power resources (IR). In the case of FH-2005, the explained part of variation varies from 11 to 46 percent.

The central problem of this study concerns the question of the extent to which the variation in the level of democratization (ID) can be traced to the hypothesized ultimate constraining factors: the variation in the average mental abilities of populations (national IQ) and the highly varying climatic conditions. The results of correlation analysis provide a partial answer to this question. As hypothesized, there are clear negative correlations between MT (annual mean temperature) and the measures of democratization and somewhat stronger positive correlations between these measures and national IQ. However, on the basis of these correlations we do not know to what extent these relationships are direct and to what extent they overlap with the even stronger correlations between the IPR and the measures of democratization. Multiple regression analysis can be used to clarify the relative significance of single explanatory variables.

The IPR is assumed to be a crucial intervening variable in the hypothesized relationship between mean temperature and ID. Therefore it is important to explore to what extent the variation in the IPR is due to the variation in national IQ and mean temperature. The results of correlation analysis support the assumption that a substantial part of the variation in resource distribution (IPR) can be traced via differences in the average mental abilities of populations (national IQ) to differences in climatic conditions (MT). Because the IPR explains nearly 70 percent of the variation in the degree of democratization (ID) in this group of 172 countries, the results support the argument that a significant part of the variation in ID can be traced to differences in mean temperature via intervening variables.

Further, we cannot know on the basis of correlations how well the average relationships between variables apply to single countries. Because a substantial part of the variation in dependent variables remains unexplained, it is clear that many countries deviate considerably from the hypothesized relationships. The results of regression analyses at the level of single countries will be used to clarify these questions. They will also disclose to what extent the most deviating countries remain the same in all regressions. If it can be shown that a substantial part of the large outliers in the regression of the IPR on national IQ are the same as the large outliers in the regression of national IQ on mean temperature, it would support the argument on the causal link between mean temperature (MT) and the IPR via national IQ. The same applies to the hypothesized causal link between mean temperature and the level of democratization via the IPR and national IQ. We shall return to these questions in later chapters of this book.

Multiple regression analysis

The results of correlation analysis do not indicate the relative significance of independent variables. Is there any direct relationship between MT and the measures of democratization that is independent from the intervening variables (national IQ and the IPR), or is the explanation provided by MT completely overlapping with the explanations provided by national IQ and the IPR? And is there any direct relationship between national IQ and the measures of democratization that is independent from the IPR? Multiple regression analysis helps to find answers to these questions. Multiple regression discloses the impact of each explanatory variable on the dependent variable when the impact of the other explanatory variables is controlled. Of the two indices of resource distribution (the IPR and the mean), only the IPR is taken into account in multiple regression analyses, and of the five measures of democratization (ID) over the years 2002–2006 (see Table 3.4), only ID-2006 is taken into account. I selected ID-2006 for this purpose because the latest data on democratization are from the year 2006. Since the measures of democratization over the period 2002–2006 are extremely strongly intercorrelated (see Table 3.3), it does not make much difference which one of them is used in multiple regression analysis. Let us start from a multiple regression analysis in which MT, national IQ, and the IPR are used to explain the variation in ID-2006 (Table 3.6).

Table 3.6 shows that the impact of MT and national IQ on ID-2006 that is independent from the IPR is insignificant (see standardized

Table 3.6. The results of multiple regression analysis in which MT, national IQ, and the IPR are used to explain variation in ID-2006 in the group of 172 countries

Variable	Coefficient	Std. Error	Std. Coeff.	t-Value	P-Value
Intercept	4.159	6.615	4.159	0.628	0.5310
MT	0.098	0.101	0.063	0.967	0.3348
National IQ	-0.069	0.073	-0.066	-0.936	0.3507
IPR	0.570	0.047	0.906	12.226	<0.0001
R = 0.816					
R squared = 0.666					

coefficients). The coefficients of MT and national IQ are not statistically significant, whereas the coefficient of the IPR is statistically highly significant. In fact, the explained part of variation in ID-2006 seems to be nearly completely due to the IPR. The multiple correlation 0.816 is only slightly higher than the simple correlation between the IPR and ID-2006 (0.813). These results show that MT and national IQ do not explain anything of the variation in ID-2006 independently from the IPR. In other words, the relationships between MT and ID-2006 and between national IQ and ID-2006 seem to completely overlap with the correlation between the IPR and ID-2006. This means that the hypothesized causal link between MT and ID is mediated by national IQ and the IPR and that the causal link between national IQ and ID is mediated by the IPR. Because the IPR is relatively strongly related to national IQ and MT, I think that it is justified to trace the causal roots of ID to national IQ and MT via the IPR.

Let us next explore the relative significance of national IQ and the IPR as explanatory factors of ID-2006 when MT is excluded from the model (Table 3.7). Is there any direct impact of national IQ on ID-2006 that is independent from the IPR?

The results of this multiple regression analysis indicate that national IQ does not explain anything of the variation in ID-2006 that is independent from the impact of the IPR. The coefficient of national IQ is not statistically significant. The impact of national IQ on ID-2006 seems to be completely mediated by IPR. The multiple correlation 0.815 is practically the same as the simple correlation between IPR and ID-2006 (0.813). Although the correlation between national IQ and ID-2006 is 0.575, the impact of national IQ on ID is insignificantly independent from

Table 3.7. The results of multiple regression analysis in which national IQ and the IPR are used to explain variation in ID-2006 in the group of 172 countries

Variable	Coefficient	Std. Error	Std. Coeff.	t-Value	P-Value
Intercept	8.215	5.128	8.215	1.602	0.1110
National IQ	-0.089	0.070	-0.086	-1.265	0.2077
IPR	0.552	0.043	0.878	12.936	<0.0001
R = 0.815					
R squared = 0.664					

the IPR. It is evident that the IPR functions as an intervening mechanism in the hypothesized causal connection between national IQ and ID.

MT and national IQ do not increase the explained part of variation in ID-2006 independently from the IPR, but are both needed to explain variation in the IPR? The multiple regression analysis in which MT and national IQ are used as independent variables and the IPR as the dependent variable answers this question (Table 3.8).

Table 3.8. The results of multiple regression analysis in which MT and national IQ are used to explain variation in the IPR in the group of 172 countries

Variable	Coefficient	Std. Error	Std. Coeff.	t-Value	P-Value
Intercept	-28.377	10.718	-28.377	-2.648	0.0089
MT	-0.869	0.153	-0.350	-5.692	<0.0001
National IQ	0.861	0.101	0.523	8.505	<0.0001
R = 0.799					
R squared = 0.638					

Table 3.8 shows that both MT and national IQ affect the variation in IPR independently from each other. The multiple correlation 0.799 is clearly higher than the simple correlation between national IQ and the IPR (0.754). The coefficients of both variables are statistically highly significant. However, the impact of national IQ on the IPR is clearly greater than the impact of MT. Taken together they seem to explain nearly two-thirds of the variation in the IPR, which means that the causal roots of national differences in the IPR can be traced to a significant extent to MT and national IQ.

The results of multiple regression analyses indicate that the explained part of variation in the level of democratization (ID) is nearly completely due to the degree of resource distribution (IPR). National IQ and mean temperature (MT) do not explain anything of the variation in ID independently from the IPR, although they are moderately correlated with ID-2006. Further, the explained part of variation in the IPR is to some extent due to both MT and national IQ (multiple correlation 0.799), but national IQ is more strongly correlated with the IPR than MT. According to my interpretation, national IQ functions as a significant intervening mechanism in the hypothesized causal connection between MT and the IPR. Figure 3.1, based on simple correlations between variables, illustrates the causal roots of democratization and causal

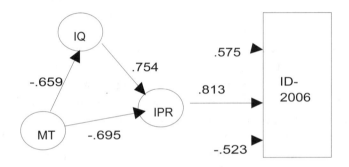

Figure 3.1. Causal roots of democratization from annual mean temperature (MT) via national IQ and IPR to ID-2006

paths between the ultimate explanatory factors and democratization.

In Figure 3.1, MT is the ultimate causal factor that temporally precedes national IQ and the IPR. It explains 43 percent of the variation in national IQ, which relationship reflects the evolutionary origin of differences in national IQs. National IQ explains 57 percent of the variation in the IPR and taken together with MT 64 percent, although the multiple correlation between MT and national IQ and the IPR (0.799) is not given in Figure 3.1. The correlation between MT and IPR is -0.695, but the results of a multiple regression analysis (Table 3.8) indicate that the impact of MT on the IPR takes place principally through national IQ. Finally, IPR explains 66 percent of the variation in ID-2006. The direct correlations between MT and ID-2006 (-0.523) and between national IQ and ID-2006 (0.575) are also given in Figure 3.1, although their impact on ID-2006 seems to take place completely via the IPR (see Table 3.6).

The results of empirical analysis imply that there are limits of democratization and that they can be traced via the IPR to national IQ and mean temperature (MT). Climatic conditions are outside human control, and differences in national IQ are most probably based to a significant extent on small evolved genetic differences between populations. Therefore, the human chances to equalize national differences in the IPR, which explains approximately 70 percent of the variation in the level of democratization, are quite limited. It is not reasonable to expect the emergence of approximately similar democracy in all countries of the world because it does not seem possible to establish equally favorable social conditions for democratization throughout the world. We are bound to live in a world in which the nature of political systems and the quality of democracy vary significantly.

However, because the level of democratization is only partly dependent on the degree of resource distribution, and because the degree of resource distribution is not completely dependent on national IQ and MT, there are chances to further democratization by appropriate social reforms and institutional selections. Therefore, it would be useful to explore factors which are related to clear deviations from the average relationship between the level of democratization and its determinants. This can be done, to some extent, by exploring the results of regression analyses at the level of single countries.

CHAPTER 4

MT As a Determinant of National IQ

The purpose of this study on the limits of democratization is to explore to what extent it is possible to trace the roots of democratization (ID) via resource distribution (IPR) to differences in national intelligence (national IQ) and climatic conditions (MT). The results of statistical analyses (Chapter 3) support the three research hypotheses formulated in Chapter 2. There seems to be a causal path from climatic conditions via national IQ and resource distribution (IPR) to the variation in the level of democratization (ID and GID), but the hypothesized causal relationships between variables are not complete. MT explains 43 percent of the variation in national IQ, national IQ explains 57 percent of the variation in the IPR, and the IPR explains 66–73 percent of the variation in the level of democratization in the period 2002–2006. This means that there is a lot of room for outlying cases and other explanatory factors. It is obvious that an average relationship between variables does not apply equally well to all single countries. In the following chapters, my purpose is to explore, on the basis of regression analyses, how well MT determines the value of national IQ at the level of single countries, how well MT and national IQ determine the value of the IPR at the level of single countries, and how well the IPR, MT, and national IQ determine the level of democratization at the level of single countries (see Figure 3.1). The examination of the most outlying countries may help to find factors which have caused some countries to deviate significantly from the regression line.

Let us start from the regression of national IQ on mean temperature (MT) because it was assumed that racial differences in intelligence emerged when people migrated out of Africa to other parts of the world and when they had to become adapted to different geographical and climatic conditions. It was assumed that selection pressure raised the average intelligence of people in cold regions of the world and that, consequently, there must be a linear causal relationship between MT and national IQ.

Satoshi Kanazawa (2007) argues that it was the evolutionary novelty of the environment which increased general intelligence rather than the cold climate and harsh winters. He measures evolutionary novelty by latitude, longitude, and distance from the ancestral environment and comes to the conclusion that annual mean temperature and evolutionary novelty simultaneously have had independent effects on average intelligence of populations. According to the results of his analysis, temperature and evolutionary novelty together explain half to two-thirds of the variance in national IQ. This would be somewhat more than what MT alone explains of the variance in national IQ, but in this connection my attention is limited to the impact of MT on national IQ.

The impact of MT on national IQ

The moderate negative correlation between MT and national IQ (-0.659) supports the first hypothesis about the negative relationship between the annual mean temperature and national IQ, but because their covariation is not more than 43 percent, many countries deviate from the average relationship. The results of regression analysis of national IQ on MT summarized in Figure 4.1 show that the negative relationship between MT and national IQ is linear, as hypothesized, and that the number of deviating countries is really large. Some of the most outlying countries are named in the figure.

Figure 4.1 illustrates the hypothesized negative correlation between MT and national IQ. National IQ is 85 or higher for nearly all countries in which annual mean temperature is lower than 15 degrees centigrade, whereas the relationship between MT and

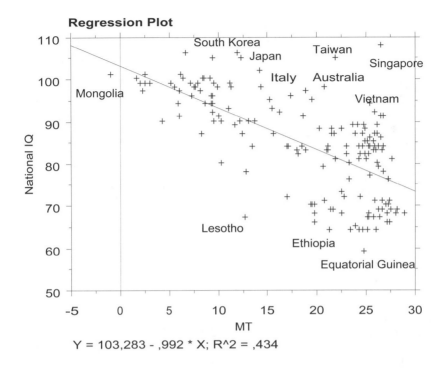

Figure 4.1. The results of regression analysis of national IQ on annual mean temperature (MT) in the group of 172 countries

national IQ is much weaker in the group of countries for which MT is higher than 15 degrees centigrade. The problem is to learn why the relationship becomes much weaker at higher levels of MT. Figure 4.1 also implies that national IQ does not rise continually with the decrease of MT. National IQ seems to have achieved the highest level in countries of temperate climate from 5 to 15 degrees centigrade. When MT drops below 5, national IQ no longer rises, but it remains at the level of 95–100. The examination of single countries may help to disclose some causes of large deviations from the regression line. The detailed results of regression analysis of national IQ on MT are given in Table 4.1.

Table 4.1. The results of regression analyses of national IQ on MT for single countries in the group of 172 countries

	Country	MT	National IQ	Residual IQ	Fitted IQ
1	Afghanistan	13.6	84	-5.8	89.8
2	Albania	13.8	90	0.4	89.6
3	Algeria	21.2	83	0.8	82.2
4	Angola	22.6	68	-12.9	80.9
5	Argentina	15.6	93	5.2	87.8
6	Armenia	9.6	94	0.2	93.8
7	Australia	20.8	98	15.4	82.6
8	Austria	6.6	100	3.3	96.7
9	Azerbaijan	12.6	87	-3.8	90.8
10	Bahamas	24.7	84	5.2	78.8
11	Bahrain	26.8	83	6.3	76.7
12	Bangladesh	25.3	82	3.8	78.2
13	Barbados	26.2	80	2.7	77.3
14	Belarus	6.2	97	-0.1	97.1
15	Belgium	9.7	99	5.3	93.7
16	Belize	26.0	84	6.5	77.5
17	Benin	27.4	70	-6.1	76.1
18	Bhutan	10.4	80	-13.0	93.0
19	Bolivia	21.6	87	5.2	81.8
20	Bosnia and Herzegovina	9.7	90	-3.7	93.7
21	Botswana	19.8	70	-13.6	83.6
22	Brazil	24.0	87	7.5	79.5
23	Brunei	26.9	91	14.4	76.6
24	Bulgaria	11.2	93	0.8	92.2
25	Burkina Faso	28.1	68	-7.4	75.4
26	Burma (Myanmar)	24.7	87	8.2	78.8
27	Burundi	21.5	69	-12.9	81.9
28	Cambodia	26.9	91	14.4	76.6
29	Cameroon	24.7	64	-14.8	78.8
30	Canada	2.6	99	-1.7	100.7
31	Cape Verde	23.4	76	-4.1	80.1
32	Central African Republic	25.2	64	-14.3	78.3
33	Chad	27.3	68	-8.2	76.2
34	Chile	10.4	90	-3.0	93.0
35	China	9.6	105	11.2	93.8
36	Colombia	24.4	84	4.9	79.1
37	Comoros	25.5	77	-1.0	78.0
38	Congo, Dem. Republic	24.0	65	-14.5	79.5

	Country	MT	National IQ	Residual IQ	Fitted IQ
39	Congo, Republic of	24.4	64	-15.1	79.1
40	Costa Rica	24.8	89	10.3	78.7
41	Côte d'Ivoire	26.4	69	-8.1	77.1
42	Croatia	12.3	90	-1.1	91.1
43	Cuba	25.2	85	6.7	78.3
44	Cyprus	18.7	91	6.3	84.7
45	Czech Republic	7.8	98	2.5	95.5
46	Denmark	7.7	98	2.4	95.6
47	Djibouti	29.0	68	-6.5	74.5
48	Dominican Republic	25.0	82	3.5	78.5
49	East Timor	26.2	87	9.7	77.3
50	Ecuador	20.4	88	5.0	83.0
51	Egypt	22.0	81	-0.4	81.4
52	El Salvador	23.3	80	-0.2	80.2
53	Equatorial Guinea	24.8	59	-19.7	78.7
54	Eritrea	25.3	68	-10.2	78.2
55	Estonia	5.3	99	1.0	98.0
56	Ethiopia	21.3	64	-18.1	82.1
57	Fiji	25.0	88	9.5	78.5
58	Finland	2.1	99	-2.2	101.2
59	France	11.4	98	6.0	92.0
60	Gabon	25.2	64	-14.3	78.3
61	Gambia	27.5	66	-10.0	76.0
62	Georgia	9.4	94	0.0	94.0
63	Germany	8.1	99	3.8	95.2
64	Ghana	26.7	71	-5.8	76.8
65	Greece	16.3	92	4.9	87.1
66	Guatemala	20.7	79	-3.7	82.7
67	Guinea	25.4	67	-11.1	78.1
68	Guinea-Bissau	26.5	67	-10.0	77.0
69	Guyana	26.0	87	9.5	77.5
70	Haiti	25.2	67	-11.3	78.3
71	Honduras	24.4	81	1.9	79.1
72	Hungary	10.0	98	4.6	93.4
73	Iceland	2.7	101	0.4	100.6
74	India	24.5	82	3.0	79.0
75	Indonesia	26.2	87	9.7	77.3
76	Iran	17.2	84	-2.2	86.2
77	Iraq	21.9	87	5.5	81.5
78	Ireland	9.5	92	-1.9	93.9
79	Israel	19.6	95	11.2	83.8

	Country	MT	National IQ	Residual IQ	Fitted IQ
80	Italy	14.3	102	12.9	89.1
81	Jamaica	26.0	71	-6.5	77.5
82	Japan	12.4	105	14.0	91.0
83	Jordan	18.6	84	-0.8	84.8
84	Kazakhstan	6.1	94	-3.2	97.2
85	Kenya	24.5	72	-7.0	79.0
86	Korea, North	6.8	106	9.5	96.5
87	Korea, South	12.1	106	14.7	91.3
88	Kuwait	25.5	86	8.0	78.0
89	Kyrgyzstan	4.4	90	8.9	98.9
90	Laos	24.2	89	9.7	79.3
91	Latvia	5.7	98	0.4	97.6
92	Lebanon	18.2	82	-3.2	85.2
93	Lesotho	12.8	67	-23.6	90.6
94	Liberia	25.9	67	-10.6	77.6
95	Libya	21.1	83	0.7	82.3
96	Lithuania	6.2	91	-6.1	97.1
97	Luxembourg	8.5	100	5.2	94.8
98	Macedonia	10.2	91	-2.2	93.2
99	Madagascar	23.1	82	1.6	80.4
100	Malawi	21.7	69	-12.7	81.7
101	Malaysia	26.0	92	14.5	77.5
102	Maldives	27.8	81	5.3	75.7
103	Mali	28.3	69	-6.2	75.2
104	Malta	18.9	97	12.5	84.5
105	Mauritania	27.4	76	-0.1	76.1
106	Mauritius	23.7	89	9.2	79.8
107	Mexico	21.6	88	6.2	81.8
108	Moldova	9.5	96	2.1	93.9
109	Mongolia	-0.8	101	-3.1	104.1
110	Montenegro	11.8	89	-2.6	91.6
111	Morocco	17.1	84	-2.3	86.3
112	Mozambique	23.5	64	-16.0	80.0
113	Namibia	19.6	70	-13.8	83.8
114	Nepal	13.0	78	-12.4	90.4
115	Netherlands	9.3	100	5.9	94.1
116	New Zealand	11.3	99	6.9	92.1
117	Nicaragua	25.1	81	2.6	78.4
118	Niger	27.6	69	-6.9	75.9
119	Nigeria	26.8	69	-7.7	76.7
120	Norway	1.8	100	-1.5	101.5

	Country	MT	National IQ	Residual IQ	Fitted IQ
121	Oman	25.9	83	5.4	77.6
122	Pakistan	21.2	84	1.8	82.2
123	Panama	25.5	84	6.0	78.0
124	Papua New Guinea	26.1	83	5.6	77.4
125	Paraguay	23.1	84	3.6	80.4
126	Peru	22.6	88	7.1	80.9
127	Philippines	26.6	86	9.1	76.9
128	Poland	7.3	99	3.0	96.0
129	Portugal	15.3	95	6.9	88.1
130	Qatar	26.9	78	1.4	76.6
131	Romania	8.8	94	-0.5	94.5
132	Russia	2.4	97	-3.9	100.9
133	Rwanda	19.5	70	-13.9	83.9
134	Saudi Arabia	25.3	84	5.8	78.2
135	Senegal	27.2	66	-10.3	76.3
136	Serbia	11.8	89	-2.6	91.6
137	Sierra Leone	26.1	64	-13.4	77.4
138	Singapore	26.6	108	31.1	76.9
139	Slovakia	7.4	96	0.1	95.9
140	Slovenia	9.4	96	2.0	94.0
141	Solomon Islands	26.3	84	6.8	77.2
142	Somalia	27.2	68	-8.3	76.3
143	South Africa	17.1	72	-14.3	86.3
144	Spain	14.4	98	9.0	89.0
145	Sri Lanka	26.3	79	1.8	77.2
146	Sudan	27.5	71	-5.0	76.0
147	Suriname	26.2	89	11.7	77.3
148	Swaziland	19.9	68	-15.5	83.5
149	Sweden	3.1	99	-1.2	100.2
150	Switzerland	6.3	101	4.0	97.0
151	Syria	18.1	83	-2.3	85.3
152	Taiwan	22.0	105	23.6	81.4
153	Tajikistan	8.4	87	-7.9	94.9
154	Tanzania	22.8	72	-8.7	80.7
155	Thailand	26.6	91	14.1	76.9
156	Togo	27.1	70	-6.4	76.4
157	Trinidad and Tobago	25.9	85	7.4	77.6
158	Tunisia	19.0	83	-1.4	84.4
159	Turkey	13.2	90	-0.2	90.2
160	Turkmenistan	15.7	87	-0.7	87.7
161	Uganda	22.6	73	-7.9	80.9

	Country	MT	National IQ	Residual IQ	Fitted IQ
162	Ukraine	8.3	97	2.0	95.0
163	United Arab Emirates	26.9	84	7.4	76.6
164	United Kingdom	8.7	100	5.4	94.6
165	United States	10.1	98	4.7	93.3
166	Uruguay	17.4	96	10.0	86.0
167	Uzbekistan	12.5	87	-3.9	90.9
168	Venezuela	25.5	84	6.0	78.0
169	Vietnam	25.5	94	16.0	78.0
170	Yemen	25.0	85	6.5	78.5
171	Zambia	20.9	71	-11.5	82.5
172	Zimbabwe	19.9	66	-17.5	83.5

Table 4.1 shows that many countries with large positive or negative residuals deviate considerably from the regression line, which implies the impact of other factors. It is reasonable to separate the more highly divergent countries from the less deviating ones and to explore what factors might explain their deviations from the regression line. Because one standard deviation for residual national IQ is 8.9, it is plausible to place countries with residuals ±8.9 or higher in the category of the most deviating countries.

Using this criterion, positive residuals are large for the following 26 countries: Australia, Brunei, Cambodia, China, Costa Rica, East Timor, Fiji, Guyana, Indonesia, Israel, Italy, Japan, North Korea, South Korea, Laos, Malaysia, Malta, Mauritius, Philippines, Singapore, Spain, Suriname, Taiwan, Thailand, Uruguay, and Vietnam.

Negative residuals are large for the following 30 countries: Angola, Bhutan, Botswana, Burundi, Cameroon, Central African Republic, Democratic Republic of Congo, Republic of Congo, Equatorial Guinea, Eritrea, Ethiopia, Gabon, Gambia, Guinea, Guinea-Bissau, Haiti, Kyrgyzstan, Lesotho, Liberia, Malawi, Mozambique, Namibia, Nepal, Rwanda, Senegal, Sierra Leone, South Africa, Swaziland, Zambia, and Zimbabwe.

For the other 116 countries, residuals are smaller than ±8.9. These countries are around the regression line. Their national IQs are approximately at the level expected on the basis of the annual mean temperature (MT). They most clearly support the first hypothesis.

It is easy to see that countries with large positive and negative residuals differ from each other geographically. Therefore it is plausible to start the analysis of single countries by dividing the total group of 172 countries into six regional and cultural subgroups: (1) European and European offshoot countries (N=48), (2) Latin American and Caribbean countries (N=27), (3) sub-Saharan African countries (N=46), (4) Middle Eastern and North African countries (N=18), (5) East Asian countries (N=6), and (6) other Asian and Pacific countries (N=27). In this classification, the European group includes Canada, the United States, Australia, and New Zealand outside Europe; Armenia, Azerbaijan, and Georgia from the Caucasus; and Cyprus and Turkey from the Mediterranean. The East Asian group includes China, Japan, North Korea, South Korea, Mongolia, and Taiwan. Singapore is in the group of other Asian and Pacific countries. The distribution of large outliers by regional groups is presented in Table 4.2.

Table 4.2. The 56 countries with large positive or negative residuals (±8.9 or higher) on the basis of the regression of national IQ on MT classified by regional groups

Regional group	N	Large positive %	N	Large negative %	N	Total %
Europe and offshoots	4	15.4	0	0	4	7.1
Latin America and the Caribbean	4	15.4	1	3.3	5	8.9
Sub-Saharan Africa	1	3.8	26	86.7	27	48.2
Middle East and North Africa	1	3.8	0	0	1	1.8
East Asia	5	19.2	0	0	5	8.9
Other Asia and Pacific	11	42.3	3	10.0	14	25.0
Total	26	100	30	100.0	56	100

Table 4.2 shows that there are striking geographical differences in the distribution of large outliers. Most countries with large positive residuals are in Asia. Of the 30 countries with large negative residuals, 26 are sub-Saharan African countries. Bhutan, Kyrgyzstan, and Nepal are from the region of the Himalaya Mountains and Haiti, with a West African and mulatto population, is from the Caribbean. This category does not include any country from the regional groups of Europe, the Middle East, and East Asia.

How to explain these geographical differences between the two categories of highly deviating countries? It seems to me that there are two principal explanatory factors behind large outliers: population migrations and the impact of mountainous regions on mean temperature in some countries. It is quite possible that large positive residuals of some tropical Latin American countries and most Southeast Asian countries reflect the history of ancient and recent migrations. The same argument concerns large negative residuals of southern African countries. The mean temperature of mountainous countries tends to be clearly lower than the mean temperature of neighboring lowland countries.

European and European offshoot countries

The regional group of European and European offshoot countries includes only four large outliers. For the other 44 countries residuals are smaller than ±8.9. Australia's large positive residual is easy to explain. Australia is inhabited by relatively recent migrants from Europe. Therefore its national IQ (98) represents the average national IQ of Europeans. In the case of Malta, it is also evident that migrants from Europe raised its national IQ (97) much higher than in the neighboring Tunisia (84). Italy and Spain are more problematic cases. Italy's national IQ (102) is exceptionally high. Ancient migrations from the north may have raised its IQ, especially so in northern Italy where mean temperature is lower than in southern Italy. It is also evident that descendants of ancient migrants from the colder regions of Europe constitute a substantial part of Spain's population (cf. Cavalli-Sforza et al. 1996, pp. 258–260). It is remarkable that the national IQ of nearly all European countries is approximately at the level expected on the basis of MT.

Latin American and Caribbean countries

In the case of American countries, it is obvious that the present populations of most countries are relatively recent ones. It was assumed in Chapter 1 that the ancestors of Amerindians migrated to America via Siberia and Alaska probably before the last ice age. They had evolved in temperate and cold climatic conditions after the "Out of Africa" migration, and their average IQ may have risen approximately to the present day level of 86 (Lynn 2006, pp. 240–243). In America these populations inhabited all climatic zones from the cold and temperate regions to the tropics. It is remarkable that the skin color of Amerindians has remained approximately the same throughout the Americas despite great climatic differences. The period of time seems to have been too short for significant morphological adaptations. The same is probably true for their mental abilities. There does not seem to be much variation in the average intelligence of Amerindian populations (see Lynn 1997, pp. 261–262; 2003, p. 137; Lynn and Vanhanen 2002, p. 23).

J. Philippe Rushton notes that Amerindians "are descendants of an archaic Mongoloid people that entered the Americas prior to the main Würm glaciation of approximately 24,000–10,000 years ago that produced the 'classical' Mongoloid features with their highly elevated cognitive abilities" (Rushton 1995, p. 230). Richard Lynn, who first proposed the cold winters theory in 1987, argues that the American Indians "escaped the full rigor of the cold northern environment by migrating into the Americas before the onset of the last ice age, which lasted between around 24,000 and 10,000 years." He emphasizes that the extreme cold of the last ice age boosted the intelligence level of the Mongoloids by a further 15 IQ points and of the European Caucasoids by a further 10 IQ points. This explains, he says, "why the first Mongoloid and Caucasoid civilizations were developed after the end of the last ice age and not during any of the warm interludes which have occurred in Eurasia during the course of the last 100,000 years" (Lynn 1997, pp. 275–276).

Europeans and Africans are even more recent migrants to the Americas, whence they migrated during the last 400 years. Most Europeans settled in the cold and temperate regions of North and South America, whereas most Africans are living in the hot and tropical regions of the Americas and the Caribbean. Africans constitute the majority of populations in the Caribbean countries (for ancient migrations, see also Howells 1992; Cavalli-Sforza and Cavalli-Sforza 1995; Cavalli-Sforza et al. 1996; Itzkoff 2000; Olson 2002; Stringer 2003; Oppenheimer 2003; Wells 2003).

Because differences in climatic conditions have not yet had time to significantly affect the morphological structures or mental abilities of the migrant populations of American countries, the variation in national IQs is mainly due to racial differences of populations. National IQs are highest (90 or higher) for the countries with cold and temperate climatic zones (Canada, the United States, Argentina, Chile, and Uruguay), in which Europeans constitute the majority of the population, and national IQs are lowest for the tropical Caribbean countries (from 67 to 84), which are inhabited mainly by Africans (the Bahamas, Barbados, Haiti, and Jamaica). For the other Latin American and Caribbean countries, national IQs vary from 79 (Guatemala) to 89 (Costa Rica). The differences in national IQs are related to the relative shares of Europeans, Africans, East Indians, and Amerindians in these countries.

All these countries are situated completely or partially (Mexico, Brazil, and Paraguay) in the tropics between the Tropic of Cancer and the Tropic of Capricorn. The mean annual temperature (MT) is lowest for mountainous Guatemala, Ecuador, and Bolivia as well as for Mexico, Brazil, and Paraguay, which are situated partly in the temperate climatic zone. For the other 14 countries MT varies from 24.4 (Colombia) to 26.2 (Surinam). Residuals are positive (mostly relatively small) for all these tropical countries except for Guatemala and El Salvador. The group includes three (Costa Rica, Guyana, and Surinam) of the four Latin American and Caribbean countries for which positive residuals are higher than 8.9. Costa Rica is inhabited mainly by Europeans. In Guyana East Indians constitute approximately half of the population. In Surinam more than 50 percent of the population belong to East Indians and Javanese. Uruguay is situated in the temperate zone of Latin America, but its residual is positive and large because it is inhabited by European migrants. Haiti is the only Latin American country for which the negative residual is higher than -8.9. The national IQ (67) of its completely African population is significantly lower than expected on the basis of MT (25.2).

According to my interpretation, positive residuals for tropical Latin American and Caribbean countries reflect the fact that these countries are inhabited by migrant populations whose mental abilities evolved in colder climates. This means that these residuals do not necessarily contradict the hypothesis.

Sub-Saharan African countries

How to explain the clustering of countries with large negative residuals in sub-Saharan Africa? The pattern of the regression plot (see Figure 4.1) provides a partial answer. Residuals are highly positive for many tropical Southeast Asian and Latin American countries, which are inhabited by recent migrants from colder climatic zones or by hybrid populations. As explained earlier, selection pressure enhanced the average intelligence of populations that migrated out of Africa to a higher degree than the case was and still is in the original environment of the human species in tropical Africa. When some of the people that migrated out of Africa later entered the tropical regions of Southeast Asia and Latin America, their enhanced level of intelligence did not decrease to the same level as it had originally been in tropical Africa. Consequently, the differences in the evolutionary history of the populations of tropical Southeast Asian, Latin American, and African countries may explain a major part of the contrast between their contemporary national IQs.

Let us examine the 26 sub-Saharan African countries with large negative residuals in greater detail. Relatively recent migrations seem to explain some extremely large negative residuals of sub-Saharan African countries. Residuals are highly negative for all southern African countries (Botswana, Lesotho, Namibia, South Africa, Swaziland, and Zimbabwe). In all these countries, the annual mean temperature (MT) is below 20 degrees centigrade. These countries are inhabited mainly by Bantus, but the Bantu expansion to central and southern Africa started only 2500–3000 years ago and reached the sparsely populated South Africa only some hundreds of years ago. This means that these six countries of southern Africa are inhabited by relatively recent migrants from the tropics (for ancient migrations in Africa, see Cavalli-Sforza et al. 1996:158–194). Their mental abilities evolved in the tropics before their migration to the colder region of southern Africa, which may explain, according to my interpretation, the extremely large negative residuals of these countries.

In the other 20 sub-Saharan African countries with large negative residuals, the annual mean temperature varies from 19.5 in Rwanda to 27.2 in Senegal. All of these countries are wholly or at least partly tropical. Note that residuals are negative for all sub-Saharan African countries, except for Madagascar and Mauritius. There is an environmental explanation for the lower than expected national IQs in sub-Saharan Africa. Richard Lynn (2006, pp. 70–71) argues that the actual mean IQ of Africans (67) is much lower than the estimated genotypic African IQ of 80. Unfavorable environmental conditions have kept national IQs below the genotypic potential in sub-Saharan Africa, by which he means that Africans could obtain the genotypic African IQ of 80 if the environments in which they were raised were the same as those of Europeans. His argument is "that adverse environmental conditions in sub-Saharan Africa impair the African IQ by around 13 IQ points" (p. 71). This difference of 13 IQ points would be enough to explain the negative residuals of sub-Saharan African countries. The adverse environmental conditions include, for example, difficult geographical and climatic conditions and tropical diseases, which hamper economic development.

The residual is slightly positive for Madagascar (1.6) and highly positive for Mauritius (9.2). Madagascar's IQ of 82 is 15 points higher than the African average of 67, and Mauritius' IQ of 89 is even higher. The populations of Madagascar and Mauritius differ racially to some extent from those of other African countries. Malayo-Indonesians constitute a significant part of Madagascar's population, while in Mauritius, recent migrants from India (68 %), Europe, and China constitute over 70 percent of the population.

The Middle East and North Africa

The national IQs of the Middle Eastern and North African countries are in better balance with the annual mean temperature than in any other regional group. Positive and negative residuals are small for nearly all countries. Positive residual is large only for Israel (11.2). Of the Jewish population of Israel, approximately half are recent migrants from the north (mainly from Europe), which has raised Israel's IQ considerably higher than in neighboring Arab countries. I think that migrations from Europe and North America provide a sufficient explanation for Israel's large positive residual.

East Asia

The actual level of national IQ is much higher than expected for all East Asian countries, except for Mongolia. The evolutionary history of East Asians may provide an explanation for these deviations. Their high level of intelligence may have evolved in much colder climatic conditions than in which they now live. Richard Lynn (2006, p. 238) notes that the winters to which archaic East Asians were exposed were much more severe than in South Asia and somewhat more severe than in Europe: "It was in response to the cold winters that the East Asians evolved the cold adaptations of the flattened nose to prevent frost bite, the short legs and thick trunk to conserve heat, the subcutaneous layer of fat that gives the skin a yellowish appearance,...." Lynn assumes it to be probable that, as with the Europeans, most of the increase in the intelligence of East Asians occurred during the main Würm glaciation. Later on they spread to somewhat warmer regions of China and East Asia.

Korea and Japan were colonized thousands of years ago by migrants who had evolved in colder regions of Asia. The positive residual is extremely large for Taiwan (23.6), which is situated at the border of the tropics. Its extremely high positive residual contradicts the hypothesis, but it should be noted that 14 percent of its population are recent immigrants from mainland China and that most of the other Taiwanese are also descendants of Chinese migrants. Chinese settlers started to arrive in Taiwan since the 7th century. The original Aboriginal people do not constitute more than 2 percent of the population (Cavalli-Sforza et al.1996: 235; *World Directory of Minorities 1997, p.* 641; *Philip's Encyclopedic World Atlas 2000, p.* 215). So nearly all Taiwanese are descendants of migrants from somewhat colder mainland China.

Other Asian and Oceanian countries

Positive residuals are large for 11 other Asian and Oceanian countries (Brunei, Cambodia, East Timor, Fiji, Indonesia, Laos, Malaysia, Philippines, Singapore, Thailand, and Vietnam), and negative residuals are large for three countries (Bhutan, Kyrgyzstan, and Nepal). Are there any explanations for these outliers?

Of the 11 Asian and Oceanian countries with large positive residuals, Singapore is inhabited by recent immigrants principally from China (78%). They are now living in a tropical country, but their mental abilities evolved in the temperate climatic conditions in China. Nearly half of Fiji's population are recent immigrants from India. A significant part of the Vietnamese seem to have migrated initially from southern China during the last thousands of years. Relatively recent Chinese immigrants constitute significant minorities also in Malaysia (30%), Brunei (15–20%), Thailand (12%), Indonesia (3–4%), and Cambodia (3%). They have raised national IQs especially in Malaysia, Brunei, and Thailand.

The East Timorese population is mainly of Malay and Papuan descent.

The origin of the Southeast Asian populations is still unclear, but most of them seem to be descendants of ancient migrants from South Asia. To some extent, they have become mixed with later migrants from southern China (see Cavalli-Sforza et al. 1996, pp. 78–83, 206–208; Oppenheimer 2003). Richard Lynn (2006, p. 232) has an explanation for the Southeast Asians' IQ of 87, which is higher than that of North Africans and South Asians 84), from whom they mostly evolved. He says: "The most probable explanation is that there is some East Asian admixture in the Southeast Asians from East Asians who have migrated south and interbred with indigenous populations." He argues that as a result of migrations and intermixing, the Southeast Asian peoples are closely related genetically to the southern Chinese. Consequently, the migration of peoples from China provides at least a partial explanation for the large positive residuals of all Southeast Asian countries. In the case of Singapore, whose positive residual 32.2 is the highest in the world, recent migrants from China provide a complete explanation for its highly outlying position.

Negative residuals are large for Bhutan, Kyrgyzstan, and Nepal. The mean temperatures of these three mountainous countries are much lower than in the South Asian lowland countries (Bangladesh, India and Pakistan), whereas national IQs are approximately at the same level. Because the contemporary populations of these countries are related to the populations of the warmer South Asian countries, it is plausible to argue that their large negative residuals are due to migrations from warmer lowlands to colder mountainous countries. The same argument applies to Afghanistan, Tajikistan, and Uzbekistan, for which residuals are negative.

Summary

The review of ancient and recent migrations shows that many contemporary countries are inhabited by people most of whose ancestors evolved in different climatic conditions. There are numerous tropical and other warm countries inhabited by ancient or recent migrants from colder regions, and there are some countries of temperate zone whose most inhabitants are descendants of the migrants from the tropics or warmer regions.

The first group of countries includes most clearly Australia and Malta in the group of European and European offshoot countries, Costa Rica, Guyana, Surinam, and Uruguay in Latin America, Mauritius in sub-Saharan Africa, Israel in the Middle East, Taiwan in East Asia, and Brunei, Cambodia, Fiji, Indonesia, Malaysia, Thailand, Singapore, and Vietnam in the group of other Asian and Oceanian countries. The second group includes most clearly six countries of southern Africa (Botswana, Namibia, Lesotho, South Africa, Swaziland, and Zimbabwe) and mountainous countries like Bhutan, Kyrgyzstan, and Nepal in South Asia and Central Asia. Migrations within more or less similar climatic conditions are not taken into account. My argument is that as a consequence of migrations between climatic zones the contemporary correlation between MT and national IQ is significantly weaker than what it would

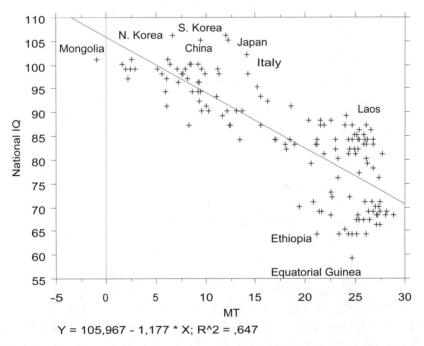

$Y = 105,967 - 1,177 * X; R^2 = ,647$

Figure 4.2. The results of regression analysis of national IQ on annual mean temperature (MT) in a group of 146 countries

be if people had remained in their original climatic zones.

The impact of ancient and recent migrations of peoples on the relationship between the mean annual temperature and national IQ can be checked by excluding the above-listed 26 countries from the analysis. In the reduced group of 146 countries, the negative correlation between MT and national IQ rises to -0.805, which means that the explained part of variation increases from 43 to 65 percent. Figure 4.2 summarizes the results of regression analysis of national IQ on MT for single countries in this reduced group of 146 countries.

We can see from Figure 4.2 that several, although not all, of the most highly deviating countries have disappeared and that the countries are more closely clustered around the regression line than in Figure 4.1. Most countries with large negative residuals are still sub-Saharan African countries, but their negative residuals are smaller than in Figure 4.1. The results imply that the original impact of climatic differences on the evolution of mental abilities of populations had been strong. The original connection between climate and national IQs may have been even stronger than this regression plot shows for the reason that migrations during the last thousands of years affected the composition of practically all national populations.

My conclusion is that there is a significant negative correlation between MT and national IQ as hypothesized and that this relationship has probably been originally even stronger than what it is now. This relationship can be regarded to be causal because climatic differences have preceded the evolution of human mental abilities and because one cannot find any mechanism by which differences in national IQ could affect climatic conditions. As a consequence of migrations of peoples during the last thousands of years, many people have moved from temperate zones to tropical countries and also from tropical countries to temperate zones. Consequently, the correlation between MT and national IQ has decreased to some extent. However, all deviations from the regression line cannot be explained by migrations of peoples. It is possible, for example, that because of difficult tropical conditions, the national IQs of sub-Saharan African countries are significantly lower than their genotypic intelligence.

CHAPTER 5

MT and IQ as Determinants of IPR

According to the first and second research hypotheses, mean temperature (MT) and national IQ are assumed to be important determinants of resource distribution (IPR). The results of correlation analysis support these hypotheses (see Chapter 3), although many countries deviate significantly from the hypothesized relationships. In this chapter, my intention is to explore, on the basis of regression analyses, the relationships between MT and IPR and between national IQ and IPR at the level of single countries. My purpose is to ascertain in which countries the level of resource distribution is approximately at the level expected on the basis of MT and national IQ and which countries deviate clearly from the regression lines. The analysis of large deviations may disclose whether there are any systematic factors behind large deviations and to what extent large deviations are the same on the basis of both MT and national IQ.

MT as a determinant of IPR

Let us start from the regression of IPR on MT, although national IQ is more strongly correlated with IPR (0.754) than MT (-0.695). MT explains 48 percent of the variation in IPR. This explanation mostly overlaps with the explanation provided by national IQ because MT and national IQ are moderately intercorrelated (-0.659). However, to some extent MT may explain the variation in IPR independently from national

IQ (see Table 3.8). The results of the regression of IPR on MT for single countries are summarized in Figure 5.1.

The figure shows that the relationship between MT and the IPR is

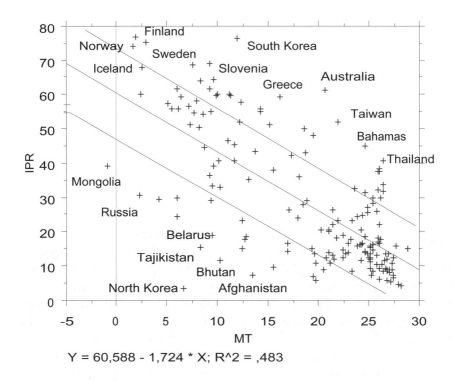

Y = 60,588 - 1,724 * X; R^2 = ,483

Figure 5.1. The results of regression analysis of IPR on annual mean temperature (MT) in the group of 172 countries

linear but not strong. Many countries deviate greatly from the regression line. Some of the most extreme deviations are shown in the figure. We can see from Figure 5.1 that the largest positive outliers are economically highly developed market economies and that most of the largest negative outliers are contemporary or former socialist countries. This observation implies that differences in economic systems matter independently from the annual mean temperature. Detailed results for single countries are given in Table 5.1.

Table 5.1. The results of regression analyses of the IPR for MT and the IPR on national IQ in the group of 172 countries

	Country	MT	IPR	Residual IPR	Fitted IPR	National IQ	Residual IPR	Fitted IPR
1	Afghanistan	13.6	7.1	-30.0	37.1	84	-20.3	27.4
2	Albania	13.8	43.3	6.5	36.8	90	8.4	34.9
3	Algeria	21.2	20.0	-4.0	24.0	83	-6.2	26.2
4	Angola	22.6	12.1	-9.5	21.6	68	4.5	7.6
5	Argentina	15.6	37.8	4.1	33.7	93	-0.8	38.6
6	Armenia	9.6	33.1	-10.9	44.0	94	-5.7	39.8
7	Australia	20.8	61.1	36.4	24.7	98	16.3	44.8
8	Austria	6.6	58.9	9.7	49.2	100	11.6	47.3
9	Azerbaijan	12.6	23.1	-15.8	38.9	87	-8.0	31.1
10	Bahamas	24.7	44.5	26.5	18.0	84	17.1	27.4
11	Bahrain	26.8	9.1	-5.3	14.4	83	-17.1	26.2
12	Bangladesh	25.3	13.1	-3.9	17.0	82	-11.8	24.9
13	Barbados	26.2	38.0	22.6	15.4	80	15.5	22.5
14	Belarus	6.2	23.9	-26.0	49.9	97	-19.7	43.6
15	Belgium	9.7	64.1	20.2	43.9	99	18.1	46.0
16	Belize	26.0	16.8	1.0	15.8	84	-10.6	27.4
17	Benin	27.4	8.4	-5.0	13.4	70	-1.6	10.0
18	Bhutan	10.4	11.4	-31.3	42.7	80	-11.1	22.5
19	Bolivia	21.6	21.6	-1.8	23.4	87	-9.5	31.1
20	Bosnia and Herzegovina	9.7	39.0	-4.9	43.9	90	4.1	34.9
21	Botswana	19.8	13.3	13.2	26.5	70	3.3	10.0
22	Brazil	24.0	24.1	4.9	19.2	87	-7.0	31.1
23	Brunei	26.9	8.3	-5.9	14.2	91	-27.8	36.1
24	Bulgaria	11.2	46.1	4.8	41.3	93	7.5	38.6
25	Burkina Faso	28.1	4.4	-7.8	12.2	68	-3.2	7.6
26	Burma (Myanmar)	24.7	18.4	0.4	18.0	87	-12.7	31.1
27	Burundi	21.5	13.0	-10.5	23.5	69	4.2	8.8
28	Cambodia	26.9	11.5	-2.7	14.2	91	-24.6	36.1
29	Cameroon	24.7	13.9	-4.1	18.0	64	11.3	2.6
30	Canada	2.6	59.8	3.7	56.1	99	13.8	46.0
31	Cape Verde	23.4	22.8	2.5	20.3	76	5.3	17.5
32	Central African Rep.	25.2	8.8	-8.4	17.2	64	6.2	2.6
33	Chad	27.3	5.2	-8.3	13.5	68	-2.4	7.6
34	Chile	10.4	32.5	-10.2	42.7	90	-2.4	34.9
35	China	9.6	18.6	-25.4	44.0	105	-34.9	53.5

	Country	MT	IPR	Residual IPR	Fitted IPR	National IQ	Residual IPR	Fitted IPR
36	Colombia	24.4	20.2	1.7	18.5	84	-7.3	27.4
37	Comoros	25.5	8.1	-8.5	16.6	77	-10.6	18.7
38	Congo, Dem. Rep.	24.0	15.7	-3.5	19.2	65	11.9	3.8
39	Congo, Rep. of	24.5	15.8	-2.7	18.5	64	13.2	2.6
40	Costa Rica	24.8	31.1	13.3	17.8	89	-2.5	33.6
41	Côte d'Ivoire	26.4	10.2	-4.9	15.1	69	1.4	8.8
42	Croatia	12.3	51.5	12.1	39.4	90	16.6	34.9
43	Cuba	25.2	15.3	-1.9	17.2	85	-13.4	28.7
44	Cyprus	18.7	49.7	21.3	28.4	91	13.6	36.1
45	Czech Republic	7.8	54.5	7.4	47.1	98	9.7	44.8
46	Denmark	7.7	68.3	21.0	47.3	98	23.5	44.8
47	Djibouti	29.0	14.8	4.2	10.6	68	7.2	7.6
48	Dominican Rep.	25.0	25.1	7.6	17.5	82	0.2	24.9
49	East Timor	26.2	8.8	-6.6	15.4	87	-22.3	31.1
50	Ecuador	20.4	20.1	-5.3	25.4	88	-12.3	32.4
51	Egypt	22.0	23.1	0.4	22.7	81	-0.6	23.7
52	El Salvador	23.3	17.6	-2.8	20.4	80	-4.9	22.5
53	Equatorial Guinea	24.8	13.5	-4.3	17.8	59	17.1	-3.6
54	Eritrea	25.3	12.1	-4.9	17.0	68	4.5	7.6
55	Estonia	5.3	56.9	5.4	51.5	99	10.9	46.0
56	Ethiopia	21.3	10.4	-13.5	23.9	64	7.8	2.6
57	Fiji	25.0	26.7	9.2	17.5	88	-5.7	32.4
58	Finland	2.1	76.6	19.6	57.0	99	30.6	46.0
59	France	11.4	59.4	18.5	40.9	98	14.6	44.8
60	Gabon	25.2	15.4	-1.8	17.2	64	12.8	2.6
61	Gambia	27.5	6.9	-6.3	13.2	66	1.8	5.1
62	Georgia	9.4	36.1	-8.3	44.4	94	-3.7	39.8
63	Germany	8.1	57.7	11.1	46.6	99	11.7	46.0
64	Ghana	26.7	11.3	-3.3	14.6	71	0.0	11.3
65	Greece	16.3	59.0	26.5	32.5	92	21.7	37.3
66	Guatemala	20.7	8.7	-16.2	24.9	79	-12.5	21.2
67	Guinea	25.4	6.8	-10.0	16.8	67	0.5	6.3
68	Guinea-Bissau	26.5	8.1	-6.8	14.9	67	1.8	6.3
69	Guyana	26.0	18.0	2.2	15.8	87	-13.1	31.1
70	Haiti	25.2	10.9	-6.3	17.2	67	4.6	6.3

	Country	MT	IPR	Residual IPR	Fitted IPR	National IQ	Residual IPR	Fitted IPR
71	Honduras	24.4	11.1	-7.4	18.5	81	-12.6	23.7
72	Hungary	10.0	59.6	16.2	43.4	98	14.8	44.8
73	Iceland	2.7	67.4	11.5	55.9	101	18.9	48.5
74	India	24.5	24.6	6.2	18.4	82	-0.3	24.9
75	Indonesia	26.2	37.3	21.9	15.4	87	6.2	31.1
76	Iran	17.2	26.0	-4.9	30.9	84	-1.4	27.4
77	Iraq	21.9	17.7	-5.1	22.8	87	-13.4	31.1
78	Ireland	9.5	54.7	10.5	44.2	92	17.4	37.3
79	Israel	19.6	47.6	20.8	26.6	95	6.5	41.1
80	Italy	14.3	54.6	18.7	35.9	102	4.8	49.8
81	Jamaica	26.0	31.7	15.9	15.8	71	20.4	11.3
82	Japan	12.4	57.5	18.3	39.2	105	4.0	53.5
83	Jordan	18.6	27.6	-0.9	28.5	84	0.2	27.4
84	Kazakhstan	6.1	29.4	-20.7	50.1	94	-10.4	39.8
85	Kenya	24.5	16.3	-2.1	18.4	72	3.8	12.5
86	Korea, North	6.8	3.0	-45.9	48.9	106	-51.7	54.7
87	Korea, South	12.1	76.1	36.4	39.7	106	21.4	54.7
88	Kuwait	25.5	14.4	-2.2	16.6	86	-15.5	29.9
89	Kyrgyzstan	4.4	29.3	-23.7	53.0	90	-5.6	34.9
90	Laos	24.2	16.0	-2.9	18.9	89	-17.6	33.6
91	Latvia	5.7	55.4	4.6	50.8	98	10.6	44.8
92	Lebanon	18.2	35.7	6.5	29.2	82	10.8	24.9
93	Lesotho	12.8	17.5	-21.0	38.5	67	11.2	6.3
94	Liberia	25.9	10.2	-5.7	15.9	67	3.9	6.3
95	Libya	21.1	20.1	-4.1	24.2	83	-6.1	26.2
96	Lithuania	6.2	61.4	11.5	49.9	91	25.3	36.1
97	Luxembourg	8.5	63.5	17.6	45.9	100	16.2	47.3
98	Macedonia	10.2	40.2	-2.8	43.0	91	4.1	36.1
99	Madagascar	23.1	13.5	-7.3	20.8	82	-11.4	24.9
100	Malawi	21.7	11.8	-11.4	23.2	69	3.0	8.8
101	Malaysia	26.0	37.4	21.6	15.8	92	0.1	37.3
102	Maldives	27.8	15.5	2.8	12.7	81	-8.2	23.7
103	Mali	28.3	3.9	-7.9	11.8	69	-4.9	8.8
104	Malta	18.9	42.8	14.8	28.0	97	-0.8	43.6
105	Mauritania	27.4	10.4	-3.0	13.4	76	-7.1	17.5
106	Mauritius	23.7	32.3	12.6	19.7	89	-1.3	33.6
107	Mexico	21.6	26.0	2.6	23.4	88	-6.4	32.4
108	Moldova	9.5	28.7	-15.5	44.2	96	-13.6	42.3
109	Mongolia	-0.8	38.9	-23.1	62.0	101	-9.6	48.5
110	Montenegro	11.8	44.9	4.6	40.3	89	11.3	33.6
111	Morocco	17.1	16.4	-14.7	31.1	84	-11.0	27.4

	Country	MT	IPR	Residual IPR	Fitted IPR	National IQ	Residual IPR	Fitted IPR
112	Mozambique	23.5	8.2	-11.9	20.1	64	5.6	2.6
113	Namibia	19.6	6.5	-20.3	26.8	70	-3.5	10.0
114	Nepal	13.0	18.2	-20.0	38.2	78	-1.8	20.0
115	Netherlands	9.3	61.3	16.7	44.6	100	14.0	47.3
116	New Zealand	11.3	59.8	18.7	41.1	99	13.8	46.0
117	Nicaragua	25.1	12.2	-5.1	17.3	81	-11.5	23.7
118	Niger	27.6	6.2	-6.8	13.0	69	-2.6	8.8
119	Nigeria	26.8	13.3	-1.1	14.4	69	4.5	8.8
120	Norway	1.8	73.8	16.3	57.5	100	26.5	47.3
121	Oman	25.9	13.0	-2.9	15.9	83	-13.2	26.2
122	Pakistan	21.2	13.7	-10.3	24.0	84	-13.7	27.4
123	Panama	25.5	28.1	11.5	16.6	84	0.7	27.4
124	Papua New Guinea	26.1	16.5	0.9	15.6	83	-9.7	26.2
125	Paraguay	23.1	16.5	-4.3	20.8	84	-10.9	27.4
126	Peru	22.6	18.8	-2.8	21.6	88	-13.6	32.4
127	Philippines	26.6	33.3	18.6	14.7	86	3.4	29.9
128	Poland	7.3	56.3	8.3	48.0	99	10.3	46.0
129	Portugal	15.3	50.7	16.5	34.2	95	9.6	41.1
130	Qatar	26.9	8.4	-5.8	14.2	78	-11.6	20.0
131	Romania	8.8	44.1	-1.3	45.4	94	4.3	39.8
132	Russia	2.4	30.1	-26.4	56.5	97	-13.5	43.6
133	Rwanda	19.5	14.6	-12.4	27.0	70	4.6	10.0
134	Saudi Arabia	25.3	11.6	-5.4	17.0	84	-15.8	27.4
135	Senegal	27.2	8.4	-5.3	13.7	66	3.3	5.1
136	Serbia	11.8	40.3	0.0	40.3	89	6.7	33.6
137	Sierra Leone	26.1	5.7	-9.9	15.6	64	3.1	2.6
138	Singapore	26.6	31.6	16.9	14.7	108	-25.6	57.2
139	Slovakia	7.4	50.7	2.9	47.8	96	8.4	42.3
140	Slovenia	9.4	68.6	24.2	44.4	96	26.3	42.3
141	Solomon Islands	26.3	17.5	2.2	15.3	84	-9.9	27.4
142	Somalia	27.2	7.6	-6.1	13.7	68	0.0	7.6
143	South Africa	17.1	14.1	-17.0	31.1	72	1.6	12.5
144	Spain	14.4	55.4	19.6	35.8	98	10.6	44.8
145	Sri Lanka	26.3	29.7	14.4	15.3	79	8.5	21.2
146	Sudan	27.5	12.2	-1.0	13.2	71	0.9	11.3
147	Suriname	26.2	21.9	6.5	15.4	89	-11.7	33.6
148	Swaziland	19.9	5.5	-20.8	26.3	68	-2.1	7.6
149	Sweden	3.1	74.9	19.7	55.2	99	28.9	46.0
150	Switzerland	6.3	55.5	5.8	49.7	101	7.0	48.5

	Country	MT	IPR	Residual IPR	Fitted IPR	National IQ	Residual IPR	Fitted IPR
151	Syria	18.1	23.8	-5.6	29.4	83	-2.4	26.2
152	Taiwan	22.0	51.6	<u>28.9</u>	22.7	105	-1.9	53.5
153	Tajikistan	8.4	15.3	<u>-30.8</u>	46.1	87	<u>-15.8</u>	31.1
154	Tanzania	22.8	13.2	-8.1	21.3	72	0.7	12.5
155	Thailand	26.6	40.5	<u>25.8</u>	14.7	91	4.4	36.1
156	Togo	27.1	13.1	-0.8	13.9	70	3.1	10.0
157	Trinidad and Tobago	25.9	25.7	9.8	15.9	85	-3.0	28.7
158	Tunisia	19.0	28.7	0.9	27.8	83	2.5	26.2
159	Turkey	13.2	35.1	-2.7	37.8	90	0.2	34.9
160	Turkmenistan	15.7	9.2	<u>-24.3</u>	33.5	87	<u>-21.9</u>	31.1
161	Uganda	22.6	14.3	-7.3	21.6	73	0.5	13.8
162	Ukraine	8.3	50.1	3.8	46.3	97	6.5	43.6
163	United Arab Emirates	26.9	5.6	-6.6	14.2	84	<u>-21.8</u>	27.4
164	United Kingdom	8.7	53.9	8.3	45.6	100	6.6	47.3
165	United States	10.1	59.9	<u>16.7</u>	43.2	98	<u>15.1</u>	44.8
166	Uruguay	17.4	41.8	11.2	30.6	96	-0.5	42.3
167	Uzbekistan	12.5	14.6	<u>-24.4</u>	39.0	87	<u>-16.5</u>	31.1
168	Venezuela	25.5	29.7	13.1	16.6	84	2.3	27.4
169	Vietnam	25.5	15.8	-0.8	16.6	94	<u>-24.0</u>	39.8
170	Yemen	25.0	13.3	-4.2	17.5	85	<u>-15.4</u>	26.7
171	Zambia	20.9	12.1	-12.5	24.6	71	0.8	11.3
172	Zimbabwe	19.9	10.4	<u>-15.9</u>	26.3	66	5.3	5.1

Table 5.1 indicates how well the average relationship between MT and the IPR applies to single countries and which countries deviate most clearly from the regression line. The most deviating countries contradict the first hypothesis about the negative relationship between MT and the IPR. We can use one standard deviation of residual IPR (±14.0) to separate the most deviating countries from the less deviating ones. In Figure 5.1, two parallel lines at the distance of approximately one standard deviation of residual IPR (±14.0) from the regression line separate the most divergent countries from the countries around the regression line. In Table 5.1, the residuals of these most divergent countries are underlined.

Large positive and negative outliers

Using this criterion, the group of large positive outliers includes 32 countries: Australia, Bahamas, Barbados, Belgium, Cyprus, Denmark, Finland, France, Greece, Hungary, Indonesia, Israel, Italy, Jamaica, Japan, South Korea, Luxembourg, Malaysia, Malta, the Netherlands, New Zealand, Norway, Philippines, Portugal, Singapore, Slovenia, Spain, Sri Lanka, Sweden, Taiwan, Thailand, and the United States.

The group of large negative outliers includes 22 countries: Afghanistan, Azerbaijan, Belarus, Bhutan, China, Guatemala, Kazakhstan, North Korea, Kyrgyzstan, Lesotho, Moldova, Mongolia, Morocco, Namibia, Nepal, Russia, South Africa, Swaziland, Tajikistan, Turkmenistan, Uzbekistan, and Zimbabwe.

The nature of the economic system seems to be the most important factor which separates large positive and negative outliers from each other. Of the 32 large positive outliers, 24 are economically highly developed market economies, whereas 12 of the 22 large negative outliers are contemporary or former socialist countries. In market economies especially, economic power resources have become more widely distributed and decentralized than in socialist economic systems. This environmental factor is nearly completely independent from mean temperature. We can see from Figure 5.1 and Table 5.1 that both types of economic systems occur at all levels of mean temperature (MT). The nature of a country's economic system is an environmental factor which is under conscious human control. Consequently, it would be possible to change this factor, and in fact it has been changed in many countries during the last decades.

Of the eight other large positive outliers, the Bahamas, Barbados, and Jamaica are Caribbean tourist countries, which have benefited from their geographical neighborhood of the United States. Indonesia, Malaysia, the Philippines, and Thailand are tropical Southeast Asian countries, which have more or less successfully adopted a market economy and which have also to some extent democratized. Sri Lanka is a South Asian tropical country, in which a high level of literacy (91%) and the dominance of family farms (FF 76%) have raised the value of IPR.

Of the ten other large negative outliers, Afghanistan, Bhutan, Guatemala, Nepal, and Morocco are mountainous countries, in which MT is some degrees lower than in neighboring lowland countries.

This geographical difference provides a sufficient explanation for their large negative residuals. Botswana, Lesotho, Namibia, South Africa, Swaziland, and Zimbabwe are southern African countries, which are inhabited by relatively recent migrants from warmer parts of sub-Saharan Africa. MT is some degrees lower in these five countries than in other parts of sub-Saharan Africa. This difference in MT explains at least a part of their large negative residuals.

It is remarkable that for the other 118 countries the actual IPR value differs less than ±14.0 IPR index points from the regression line. This observation indicates that differences in the level of resource distribution are moderately related to differences in the annual mean temperature. Economic and intellectual power resources tend to be more widely distributed in temperate and cold countries than in tropical countries. The relationship is not strong but moderate. Since we cannot change existing climatic differences, it is justified to conclude that differences in climatic conditions will most probably constrain human chances to equalize the level of resource distribution (IPR) in the world in the future.

In the reduced group of 146 countries (see Chapter 4), from which some mountainous countries and the countries most affected by relatively recent migrations have been excluded, the correlation between MT an IPR rises to 0.766 and their covariation to 59 percent. This implies that the impact of annual mean temperature to the level of IPR may be stronger than the correlation between MT and IPR in the group of 172 countries indicates.

National IQ as a determinant of IPR

National IQ is another hypothesized determinant of IPR. It is more strongly correlated with IPR than MT, but, on the other hand, a significant part of the variation in national IQ seems to be causally related to MT (see Chapter 4). Therefore, it is difficult to separate the impacts of MT and national IQ from each other.

National IQ explains 57 percent of the variation in IPR, which means that 43 percent of the variation is due to other factors. National IQ and MT taken together explain 64 percent of the variation in IPR, but still 36 percent remains unexplained. The problem is what other factors affect the level of IPR independently from national IQ and MT. Regression analysis of IPR on national IQ can be used to clarify this problem. The results of regression analysis show how well the average relationship between variables applies to single countries and which countries deviate most from the average relationship (regression line). The analysis of the most divergent cases may provide hints about factors that are related to great deviations. The results of the regression of IPR on national IQ for single countries are presented in Figure 5.2 and in Table 5.1.

Figure 5.2 shows that the relationship between national IQ and IPR is slightly curvilinear. IPR starts to rise steeply when national IQ rises above the level of 85–90. Some of the most highly outlying countries are named in Figure 5.2. The relationship between the two variables is slightly curvilinear, but because the hypothesis is linear, I analyze the results on the basis of the linear regression line. Large negative outliers

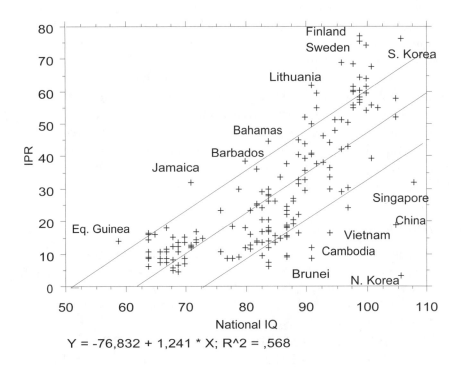

$Y = -76,832 + 1,241 * X; R^2 = ,568$

Figure 5.2. The results of regression analysis of IPR on national IQ in the group of 172 countries

are most frequent at the national IQ level from 80 to 90, whereas nearly all large positive outliers appear above the national IQ level of 90. This difference reflects the curvilinear pattern of the actual relationship between national IQ and IPR.

A central purpose of this study is to explore to what extent differences in national IQs could explain the great national variation in the degree of resource distribution (IPR). Therefore it is useful to explore the problem at the level of single countries on the basis of the regression of IPR on national IQ. Because our operational measures are not complete substitutes for the hypothetical concepts and because there are certainly measurement errors in empirical data on variables, we do not need to pay attention to relatively small deviations from the regression line. The level of IPR is more or less in balance with the level of national IQ in such countries.

It is reasonable to focus on the most extremely deviating countries, which deviate from the regression line one standard deviation (±12.8) or more. They contradict most clearly the hypothesis on the causal relationship between national IQ and IPR because national IQ has failed to predict the level of resource distribution (IPR) satisfactorily for these countries. In Figure 5.2, two parallel lines approximately at a distance of one standard deviation (±12.8) from the regression line separate the most deviating countries from the less deviating ones. In Table 5.1, the residuals of these highly divergent countries are underlined. The problem is why the degree of resource distribution differs so much from the predicted level. I try to explore what factors might be connected with these extremely deviating cases.

Large positive and negative outliers

Positive residuals are 12.8 or higher for the following 27 countries: Australia, the Bahamas, Barbados, Belgium, Canada, Republic of Congo, Croatia, Cyprus, Denmark, Equatorial Guinea, Finland, France, Gabon, Greece, Hungary, Iceland, Ireland, Jamaica, South Korea, Lithuania, Luxembourg, the Netherlands, New Zealand, Norway, Slovenia, Sweden, and the United States.

Negative residuals are -12.8 or larger for the following 26 countries: Afghanistan, Bahrain, Belarus, Brunei, Cambodia, China, Cuba, East Timor, Guyana, Iraq, North Korea, Kuwait, Laos, Moldova, Oman, Pakistan, Peru, Russia, Saudi Arabia, Singapore, Tajikistan, Turkmenistan, the United Arab Emirates, Uzbekistan, Vietnam, and Yemen.

Let us first examine the regional distribution of the 53 extremely deviating countries presented in Table 5.1 (see Table 5.2).

Table 5.2. The 53 countries with large positive or negative residuals (±12.8 or higher) on the basis of the regression of IPR on national IQ by regional groups

Regional group	N	Large positive %	N	Large negative %	N	Total
Europe and offshoots	20	74.1	3	11.5	23	43.4
Latin America and the Caribbean	3	11.1	3	11.5	6	11.3
Sub-Saharan Africa	3	11.1	-	-	3	5.7
Middle East and North Africa	-	-	7	26.9	7	13.2
East Asia	1	3.7	2	7.7	3	5.7
Other Asia and Oceania	-	-	11	42.3	11	20.7
Total	27	100.0	26	100	53	100.0

Large outliers are not evenly distributed around the world; they constitute 30.8 percent of the total number of countries, but are considerably overrepresented in the regional groups of European, Middle Eastern, and other Asian and Oceanian countries. The IPRs of the Latin American, Caribbean, and sub-Saharan African countries are in better balance with national IQs. Besides, most large positive outliers are in the European group, and nearly all negative outliers (77%) are in the three regional groups of Asian countries. What are the factors that could explain the drastic contrasts between regional groups and between large positive and negative outliers?

All 20 European and European offshoot countries with large positive residuals are stabilized democracies, in which the level of education is at the highest level in the world and in which agricultural land and other economic power resources are widely distributed. South Korea belongs to the same category of countries. The IPR values of these countries are much higher than expected on the basis of the average relationship between national IQ and the IPR. It is remarkable that a national IQ is higher than 90 for all of them. The pattern of the residual plot in Figure 5.2 raises the question about a possible IQ threshold of accelerated socio-economic development. Figure 5.2 implies that a national IQ level of 90 might represent such a threshold. National IQ is above 90 for 21 out of the 27 large positive outliers and between 80 and 90 for most large negative outliers.

However, there are nine negative outliers above the national IQ level of 90 (Belarus, Cambodia, China, Brunei, Moldova, North Korea, Russia, Singapore, and Vietnam). It is remarkable that seven of them are contemporary or former socialist countries. This observation implies that the nature of an economic system matters. Besides, there are five other socialist or former socialist countries below the IQ level of 90 in the category of large negative outliers (Cuba, Laos, Tajikistan, Turkmenistan, and Uzbekistan). The transformation of several former socialist systems into market economies is still so much unfinished that the degree of resource distribution is significantly lower than in the stabilized European market economies, although differences in the levels of education and in the distribution of intellectual power resources are relatively small. Notice that some former socialist countries have already been quite successful in their transition to democracy and a market economy. Two former socialist countries (Lithuania and Slovenia) are in the group of large positive outliers.

Six other countries with large positive residuals (the Bahamas, Barbados, Republic of Congo, Equatorial Guinea, Gabon, and Jamaica) are different cases. The Bahamas, Barbados, and Jamaica have benefited from tourism and from their geographical proximity to the United States. Equatorial Guinea's large positive residual is principally due to its exceptionally low national IQ value (59). Its IPR value (13.4) is approximately at the same level as in most other sub-Saharan African countries. A high level of literacy (83%) has raised the IPR value of the Republic of Congo, and Gabon has benefited from oil exports, which have helped to raise its IPR a little higher than in most other sub-Saharan African countries.

Socialist and former socialist countries (12) comprise nearly half of the large negative outliers. Of the other 14 large negative outliers, 8 are Middle Eastern and other oil producing countries (Bahrain, Brunei, Iraq, Kuwait, Oman, Saudi Arabia, the United Arab Emirates, and Yemen), in which the ownership and control of crucial oil resources is extremely highly concentrated in the hands of the governments or ruling families. In these countries, important economic power resources have been as highly concentrated in the hands of the rulers as in socialist systems. This factor explains their much lower than expected IPR values.

Afghanistan, East Timor, Guyana, Pakistan, Peru, and Singapore are different cases. Afghanistan and East Timor have suffered from long and bloody civil wars, which have hampered socioeconomic development. In Guyana and Peru, the concentration of landownership and other economic power resources has lowered the IPR values. Pakistan's low IPR value is principally due to the low level of education. Singapore's IPR (31.6) is relatively high, but is much lower than expected on the basis of its extremely high national IQ (108). Singapore's national IQ may be lower than shown or other factors may be involved.

The results of empirical analysis support the second hypothesis about the positive relationship between national IQ and the IPR. Residuals are small or only moderate for most countries. The analysis of highly deviating countries has disclosed that, in addition to national IQ, there are other factors affecting the degree of resource distribution. Some of those other factors may be only locally important or otherwise limited to certain countries and regions. The nature of the economic system seems to be the most important of those other factors. Power resources tend to be more widely distributed in market economies than in socialist and other command economies, and this difference in economic systems affects the chances to establish and maintain democratic political institutions.

Nearly all large positive outliers are economically and socially highly developed European and European offshoot countries, in which the degree of resource distribution is significantly higher than expected on the basis of national IQs. Nearly half of the large negative outliers are contemporary or former socialist countries, in which the concentration of economic power resources into the hands of the government especially reduces the IPR values, and most of the other large negative outliers are autocratically ruled oil-producing countries in which the ownership and control of crucial oil industries is highly concentrated. It is obvious that the nature of the economic system matters to some extent independently from national IQ. However, in some of these cases the economic system may be only a temporarily important factor. When former socialist countries reject socialist economic structures and transition to a free market-economy, economic power resources become more widely distributed and their IPR values will rise.

Besides, it was observed that a national IQ level of 90 constitutes some kind of threshold of accelerated socioeconomic development. Residuals are positive for nearly all countries above the national IQ level of 90, and they are negative for most countries with IQs between 75 and 90.

The observation that more than half of the variation in the IPR can be traced to differences in national IQ means that national IQ constitutes a permanent constraint for democratization through the IPR, largely because relative differences in national IQs change slowly. Because of this constraint, it is not realistic to expect resource distribution to become equalized in the world and that all countries could establish democratic systems or achieve the same quality of democracy. The evolved differences in the mental abilities of populations have constrained until now and will constrain in the future the possibilities of establishing equally democratic political systems in all countries of the world.

Overlapping of explanations based on MT and national IQ

The results of empirical analysis indicate that the index of power resources (IPR) is causally related to both mean temperature (MT) and national IQ, as hypothesized. The relationship between national IQ and IPR is stronger than that between MT and the IPR, but national IQ does not explain resource distribution independently from MT. The moderate negative correlation between MT and national IQ means that a significant part of the variation in national IQ is due to the variation in mean temperature (MT). Consequently, the impact of MT on the IPR can be assumed to take place principally through national IQ and that the explanations of the IPR provided by MT and national IQ would overlap in most cases. We can check this assumption from the results of the two regression analyses given in Table 5.1.

The large residuals (one standard deviation or higher) produced by the two regression analyses are underlined in Table 5.1, so it is easy to check to what extent the same countries have large residuals on the basis of both regression equations and to what extent the same countries have residuals smaller than one standard deviation.

Table 5.1 shows that both residuals are smaller than one standard deviation for 93 countries and that both residuals are large for 29 countries. Besides, positive residuals are large for 20 countries and negative residuals large for other 30 countries. These 50 countries deviate less than the 29 countries for which both residuals are large.

Table 5.3. The 93 countries with residuals smaller than one standard deviation on the basis of the regressions of the IPR on MT and on national IQ classified by regional groups

Regional group	N	%	Total
Europe and offshoots	20	41.7	48
Latin America and the Caribbean	20	74.1	27
Sub-Saharan Africa	38	82.6	46
Middle East and North Africa	9	50.0	18
East Asia	0	0	6
Other Asia and Oceania	6	22.2	27
Total	99	-	172

Countries around the regression line

The evolutionary roots of resource distribution can be most reliably traced to MT and national IQ in the 93 cases in which both residuals are smaller than one standard deviation. In these countries, the level of resource distribution deviates only moderately from the level expected on the basis of MT and national IQ. The group includes countries from all climatic zones and from all levels of national IQ, but there are significant regional differences in the distribution of these 93 countries (Table 5.3).

Table 5.3 shows that MT and national IQ have predicted the actual level of resource distribution (IPR) quite well for single countries in the regional groups of Latin America, the Caribbean, and sub-Saharan Africa, whereas predictions have been most inaccurate for East Asian and most other Asian and Oceanian countries. In two other regional groups (Europe and offshoots and the Middle East and North Africa), the percentages of countries with small residuals differ only slightly from the global average of 54.1 percent. I think that significant regional differences in the accuracy of predictions reflect the impact of some other factors. As noted earlier, one of these factors seems to be related to the nature of economic system. Socialist experiments have been principally limited to Europe and Asia and have been rare in Latin America and sub-Saharan Africa. This observation implies that without the impact of socialist experiments, the dependence of the IPR on MT and national IQ would probably be even stronger.

The most deviating countries

The 29 countries for which both residuals are large constitute the group of the most deviating countries. Both residuals are positive and large for Australia, the Bahamas, Barbados, Belgium, Cyprus, Denmark, Finland, France, Greece, Hungary, Jamaica, South Korea, Luxembourg, the Netherlands, New Zealand, Norway, Slovenia, Sweden, and the United States. Both residuals are negative and large for Afghanistan, Belarus, China, North Korea, Moldova, Russia, Tajikistan, Turkmenistan, and Uzbekistan.

The most conspicuous environmental factor which separates these two groups of countries from each other concerns the nature of their economic systems. All 19 countries with large positive residuals are market economies, and 16 of them are economically highly developed countries. The Bahamas, Barbados, and Jamaica are Caribbean tourist countries. It is remarkable that, except for the Caribbean countries, the national IQ for this group is higher than 90. The national IQ level of 90 seems to constitute a threshold above which socioeconomic development has started to accelerate and has made it possible for countries to deviate from the average relationship between national IQ and the IPR. Note also that residuals are positive, although smaller than one standard deviation, for nearly all other socioeconomically highly developed market economies.

Eight of the nine countries with large negative residuals are contemporary or former socialist countries. Afghanistan is a country ravaged by long civil wars, but it experimented with socialism during the 1980s. Socialist systems are characterized by the concentration of economic power resources in the hands of the government, which has decreased their IPR values. Besides, the socialist system seems to have hampered economic development. The residuals of other socialist countries are also negative in nearly all cases. The impact of the socialist system has been opposite to the impact of the market economy. This observation leads to the conclusion that the adoption of a market economy would help former socialist countries to accelerate their socioeconomic development, to raise their IPR values, and to decrease their negative residuals.

Singapore is an exceptional case. Its residual based on MT is highly positive, whereas its residual based on national IQ is even more strongly negative. As noted earlier, Singapore is inhabited by recent immigrants mainly from China. This explains its high national IQ in a tropical country and its large positive residual based on MT. On the other hand, its IPR is much lower than expected on the basis of national IQ. This discrepancy is probably because Singapore's national IQ may be lower than indicated.

Partly deviating countries

One positive residual is large for 20 countries, although the residual produced by the other regression equation is smaller than one standard deviation. To some extent, these countries illustrate different impacts of MT and national IQ.

Large positive residuals are based on MT in 12 cases (Indonesia, Italy, Israel, Japan, Malaysia, Malta, the Philippines, Portugal, Spain, Sri Lanka, Taiwan, and Thailand). Seven of these 12 countries are socioeconomically highly developed market economies. Their high MT values predict a lower level of resource distribution (IPR), whereas their actual IPR values are only moderately (if at all) higher than expected on the basis of national IQs (see Table 5.1). The impact of national IQ seems to have overcome the impact of mean temperature in these cases. The same argument applies to Indonesia, Malaysia, the Philippines, Sri Lanka, and Thailand. Indonesia, Malaysia, the Philippines, and Thailand are tropical Southeast Asian countries, in which the level of resource distribution is only slightly (if at all) higher than expected on the basis of national IQ. In Sri Lanka the level of IPR is also in better balance with national IQ than with MT.

In eight countries (Canada, Republic of Congo, Croatia, Equatorial Guinea, Gabon, Iceland, Ireland, and Lithuania) IPR values are much higher than expected on the basis of national IQ, whereas residuals based on MT are in most cases small and even slightly negative. Canada and Iceland are among the socioeconomically most highly developed countries in the world but also among the coldest. Their IPR values are only moderately higher than expected on the basis of mean temperature (MT). In the case of Ireland, the discrepancy may be due to the country's low IQ value (92), which is probably lower than it really is. The same applies to Lithuania and Equatorial Guinea, whose national IQs are considerably lower than in neighboring countries. Therefore, their large positive residuals based on national IQ may be due to measurement errors in national IQ. I do not have any particular explanation for the large positive residuals of the Republic of Congo, Croatia, and Gabon, but it should be noted that because of oil production Gross National Income (GNI) per capita in Gabon is much higher than in neighboring sub-Saharan African countries and it may have raised its IPR value.

One negative residual is larger than one standard deviation for 30 partly deviating countries. In 14 cases, large negative residuals are based on MT: Azerbaijan, Bhutan, Botswana, Guatemala, Kazakhstan, Kyrgyzstan, Lesotho, Mongolia, Morocco, Namibia, Nepal, South Africa, Swaziland, and Zimbabwe. In these countries, the level of resource distribution is considerably lower than expected on the basis of MT. How to explain these deviations? Most are clearly related to geographical conditions. Bhutan, Kazakhstan, Kyrgyzstan, and Nepal are mountainous countries in which annual mean temperature is somewhat lower than in neighboring lowland countries, whereas their national IQ is approximately the same as in neighboring lowland countries. To some extent, the same argument applies also to mountainous countries like Azerbaijan, Guatemala, and Morocco. Mongolia's mean temperature is the lowest in the world, and, consequently, the predicted IPR (62.0) is the highest in the world. Mongolia's geographical isolation may have hampered socioeconomic development; exceptional geographical circumstances are sufficient to explain the differences between the residuals based on MT and national IQ. Their negative residuals based on national IQ are smaller than one standard deviation, which implies that national IQ has been the principal determinant of IPR in these cases. Botswana, Lesotho, Namibia, South Africa, Swaziland, and Zimbabwe are southern African countries inhabited by relatively recent Bantu immigrants from tropical regions of Africa. The mean temperature of these countries is clearly colder than that of tropical African countries, whereas national IQs are at the same level as in tropical African countries. Consequently, the regression of IPR on MT has produced large negative residuals for these countries, whereas residuals based on national IQ are positive or only slightly negative (see Table 5.1).

For 16 other countries, negative residuals based on national IQ are large, whereas negative residuals based on MT are small or only moderate. This group includes Bahrain, Brunei, Cambodia, Cuba, East Timor, Guyana, Iraq, Kuwait, Laos, Oman, Pakistan, Peru, Saudi Arabia, the United Arab Emirates, Vietnam, and Yemen. How to explain large negative residuals based on national IQ in these countries? Bahrain, Iraq, Kuwait, Oman, Saudi Arabia, the United Arab Emirates, and also Yemen are oil-producing Arab countries in which economic power resources have been highly concentrated. Brunei in Southeast Asia belongs to the same category. The concentration of crucial economic power resources has decreased the level of resource distribution (IPR) much lower than expected on the basis of national IQ. On the other hand, because MT is relatively high in all these countries, negative residuals based on MT are small or only moderate. Cambodia, Cuba, Laos, and Vietnam are socialist or former socialist countries, in which the concentration of economic power resources has decreased the level of resource distribution (IPR) much lower than expected on the basis of national IQ. Because these are hot tropical countries, their low IPR values are approximately in balance with MT. East Timor and Pakistan are poor South Asian and Southeast Asian countries, which have failed to raise the value of IPR to the level expected on the basis of national IQ. In Guyana and Peru, as noted earlier, the concentration of economic power resources has kept the level of resource distribution lower than expected on the basis of national IQ. Their IPR values are in balance with MT.

Summary

The results of this analysis indicate that the evolutionary roots of global differences in IPR can be traced, to a significant extent, to national differences in MT and national IQ. Together these two variables explain 64 percent of the variation in IPR in the group of 172 countries, which represents a high level of explanation. The impact of MT on IPR is assumed to take place principally through national IQ, but to some extent also independently from national IQ.

The unexplained part of the variation in IPR (36%) leaves room for the impact of various other explanatory factors, measurement errors, and also accidental factors. I tried to explore what kinds of factors might affect IPR independently from MT and national IQ and was able to discover some systematic factors which are related to large deviations. The nature of the economic system seems to be the most significant additional factor. At the same level of national IQ, the level of resource distribution (IPR) tends to be much higher for market economies than for countries with a socialist economic system. This is especially true at higher levels of national IQ. The concentration of economic power resources in the hands of governments and rulers in oil-producing

Arab countries as well as in some other oil-producing countries is a structural factor which has decreased the level of resource distribution and produced large negative residuals. In some cases, great deviations from the regression line seem to be due to various geographical factors. For example, it has been difficult for some exceptionally cold countries (Mongolia) as well as for several mountainous countries to achieve as high a level of IPR as expected on the basis of MT.

Because the nature of a country's economic system and some other environmental factors affecting the level of resource distribution are under conscious human control, it would be possible to decrease negative residuals by appropriate economic and political reforms. Such reforms have already been made or at least attempted in several countries. We can expect that changes will continue in relevant factors that are under human control, which means that contemporary IPR values are not fixed. In some countries, the level of resource distribution may rise independently from MT and national IQ, and in some other countries it may decrease. However, a major part of variation in IPR can be traced to differences in MT and national IQ, and because these factors are almost completely outside conscious human control, we cannot expect the disappearance of great differences in the level of resource distribution. Thus a major result of this study is the observation that the level of resource distribution, which is the most significant determinant of the level of democratization, is causally related to factors which are almost completely outside conscious human control.

CHAPTER 6

IPR As a Determinant of Democratization

According to the third hypothesis, the level of democratization is expected to be higher, the higher the degree of resource distribution (IPR). The results of correlation analysis support this hypothesis strongly (see Chapter 3). The explained part of variation in ID-2006 rises to 66 percent and in GID-2006 to 67 percent. The explained part of variation in ID and GID measures varied from 66 to 73 percent in the period 2002–2006. According to the first and second hypotheses, MT and national IQ are also assumed to be causally related to the measures of democracy. The results of correlation analysis support these hypotheses, too. The correlation between MT and ID-2006 is -0.523 and between national IQ and ID-2006 is 0.575. A multiple regression analysis carried out in Chapter 3 indicates, however, that the impact of MT and national IQ on democratization takes place completely through IPR and does not explain the variation in ID to any significant extent independently from IPR. The explanations provided by MT and national IQ overlap completely with the explanation provided by IPR. Therefore, I focus in this chapter on the impact of IPR on the measures of democracy.

The relationship between IPR and ID-2006 will be examined at the level of single countries in order to see to what extent it is possible to trace the path of causation via IPR and national IQ to mean temperature (MT). The analysis of the two determinants of IPR in Chapter 5 showed that, to a significant extent, the causal roots of differences in

IPR can be traced to national IQ and MT at the level of single countries. This analysis will be limited to the relationship between IPR and ID-2006 because 2006 is the latest year of observation. Let us start from the regression plot which summarizes the results of regression analysis of ID-2006 on IPR (Figure 6.1).

Figure 6.1 shows that most countries are relatively close to the regression line, although there are also many greatly divergent countries. The relationship between IPR and ID-2006 is not complete. In the

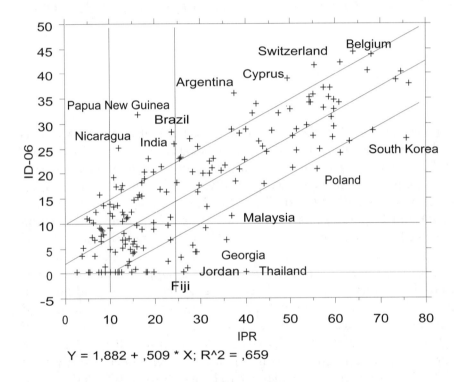

$$Y = 1,882 + ,509 * X; R^2 = ,659$$

Figure 6.1. The results of regression analysis of ID-2006 on IPR in the group of 172 countries

category of countries for which IPR values are below 30 index points, the relationship between IPR and ID seems to be much weaker than in the total group of countries. The IPR level from approximately 10 to

25 index points constitutes a transition level of resource distribution, which separates most democracies from nondemocracies. This transition level of IPR is indicated in Figure 6.1 by vertical lines. In fact, nearly all countries below the IPR level of 10 are nondemocracies, and nearly all countries above the IPR level of 25 are democracies. The approximate minimum threshold of democracy is indicated in Figure 6.1 by a horizontal line at the level of 10 ID index points. The detailed results of regression analysis of ID-2006 on IPR for single countries are given in Table 6.1, which also includes data on the two components of ID: Competition 2006 and Participation 2006. They are important components to take into account because the threshold of democracy used in this study is based on their values, not on the value of ID.

Table 6.1. The results of regression analysis of ID-2006 on IPR for single countries in the group of 172 countries

	Country	C-2006	P-2006	IPR	ID-2006	Residual ID	Fitted ID
1	Afghanistan	48.8	24.6	7.1	12.0	6.5	5.5
2	Albania	60.0	43.8	43.3	26.3	2.4	23.9
3	Algeria	31.9	27.4	20.0	8.7	-3.4	12.1
4	Angola	0	0	12.1	0	-8.0	8.0
5	Argentina	70.0	51.5	37.8	35.8	14.6	21.2
6	Armenia	51.3	40.7	33.1	20.9	2.1	18.8
7	Australia	59.1	57.4	61.1	33.9	0.8	33.1
8	Austria	64.3	54.6	58.9	35.1	3.2	31.9
9	Azerbaijan	31.0	30.1	23.1	9.3	-4.3	13.6
10	Bahamas	49.2	35.9	44.5	17.7	-6.9	24.6
11	Bahrain	14.4	7.8	9.1	1.1	-5.4	5.5
12	Bangladesh	40.0	43.3	13.1	17.3	8.8	8.5
13	Barbados	44.2	41.4	38.0	18.3	-3.0	21.3
14	Belarus	17.0	65.3	23.9	11.1	-3.0	14.1
15	Belgium	70.0	63.2	64.1	44.2	9.6	34.6
16	Belize	46.8	33.2	16.8	15.5	5.1	10.4
17	Benin	30.2	28.8	8.4	6.7	2.6	6.1
18	Bhutan	0	0	11.4	0	-7.7	7.7
19	Bolivia	46.3	35.6	21.6	16.5	3.6	12.9
20	Bosnia and Herzegovina	70.0	39.7	39.0	27.8	6.0	21.8
21	Botswana	48.3	25.0	13.3	12.1	3.5	8.6

	Country	C-2006	P-2006	IPR	ID-2006	Residual ID	Fitted ID
22	Brazil	54.6	51.4	24.1	28.1	13.9	14.2
23	Brunei	0	0	8.3	0	-6.1	6.1
24	Bulgaria	69.0	46.8	46.1	32.3	6.9	25.4
25	Burkina Faso	34.2	14.4	4.4	4.9	0.8	4.1
26	Burma (Myanmar)	0	0	18.4	0	-11.2	11.2
27	Burundi	42.2	39.1	13.0	16.5	8.0	8.5
28	Cambodia	20.3	19.9	11.5	4.0	-3.7	7.7
29	Cameroon	29.2	22.7	13.9	6.6	-2.3	8.9
30	Canada	63.7	45.7	59.8	29.1	-3.3	32.4
31	Cape Verde	47.7	34.0	22.8	16.2	2.7	13.5
32	Central African Republic	30.5	24.8	8.8	7.6	1.2	6.4
33	Chad	35.3	30.3	5.2	10.7	6.2	4.5
34	Chile	46.6	42.3	32.5	19.7	1.3	18.4
35	China	0	0	18.6	0	-11.3	11.3
36	Colombia	37.8	26.1	20.2	9.9	-2.3	12.2
37	Comoros	37.9	23.4	8.1	8.9	2.9	6.0
38	Congo, Dem. Republic	51.0	28.4	15.7	14.5	4.6	9.9
39	Congo, Republic of	10.6	38.8	15.8	4.1	-5.8	9.9
40	Costa Rica	59.5	33.2	31.1	19.8	2.1	17.7
41	Côte d'Ivoire	0	0	10.2	0	-7.1	7.1
42	Croatia	45.8	53.6	51.5	24.5	-3.7	28.2
43	Cuba	0	70.0	15.3	0	-9.7	9.7
44	Cyprus	68.9	56.1	49.7	38.7	11.5	27.2
45	Czech Republic	64.6	52.4	54.5	33.9	4.3	29.6
46	Denmark	70.0	62.2	68.3	43.5	6.8	36.7
47	Djibouti	37.3	12.1	14.8	4.5	-4.9	9.4
48	Dominican Republic	42.9	41.2	25.1	17.9	3.2	14.7
49	East Timor	27.4	49.3	8.8	13.5	7.2	6.3
50	Ecuador	43.3	46.3	20.1	20.0	7.9	12.1
51	Egypt	21.5	10.8	23.1	2.3	-11.3	13.6
52	El Salvador	51.6	34.8	17.6	18.0	7.2	10.8
53	Equatorial Guinea	18.3	42.4	13.5	7.8	-0.9	8.7
54	Eritrea	0	0	12.1	0	-8.0	8.0
55	Estonia	70.0	35.3	56.9	24.7	-6.2	30.9
56	Ethiopia	37.8	31.2	10.4	11.8	4.6	7.2
57	Fiji	0	0	26.7	0	15.5	15.5
58	Finland	70.0	53.7	76.6	37.6	-3.4	41.0
59	France	70.0	44.4	59.4	31.1	-1.1	32.2

	Country	C-2006	P-2006	IPR	ID-2006	Residual ID	Fitted ID
60	Gabon	26.2	19.3	15.4	5.1	-4.6	9.7
61	Gambia	19.5	16.6	6.9	3.2	-2.2	5.4
62	Georgia	17.7	37.1	36.1	6.6	-13.7	20.3
63	Germany	64.8	57.1	57.7	37.0	5.7	31.3
64	Ghana	46.0	41.6	11.3	19.1	11.5	7.6
65	Greece	53.5	69.0	59.0	36.9	4.9	32.0
66	Guatemala	46.0	18.0	8.7	8.3	2.0	6.3
67	Guinea	14.8	44.0	6.8	6.6	1.3	5.3
68	Guinea-Bissau	51.3	30.4	8.1	15.6	9.6	6.0
69	Guyana	44.9	41.7	18.0	18.7	7.7	11.0
70	Haiti	48.8	23.1	10.9	11.3	3.9	7.4
71	Honduras	50.1	26.3	11.1	13.2	5.7	7.5
72	Hungary	50.5	53.5	59.6	27.0	-5.3	32.3
73	Iceland	66.3	61.8	67.4	40.4	4.1	36.3
74	India	70.0	36.5	24.6	25.6	11.2	14.4
75	Indonesia	54.7	52.5	37.3	28.7	7.8	20.9
76	Iran	17.3	17.5	26.0	3.0	-12.1	15.1
77	Iraq	20.6	23.6	17.7	4.9	-6.0	10.9
78	Ireland	58.5	58.3	54.7	34.1	4.3	29.8
79	Israel	70.0	45.5	47.6	31.9	5.7	26.2
80	Italy	50.2	70.0	54.6	35.1	5.4	29.7
81	Jamaica	47.6	27.6	31.7	13.1	-4.9	18.0
82	Japan	61.8	53.1	57.5	32.8	1.6	31.2
83	Jordan	8.2	12.2	27.6	1.0	-14.9	15.9
84	Kazakhstan	8.9	45.0	29.4	4.0	-12.9	16.9
85	Kenya	39.4	23.8	16.3	9.4	-0.8	10.2
86	Korea, North	0	0	3.0	0	-3.4	3.4
87	Korea, South	56.4	47.6	76.1	26.8	-13.9	40.7
88	Kuwait	24.6	6.2	14.4	1.9	-7.7	9.2
89	Kyrgyzstan	10.5	38.9	29.3	4.1	-12.7	16.8
90	Laos	1.4	48.6	16.0	0.7	-9.3	10.0
91	Latvia	70.0	39.2	55.4	27.4	-2.7	30.1
92	Lebanon	70.0	30.7	35.7	21.5	1.4	20.1
93	Lesotho	35.8	23.9	17.5	8.6	-2.2	10.8
94	Liberia	55.3	24.8	10.2	13.7	6.6	7.1
95	Libya	0	0	20.1	0	-12.1	12.1
96	Lithuania	70.0	34.1	61.4	23.9	-9.3	33.2
97	Luxembourg	63.9	41.0	63.5	26.2	-8.1	34.3
98	Macedonia	52.4	43.2	40.2	22.6	0.2	22.4
99	Madagascar	45.2	25.7	13.5	11.6	2.9	8.7
100	Malawi	64.1	25.7	11.8	17.1	9.2	7.9

	Country	C-2006	P-2006	IPR	ID-2006	Residual ID	Fitted ID
101	Malaysia	37.6	30.4	37.4	11.4	-9.6	21.0
102	Maldives	9.7	38.3	15.5	3.7	-6.1	9.8
103	Mali	35.0	9.7	3.9	3.4	-0.4	3.8
104	Malta	48.2	70.0	42.8	33.7	10.0	23.7
105	Mauritania	28.4	16.4	10.4	4.7	-2.5	7.2
106	Mauritius	40.0	55.3	32.3	22.1	3.8	18.3
107	Mexico	63.6	36.3	26.0	23.1	8.0	15.1
108	Moldova	54.8	37.1	28.7	20.0	3.5	16.5
109	Mongolia	51.8	39.7	38.9	20.6	-1.1	21.7
110	Montenegro	43.1	43.0	44.9	24.0	-0.8	24.8
111	Morocco	42.3	12.1	16.4	5.1	-5.1	5.2
112	Mozambique	37.2	16.5	8.2	6.1	0.1	6.0
113	Namibia	23.8	42.1	6.5	10.0	4.8	5.2
114	Nepal	45.8	38.7	18.2	17.7	6.6	11.1
115	Netherlands	70.0	60.0	61.3	42.0	8.8	33.2
116	New Zealand	58.9	55.5	59.8	32.7	0.3	32.4
117	Nicaragua	61.9	40.1	12.2	24.8	16.7	8.1
118	Niger	34.5	20.6	6.2	7.1	2.1	5.0
119	Nigeria	38.1	31.6	13.3	12.0	3.4	8.6
120	Norway	67.3	57.4	73.8	38.6	-0.9	39.5
121	Oman	0	5.4	13.0	0	-8.5	8.5
122	Pakistan	20.3	28.0	13.7	5.7	-3.1	8.8
123	Panama	52.6	50.8	28.1	26.7	10.5	16.2
124	Papua New Guinea	70.0	45.1	16.5	31.6	21.3	10.3
125	Paraguay	62.7	24.1	16.5	15.1	4.8	10.3
126	Peru	47.4	48.1	18.8	22.8	11.4	11.4
127	Philippines	60.0	38.0	33.3	22.8	3.9	18.9
128	Poland	58.0	35.7	56.3	20.7	-9.9	30.6
129	Portugal	51.5	52.9	50.7	27.2	-0.5	27.7
130	Qatar	0	0	8.4	0	-6.1	6.1
131	Romania	55.8	45.4	44.1	25.3	0.9	24.4
132	Russia	39.4	43.8	30.1	17.3	0.1	17.2
133	Rwanda	14.8	45.1	14.6	6.7	-2.6	9.3
134	Saudi Arabia	0	0	11.6	0	-7.8	7.8
135	Senegal	41.5	17.4	8.4	7.2	1.1	6.1
136	Serbia	67.2	42.5	40.3	28.6	6.2	22.4
137	Sierra Leone	27.9	38.0	5.7	10.6	5.8	4.8
138	Singapore	33.4	27.0	31.6	9.0	-9.0	18.0
139	Slovakia	55.1	38.0	50.7	20.9	-6.8	27.7
140	Slovenia	56.8	50.2	68.6	28.5	-8.4	36.9
141	Solomon Islands	40.0	38.0	17.5	15.3	4.5	10.8

	Country	C-2006	P-2006	IPR	ID-2006	Residual ID	Fitted ID
142	Somalia	70.0	0	7.6	0	-5.7	5.7
143	South Africa	30.3	35.5	14.1	10.8	1.8	9.0
144	Spain	56.7	62.8	55.4	35.6	5.5	39.1
145	Sri Lanka	52.0	48.6	29.7	25.3	8.3	17.0
146	Sudan	0	0	12.2	0	-8.1	8.1
147	Surinam	54.9	38.7	21.9	21.2	8.2	13.0
148	Swaziland	0	3.4	5.5	0	-4.7	4.7
149	Sweden	65.0	61.7	74.9	40.1	0	40.1
150	Switzerland	70.0	59.1	55.5	41.4	11.2	30.2
151	Syria	16.8	39.4	23.8	6.6	-7.4	14.0
152	Taiwan	57.2	50.1	51.6	28.7	0.5	28.2
153	Tajikistan	28.1	42.9	15.3	12.1	2.4	9.7
154	Tanzania	15.5	30.7	13.2	4.8	-3.8	8.6
155	Thailand	0	0	40.5	0	-22.5	22.5
156	Togo	25.5	40.0	13.1	10.2	1.7	8.5
157	Trinidad and Tobago	49.3	46.5	25.7	22.9	7.9	15.0
158	Tunisia	12.5	43.6	28.7	5.5	-11.0	16.5
159	Turkey	59.1	34.5	35.1	20.4	0.6	19.8
160	Turkmenistan	0	0	9.2	0	-6.5	6.5
161	Uganda	40.7	26.7	14.3	10.9	1.8	9.1
162	Ukraine	58.2	56.1	50.1	32.6	5.2	27.4
163	United Arab Emirates	0	0	5.6	0	-4.7	4.7
164	United Kingdom	64.8	45.5	53.9	29.5	0.1	29.4
165	United States	49.3	70.0	59.9	34.5	2.1	32.4
166	Uruguay	49.3	64.6	41.8	31.8	8.6	23.2
167	Uzbekistan	4.3	48.7	14.6	2.1	-7.2	9.3
168	Venezuela	37.1	43.3	29.7	16.1	-0.9	17.0
169	Vietnam	10.3	60.0	15.8	6.2	-3.7	9.9
170	Yemen	21.9	29.1	13.3	6.4	-2.2	8.6
171	Zambia	53.9	25.1	12.1	13.5	5.5	8.0
172	Zimbabwe	42.1	20.8	10.4	8.8	1.6	7.2

The results of regression analysis show how well it was possible to predict the value of ID-2006 for single countries on the basis of the average relationship between IPR and ID-2006. Positive residuals vary from zero to 21.3 (Papua New Guinea) and negative residuals from zero to -22.5 (Thailand). In the countries with small residuals, the level of democratization is approximately in balance with the degree of resource distribution. A large residual indicates that IPR does not provide a satisfactory explanation for the country's level of democratization. Some other factors have increased the level of ID much higher than expected on the basis of IPR or decreased it much lower than expected. The examination of large outliers may help to find out what those other relevant factors might be. As in previous cases, we can use one standard deviation of ID-2006 residual (±7.1) to separate large outliers from countries which deviate only a little or moderately from the regression line. Two parallel lines at the distance of approximately ±7.1 ID-2006 index points from the regression line separate large outliers from less deviant countries in Figure 6.1.

Positive residuals are 7.1 or higher for the following 26 countries: Argentina, Bangladesh, Belgium, Brazil, Burundi, Cyprus, East Timor, Ecuador, El Salvador, Ghana, Guinea-Bissau, Guyana, India, Indonesia, Malawi, Malta, Mexico, the Netherlands, Nicaragua, Panama, Papua New Guinea, Peru, Sri Lanka, Surinam, Switzerland, and Uruguay.

Negative residuals are -7.1 or higher for 31 countries: Angola, Bhutan, Burma (Myanmar), China, Côte d'Ivoire, Cuba, Egypt, Eritrea, Fiji, Georgia, Iran, Jordan, Kazakhstan, South Korea, Kuwait, Kyrgyzstan, Laos, Libya, Lithuania, Luxembourg, Malaysia, Oman, Poland, Saudi Arabia, Singapore, Slovenia, Sudan, Syria, Thailand, Tunisia, and Uzbekistan.

A problem is whether there are any systematic factors which differentiate these two groups of large outliers from each other. We can start by examining the regional distribution of the 57 large outliers (Table 6.2).

Large outliers are relatively well distributed around the world, although there are clear regional differences between positive and negative outliers. Most of the large positive outliers are in the groups of European, Latin American, and other Asian countries, whereas most of the large negative outliers are in the groups of Middle Eastern and other Asian countries. To some extent, this difference reflects the regional pattern of large residuals based on the regression of IPR on national IQ in Table 6.2. It shows that 20 out of 27 large positive outliers are in the regional group of Europe and that 18 out of 26 large negative outliers are in the regional groups of the Middle East and other Asian countries. The reasons for large residuals seem to be partly similar as in the regression of IPR on national IQ, but certainly there are also differences in explanatory factors. Therefore, it is useful to examine each deviating

Table 6.2. The 57 countries with large positive or negative residuals (±7.1 or higher) in the regression of ID-2006 on IPR by regional groups

Regional group	N	Large positive %	N	Large negative %	N	Total
Europe and offshoots	5	19.2	5	16.1	10	17.5
Latin America and the Caribbean	11	42.3	1	3.2	12	21.1
Sub-Saharan Africa	4	15.4	4	12.9	8	14.0
Middle East and North Africa	-	-	9	29.0	9	15.8
East Asia	-	-	2	6.5	2	3.5
Other Asia and Oceania	6	23.1	10	32.3	16	28.1
Total	26	100.0	31	100.0	57	100.0

country separately in order to find out whether some special local factor might explain a country's large positive or negative deviation from the regression line. In principle, a large positive residual predicts a decrease of democratization, and a large negative residual predicts a rise in the level of democratization.

Large positive outliers

Argentina's large positive residual is mainly due to the country's electoral system in presidential elections. The candidate who gets more votes than any other candidate will be elected, although he gets less than 50 percent of the votes. In the 2003 election, the winning candidate received only 22 percent of the votes, which temporarily inflated Argentina's ID value. In the previous 1999 election, the winning candidate received 48.5 percent of the votes, and Argentina's positive residual was small. Argentina's large positive residual disappeared again in the 2007 presidential election. This shows that sometimes temporary and accidental factors affect ID values significantly.

Bangladesh. Democracy in Bangladesh is still fragile. The country has been able to maintain a democratic system since the 1990s, but politics is violent and extremely polarized between the two major parties. The actual level of ID-2006 was two times higher than expected on the basis of IPR, which predicted a decline in the level of democratization. In fact, the military's take-over on January 11th, 2007 dropped the ID value to zero (*The Economist,* February 20 2007, pp. 55–57), and Bangladesh's residual turned negative. IPR predicted a decrease in the level of democratization, but not a drop to zero.

Belgium's large positive residual is due to its ethnically fragmented party system. The largest party's share of votes is less than 30 percent, which inflates its ID value. Besides, its compulsory voting system has retained the level of electoral participation exceptionally high. I think that these local institutional factors explain Belgium's moderately outlying position. We do not need to expect any decline in Belgium's ID value.

Brazil's large positive residual is partly related to the country's fragmented party system, which has raised the value of ID, and partly to the concentration of economic power resources, especially of land ownership, which has decreased the value of IPR. Because both of these local factors are relatively permanent, we can expect that Brazil remains as an outlying country. However, Brazil's IPR predicts a decline in its level of democratization (ID).

Burundi's residual turned positive and high as a consequence of the introduction of democratic institutions through the 2005 parliamentary elections. Its ID value is two times higher than expected on the basis of IPR. The future will show whether Burundi is able to maintain its much higher than expected level of democratization. It should be noted that the 2005 elections were supervised by the United Nations peacekeeping mission (see Banks et al. 2007, pp. 183–284). The survival of new democratic institutions will be tested in the next elections. Burundi's transition to some kind of democracy in 2005 indicates that drastic changes in a country's ID value are possible.

Cyprus. The significantly higher than expected level of democratization is principally due to the country's ideologically fragmented party system and to a high level of electoral participation. Because of its high degree of resource distribution, the survival of democracy is secure in Cyprus. The large positive residual seems to be related to local and relatively permanent political and institutional factors.

East Timor's positive residual is two times higher than expected on the basis of its relatively low IPR value (8.8), which does not presuppose a democratic system. In fact, East Timor was below the Competition threshold of democracy in 2006, but in the 2007 presidential and parliamentary elections the country crossed the threshold of democracy and became an even more deviating case.

Ecuador. A significant increase in the electoral participation in the 2002 and 2006 presidential elections made Ecuador a clearly deviating country. It is a democracy as expected on the basis of its IPR (20.1), but the level of democratization is clearly higher than expected. Residuals are also positive and large for several other Latin American countries, which reflects the stabilization of democratic systems in Latin America.

El Salvador is a similar case. An exceptionally high level of electoral participation in the 2004 presidential election inflated El Salvador's positive residual. These observations imply that the level of democratization and residuals may fluctuate considerably in Latin American countries depending on temporary and accidental changes in the level of electoral participation. The country's relatively low IPR value is principally due to the concentration of economic power resources as in several other Latin American countries.

Ghana's actual level of democratization has been much higher than expected since the 1996 democratic elections. Its large positive residual predicts a decrease in the level of democratization if the level of resource distribution does not rise. The credit for the success of democracy in Ghana is principally due to Ghanaian politicians, who have learned to make compromises and to respect the results of free elections.

Guinea-Bissau's large positive residual indicates a much higher than expected level of democracy, but it should be noted that since 1994 military coups have already interrupted democratic politics two times. Guinea-Bissau has been a large positive outlier only since the 2005 presidential election. The social basis of democratic institutions is still fragile, and new military coups are possible. Its low IPR value (8.1) does not yet presuppose democracy.

Guyana has remained above the minimum threshold of democracy since 1992. Resource distribution among ethnic groups is the major factor supporting democratic politics in Guyana. Because of ethnic tension, the struggle for power has been bitter and sometimes violent, but the country's ethnic political parties have gradually learned to make compromises and to share power through elections. The fragmentation of the party system along ethnic lines constitutes a local institutional factor which has raised Guyana's ID value (cf. Banks et al. 2007, pp. 204–205).

India. The fragmentation of India's party system has increased its ID value and made India's positive residual large. It is possible that, because of many and deep ethnic cleavages, important power resources are in India more widely distributed than IPR indicates. Therefore, my prediction is that India can maintain its present relatively high level of democratization, although its negative residual predicts a decline in ID.

Indonesia's level of democratization (ID) is also higher than expected, but Indonesia's positive residual has been large only since the highly competitive 2004 elections. It is not yet clear how well Indonesia is able to stabilize its democratic institutions. It is reasonable to assume that geographical and ethnic cleavages will support multiparty politics in Indonesia as in India. The establishment of democratic institutions in Indonesia indicates that democratization is possible in Islamic countries, too. Douglas Webber (2006) emphasizes that Indonesia has undergone a successful transition to polyarchal democracy.

Malawi has been exceptionally successful in its efforts to maintain democracy since 1994 when Hastings Banda's long period of autocratic rule ended. Malawi's regionally and ethnically based party system supports competitive politics. The low IPR value (11.8) does not presuppose so high a level of democracy, but the competitive democratic system has survived, although the level of ID-2006 is two times higher than expected on the basis of IPR. Credit for the success of democracy in Malawi should be given to the country's politicians, who have learned to accept the results of free elections.

Malta has been a stabilized democracy since its independence in 1964. The tight competition between the two major parties and an exceptionally high level of electoral participation have raised the country's ID value much higher than expected on the basis of IPR. However, because of stabilized political and social conditions in Malta, there is no reason to expect any drastic decline in its level of democratization (ID).

Mexico's residuals remained negative a long time, but the process of democratization, which started in 1988, turned them positive. Now the level of democratization is clearly higher than expected on the basis of IPR. The concentration of economic power resources has kept the IPR value relatively low. My prediction is that Mexico is able to maintain its somewhat higher than expected level of democracy. Its neighborhood of the United States may support the survival of democracy in Mexico. Besides, Mexico's level of resource distribution (IPR 26.0) is already high enough to maintain democracy.

The Netherlands' somewhat higher than expected ID value is principally due to the country's fragmented party system and very high level of electoral participation. As a stabilized democracy, the Netherlands will probably remain as a positive outlier.

Nicaragua's residuals have been positive since 1984 when the country crossed the threshold of democracy after the period of Somoza's dictatorship. Although its level of democratization is relatively low, it is three times higher than expected on the basis of IPR. The discrepancy is principally due to Nicaragua's low level of resource distribution, particularly to the concentration of economic power resources. Nicaragua's political leaders have learned, after long periods of dictatorship and a civil war, to compromise and to respect constitutional rules of governance. However, the large negative residual predicts a decline in the level of democratization.

Panama's ID is somewhat higher than expected on the basis of IPR. Panama has been a positive outlier since the highly competitive presidential election of 1994. A competitive democratic system seems to have become stabilized in Panama, but its large positive residual predicts a decrease in the ID value.

Papua New Guinea was the largest positive outlier in the world in 2006. Its extremely fragmented party system is principally due to the population's ethnic heterogeneity, which has prevented the emergence of big national parties. I believe that ethnic heterogeneity and poor communications within the country provide a sufficient local explanation for the fragmentation of the party system and for the three times higher than expected level of democratization. Because of ethnic heterogeneity, politically relevant power resources may be more widely distributed than my IPR indicates. Benjamin Reilly (2006: 6) emphasizes the unique achievement of Papua New Guinea. It is "on some measures the most ethno-linguistically fragmented country to be found anywhere in the world, and one of the very few post-colonial states to have maintained an unbroken record of democracy since independence." An additional factor has probably been the economic and administrative support provided by Australia, which has helped to maintain national institutions.

Peru recrossed the threshold of democracy in the highly competitive presidential election of 2001. Its actual ID value is two times higher than expected on the basis of IPR. The concentration of economic power resources keeps the country's IPR value relatively low (18.8). Because the level of resource distribution presupposes a significantly lower level of democratization, Peru may not remain as a large positive outlier permanently.

Sri Lanka has been a democracy since its independence in 1948, but it has not always been a large positive outlier. Ideological cleavages within the Sinhalese majority have maintained a highly competitive party system and a high level of electoral participation. It is remarkable that despite the long ethnic civil war, Sri Lanka has been able to maintain a constitutional system and democratic institutions. Because of its relatively high level of resource distribution (IPR 29.7), I expect that democratic institutions will survive in Sri Lanka, although its positive residual will decline.

Surinam's large positive residual is, just as is in the case of Guyana, mainly due to its ethnically fragmented party system, which supports competitive politics. Surinam has been above the threshold of democracy since 1991 and it most probably will survive as a democracy, but its positive residual may drop in the future.

Switzerland is one of the most stabilized democracies in the world. Its exceptionally high level of democratization is due to the population's ethnic cleavages, which maintain a highly competitive multiparty system, and to numerous national referendums, which have raised the level of participation. Because of these local factors, it is reasonable to expect that residuals will remain positive for Switzerland.

Uruguay has been a positive outlier since its return to democracy in 1984. Its stabilized and highly competitive multiparty system maintains high levels of competition and participation. It is reasonable to expect that Uruguay will also remain as a positive outlier in the future.

The above review of large positive outliers discloses that in several cases the considerably higher than expected level of democratization can be traced to some local factors affecting resource distribution and even more to temporary and partly accidental fluctuation in institutional or other political factors, which include differences in electoral and party systems, ethnic heterogeneity of the population, and also exceptional impacts of political leaders. It was not possible to find any common factor which could explain most of the deviations, although it was noted that residuals are positive for most European market economies and also for most Latin American countries. The fact that the group of large positive outliers includes some economically highly developed market economies but not any socialist or former socialist countries reflects the impact of the economic system.

It is remarkable that relatively few countries seem to remain in the category of large positive outliers over many years. Of the 27 large positive outliers of the year 2006, only nine (Bangladesh, Brazil, Cyprus, Malawi, Nicaragua, Panama, Papua New Guinea, Peru, and Uruguay) were on the list of large positive outliers on the basis of ID-2001 on IPR (see Vanhanen, 2003, pp. 141–144). The other 18 countries had become large positive outliers in the period 2002–2006, and, on the other hand, most of the large positive outliers in 2001 had ceased to be large positive outliers in the period 2002–2006. I think that numerous changes in the lists of large positive outliers reflect the impact of temporary and also accidental factors on the values of Competition and Participation, but partly the variation is due to changes in IPR values, too.

Because many local and temporary factors will also affect resource distribution and election results in the future, it would not be reasonable to expect any significant increase in the explained part of variation. Some 30 percent of the variation in the level of democratization may remain unexplained in the future, too. Besides, a part of the unexplained variation may be due to measurement errors. Both IPR and ID are incomplete substitutes for the hypothetical concepts "resource distribution" and "level of democratization."

Large negative outliers

Angola's ID level is zero because the country has not been able to organize new presidential and legislative elections since 1992. The opposition did not accept the results of the 1992 presidential election, and a long and bloody ethnic civil war followed. After the death of UNITA's leader Jonas Savimbi in 2002, attempts were made to re-establish democratic institutions, but Angola was still without a democratically elected government at the end of 2006. Its IPR (12.1) may still be too low for a democratic system, but it presupposes attempts at democratization.

Bhutan is a traditional and autocratically ruled country without any legal parties, but its IPR presupposes some democratization. In fact, the king has started a constitutional reform intended to establish a "democratic constitutional monarchy" in which political parties would be allowed to contest National Assembly elections (Banks et al. 2007, pp. 125). It is reasonable to expect some kind of democratization in Bhutan in the near future.

Burma (Myanmar) has been ruled by military governments since the 1960s. Social conditions (IPR 18.4) presuppose a more democratic political system, and popular pressure for democratization is strong in Myanmar. The continual violent struggle with separatist ethnic groups is a local factor which has strengthened the position of the military. The extensive popular demonstrations in the autumn of 2007 anticipated a collapse of military autocracy. On the basis of the large negative residual, I have to predict democratization in Burma.

China is one of the remaining communist countries in which democratic politics has been prohibited for ideological reasons and in which the concentration of economic and coercive power resources supports the survival of an authoritarian political system. However, the spread of education and decentralization of economic power resources undermine the system. The distribution of intellectual power resources (IR 53.0) already presupposes democracy. We can expect an increasing pressure for democratization in China.

Côte d'Ivoire turned into a negative outlier in 2006. President Gbagbo's term had ended in 2005 and the country, because of an ethnic civil war, was unable to organize new elections. It is probable that Côte d'Ivoire will remain as a large negative outlier only a short period. The country has a multiparty system, and we can expect the re-establishment of democratic institutions (cf. Banks et al. 2007, pp. 301–302).

Cuba is a similar case to China. Economic power resources are still highly concentrated, but the distribution of intellectual power resources (IR 76.5) presupposes a democratic system. We can expect democratization in Cuba.

Egypt is an Arab country in which the distribution of both intellectual and economic power resources predicts democratization. Because of the lack of significant oil resources, economic power resources are in Egypt more widely distributed than in oil-rich Arab countries. Egypt has already started the process of democratization by allowing limited competition in both presidential and legislative elections, but in 2006 the country was still dominated by President Mubarak and his hegemonic party.

Eritrea has been a negative outlier since its independence in 1993. The country is ruled autocratically by president Isaias Awerki's transitional government and the Eritrean People's Liberation Front, which had led the war of independence against Ethiopia. There are no legal opposition parties, but there are several illegal opposition groups, which demand democratic elections. We can expect some kind of democratization or at least attempts at democratization in Eritrea.

Fiji turned from a large positive outlier into a large negative outlier in December 2006 when the military usurped power and displaced democratic institutions. Politics in Fiji has been highly polarized because of the ethnic tension between indigenous Fijians and Indian migrants, but they were able to maintain democratic institutions with some interruptions. Because of the ethnic cleavage, important power resources may be more widely distributed than IPR indicates, but, on the other hand, the unsolved ethnic conflict endangered the survival of democratic institutions. The military usurped power in 2006, but probably only temporarily. Fiji's high IPR value predicts a return to democracy.

Georgia is probably only a temporarily deviating country. Its large negative residual is due to Mikhail Saakashvili's overwhelming victory (96.9%) in the 2004 presidential election, which took place after the former President Shevardnadze had been forced to resign by mass demonstrations. It is reasonable to expect that Georgia will return to competitive politics in the next presidential and legislative elections. Georgia's high IPR value presupposes democracy.

Iran has an exceptional theocratic political system. The supreme power is in the hands of the Supreme Leader elected by a small group of clerics. The competition in legislative and presidential elections indicates that Iran would be ripe for and capable of competitive democratic politics. However, the hard-line clerical establishment has so far been able to keep political parties banned. We can expect increasing pressure for democratization in Iran. In fact, there has already been strong popular pressure for democratization (see Ganji 2005; Sazegara 2005).

Jordan is the most deviating Arab country. The relatively high level of resource distribution (IPR 27.6) presupposes democracy, but crucial powers are still in the hands of King Abdullah. There is an elected lower house of parliament, but its powers are limited. The fact that Jordanians of Palestinian descent constitute a significant part of the population may hinder democratization. The monarchy's traditional support base is in Transjordanian tribal groups, which constitute a relatively small part of the population. The present electoral system, for example, is heavily skewed to favor the monarchy's traditional support base (see *Freedom House 2005*, p. 332; Lust-Okar 2006). We can expect increasing popular pressure for democratization.

Kazakhstan is one of the former Central Asian Soviet republics which became independent in 1991 but in which socialist economic structures remained more or less intact. Economic power resources are still heavily concentrated in the hands of the government, although some privatization has taken place. Competition in elections is limited, and political power is concentrated in the hands of President Nazarbayev. However, intellectual power resources are widely distributed (IR 73.5). It means that there is human potential for democratization. The pressure for democratization can be expected to increase.

South Korea's large negative residual is due to its probably too high IPR value (76.1). The exceptionally high level of tertiary education (89) has inflated South Korea's IPR value. Therefore I do not regard South Korea as a seriously deviating case. Democratic institutions have already become stabilized in South Korea.

Kuwait is an oil-producing Arab country in which the ownership and control of the most important economic power resources are highly concentrated in the hands of the government and rulers. Most people are economically dependent on the government in such a country, and it is difficult to establish independent political opposition groups. However, intellectual power resources are more widely distributed, which supports democratization. Kuwait's level of resource distribution (IPR) presupposes a somewhat more democratic system.

Kyrgyzstan belongs to the same category of former Soviet republics as Kazakhstan. Economic power resources are highly concentrated in the hands of the government, and political power is concentrated in the hands of the president. The transfer of power from the deposed President Akayev to Bakiyev in 2005 did not democratize the system (see Radnitz 2006). The large negative residual predicts emergence of a more democratic political system. The country already has a multiparty system (see Banks et al. 2007, pp. 687–690).

Laos belongs to the same category of remaining socialist countries as China. Its relatively low level of resource distribution (IPR) does not presuppose a fully democratic political system, but some democratic institutions might be possible. We can expect efforts at democratization in Laos, too.

Libya represents oil-producing Arab countries in which economic *power* resources are highly concentrated in the hands of the government but in which intellectual power resources are more widely distributed and predict democratization. Camilla Sandbakken (2006, p. 146) argues that in a rentier state like Libya, in which the majority of the population is financially dependent on the state, "there is no social group where democratic opposition might surface." However, because of its large negative residual, I have to predict some popular pressure for democratization, although Libya's present level of resource distribution may be too low to support a fully democratic system.

Lithuania's large negative residual is mainly due to the exceptionally low level of electoral participation (34.1%) in the 2004 parliamentary elections. Therefore, Lithuania is probably only temporarily a large negative outlier. If the level of participation rises in the next elections, it ceases to be a large negative outlier.

Luxembourg is a similar case to Lithuania. A moderate rise in the level of electoral participation would decrease its negative residual. I assume that Luxembourg is only temporarily a large negative outlier.

Malaysia's negative residual reflects the dominance of the ruling multi-ethnic National Front, which is the alliance of Malay, Chinese, and Indian parties (see Reilly 2006: 147–148). The dominance of the National Front has decreased the level of electoral participation (cf. Thirkell-White 2006). Thomas B. Pepinsky (2007) notes that the ruling coalition has been unwilling to adopt fair electoral practices. Malaysian law "features a number of repressive ordinances that the regime has used selectively to intimidate or sideline political opposition" (p. 117; cf. Reilly 2006, p. 148).

Oman is another oil-producing Arab country. The concentration of economic power resources is in harmony with the country's autocratic political system, whereas intellectual power resources are more widely distributed, which is conducive to democratization. Because Oman's IPR (13.0) is still at the transition level of IPR, I cannot predict successful democratization.

Poland's large negative residual is mainly due to the significant decrease of electoral participation in the 2005 parliamentary elections. As a consequence of the new parliamentary elections in 2007, Poland ceased to be a large negative outlier.

Saudi Arabia is an oil-producing Arab country similar to Kuwait. Crucial economic power resources are highly concentrated, but intellectual power resources are more widely distributed, which provides some basis for opposition. However, because Saudi Arabia's IPR (11.6) is only slightly above the lower limit of transition level of IPR, I cannot predict democratization for Saudi Arabia.

Singapore's large negative residual is due to the hegemony of the Chinese-dominated Peoples' Action Party. The level of resource distribution, especially the distribution of intellectual power resources, presupposes a competitive democracy. Singapore was a highly deviating nondemocracy for several years. However, the ruling party's share of the votes decreased in the 2006 parliamentary elections, and Singapore recrossed the threshold of democracy, although only slightly. Singapore's "party block" electoral system "has hugely benefited Singapore's ruling Peoples' Action Party (PAP), which regularly wins over 90 per cent of seats in parliament" (Reilly 2006, p. 109). IPR predicts a more democratic system.

Slovenia is a stabilized democracy, although its level of democracy is clearly lower than expected on the basis of IPR. Just like in the case of South Korea, a very high level of tertiary education (70) has inflated its IPR (68.6) value. In other words, Slovenia's estimated level of resource distribution may be too high.

Sudan's low IPR value (12.2) does not presuppose a democratic system, and it is not a democracy, but its large negative residual implies that a system could be a little more democratic. In fact, a process of democratization was started after the peace agreement reached on January 9, 2005, between the government and the Sudanese Peoples' Liberation Movement (SPLM). A transitional government based on a power-sharing quota was established. Sudan already has a multiparty system based principally on deep ethnic divisions in the country (Banks et al. 2007, pp. 1167–178). Because of very deep ethnic cleavages, democratization can be expected to fail in Sudan.

Syria's large negative residual reflects the hegemonic position of president Bashar al-Assad and his National Progressive Front party. There are opposition parties, but they are without real chances to compete in elections (see Banks et al. 2007, pp. 1202–1203). Syria's relatively high IPR (23.8) predicts a more democratic system.

Thailand's negative residual for 2006 (-22.5) is the highest in the world as a consequence of the military coup of September 2006. The military coup dropped Thailand's ID value to zero, and its negative residual became extremely large. A high level of resource distribution (IPR 40.5) presupposes democracy in Thailand, and we can expect a return to democracy through competitive elections. Thailand's problem is that the position of the king and the military is too dominant.

Tunisia's large negative residual indicates that we can expect democratization in Tunisia. The level of resource distribution (IPR 28.7) presupposes a democratic political system. Tunisia should be among the first Arab countries to cross the threshold of democracy.

Uzbekistan is a former Soviet republic in which old power structures have survived. Intellectual power resources are relatively widely distributed, whereas economic power resources are still highly concentrated in the hands of the government, which supports the survival of an autocratic political system. Because Uzbekistan is still at the transition level of IPR, I cannot predict democratization, although popular pressure for democratization may increase.

The review of large negative outliers shows that it is difficult to indicate any single factor which could explain the emergence of large negative residuals in most cases. However, some common characteristics are related to several of these countries. Ten of the 31 large negative outliers were contemporary or former socialist countries in 2006 (China, Cuba, Georgia, Kazakhstan, Kyrgyzstan, Laos, Lithuania, Poland, Slovenia, and Uzbekistan). Nine of the other large negative outliers (Egypt, Iran, Jordan, Kuwait, Libya, Oman, Saudi Arabia, Syria, and Tunisia) are Middle Eastern and Arab countries which have so far resisted the social pressure for a more democratic political system (cf. Volpi and Cavatorta 2006; Hinnebusch 2006). According to rentier state theory, oil wealth prevents democracy (Sandbakken 2006), which is in harmony with my resource distribution theory of democratization. Mark Tessler and Eleanor Gao (2005) refer to survey findings, according to which "large majorities in many Arab countries want their countries to be ruled by democratic systems, and that desire does not diminish among support-ers of political Islam" (p. 93). Such an observation implies that there is human potential for democratization in Arab countries. Further, local variation in electoral and party systems as well as accidental fluctuation in the support of the largest party and in electoral participation seems to be related to large negative residuals in Georgia, Lithuania, Luxembourg, Malaysia, Poland, Singapore, and Slovenia. Civil wars or military coups dropped ID values to zero and made residuals highly negative in Angola, Côte d'Ivoire, Eritrea, Sudan, Burma, Fiji, and Thailand.

Large negative outliers seem to be more persistent than large positive outliers, although only eight of the 31 large negative outliers in 2006 had also been in the category of large negative outliers on the basis of ID-2001 on IPR (Burma, China, Egypt, Jordan, Singapore, Syria, Thailand, and Tunisia). However, residuals were also negative for most of the other countries in 2001, especially for Angola, Bhutan, Cuba, Eritrea, Georgia, Iran, South Korea, Laos, Libya, Oman, Saudi Arabia, and Sudan (see Vanhanen 2003, pp. 141–144). Residuals were only slightly negative or positive for 11 of these countries in 2001, which indicates the impact of temporary and accidental factors.

One clear difference between large positive and negative outliers concerns the level of democratization. All positive outliers were democracies and almost all negative outliers were nondemocracies in 2006. South Korea, Lithuania, Luxembourg, Malaysia, Poland, Singapore, and Slovenia were the only democracies in the category of large negative outliers in 2006. Nearly all large positive outliers were democracies, as expected on the basis of their IPR values, which are for them above the transition level of resource distribution from 10 to 25 IPR points or at least within the transition level. East Timor, Guinea-Bissau, and Malawi are the only clearly deviating democracies for which IPR values are below 10 index points.

Of the large negative outliers, Fiji, Georgia, Iran, Jordan, Kazakhstan, Kyrgyzstan, Thailand, and Tunisia are clearly deviating nondemocracies because their IPR values are above 25. On the other hand, South Korea, Lithuania, Luxembourg, Malaysia, Poland, Singapore, and Slovenia were, despite their large negative residuals, democracies, as expected because their IPR values are above 25. The IPR values of the other 16 large negative outliers are at the transition level from 10 to 25 index points, which means that the degree of resource distribution is not yet secure for democracy. Countries can be democracies or nondemocracies at the transition level of resource distribution. We can expect struggle for democracy and attempts to establish and stabilize democratic institutions at this level of resource distribution.

Summary

Large positive and negative residuals comprise 57 countries, but residuals are small or only moderate for the other 115 countries. These 115 countries support the third hypothesis most clearly and indicate that the level of resource distribution (IPR) can provide a satisfactory explanation for the variation in the level of democratization. The 115 countries are relatively evenly distributed around the world, as Table 6.3 shows. The relative frequency of countries with small and moderate residuals is highest in the regional groups of European and sub-Saharan African countries and smallest in the regional group of other Asian and Oceanian countries.

The level of democratization tends to rise with the level of resource distribution. The strength of this relationship (66%) explains the stability of differences in the level of democracy in the world. It would not be

Table 6.3. The 115 countries with small or moderate residuals (smaller than ±7.1) on the basis of the regression of ID-2006 on IPR by regional groups

Regional group	N	%	Total
Europe and offshoots	38	79.2	48
Latin America and the Caribbean	15	55.6	27
Sub-Saharan Africa	38	82.6	46
Middle East and North Africa	9	50.0	18
East Asia	4	66.7	6
Other Asia and Oceania	11	40.7	27
Total	115	66.9	172

reasonable to expect an equalization in the level of democratization as long as significant national differences in resource distribution continue. And it is not reasonable to expect the disappearance of national differences in resource distribution since the evolutionary roots of differences in resource distribution (IPR) can be traced to differences in national IQs and in climatic conditions.

We have already analyzed the evolutionary roots of the Index of Power Resources (IPR) in Chapter 5 and showed that 64 percent of the variation in IPR can be traced to the combined impact of mean temperature (MT) and national IQ. The impact of MT and national IQ on the measures of democracy takes place completely through IPR, as indicated in Chapter 3, but it would be interesting to see the direct relationships between MT and ID-2006 and between national IQ and ID-2006, although these relationships do not increase the explained part of variation in ID-2006. The explanations provided by MT and national IQ overlap completely with the explanation provided by IPR. The direct impacts of MT and national IQ on ID-2006 will be analyzed in the next chapter.

CHAPTER 7

MT and National IQ As Background Factors of Democratization

In the previous chapters, I traced the evolutionary roots of democratization to climatic differences (MT) and national IQ via the Index of Power Resources (IPR) and argued that they constitute the ultimate evolutionary constraints for democratization. Because of those limiting factors, it does not seem possible to achieve the same level and quality of democracy in all countries of the world. However, MT and national IQ do not increase the explained part of variation in the measures of democratization independently from IPR, although they are directly related to ID-2006 as hypothesized (see Figure 3.1). Correlations are moderate. Taken together, MT and national IQ explain 37 percent of the variation in ID-2006 (multiple correlation 0.606). The impact of MT on ID-2006 seems to take place principally through national IQ. As indicated in Chapter 4, MT explains 43 percent of the variation in national IQ. In this chapter, my intention is to analyze direct relationships between MT and ID-2006 and between national IQ and ID-2006 and to compare these relationships to that between IPR and ID-2006 analyzed in Chapter 6. The purpose is to see to what extent the same countries cluster around the regression lines or deviate from the regression lines on the basis of these three different regressions.

MT *as a determinant of democratization*

Let us start from the regression of ID-2006 on MT. According to the first hypothesis, the level of democratization should be negatively related to the level of MT. Figure 7.1 summarizes the results of regression analysis. The results are presented for single countries in Table 7.1.

Figure 7.1 indicates a relatively weak negative relationship between

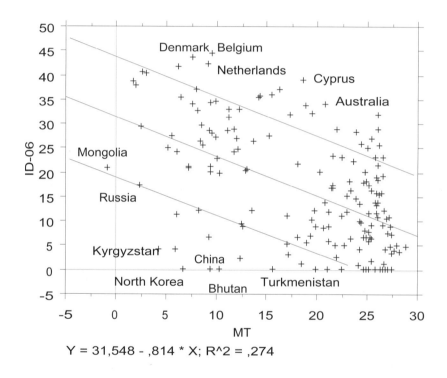

$$Y = 31,548 - ,814 * X; R^2 = ,274$$

Figure 7.1. The results of regression analysis of ID-2006 on MT in the group of 172 countries

MT and ID-2006. Many highly deviating countries contradict the first hypothesis. The covariation between MT and ID-2006 is only 27 percent. The predictive power of MT is not great, but it is interesting to see what countries are clustered around the regression line and what countries deviate greatly from the average pattern. Some of the most highly deviating countries are named in Figure 7.1. Detailed results are given in Table 7.1.

Table 7.1. The results of regression analyses of ID-2006 on MT and of ID-2006 on national IQ for single countries in the group of 172 countries.

	Country	MT	ID - 2006	Residual ID-06	Fitted ID-06	Nat. IQ	Residual ID-06	Fitted ID-06
1	Afghanistan	13.6	12.0	-8.5	20.5	84	-3.9	15.9
2	Albania	13.8	26.3	6.0	20.3	90	6.9	19.4
3	Algeria	21.2	8.7	-5.6	14.3	83	-6.6	15.3
4	Angola	22.6	0	-13.1	13.1	68	-6.3	6.3
5	Argentina	15.6	35.8	16.9	18.9	93	14.6	21.2
6	Armenia	9.6	20.9	-2.9	23.8	94	-0.9	21.8
7	Australia	20.8	33.9	19.3	14.6	99	9.7	24.2
8	Austria	6.6	35.1	8.9	26.2	100	9.7	25.4
9	Azerbaijan	12.6	9.3	-12.0	21.3	87	-8.4	17.7
10	Bahamas	24.7	17.7	6.3	11.4	84	1.8	15.9
11	Bahrain	26.8	1.1	-8.6	9.7	83	-14.2	15.3
12	Bangladesh	25.3	17.3	6.4	10.9	82	2.6	14.7
13	Barbados	26.2	18.3	8.1	10.2	80	4.8	13.5
14	Belarus	6.2	11.1	-15.4	26.5	97	-12.5	23.6
15	Belgium	9.7	44.2	20.5	23.7	99	19.4	24.8
16	Belize	26.0	15.5	5.1	10.4	84	-0.4	15.9
17	Benin	27.4	8.7	-0.5	9.2	70	1.2	7.5
18	Bhutan	10.4	0	-23.1	23.1	80	-13.5	13.5
19	Bolivia	21.6	16.5	2.5	14.0	87	-1.2	17.7
20	Bosnia and Herzgovina	9.7	27.8	4.1	23.7	90	8.4	19.4
21	Botswana	19.8	12.1	-3.3	15.4	70	4.6	7.5
22	Brazil	24.0	28.1	16.1	12.0	87	10.4	17.7
23	Brunei	26.9	0	-9.6	9.6	91	-20.0	20.0
24	Bulgaria	11.2	32.3	9.9	22.4	93	11.1	21.2
25	Burkina Faso	28.1	4.9	-3.8	8.7	68	-1.4	6.3
26	Burma (Myanmar)	24.7	0	-11.4	11.4	87	-17.7	17.7
27	Burundi	21.5	16.5	2.5	14.0	69	9.6	6.9
28	Cambodia	26.9	4.0	-5.6	9.6	91	-16.0	20.0
29	Cameroon	24.7	6.6	-4.8	11.4	64	2.6	4.0
30	Canada	2.6	29.1	-0.4	29.5	99	4.3	24.8
31	Cape Verde	23.4	16.2	3.7	12.5	76	5.1	11.1
32	Central African Rep.	25.2	7.6	-3.4	11.0	64	3.6	4.0
33	Chad	27.3	10.7	1.4	9.3	68	4.4	6.3
34	Chile	10.4	19.7	-3.4	23.1	90	0.3	19.4

35	China	9.6	0	-23.8	23.8	105	-28.4	28.4
36	Colombia	24.4	9.9	-1.8	11.7	84	-6.0	15.9
37	Comoros	25.5	8.9	-1.9	10.8	77	-2.8	11.7
38	Congo, Dem. Rep.	24.0	14.5	2.5	12.0	65	9.9	4.6
39	Congo, Republic	24.4	4.1	-7.6	11.7	64	0.1	4.0
40	Costa Rica	24.8	19.8	8.5	11.3	89	0.9	18.9
41	Côte d'Ivoire	26.4	0	-10.0	10.0	69	-6.9	6.9
42	Croatia	12.3	24.5	3.0	21.5	90	5.1	19.4
43	Cuba	25.2	0	-11.0	11.0	85	-16.5	16.5
44	Cyprus	18.7	38.7	22.4	16.3	91	18.0	20.0
45	Czech Republic	7.8	33.9	8.7	25.2	98	9.7	24.2
46	Denmark	7.7	43.5	18.2	25.3	98	19.3	24.2
47	Djibouti	29.0	4.5	-3.4	7.9	68	-1.8	6.3
48	Dominican Republic	25.0	17.9	6.7	11.2	82	3.2	14.7
49	East Timor	26.2	13.5	3.3	10.2	87	-4.2	17.7
50	Ecuador	20.4	20.0	5.1	14.9	88	1.7	18.3
51	Egypt	22.0	2.3	-11.3	13.6	81	-11.8	14.1
52	El Salvador	23.3	18.0	5.4	12.6	80	4.5	13.5
53	Equatorial Guinea	24.8	7.8	-3.5	11.3	59	6.8	1.0
54	Eritrea	25.3	0	-10.9	10.9	68	-6.3	6.3
55	Estonia	5.3	24.7	-2.5	27.0	99	-0.1	24.8
56	Ethiopia	21.3	11.8	-2.4	14.2	64	7.8	4.0
57	Fiji	25.0	0	-11.2	11.2	88	-18.3	18.3
58	Finland	2.1	37.6	7.7	29.9	99	12.8	24.8
59	France	11.4	31.1	8.8	22.3	98	6.9	24.2
60	Gabon	25.2	5.1	-5.9	11.0	64	1.1	4.0
61	Gambia	27.5	3.2	-5.9	9.1	66	-2.0	5.2
62	Georgia	9.4	6.6	-17.3	23.9	94	-15.2	21.8
63	Germany	8.1	37.0	12.0	25.0	99	12.2	24.8
64	Ghana	26.7	19.1	9.3	9.8	71	11.0	8.1
65	Greece	16.3	36.9	18.6	18.3	92	16.3	20.6
66	Guatemala	20.7	8.3	-6.4	14.7	79	-4.6	12.9
67	Guinea	25.4	6.6	-4.3	10.9	67	0.9	5.7
68	Guinea-Bissau	26.5	15.6	5.6	10.0	67	9.9	5.7
69	Guyana	26.0	18.7	8.3	10.4	87	1.0	17.7
70	Haiti	25.2	11.3	0.3	11.0	67	5.6	5.7
71	Honduras	24.4	13.2	1.5	11.7	81	-0.9	14.1
72	Hungary	10.0	27.0	3.6	23.4	98	2.8	24.2
73	Iceland	2.7	40.4	11.0	29.4	101	14.4	26.0

74	India	24.5	25.6	14.0	11.6	82	10.9	14.7
75	Indonesia	26.2	28.7	18.5	10.2	87	11.0	17.7
76	Iran	17.2	3.0	-14.5	17.5	84	-12.9	15.9
77	Iraq	21.9	4.9	-8.8	13.7	87	-12.8	17.7
78	Ireland	9.5	34.1	10.3	23.8	92	13.5	20.6
79	Israel	19.6	31.9	16.3	15.6	95	9.5	22.4
80	Italy	14.3	35.1	15.2	19.9	102	8.5	26.6
81	Jamaica	26.0	13.1	2.7	10.4	71	5.0	8.1
82	Japan	12.4	32.8	11.3	21.5	105	4.4	28.4
83	Jordan	18.6	1.0	-15.4	16.4	84	-14.9	15.9
84	Kazakhstan	6.1	4.0	-22.6	26.6	94	-17.8	21.8
85	Kenya	24.5	9.4	-2.2	11.5	72	0.7	8.7
86	Korea, North	6.8	0	-26.0	26.0	106	-29.0	29.0
87	Korea, South	12.1	26.8	5.1	21.7	106	-2.2	29.0
88	Kuwait	25.5	1.5	-9.3	10.8	86	-15.6	17.1
89	Kyrgyzstan	4.4	4.1	-23.9	28.0	90	-15.3	19.4
90	Laos	24.2	0.7	-11.1	11.8	89	-18.2	18.9
91	Latvia	5.7	27.4	0.5	26.9	98	3.2	24.2
92	Lebanon	18.2	21.5	4.8	16.7	82	6.8	14.7
93	Lesotho	12.8	8.6	-12.5	21.1	67	2.9	5.7
94	Liberia	25.9	13.7	3.3	10.4	67	8.0	5.7
95	Libya	21.1	0	-14.4	14.4	83	-15.3	15.3
96	Lithuania	6.2	23.9	-2.6	26.5	91	3.9	20.0
97	Luxembourg	8.5	26.2	1.6	24.6	100	0.8	25.4
98	Macedonia	10.2	22.6	-0.7	23.3	91	2.6	20.0
99	Madagascar	23.1	11.6	-1.1	12.7	82	-3.1	14.7
100	Malawi	21.7	17.1	3.2	13.9	69	10.2	6.9
101	Malaysia	26.0	11.4	1.0	10.4	92	-9.2	20.6
102	Maldives	27.8	3.7	-5.2	8.9	81	-10.4	14.1
103	Mali	28.3	3.4	-5.1	8.5	69	-3.5	6.9
104	Malta	18.9	33.7	17.5	16.2	97	10.1	23.6
105	Mauritania	27.4	4.7	-4.5	9.2	76	-6.4	11.1
106	Mauritius	23.7	22.1	9.9	12.2	89	3.2	18.9
107	Mexico	21.6	23.1	9.1	14.0	88	4.9	18.2
108	Moldova	9.5	20.0	-3.8	23.8	96	-3.0	23.0
109	Mongolia	-0.8	20.6	-11.6	32.2	101	-5.4	26.0
110	Montenegro	11.8	24.0	2.0	22.0	89	5.1	18.9
111	Morocco	17.1	5.1	-12.5	17.6	84	-10.8	15.9
112	Mozambique	23.5	6.1	-6.3	12.4	64	2.1	4.0
113	Namibia	19.6	10.0	-5.6	15.6	70	2.5	7.5
114	Nepal	13.0	17.7	-3.3	21.0	78	5.4	12.3
115	Netherlands	9.3	42.0	18.0	24.0	100	16.6	25.4
116	New Zealand	11.3	32.7	10.3	22.4	99	7.9	24.8

117	Nicaragua	25.1	24.8	_13.7_	11.1	81	_10.7_	14.1
118	Niger	27.6	7.1	-2.0	9.1	69	0.2	6.9
119	Nigeria	26.8	12.0	2.3	9.7	69	5.1	6.9
120	Norway	1.8	38.6	8.5	30.1	100	_13.2_	25.4
121	Oman	25.9	0	-10.4	10.4	83	_-15.3_	15.3
122	Pakistan	21.2	5.7	-8.6	14.3	84	_-10.2_	15.9
123	Panama	25.5	26.7	_15.9_	10.8	84	_10.8_	15.9
124	Papua New Guinea	26.1	31.6	_21.3_	10.3	83	_16.3_	15.3
125	Paraguay	23.1	15.1	2.4	12.7	84	-0.8	15.9
126	Peru	22.6	22.8	9.7	13.1	88	4.5	18.3
127	Philippines	26.6	22.8	_12.9_	9.9	86	5.7	17.1
128	Poland	7.3	20.7	-4.9	25.6	99	-4.1	24.8
129	Portugal	15.3	27.2	8.1	19.1	95	4.8	22.4
130	Qatar	26.9	0	-9.6	9.6	78	_-12.3_	12.3
131	Romania	8.8	25.3	0.9	24.4	94	3.5	21.8
132	Russia	2.4	17.3	_-12.3_	29.6	97	-6.3	23.6
133	Rwanda	19.5	6.7	-9.0	15.7	70	-0.8	7.5
134	Saudi Arabia	25.3	0	-10.9	10.9	84	_-15.9_	15.9
135	Senegal	27.2	7.2	-2.2	9.4	66	2.0	5.2
136	Serbia	11.8	28.6	6.6	22.0	89	9.7	18.9
137	Sierra Leone	26.1	10.6	0.3	10.3	64	6.6	4.0
138	Singapore	26.6	9.0	-0.9	9.9	108	_21.2_	30.2
139	Slovakia	7.4	20.9	-4.6	25.5	96	-2.1	23.0
140	Slovenia	9.4	28.5	4.6	23.9	96	5.5	23.0
141	Solomon Islands	26.3	15.3	5.2	10.1	84	-0.6	15.9
142	Somalia	27.2	0	-9.4	9.4	68	-6.3	6.3
143	South Africa	17.1	10.8	-6.8	17.6	72	2.1	8.7
144	Spain	14.4	35.6	_15.8_	19.8	98	_11.4_	24.2
145	Sri Lanka	26.3	25.3	_15.2_	10.1	79	_12.4_	12.9
146	Sudan	27.5	0	-9.1	9.3	71	-8.1	8.1
147	Surinam	26.2	21.2	11.0	10.2	89	2.3	18.9
148	Swaziland	19.9	0	_-15.3_	15.3	68	-6.3	6.3
149	Sweden	3.1	40.1	11.0	29.1	99	_15.3_	24.8
150	Switzerland	6.3	41.4	15.0	26.4	101	_15.4_	26.0
151	Syria	18.1	6.6	-10.2	16.8	83	-8.7	15.3
152	Taiwan	22.0	28.7	_15.1_	13.6	105	0.3	28.4
153	Tajikistan	8.4	12.1	_-12.6_	24.7	87	-5.6	17.7
154	Tanzania	22.8	4.8	-8.2	13.0	72	-3.9	8.7
155	Thailand	26.6	0	-9.9	9.9	91	_-20.0_	20.0
156	Togo	27.1	10.2	0.7	9.5	70	2.7	7.5

157	Trinidad and Tobago	25.9	22.9	12.5	10.4	85	6.4	16.5
158	Tunisia	19.0	5.5	-10.6	16.1	83	-9.8	15.3
159	Turkey	13.2	20.4	-0.4	20.8	90	1.0	19.4
160	Turkmenistan	15.7	0	-18.8	18.8	87	17.7	17.7
161	Uganda	22.6	10.9	-2.2	13.1	73	1.6	9.3
162	Ukraine	8.3	32.6	7.8	24.8	97	9.0	23.6
163	United Arab Emirates	26.9	0	-9.6	9.6	84	-15.9	15.9
164	United Kingdom	8.7	29.5	5.0	24.5	100	4.1	25.4
165	United States	10.1	34.5	11.2	23.3	98	10.3	24.2
166	Uruguay	17.4	31.8	14.4	17.4	96	8.8	23.0
167	Uzbekistan	12.5	2.1	-19.3	21.4	87	15.6	17.7
168	Venezuela	25.5	16.1	5.3	10.8	84	0.2	15.9
169	Vietnam	25.5	6.2	-4.6	10.8	94	-15.6	21.8
170	Yemen	25.0	6.4	-4.8	11.2	85	-10.1	16.5
171	Zambia	20.9	13.5	-1.0	14.5	71	5.4	8.1
172	Zimbabwe	19.9	8.8	-6.5	15.3	66	3.6	5.2

Table 7.1 discloses the countries in which the level of democratization is more or less in balance with the mean annual temperature as well as the countries which deviate clearly from the regression line and contradict the hypothesis. In Figure 7.1, two parallel lines at a distance of approximately one standard deviation of residual ID-2006 (±12.2) from the regression line separate the most deviating countries from the less deviating ones. In Table 7.1, large positive and negative outliers are underlined.

Using this criterion, the group of large positive outliers comprises 23 countries: Argentina, Australia, Belgium, Brazil, Cyprus, Denmark, Greece, India, Indonesia, Israel, Italy, Malta, the Netherlands, Nicaragua, Panama, Papua New Guinea, the Philippines, Spain, Sri Lanka, Switzerland, Taiwan, Trinidad and Tobago, and Uruguay.

The group of large negative outliers comprises 18 countries: Angola, Belarus, Bhutan, China, Georgia, Iran, Jordan, Kazakhstan, North Korea, Kyrgyzstan, Lesotho, Libya, Morocco, Russia, Swaziland, Tajikistan, Turkmenistan, and Uzbekistan.

It is easy to note that there are some clear differences in the nature of large positive and negative outliers. All positive outliers were above the threshold of democaracy, whereas all negative outliers, except Russia, were below the threshold of democracy in 2006. Of the 23 positive outliers, 10 are economically highly developed European and European offshoot countries. Taiwan is an economically highly developed East Asian country. Argentina, Brazil, Israel, and Uruguay are countries inhabited mainly by relatively recent immigrants from colder climatic zones. Ethnically highly heterogeneous countries like India, Indonesia, Papua New Guinea, Sri Lanka, and Trinidad and Tobago have succeeded in establishing and maintaining multiparty systems and raising the level of democratization considerably higher than expected on the basis of MT.

It is characteristic for large negative outliers that ten of them are socialist or former socialist countries. Iran, Jordan, Libya, and Morocco are Middle Eastern Muslim countries in which democratization has been exceptionally difficult, Bhutan is a mountainous country, and Lesotho and Swaziland are southern African countries inhabited by relatively recent migrants from tropical Africa.

This brief review of most deviating countries implies that there are various intervening variables which weaken the relationship between mean temperature and democratization. For example, migrations of people between different climatic zones seem to be related to some large outliers. In Chapter 4, I separated 26 countries whose populations originated at least partly from clearly different climatic zones. Six of the 17 countries whose populations originated at least partly from colder climatic zones are among the large positive outliers on the basis of this regression (Australia, Indonesia, Israel, Malta, Taiwan, and Uruguay), and four of the nine countries whose populations originated at least partly from tropical or other warmer regions are among the large negative outliers (Bhutan, Kyrgyzstan, Lesotho, and Swaziland).

National IQ as a determinant of democratization

Let us next examine how well national IQ explains the variation in the level of democratization and which countries deviate most from the average relationship between national IQ and ID-2006. According to the second hypothesis, the level of democratization is expected to rise with the level of national IQ. Figure 7.2 summarizes the results of regression analysis of ID-2006 on national IQ, and detailed results that were given in Table 7.1.

We can see from Figure 7.2 that the level of democratization tends to rise with national IQ as hypothesized, but there are several highly

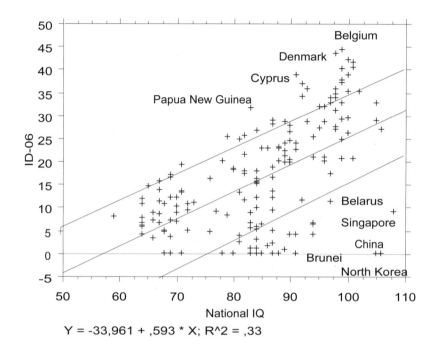

$$Y = -33,961 + ,593 * X; R^2 = ,33$$

Figure 7.2. The results of regression analysis of ID-2006 on national IQ in the group of 172 countries

deviating countries. Most of the highest positive outliers are at the upper level of national IQ, and most of the largest negative outliers are at the middle level of national IQ, although the most extreme negative outliers are at the highest level of national IQ.

Table 7.1 shows in which countries the level of democratization is more or less in balance with national IQ and which countries contradict the hypothesis (large residuals). We can again use one standard deviation of residual ID-2006 (±10.0) to separate most deviating countries from the less deviating ones. In Figure 7.2, two parallel lines at a distance of ±10.0 ID index points from the regression line separate the most deviating cases from the countries around the regression line. In Table

7.1, large positive and negative outliers are underlined.

Using this criterion, the group of large positive outliers includes the following 26 countries: Argentina, Belgium, Brazil, Bulgaria, Cyprus, Denmark, Finland, Germany, Ghana, Greece, Iceland, India, Indonesia, Ireland, Malawi, Malta, Netherlands, Nicaragua, Norway, Panama, Papua New Guinea, Spain, Sri Lanka, Sweden, Switzerland, and the United States.

The group of large negative residuals includes the following 33 countries: Bahrain, Belarus, Bhutan, Brunei, Burma, Cambodia, China, Cuba, Egypt, Fiji, Georgia, Iran, Iraq, Jordan, Kazakhstan, North Korea, Kuwait, Kyrgyzstan, Laos, Libya, Maldives, Morocco, Oman, Pakistan, Qatar, Saudi Arabia, Singapore, Thailand, Turkmenistan, the United Arab Emirates, Uzbekistan, Vietnam, and Yemen.

The characteristics which separate large positive and negative outliers from each other are partly similar, as in the previous regression of ID-2006 on MT. The group of positive outliers is dominated by economically highly developed European and European offshoot democracies (16). The group of negative outliers is dominated by socialist and former socialist countries (12) and by oil-producing and other Middle Eastern Muslim countries (13).

Causal path from MT via national IQ and IPR to ID-2006

The results of regression analyses of ID-2006 on MT and on national IQ (Table 7.1) and ID-2006 on IPR (Table 6.1) for single countries make it possible to explore to what extent we can trace the roots of differences in the level of democratization through IPR to national IQ and MT. It is reasonable to assume that a causal path of democratization extends to national IQ and MT most clearly in countries which are relatively close to the regression line on the basis of all three regression analyses. One standard deviation of residual ID-2006 (± 12.2 for MT, ± 10.0 for national IQ, and ± 7.1 for IPR) can be used as the criterion for "relatively close to the regression line." In other words, the countries for which all three residuals are smaller than one standard deviation of residual ID-2006 constitute the category of countries in which the level of democratization is more or less in balance, not only with the level of IPR, but also with the levels of national IQ and MT (annual mean temperature). In such countries, the evolutionary roots of democratization can be clearly traced to national IQ and MT. The countries for which one, two, or all three residuals are larger than one standard deviation of residual ID-2006 deviate more clearly from the hypothesized pattern and contradict one or more hypotheses. The countries for which all three residuals are larger than one standard deviation constitute the group of the most contradictory countries. In such countries, some other factors seem to have affected the level of democratization more than IPR, national IQ, and MT.

For 81 countries all three residuals are smaller than one standard deviation, for 50 countries one of the three residuals is larger than one standard deviation, for 19 countries two of the three residuals are larger than one standard deviation, and for 22 countries all three residuals are larger than one standard deviation. It is useful to examine the hypothesized evolutionary roots and constraints of democratization separately in these four groups of countries, but let us first see the regional distribution of countries by the number of large residuals (Table 7.2).

Table 7.2 shows that countries with small and large residuals are distributed around the world, but there are clear regional differences in the frequency of cases. Countries with small residuals are overrepresented in the sub-Saharan African group and underrepresented in the three regional groups of Middle Eastern and Asian countries. Correspondingly, countries with large residuals are underrepresented in the sub-Saharan African group and especially overrepresented in the regional groups of the Middle East and North Africa and other Asian and Oceanian countries. The evolutionary roots of democratization extend to national IQ and MT more clearly in the first three regional groups than in the three last regional groups.

The correspondence of residuals supports to a significant extent the central theoretical argument of this study, according to which the causal path of democracy can be traced from IPR to national IQ and MT. It would be interesting to see which one of the three explanatory variables has predicted the ID value for a country most accurately. Is the actual level of democratization in a country best in balance with the degree of resource distribution (IPR), national IQ, or the annual mean temperature (MT)? Such a comparison would provide additional information to evaluate the chances of democracy and potential for democracy in different countries. For example, if a present low level of democratization in a country is in balance with the degree of resource distribution (IPR), but national IQ and MT presuppose a considerably

Table 7.2. The regional distribution of 172 countries by the number of small and large residuals based on the regressions of ID-2006 on MT, ID-2006 on national IQ, and ID-2006 on IPR

Regional group	Small	1 large residual	2 large residuals	3 large residuals	Total residuals
Europe and offshoots	23	15	4	6	48
%	47.9	31.2	8.3	12.5	100.0
Latin America and the Caribbean	14	8	1	4	27
%	51.9	29.6	3.7	14.8	100.0
Sub-Saharan Africa	37	6	3	0	46
%	80.4	13.0	6.5	0	100
The Middle East and North Africa	2	8	5	3	18
%	11.1	44.4	27.8	16.7	100.0
East Asia	2	2	1	1	6
%	33.3	33.3	16.7	16.7	100
Other Asia and the Pacific	3	11	5	8	27
%	11.1	40.7	18.5	29.6	100
Total	81	50	19	22	172
%	47.1	29.1	11.0	12.8	100.0

higher level of democratization, it would be reasonable to expect increasing pressure for democratization.

My argument is that if all three residuals are smaller than one standard deviation, it is justified to trace the causal explanation of the level of democratization to national IQ and MT via IPR. Since changes in MT and national IQ are slow, it means that they would constrain chances to raise or lower the level of democratization. In other words, it would not be justified to expect that countries at different levels of MT and national IQ could achieve the same level of democratization. These two ultimate causal factors constitute permanent limits of democratization. The appearance of large residuals indicates the impact of some other factors of democratization, which factors may have furthered (positive residuals) or obstructed (negative residuals) democratization. It would be interesting to explore what those other factors may be in different cases and to what extent they are under conscious human control.

Countries with small and moderate residuals

In the European group, all three residuals are smaller than one standard deviation for the following 23 countries: Albania, Armenia, Austria, Azerbaijan, Bosnia and Herzegovina, Canada, Croatia, Czech Republic, Estonia, France, Hungary, Latvia, Macedonia, Moldova, Montenegro, New Zealand, Portugal, Romania, Serbia, Slovakia, Turkey, Ukraine, and the United Kingdom. The group includes nearly all former East European socialist countries and former Soviet republics, but only a few of the old economically highly developed European democracies. In these 23 countries, the relatively high level of democratization is approximately in balance with the index of power resources, national IQ, and annual mean temperature. Therefore, we cannot expect any drastic changes in the level of democratization, although there are certainly possibilities for improving or worsening the quality of democracy.

In the Latin American and Caribbean group, all residuals are small or only moderate for the following 14 countries: the Bahamas, Barbados, Belize, Bolivia, Chile, Colombia, Costa Rica, Dominican Republic, Guatemala, Haiti, Honduras, Jamaica, Paraguay, and Venezuela. The values of explanatory variables vary significantly in this group, as does the level of democratization. All of these countries, except Guatemala, were above the threshold of democracy in 2006, but several have had troubles in their attempts to maintain democratic institutions. Democracy has not yet become consolidated in all those countries. Because the present level of democratization is approximately in balance with the values of explanatory variables, troubles can be expected to continue.

In the sub-Saharan African group, all residuals are small or moderate for 37 countries: Benin, Botswana, Burkina Faso, Cameroon, Cape Verde, the Central African Republic, Chad, Comoros, the Democratic Republic of Congo, the Republic of Congo, Djibouti, Equatorial Guinea, Ethiopia, Gabon, Gambia, Guinea, Kenya, Liberia, Madagascar, Mali, Mauritania, Mauritius, Mosambique, Namibia, Niger, Nigeria, Rwanda, Senegal, Sierra Leone, Somalia, South Africa, Swaziland, Tanzania, Togo, Uganda, Zambia, and Zimbabwe. Many of them were more or less below the threshold of democracy in 2006 (competition 30 and participation 20), but Benin, Botswana, Burundi, Cape Verde, the Central African Republic, Chad, Comoros, the Democratic Republic of Congo, Ethiopia, Ghana, Guinea-Bissau, Kenya, Lesotho, Liberia, Madagasgar, Malawi, Mauritius, Niger, Nigeria, South Africa, Uganda, Zambia, and

Zimbabwe were above the threshold of democracy. However, all these countries, except Mauritius, were only slightly above the threshold of democracy, and several had crossed the minimum threshold quite recently. The fact that all three residuals are smaller than one standard deviation for 80 percent of sub-Saharan African countries indicates that the lack of democracy or a low level of democratization are approximately in balance with the three explanatory variables. Because the causal roots of democratization seem to extend to national IQ and MT, we cannot expect any drastic rise in the level of democratization. The ultimate causal factors (MT and national IQ) constrain the chances to raise the level of resource distribution (IPR) and through it the level of democratization.

In the group of Middle Eastern and North African countries, all three residuals are small only for Algeria and Lebanon. Algeria was slightly above the threshold of democracy in 2006 and Lebanon clearly above the threshold. The small number of countries with small and moderate residuals implies that the present low level of democratization deviates from the level presupposed by one or more explanatory variables in most countries of this regional group.

In East Asia, all three residuals are small for Japan and Mongolia. These two countries have good chances to maintain their high level of democratization.

In the group of other Asian and Oceanian countries, all three residuals are small only for Afghanistan, Nepal, and the Solomon Islands. All of them were above the threshold of democracy in 2006. In Afghanistan, democratic institutions were still fragile and protected by foreign troops.

My general conclusion is that because the present level of democratization is more or less in balance not only with IPR but also with national IQ and MT in this category of 81 countries, we cannot expect any drastic changes in the level of democratization. National IQ and MT constitute background factors that are outside conscious human control.

Countries with one large residual

In the category of 50 countries with one large residual, the level of democratization clearly deviates from the level expected on the basis of one explanatory variable. However, because two other residuals are smaller than one standard deviation, these 50 countries only partly contradict the hypothesized causal path of democratization. It is useful to see from which explanatory variable the level of democratization deviates and in what direction. The countries in this category are relatively evenly distributed around the world. Of the 50 large residuals, 25 are positive and 25 negative: nine are based on the regression of ID-2006 n MT, 19 on the regression of ID-2006 on national IQ, and 22 on the regression of ID-2006 on IPR. In the following, I refer to each country with one large residual, starting from residuals based on MT.

Large residuals based on MT are positive for six countries (Australia, Israel, Italy, the Philippines, Taiwan, and Trinidad and Tobago). In these countries, the level of democratization is considerably higher than expected on the basis of MT. Relatively recent immigrants from colder climatic regions constitute a significant part of the population especially in Australia, Israel, and Trinidad and Tobago, which may partly explain their higher than expected level of ID. The three other countries are more ambiguous cases. The fragmentation of the party system has especially raised the level of democratization (ID) in Italy. Large positive residuals predict a decline in the level of democratization, but because residuals are small or moderate on the basis of two other explanatory variables, this does not need to happen.

Large residuals based on MT are negative for Lesotho, Russia, and Tajikistan. Russia and Tajikistan are former socialist countries, in which the institutional heritage of the socialist system has hampered democratic development. Besides, Tajikistan is a mountainous country in which the annual mean temperature is lower than in neighboring countries from which its population originated. The people of Lesotho are Bantu migrants from tropical regions of sub-Saharan Africa, which means that Lesotho's national IQ presupposes a much lower level of democratization than MT.

It is obvious that in at least four of these nine countries, large positive or negative residuals based on MT are related to migration of people from different climatic zones or to exceptional geographical conditions. Therefore, these countries are not serious outliers from the theoretical point of view.

Large residuals based on national IQ are positive for eight countries and negative for 11. Large residuals are positive for Finland, Bulgaria, Germany, Iceland, Ireland, Norway, Sweden, and the United States.

All these countries are economically highly developed European and European offshoot countries, which have achieved a significantly higher level of democratization than expected on the basis of national IQ. However, because the level of democratization is approximately in balance with the two other explanatory variables, I do not regard them as seriously deviating countries. They have good chances to maintain their high level of democratization.

Large residuals based on national IQ are negative for Bahrain, Brunei, Cambodia, Iraq, Maldives, Pakistan, Qatar, Turkmenistan, the United Arab Emirates, Vietnam, and Yemen. Why have these countries not been able to achieve the level of democratization expected on the basis of their national IQs? It is characteristic of these countries that six (Bahrain, Brunei, Iraq, Qatar, the United Arab Emirates, and Yemen) are oil-producing Muslim countries in which economic and coercive power resources are highly concentrated in the hands of the rulers. This concentration of power resources has prevented democratization until now, but large negative residuals based on national IQ indicate that there is human potential for a more democratic political system. We can expect increasing popular pressure for democratization in these countries. Cambodia is a poor country that has suffered from a long civil war and has not yet been able to stabilize a democratic system. The Maldives and Pakistan are poor Muslim countries in which it has been difficult to establish and maintain democratic institutions. The struggle for democracy has been intensive in Pakistan. Turkmenistan is a former socialist country in which economic power resources are still concentrated in the hands of the government. Vietnam is a socialist country dominated by the ruling Communist party. Large negative residuals based on national IQs predict democratization in all these countries, but their nondemocratic systems are still more or less in balance with the values of the two other explanatory variables, especially with IPR.

Large residuals based on IPR are positive for 11 countries and negative for 11 others. Residuals are positive for Bangladesh, Burundi, East Timor, Ecuador, El Salvador, Guinea-Bissau, Guyana, Mexico, Peru, Suriname, and Uruguay. The group includes four poor Asian and African countries and seven Latin American countries in which the level of democratization in 2006 was much higher than expected on the basis of IPR, whereas it was relatively well in balance with MT and national IQ.

Large residuals are negative for Cote d'Ivoire, Eritrea, South Korea, Lithuania, Luxembourg, Malaysia, Poland, Slovenia, Sudan, Syria, and Tunisia. ID-2006 was zero or almost zero in five of these (Cote d'Ivoire, Eritrea, Sudan, Syria, and Tunisia). Five other countries are economically highly developed market economies in which the level of democratization in 2006 was, for various local and temporary reasons, somewhat lower than expected. Malaysia's large negative residual reflects the dominance of the ruling National Front as explained in Chapter 6.

Countries with two large residuals

The 19 countries with two large residuals contradict the hypothesis on the evolutionary roots of democracy more seriously than do the 50 countries with only one large residual. These 19 countries are evenly distributed around the world. Two large residuals are positive for 12 countries and negative for 11. Positive residuals predict a decline in the level of democratization and a rise in negative residuals. There are three combinations of large positive residuals, and similarly, three combinations of large negative residuals (MT and national IQ, MT and IPR, and national IQ and IPR).

Positive residuals based on MT and national IQ are large for Denmark, Greece, and Spain. These three countries are economically highly developed European democracies, in which the level of democratization has risen much higher than expected on the basis of MT and national IQ. However, because the level of democratization is approximately in balance with the degree of resource distribution, there is no reason to expect a decline of democracy in these countries.

Negative residuals based on MT and national IQ are large for Belarus, North Korea, and Morocco. These three countries are below the threshold of democracy, but on the basis of MT and national IQ, they should be democracies. Belarus is slightly below the Competition threshold for democracy, while North Korea is the most highly deviating country, its autocratic system being especially inconsistent with its very high level of national IQ. Noted that the lack of democracy in Belarus and North Korea is in harmony with the concentration of economic power resources. The same concerns Morocco, although to a lesser degree. The lack of democracy in these countries is more or less in harmony with the concentration of power resources (IPR), but because MT and national

IQ presuppose a democratic system, we can expect popular pressure for democratization. There is human potential for more democratic political systems, especially in Belarus and North Korea.

Negative residual based on MT and IPR is large for Angola, whereas the lack of democracy in Angola is in better balance with the country's low national IQ. We can expect increasing pressure for democratization in Angola.

Finally, positive residuals based on national IQ and IPR are large for Ghana and Malawi. The level of democratization is much higher than expected on the basis of national IQ and IPR in these two countries, and it would be reasonable to expect some decline in their ID values. In fact, these countries crossed the minimum threshold of democracy quite recently and have been exceptionally successful in democratization.

Negative residuals based on national IQ and IPR are large for ten countries: Burma, Cuba, Egypt, Fiji, Kuwait, Laos, Oman, Saudi Arabia, Singapore, and Thailand. Both national IQ and IPR presuppose a higher level of democratization in these countries, and we can expect increasing pressure for democracy. The lack of democracy in Burma is due to the ability of the military government to remain in power. The long ethnic civil war between the Burmese government forces and separatist ethnic rebels strengthened the dominant position of the military. The military has needed violent means to suppress popular pressure for democratization in Burma. Cuba and Laos are socialist countries in which the concentration of economic power resources has supported the hegemony of ruling parties, but both national IQ and IPR predict democratization. Limited attempts at democratization have been made in Egypt, but the system was still autocratic in 2006. Fiji dropped below the threshold of democracy in 2006, probably only temporarily, as a consequence of a military coup. Kuwait, Oman, and Saudi Arabia are autocratically ruled oil-producing Arab countries where national IQ in particular presupposes some democratization. Singapore is an anomalous case. Its present level of democratization is too low, according to national IQ and IPR, whereas in fact, Singapore is one of the most highly divergent countries in the world and it is reasonable to expect a significant rise in the level of democratization. Thailand, like Fiji, dropped below the threshold of democracy in 2006 as a consequence of a military coup supported by the king. Large negative residuals predict some democratization in all these countries.

Various local and temporary factors seem to be related to large positive and negative residuals in many cases. It is not possible to find any common factor which could provide a satisfactory explanation for all large positive or negative residuals, although several of those countries have some common characteristics.

Countries with three large residuals

All three residuals are large for 22 countries, which most clearly contradict the hypothesis on the evolutionary roots of democracy. Large residuals are positive for 13 countries and negative for nine countries. These highly deviant countries are not evenly distributed around the world, but are overrepresented in the regional groups of Europe and European offshoot countries and of other Asian and Oceanian countries.

Five of the 13 countries with three large positive residuals are economically highly developed European democracies (Belgium, Cyprus, Malta, the Netherlands, and Switzerland). The level of democracy in these countries is much higher than expected on the basis of all three explanatory variables, but we do not need to expect any significant decline in the level of democratization for the reason that these countries already have been positive outliers for a long period. It may be that some crucial power resources are even more widely distributed in these countries than my IPR indicates. In fact, residuals are positive for nearly all Western European democracies. All residuals are also large for four Latin American countries: Argentina, Brazil, Nicaragua, and Panama. Argentina was only a temporarily highly deviating country in 2006, as explained in Chapter 6. Brazil's deviating position is mainly due to its highly fragmented party system, which has raised the level of competition. Some temporary and accidental factors may explain Nicaragua's and Panama's high-positive residuals. In Nicaragua, the level of competition rose exceptionally high in the 2006 presidential election. Panama's deviating position is partly caused by its system of presidential election. There is only one round of voting in a presidential election, and the winning candidate does not need to get a majority of the votes. As a consequence, the value of the Competition variable tends to rise somewhat higher than in other Latin American countries, in which the winning candidate needs more than 50 percent of the votes.

India, Indonesia, Papua New Guinea, and Sri Lanka are the four Asian and Oceanian countries for which all three positive residuals are large; they are much more democratized than expected. In India, the level of competition rose significantly in the 2004 parliamentary election and made India a highly deviating country. Indonesia has been a positive outlier since 2004, when both president and parliament were chosen by competitive elections. Large positive residuals predict a decline in the level of democratization, but the adaptation of the country's party system to the ethnic heterogeneity of the population may support the survival of democratic institutions and competitive elections. Papua New Guinea's much higher than expected level of democratization is related to the extreme ethnic heterogeneity of its population, which has prevented the emergence of large national parties. Consequently, the share of the largest party is low and the degree of competition high. Because of its ethnically fragmented party system, Papua New Guinea may be able to maintain a much higher level of democratization than the three explanatory variables predict. Sri Lanka has succeeded in maintaining its democratic institutions despite a long ethnic civil war, which is a significant achievement. Deep ethnic and ideological cleavages have maintained a highly competitive party system.

Five of the nine countries with large negative residuals are contemporary or former socialist countries: China, Georgia, Kazakhstan, Kyrgyzstan, and Uzbekistan. The heritage of socialist economic and political structures has hampered the development of competitive politics in these countries. However, large negative residuals predict increasing popular pressure for democratization. China is a highly anomalous country. Its negative residuals based on national IQ and MT are extremely high, which means that there is more human potential for democratization than China's relatively low IPR value indicates. The economic transformation taking place in China precedes democratization, which will follow sometime later. Countries like North Korea and China with highly intelligent populations cannot remain forever as extreme outliers. As emphasized earlier, Georgia is probably only a temporarily deviating country. Its much lower than expected level of democratization is due to the 2004 exceptional presidential election, in which the opposition's candidate Mikhail Saakashvili won 96 percent of the votes (see *Keesing's Record of World Events* 2004, p. 45820). Most probably Georgia will recross the threshold of democracy in the next election. Bhutan's lack of democracy reflects the traditional autocratic rule of the king, but some years ago the king started a process of democratization whose purpose is to transform Bhutan into a constitutional monarchy. Iran, Jordan, and Libya are Middle Eastern and North African Muslim countries in which democratization has been exceptionally difficult. It is justified to expect increasing popular pressure for democratization in all these countries.

Various local, temporary, and accidental factors have caused some countries to deviate greatly from the regression lines of the three regression equations, but it was possible to find some common factors that characterize several positive and negative outliers. Most of the large positive outliers are economically highly developed European or Latin American democracies, whereas most of the large negative outliers are contemporary or former socialist or oil-producing Middle Eastern and North African countries. Numerous highly deviating countries emphasize the fact that the hypothesized causal relationship between the explanatory variables and the measures of democracy is not complete and that some other factors may affect the relationship significantly. I would also like to emphasize that because of the impact of temporary and accidental factors, the residuals of countries fluctuate considerably.

Conclusion

My purpose in this chapter was to explore to what extent it is possible to trace the causal path of democratization from the principal explanatory variable, the index of power resources (IPR), to the evolutionary background factors, the annual mean temperature and national IQ, which explain a significant part of the variation in IPR. This was done by comparing the results of regression analyses of ID-2006 on MT, ID-2006 on national IQ, and ID-2006 on IPR at the level of single countries. It was argued that it is justified to trace the evolutionary roots of democratization from IPR to national IQ and MT if the same countries cluster around the regression line according to all three regression equations.

In the first section, the results of the regression of ID-2006 on MT were examined at the level of single countries. The results show that the most deviating positive and negative outliers clearly differ from each other in some respects. Most of the largest positive outliers are European and other economically highly developed democracies, but the group also includes some countries which have benefited from immigrants from colder climatic zones. Most of the large negative outliers are socialist or former socialist countries and Middle Eastern Muslim countries. The group also includes some countries that have suffered from long ethnic and other civil wars, which have hampered economic and political development. These observations on the characteristics of the countries that deviate most from the regression line refer to some other factors that have affected the nature of political systems independently from the annual mean temperature.

In the next section, the results of the regression of ID-2006 on national IQ were examined at the level of single countries. The correlation between national IQ and the level of democratization is significantly stronger than between MT and the level of democratization. The observations on the nature of the most deviating countries are principally similar, as in the case of MT. Most of the large positive outliers are economically highly developed European and European offshoot democracies, and most of the large negative outliers are socialist or former socialist countries and Middle Eastern Muslim countries. These observations imply that similar factors have caused most of the large deviations in both regressions. It should be noted that the examination of the results of the regression of ID-2006 on IPR in Chapter 6 disclosed similar factors that are related to large outliers.

In the third section, the results of the three regression analyses were combined in order to see to what extent the same countries cluster around the regression line or deviate greatly from the regression line according to all three regressions. The results show that the residuals of all three regression analyses were smaller than one standard deviation for 81 countries in 2006. In these cases, the causal path of democratization and constraints of democratization can be most reliably traced from IPR to national IQ and MT. A low or high level of democratization is related not only to the degree of resource distribution but also to the level of national IQ and the mean annual temperature. Because these background factors are outside conscious human control, they constitute constraints that maintain the persistence of great differences in the level of resource distribution (IPR) and through it in the level of democratization and the quality of democracy.

However, the level of democratization is not adapted to this pattern in all countries of the world. The comparison of residuals disclosed that one of the three residuals is larger than one standard deviation in 50 cases and that two residuals are large in 19 cases and all three residuals in 22 cases. These exceptions leave room for the impact of other factors, for conscious human choices, and also for various local, temporary, and accidental factors.

The 41 countries for which two or three residuals are larger than one standard deviation are more serious outliers than the 50 countries for which only one residual is large. The examination of the 41 most outlying countries disclosed that there are some common factors related respectively to large positive and negative outliers. Eight of the 18 large positive outliers are economically highly developed European democracies, whereas 16 of the 23 large negative outliers are socialist or former socialist countries or Middle Eastern Muslim countries. The rest of the large positive and negative outliers seems to be due to more temporary and accidental factors or particular local factors.

According to my interpretation, the extensive correspondence of residuals means that the explanation of democratization based on the degree of resource distribution (IPR) can to a significant extent be traced to the two background factors, national IQ and MT, which explain 64 percent of the variation in IPR. Because the values of national IQ and MT are nearly completely outside conscious human control, they are constants that constrain the chances to equalize the level and quality of democracy in the world. However, the appearance of numerous deviating cases indicates that, to some extent, it has been possible and will be possible in the future to break these constraints. However, despite several exceptions, these constraints seem to be strong enough to maintain a great variation in the level and quality of democracy. An interesting question is how these constraints are reflected in political practices. These problems will be preliminarily discussed in the next chapters.

CHAPTER 8

The Quality of Democracy by the Level of National IQ

The results of this study show that the level of democratization does not vary at random, but is strongly related to the degree of resource distribution (IPR) within societies and further to the average intelligence of a nation (national IQ) and annual mean temperature (MT). My theoretical argumentation, inspired by Montesquieu's idea of the impact of climatic conditions on human nature and institutions, led me to seek an ultimate explanation for the persistent variance in the degree of resource distribution and through it in the level of democratization. These factors derive from the evolved differences in the average mental abilities of populations (national IQ) and from differences in climatic conditions (MT), which are assumed to have generated evolved differences in national IQs (see Lynn 2006). Since these explanatory background factors are nearly constant and explain a considerable part of the variation in the level of democratization via IPR, I came to the conclusion that they constitute permanent limits of democratization.

Because of these constraints, it is improbable that all countries could ever achieve the same level of democratization or the same quality of democracy. Thus my argument is that the ultimate limits of democratization can be traced to national IQ and through it to differences in mean temperature (MT). Because the impact of mean temperature on resource distribution and democratization seems to take place principally through national IQ, it is enough to focus on the relationship between national IQ and the level and quality of democracy. According to my hypothesis, national IQ constrains democratization via IPR in such a way that the level and quality of democracy tend to be higher, the higher the level of national IQ.

The results of correlation analysis (Chapter 3) have already indicated that national IQ, the level of resource distribution (IPR), and the level of democratization are positively correlated as hypothesized. In this chapter, my purpose is to focus on various measures of the quality of democracy and to test the hypothesis by comparing the means of explanatory and dependent variables at different levels of national IQ. For this purpose, the 172 countries of this study are divided into seven national IQ categories: (1) national IQ 59–69 (N = 30), (2) national IQ 70–79 (N = 20), (3) national IQ 80–84 (N = 33), (4) national IQ 85–89 (N = 26), (5) national IQ 90–94 (N = 22), (6) national IQ 95–99 (N = 26), and (7) national IQ 100–108 (N = 15). The hypothesis presupposes that the means of variables rise systematically from the national IQ category 1 to the national IQ category 7. This hypothesized relationship is assumed to reflect the constraining impact of national IQ (and MT) on the quality of democracy.

A big problem is how to measure the quality of democracy. I assume that the quality of democracy is strongly related to the level of democracy, which has been measured by my indicators of democratization as well as by some other indicators of democracy yet these indicators do not take into account all important aspects of the quality of democracy. It is therefore useful to explore what other indicators might be related to the quality of democracy. For this purpose, I shall first review some studies of the quality of democracy, after which it is possible to define empirical indicators which will be used in this study to measure the quality of democracy from various perspectives. The hypothesis is tested by using data on available indicators of the quality of democracy but also on the components of IPR. However, because empirical indicators take only some aspects of the quality of democracy into account, I try to complement the analysis in the next chapter by describing the quality of democracy in single countries at different levels of national IQ. My purpose is to highlight the fact that significant and persistent differences in the quality of democracy are systematically related to the level of national IQ.

Studies on the quality of democracy

It has been observed in studies of democracy since the 1960s that the level of democratization varies greatly in the world. It was also found that differences in the level of democracy reflect differences in the quality of democracy. All countries that fulfill minimum criteria for democracy have not achieved the same quality of democracy. So the problem is why the quality of democracy varies greatly and why it has not been possible to achieve the same quality of democracy in all parts of the world. But what is meant by the quality of democracy? It has been difficult to define the quality of democracy and even more difficult to measure it. I refer to some studies in which these problems are discussed from various perspectives.

Robert A. Dahl (1989) discusses the limits and possibilities of democracy and presents a list of seven institutions of polyarchy (elected officials, free and fair elections, inclusive suffrage, right to run for office, freedom of expression, alternative information, and association autonomy). He notes that it might be possible to rank the countries of the world approximately according to the extent to which each of the institutions is present in a realistic sense. Thus these institutions could serve as criteria "for deciding which countries are governed by polyarchy today or were in earlier time" (p. 221). Dahl emphasizes that "countries vary enormously in the extent to which their governments meet the criteria of the democratic process or, more narrowly, sustain the institutions necessary to polyarchy" (p. 233). He did not try to rank countries according to these criteria, but I think that if it were possible to make such a ranking, its correlations with MT and national IQ would be approximately the same as the correlations between these two constraints of democratization and various indicators of democracy observed in this study (see Chapter 3).

In their book *Politics in Developing Countries: Comparing Experiences with Democracy,* Diamond et al. (1995) seek to explain whether, why, and to what extent democracy has evolved and taken root in the vastly different cultural and historical soils (p. 1). They pay attention to the fact that the level of democracy varies. All countries have not been able to achieve full democracy; there are low-quality democracies, hegemonic party systems, pseudodemocracies, and totalitarian regimes. They present a list of facilitating and obstructing factors for democratic development (legitimacy and performance, political leadership, political culture, social structure and socioeconomic development, population growth, civil society, state and society, political institutions, ethnic and regional conflict, the military, and international factors). They do not take into account the possibility that differences in the mental abilities of populations might affect the nature of political systems, but I assume that at least some of their facilitating and obstructing factors would be significantly related to national IQ (see also Linz and Stepan 1996; Stepan 2001).

Larry Diamond (1999) makes an interesting distinction between "liberal democracies," which fulfill the most criteria of democratic governance, and "electoral democracies," which fulfill only some minimal requirements of democracy. This distinction refers to qualitative differences between democracies. His categories of liberal and electoral democracies are based on Freedom House ratings (cf. Diamond 2002; Levitsky and Way 2002). Ronald Inglehart (2000) argues that some cultures are more conducive to democracy than some others and that the quality of democracy depends on the cultural values and beliefs of ordinary citizens (see also Huntington 1996; Inglehart and Welzel 2005; Welzel 2007). It would be interesting to know to what extent cultural values and beliefs of ordinary citizens are related to MT and national IQ.

Arend Lijphart (1999) examines the patterns of democracy by comparing majoritarian and consensus democracies. He comes to the conclusion that the quality of democracy is somewhat better in consensus democracies than in majoritarian democracies. Such qualitative differences are often due to electoral laws. Lauri Karvonen and Carsten Anckar (2002) explore to what extent the variation in democratization in Third World countries might be related to differences in party systems. They found that party system characteristics fail to explain variation in democratic development, although they seem to play a role in certain contexts. They come to the conclusion that the electoral system is more important than the form of government. One of their findings is that "in proportional electoral systems the legitimacy of the democratic form of government is not called into question, despite high levels of party system fragmentation" (p. 27).

Adam Przeworski et al. (2000) classify political systems into democracies and dictatorships, which classification refers to qualitative differences between regimes from the perspective of democracy.

They use the impact of economic performance to explain the difference between democracies and dictatorships, but their lists of regimes imply that MT and national IQ would explain a significant part of the difference between the two categories of regimes.

David Altman and Aníbal Pérez-Liñán (2002) explore the problem of conceptualizing and measuring the quality of democracy in Latin America. They note that there is a substantial difference between the quality of democracy and the level of democratization. Every analysis of the quality of democracy is based on the assumption that countries have already achieved a minimum degree of democratization. Their attention is focused on the question in which countries democracy performs better given some normative standards, but it is problematic how to identify these normative standards. In their empirical study of 18 Latin American countries, they take into account three dimensions of the quality of democracy: civil rights, participation, and effective competition inferred from Dahl's concept of polyarchy. Two of these dimensions are in principle the same as my two components (competition and participation) of the index of democratization (ID), although they use different indicators to measure them. Civil rights represents an additional dimension. They admit that these three dimensions are not enough to fully describe the complexities of democratic life, although they are well-grounded in democratic theory. Consequently, we are still far from settling the question of how to measure the quality of democracy. It is certainly possible to identify various dimensions of the quality of democracy, but the problem is how to measure them.

The Quality of Democracy: Theory and Applications, edited by Guillermo O'Donnell et al. (2004), is based on the discussions in the workshop on the quality of democracy and human development in Latin America held in Costa Rica in 2002. O'Donnell (2004) links democracy to human rights and human development in his theoretical chapter and presents a long list of standards for democracy. He emphasizes especially the significance of the rule of law and the temporal sequence of rights from civil rights to political rights and finally to social rights. However, it is not clear to what extent it might be possible to quantify his standards of democracy and to use them in comparative studies. Jorge Vargas Cullell (2004) reports on the methods and results of the experimental Citizen Audit of the Quality of Democracy in Costa Rica. This audit covers more than 200 indicators, which have been reduced to 32 standards of democracy. I think that the large number of standards makes it impossible to use them in comparative studies. He concludes that "the democratization of political regimes does not necessarily lead to improvement in the quality of democracy" (p. 145). It is an important observation.

Several scholars have commented on O'Donnell's and Cullell's articles. Ippolito (2004) notes that the question underlying O'Donnell's chapter is this: "How do we account for the coexistence of a democratic political regime based on the idea of citizenship or political equality in a context of high socioeconomic inequality and/or violation of fundamental human rights?" (p. 170). Juan E. Mendez (2004) pays attention to the same problems, saying that it is difficult to explain why Latin American democracies seem defenseless against growing poverty and even seem to favor the regressive distribution of income (p. 201).

I try to show in this study that because of evolved human diversity, it is not possible to achieve the same quality of democracy in all parts of the world. Terry Lynn Karl (2004) emphasizes as a standard of democracy the crucial significance of the extent to which the poor in alliance with other groups have been able to organize themselves (p. 192). The extent of grassroots organizations certainly measures the quality of democracy, but, unfortunately, we do not have comparable empirical data on the extent and importance of such organizations. Finally, I agree with Michael Coppedge's (2004) argument that comparative study of the quality of democracy presupposes the standardization of the criteria for democracy, as well as with his argument that social and economic conditions should be kept analytically separate in measurements of the quality of democracy.

In the workshop on the quality of democracy in 2003, organized by the Center on Democracy, Development, and the Rule of Law, Stanford University, scholars discussed several dimensions of the quality of democracy. David Beetham (2003) stresses that because we claim a universal value for democracy, it follows that, in the assessment of democratic quality, common standards can be applied equally to established and recent transitional democracies. He pays attention especially to freedom and rights as criteria for the quality for democracy. G. Bingham Powell (2003) argues that responsiveness of policymakers constitutes an important aspect of democratic quality. Dietrich Rueschemeyer (2003) regards political equality to be one of the critical dimensions of the quality of democracy. Democracy creates some equality in the political sphere by giving every adult an equal vote, but the democratic ideal demands much more. Ultimately it is measured by the responsiveness of the government to the preferences of its citizens. Philippe C. Schmitter (2003) refers to accountability as an important dimension of the quality of democracy.

Larry Diamond and Leonardo Morlino's (2004) working paper "The Quality of Democracy" summarizes debates on the content of democratic quality and provides a systematic overview of the crucial dimensions of the quality of democracy. They identify and define eight dimensions in which democracies vary in quality. The first five are procedural dimensions: the rule of law, participation, competition, vertical accountability, and horizontal accountability. They describe the nature of each dimension and refer to the means by which each of them is commonly subverted, and indicate a myriad of ways to subvert the rule of law and other procedural dimensions of democratic quality. In addition to these five procedural dimensions, there are two substantive dimensions: respect for civil and political freedoms, and the implementation of greater political (and underlying it, social and economic) equality. Both are indispensable for a good democracy. Diamond and Morlino's final dimension, responsiveness, links the procedural dimensions to the substantive ones by measuring the extent to which public policies correspond to citizen demands and preferences. However, it is impossible for government to be responsive to all interests because people have many different and often contradictory interests. They emphasize the multidimensional nature of the quality of democracy. It is not possible to identify a single measurement framework of democratic quality, although the eight dimensions of democratic quality interact and reinforce one another. I think that the eight dimensions formulated and described by Diamond and Morlino provide excellent standards against which we could evaluate defects of democratic quality in single countries.

Dirk Berg-Schlosser (2004) refers to several indicators of democracy and good governance and uses them to evaluate the quality of governance in sub-Saharan African countries. He pays attention especially to the corruption perception index and to the World Bank data on government effectiveness, regulatory quality, rule of law, and control of corruption. He emphasizes that "democraticness" and "good governance" should be kept conceptually apart and analyzed separately in each case (see also Berg-Schlosser 2005, pp. 413–414).

Gianfranco Pasquino (2005) notes that scholars have always compared political systems, but the idea of more precisely evaluating the quality of democracy is quite recent. This debate started in the 1990s. His discussion indicates that it has been difficult for scholars to define the content of the quality of democracy and even more difficult to find indicators by which to measure differences in the quality of democracy. Pasquino focuses on three aspects of the quality of democracy: competition, participation, and accountability. In the case of political competition, he pays attention not only to electoral competition but also to the nature of party systems, the impact of electoral systems (majoritarian and proportional), the likelihood of alternation, the systems of government (presidential, semipresidential, and parliamentary), and their decision-making effectiveness and efficacy.

In the case of participation, he emphasizes that the right to participate is not enough; citizens' political participation should be meaningful and productive of consequences. His argument is that the vote remains the single most important, and perhaps the most important, act performed in democratic countries. Participation has many aspects. Pasquino refers to the debate on the desirable amount of political participation, to the identification of the obstacles to participation, to the role of parties and associations, to the impact of electoral systems, and to referendums. In particular, he emphasizes the significance of associational life and says that one should be worried for the quality of democracy whenever the number of associations declines and their internal life becomes atrophied. A problem with the numerous aspects of the quality of democracy discussed by Pasquino is that it would be difficult or impossible to find satisfactory empirical indicators to measure them.

Staffan I. Lindberg (2006) emphasizes the importance of elections in the process of democratization. An uninterrupted sequence of elections improves the quality of democracy. His argument is that "elections seem to have the power to expand and improve democracy writ large" (p. 141). Charles Tilly (2007) formulates a process-oriented definition of democracy, according to which "a regime is democratic to the degree that political relations between the state and citizens feature broad, equal, protected and mutually binding consultation," and "net movement of a regime toward higher ends of the four dimensions qualifies as democratization" (pp. 13–15, 189). Again, a problem is how to measure these dimensions of democratization and the quality of democracy.

Tilly illustrates the use of his criteria by describing the processes of democratization and de-democratizations in various countries. To some extent, he supports his descriptions with Freedom House ratings of political rights and civil liberties.

Measures of the quality of democracy

The studies reviewed above indicate that the concept of the quality of democracy is multidimensional and that the number of empirical variables with which we could measure differences in the quality of democracy is quite limited. Most dimensions of democratic quality discussed in these studies are such that it would not be possible to measure them by quantitative indicators. However, of these some dimensions are measurable, at least to some extent.

The two components of my index of democratization (ID), Competition and Participation, measure not only the level of democratization but also differences in the quality of democracy. It is reasonable to argue that a low level of electoral competition indicates a low quality of democracy because many groups representing different ideas and sections of the population are excluded from the democratic process. Similarly, it is reasonable to argue that a low level of electoral participation indicates a defect in the quality of democracy because a significant part of the population, maybe a majority, is excluded from the democratic decision-making process, which takes place through elections. However, this argument is valid only in countries in which all interested political groups have the right and opportunity to compete in elections. Thus my argument is that competition and participation measure not only the level of democratization, but also, to some extent, differences in the quality of democracy. The same concerns the combined index of democratization (ID). Besides, the gender-weighted index of democratization (GID) defined in Chapter 2 can be used to measure the quality of democracy from a slightly different perspective.

In addition to competition, participation, ID, and GID, I will use the Freedom House ratings of political rights and civil liberties to measure the quality of democracy. Political rights and civil liberties represent crucial aspects of the quality of democracy. In a good democracy, political rights and civil liberties should be extensive and guaranteed. People need political rights and civil liberties to participate in local and national politics. In practice, the existence of such freedoms and rights varies greatly. Freedom House's *Freedom in the World* reports provide ample material on the extent and limitations of political rights and civil liberties among all countries of the world. Freedom House's annual reviews of freedom are based on information from a wide range of sources, including many human rights activists, journalists, and political figures who keep the Freedom House analysts informed of the human rights situations in their respective countries. The survey team consults a vast array of published materials, and they make fact-finding missions to gain more in-depth knowledge of the vast political transformations in the world. In these investigations, they make "every effort to meet a cross-section of political parties and associations, human rights monitors, religious figures, representatives of both the private sector and trade union movements, academics, and journalists" (*Freedom in the World 2003*, p. 1).

Freedom in the World annual reviews describe and analyze the state of political rights and civil liberties separately in each country. Their reviews illustrate the great variation in the extent of freedoms and provide detailed information on the measures by which these freedoms are limited. For example, in the case of Indonesia, the 2003 review notes that Indonesians "can choose their legislators in free and reasonably fair elections and will be able to elect their president directly for the first time in 2004." After this general statement, which indicates the existence of democratic institutions in Indonesia, the review refers to many defects and limitations of freedoms. They note, for example, that "the rule of law continues to be weak throughout the archipelago," and that in Aceh "the army continued to be implicated in extrajudicial killings, disappearances, tortures, rapes, illegal detentions, and other abuses against the suspected guerrillas or sympathizers of the pro-independence Free Aceh Movement." They continue that security forces enjoy near impunity even in nonconflict areas, and that the "military and police also often torture criminal suspects, independence supporters in Aceh, and ordinary Indonesians involved in land or labor disputes."

They refer to the lack of judicial independence and note that "low judicial salaries lead to widespread corruption, and due process safeguards often are inadequate to ensure fair trials...." Further, sporadic violence along ethnic or sectarian lines continued in many parts of the country, in which conflicts thousands of people were killed. However, despite "the problems of military impunity and violent conflicts in some areas, Indonesia has evolved from a tightly controlled to a politically open society." It is significant that the private press "reports aggressively on government policies, corruption, political protests, civil conflicts, and other formerly taboo topics" (*Freedom in the World 2003*, pp. 260–265; cf. *Freedom in the World 2000–2001*, pp. 258–261; *Freedom in the World 2005*, pp. 292–299). The information given in the reviews shows that freedom is still limited in many ways in Indonesia and that these defects and limitations reduce the quality of democracy.

The Freedom House annual reviews include similar descriptions and evaluations of the state of political rights and civil liberties from all countries of the world. Thus they provide rich source material to compare the extent of freedoms in the world and the differences in the quality of democracy. They help this comparison by providing numerical ratings between 1 and 7 for each country, with 1 representing the most free and 7 the least free (for ratings, see *Freedom in the World 2003*, pp. 700–701).

The corruption perception index (CPI) combined by the Transparency International organization measures the quality of democracy from one particular perspective. According to their definition, "Corruption is the abuse of entrusted power for private gain. It hurts everyone whose life, livelihood or happiness depends on the integrity of people in a position of authority." The CPI score relates to perceptions of the degree of corruption as seen by business people and country analysts and ranges between 10 (highly clean) and 0 (highly corrupt). The Transparency International corruption perceptions index has been published annually since 1995 (see http://www.transparency.org/). It is reasonable to argue that corruption does not belong to a good democratic system and that, consequently the quality of democracy is better in a country in which the level of corruption is low than in a country in which it is high.

Thus we have seven empirical variables which can be assumed to measure the quality of democracy from various perspectives: (1) competition (C) 2006, (2) participation (P) 2006, (3) index of democratization (ID) 2006, (4) gender-weighted index of democratization (GID) 2006, (5) political rights (PR) 2005, (6) civil liberties (CL) 2005, and (7) corruption perception index (CPI) 2007.

Empirical data on Vanhanen's four measures of democracy for 2006 are derived from FSD1289, *Measures of Democracy 1810–2006*, (http://www.fsd.uta.fi) and FSD2140 *Gender-Weighted Index of Democratization*

1995–2006 (http://www.fsd.uta.fi). Data on Freedom House ratings of political rights and civil liberties for 2005 are from Freedom House's *Freedom in the World 2006*. Data on CPI Score 2007 are from Transparency International *Corruption Perception Index 2007* (http://www.transparency.org). CPI data are lacking for four countries in this study (the Bahamas, Brunei, Fiji, and North Korea). I estimated CPI scores for each of these four countries on the basis of a neighboring country: the Bahamas 3.0 (Dominican Republic), Brunei 5.1 (Malaysia), Fiji 2.8 (the Solomon Islands), and North Korea 5.1 (South Korea).

These variables are not able to take all important aspects of the quality of democracy into account, but certainly they indicate something about the differences in the quality of democracy. Competition and participation measure two crucial dimensions of democracy. I assume that their combined index (ID) measures not only the level of democratization but also differences in the quality of democracy. It is also reasonable to argue that the quality of democracy is better in countries in which women are adequately represented in political decision-making institutions than in countries in which their representation is meagre or they are completely excluded. Further, political rights and civil liberties represent important aspects of the quality of democracy. Since the numerical values of the Freedom House ratings of political rights and civil liberties rise when the level of democracy decreases, they should be positively correlated with MT and negatively with national IQ and IPR.

Statistical analysis

Let us first see how strongly the above-defined seven measures of the quality of democracy are intercorrelated with each other and correlated with MT, national IQ, and IPR, which are the three principal explanatory variables. The intercorrelations of the seven measures of the quality of democracy in the group of 172 countries are given in Table 8.1 and their correlations with the three explanatory variables in Table 8.2.

We can see from Table 8.1 that the seven measures of the quality of democracy are moderately or strongly intercorrelated. Competition and participation are only moderately correlated (0.570), whereas the Freedom House political rights and civil liberties variables are extremely strongly correlated (0.949). The corruption perception index (CPI) is moderately correlated with the six other variables. Correlations between my four measures of democracy and Freedom House's two measures vary from -0.575 to -0.798. Because most correlations are only moderate, this means that the seven variables measure the quality of democracy to some extent from different perspectives.

Table 8.2 shows that all measures of the quality of democracy are positively or negatively correlated, as hypothesized, with the three explanatory variables. In the cases of MT and national IQ, correlations are only moderate, whereas correlations with IPR are much stronger. The quality of democracy measured by these variables is dependent on IPR and further on national IQ and MT to a significant extent. National IQ can be regarded as the ultimate constraining factor because the impact of MT on IPR takes place mostly through national IQ.

Seven national IQ levels

My purpose in this chapter is to deepen the analysis by comparing the means of explanatory and dependent variables between different levels of national IQ on the basis of the hypothesis according to which the means of the variables are expected to rise or decrease systematically from the national IQ level 1 to the national IQ level 7. We can start by comparing the means of MT and of the components of resource distribution with the seven national IQ categories defined in a previous section. The means should be systematically lower at low levels of IQ than at high levels of IQ, except in the case of MT, which is negatively correlated with national IQ (Table 8.3).

Table 8.3 shows that the annual mean temperature declines systematically from IQ level 1 to IQ levels 6 and 7, but the decline is relatively slight until IQ level 4 (IQ 85–89). MT drops sharply when IQ rises above 90. Most nations with national IQs above 90 live in temperate and cold climatic conditions. The correlation between the means of MT and national IQ is -0.912 in this group of seven IQ categories. MT is the independent variable in the relationship between MT and national IQ. The pattern of means indicates that the values of national IQs are indeed dependent on MT to a significant extent.

The means of all measures of resource distribution rise almost regularly from one IQ level to the next until IQ level 6. The means of IQ level 7 are in most points slightly lower than the means of IQ level 6. This discrepancy is principally due to the impact of China and North

Table 8.1. Intercorrelations of the seven measures of the quality of democracy in the group of 172 countries

Measures of the quality of democracy	C-06	P-06	ID-06	GID-06	PR-05	CL-05	CPI-07
Competition 2006	1.000	0.570	0.854	0.829	-0.755	-0.725	0.413
Participation 2006		1.000	0.788	0.780	-0.575	-0.594	0.421
ID-2006			1.000	0.989	-0.794	-0.798	0.617
GID-2006				1.000	-0.781	-0.787	0.656
Political rights 2005					1.000	0.949	-0.602
Civil liberties 2005						1.000	-0.636
CPI-2007							1.000

Table 8.2. Correlations between seven measures of the quality of democracy and MT, national IQ, and IPR in 172 countries

Measures of the quality of Democracy	Mean temperature (MT)	National IQ	IPR
Competition 2006	-0.366	0.337	0.606
Participation 2008	-0.426	0.480	0.632
ID-2006	-0.523	0.576	0.813
GID-2006	-0.538	0.608	0.819
Political rights 2005	0.331	-0.428	-0.678
Civil liberties 2005	0.375	-0.458	-0.712
CPI 2007	-0.497	0.608	0.738

Table 8.3. Arithmetic means of MT and of various components of IPR and Mean in the seven categories of national IQ

Variable	Category of national IQ						
	1	2	3	4	5	6	7
	(59–69)	(70–79)	(80–84)	(85–89)	(90–94)	(95–99)	(100–108)
N	30	20	33	26	22	26	15
MT	24.7	23.2	22.7	21.5	14.4	9.7	9.8
Tertiary enrollment	2.5	6.4	21.0	20.3	35.9	59.2	51.3
Adult literacy rate	53.9	67.9	75.7	88.7	95.0	98.1	97.7
IR	28.2	37.1	48.3	54.5	65.5	78.7	74.5
Family farms	43.1	43.7	45.4	42.2	57.4	52.3	68.1
DD	19.4	31.8	36.9	40.2	55.6	70.7	64.7
ER	37.2	39.4	41.9	41.6	56.9	69.0	66.3
IPR	10.2	14.4	19.8	22.6	38.0	54.4	51.1
Mean	30.2	37.4	44.7	47.9	61.0	70.0	70.4

Korea on the means of variables in the group of 15 countries at IQ level 7. Without China and North Korea, nearly all means would be clearly higher than at IQ level 6. This observation highlights the exceptional position of China and North Korea. The data presented in Table 8.3 shows that various dimensions of resource distribution are related to the level of national IQ as hypothesized.

The causal relationship between the level of national IQ and various measures of resource distribution is strong, although the use of group means exaggerates the strength of these relationships. It should be noted that many countries deviate greatly from the group means at all levels of national IQ, which weakens the correlations based on single countries. Anyway, because the level of democratization depends to a significant extent on the degree of resource distribution, it is justified to conclude that national IQ constrains the level of democratization and the quality of democracy through its impact on the measures of resource distribution, especially on IPR. Table 8.3 shows that the group means of IPR rise regularly from IQ level 1 (10.2) to IQ level 6 (54.4). Figure 8.1 illustrates the strength of this relationship (correlation 0.935). IQ levels 3 and 4 are clearly below and IQ level 6 is clearly above the regression line, which indicates a slightly curvilinear relationship between national IQ and IPR.

Let us next test the hypothesis for the impact of national IQ on the quality of democracy by comparing the means of seven indicators of the quality of democracy between the seven IQ categories. According to the hypothesis, the means of each indicator are expected to rise systematically from one IQ category to the next one. The means of the seven indicators of the quality of democracy are presented in Table 8.4. In addition to means, standard deviations of all indicators are also given in Table 8.4. They indicate that the actual values of indicators vary greatly around the mean at each IQ level.

Table 8.4 shows that at most points the means of the seven indicators of the quality of democracy rise with the category of national IQ as hypothesized. The correlations between the means of national IQs and of the seven indicators vary from 0.768 (C-2006) to 0.914 (ID-2006) in this group of seven IQ categories. The relationships between the means are strong but not complete. There is room for discrepancies, the most

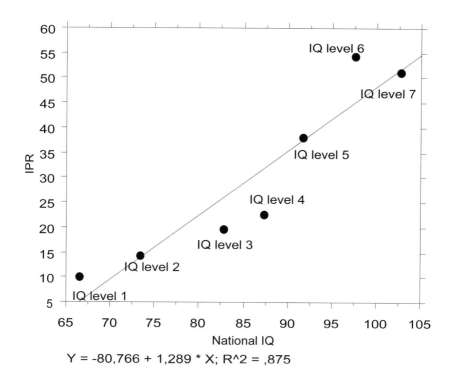

Figure 8.1. The results of regression analysis of IPR for national IQ in the group of seven national IQ levels

serious of which concerns IQ category 7. Contrary to the hypothesis, almost all means of indicators at IQ level 7 are somewhat smaller than at IQ level 6, but still higher than at IQ level 5. As noted earlier, this discrepancy is principally due to the impact of China and North Korea, for which the values of indicators are much lower than for the other countries at IQ level 7. Without China and North Korea, the means of all indicators would be as high as or a little higher than for IQ level 6. Another significant discrepancy concerns the corruption perception index (CPI). Table 8.4 shows that the mean of CPI-2007 remains approximately at the same level through national IQ levels from 1 to 4, but rises sharply at national IQ level 5. This observation implies that a relatively high level of national IQ is needed to hamper corruption. It should be noted that the lower the level of corruption, the higher the value of CPI.

As standard deviations of indicators given in Table 8.4 show, the variation around the mean is significant in all measures of the quality of democracy and at all levels of national IQ. Some countries seem to have established, at least temporarily, a democratic system at even the lowest national IQ levels, and on the other hand, there are nondemocracies at even the highest IQ level (China and North Korea). Therefore, it is evident that national IQ does not determine the level of democracy in all cases. The level and quality of democracy also depends on various local factors which are under more or less conscious human control.

Table 8.4. Arithmetic means and standard deviations of the seven indicators of the quality of democracy in the seven categories of national IQ

Variable	Category of national IQ						
	1 (59–69)	2 (70–79)	3 (80–84)	4 (85–89)	5 (90–94)	6 (95–99)	7 (100–108)
N	30	20	33	26	22	26	15
Competition 2006							
Mean	32.3	34.2	33.8	34.2	42.6	58.1	51.8
Standard deviation	18.3	17.1	22.6	22.4	24.8	12.0	23.1
Participation 2006							
Mean	21.7	28.6	26.8	35.9	40.5	52.8	44.4
Standard deviation	12.9	13.2	15.3	18.3	17.0	10.6	20.8
ID 2006							
Mean	7.5	10.5	11.2	14.2	19.3	30.3	27.1
Standard deviation	5.1	6.1	9.0	10.4	12.7	7.9	14.0
GID 2006							
Mean	8.6	12.0	12.6	16.8	22.3	37.3	33.6
Standard deviation	5.9	6.5	10.0	12.2	15.2	11.9	18.5
Freedom House political rights 2005							
Mean	4.9	3.7	4.2	3.9	3.2	1.6	2.1
Standard deviation	1.2	2.0	1.9	2.0	1.9	1.6	2.2
Freedom House civil liberties 2005							
Mean	4.6	3.5	4.0	3.7	2.9	1.5	2.1
Standard deviation	1.2	1.5	1.6	1.9	1.4	1.3	2.0
Corruption Perception Index (CPI) 2007							
Mean	2.4	3.3	3.3	2.9	3.9	6.3	7.0
Standard deviation	0.5	1.2	1.2	1.0	1.5	2.2	2.2

Consequently, it would be useful to examine structures, institutions, and policies which could further democratization and improve the quality of democracy as well as structures, institutions, and policies which obstruct or prevent democratization. I want to emphasize that there is always room for human choices and also for accidental factors.

However, Table 8.4 makes it clear that the relationship between the level of national IQ and the means of all indicators of the quality of democracy is strong. Because the evolved differences in the average intelligence of nations certainly preceded the contemporary differences in political systems, it is justified to argue that national IQ is the independent variable in this relationship and that the relationships between the national IQ categories and the means of indicators of the quality of democracy are causal. The quality of democracy tends to rise with the level of national IQ. Single countries may deviate from this pattern significantly, but the relationship between the means remains strong, which implies that the level of national IQ constrains the chances of a country to achieve a higher level of the quality of democracy than is common for countries at the same level of national IQ. Since the level of national IQ is nearly constant, or changes only slowly, it constitutes a persistent and permanent limiting factor. Consequently, I have to conclude that we cannot expect the equalization of the level of democratization and of the quality of democracy in the world, although significant changes in single cases are always possible. Figure 8.2 illustrates the strong causal relationship between the level of national IQ and the mean of the Index of Democratization (ID-2006).

The pattern of relationship between variables in Figure 8.2 is quite similar to the pattern in Figure 8.1, which is natural considering the fact that IPR and ID-2006 are highly intercorrelated (0.992) in this group of seven national IQ categories. IQ levels 3, 4, and 6 deviate most clearly from the regression line, whereas the means of ID-2006 are close to the regression line at IQ levels 1, 2, 5, and 7. The nearly regular pattern of relationship between variables in Figure 8.2 illustrates the constraining power of national IQ. On the basis of this figure, it is highly improbable that the average level of democratization and the quality of democracy in the countries at IQ level 1 could ever rise to the average level of the countries at IQ levels 5–7. Because of this strong relationship, it is reasonable to expect that significant average differences in the level and quality of democracy between the groups of countries at different

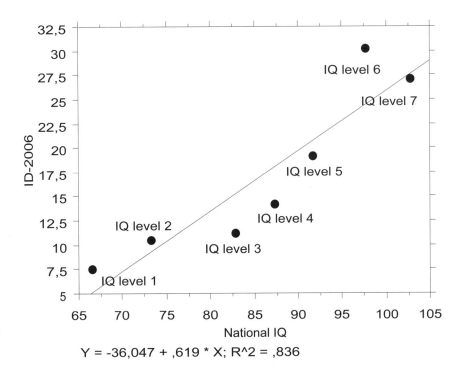

Y = -36,047 + ,619 * X; R^2 = ,836

Figure 8.2. The results of regression analysis of ID-2006 on national IQ in the group of seven national IQ levels

national IQ levels will persist.

Figure 8.2 illustrates the relationship between the means of national IQ and the means of ID-2006 in the group of seven national IQ categories, but the same pattern is repeated, with some variations, in the cases of the six other measures of the quality of democracy used in this analysis. The means of the seven indicators are moderately or strongly intercorrelated. Their intercorrelations vary from 0.518 (participation 2006 and competition 2006) to 0.999 (ID-2006 and GID-2006). The pattern seems to remain approximately the same no matter what indicator is used to measure differences in the quality of democracy. The level of national IQ (and through it MT) matters and maintains differences in the quality of democracy.

Deficiencies in key institutions of democracy

Another strategy to explore the constraining impact of MT and national IQ on the quality of democracy is to focus on some measurable deficits in key institutions of democracy. It can be assumed that differences in the quality of democracy are reflected in the nature and function of institutions needed in democratic politics. UNDP's *Human Development Report 2002: Deepening Democracy in a Fragmented World* reviews the nature and extent of such deficiencies and provides empirical data and observations on them. The review starts by listing the key institutions of democratic governance (p. 4):

- A system of representation, with well-functioning parties and interest associations.

- An electoral system that guarantees free and fair elections as well as universal suffrage.

- A system of checks and balances based on the separation of powers, with independent judicial and legislative branches.

- A vibrant civil society, able to monitor government and private business—and provide alternative forms of political participation.

- A free, independent media.

- Effective civilian control over the military and other security forces.

I think that the UNDP's list covers the most important institutions needed for good democratic governance and provides standards to evaluate the sufficiency of democratic institutions in particular countries as well as their deficiencies. The fact is that there are more or less serious deficiencies in these key institutions of democracy in most countries of the world, but the extent of shortages varies greatly, and it would be interesting to find out to what extent those shortages are related to the ultimate constraints of democracy: MT and national IQ.

In many countries, there are various defects in the system of representation. Political parties are unstable and without effective local organizations. Interest associations are often weak, or the government does not allow citizens to establish independent interest associations.

Elections are less than free and fair in many countries, and there may be significant restrictions to universal suffrage or to the possibilities to vote. A constitutional system of checks and balances may not function in practice; executive and legislative powers may be concentrated in the hands of the chief executive; and the judicial branch is often less than independent. Civil society is suppressed and unable to monitor government and private business, and alternative forms of political participation are quite limited. Media are less than free and independent in many countries. The military and other security forces are often not under effective civilian control. Innumerable studies describe these and other deficits in key institutions of democracy in particular countries, regions, and historical periods. The existence of differences between countries in the extent of democratic deficiencies is a fact, but it is another matter to measure such differences.

UNDP's *Human Development Report 2002* includes many references to such deficiencies. The report states that, of the 81 new democracies, only 47 are fully democratic; 61 countries still do not have a free press; 106 countries still restrict important civil and political freedoms; and worldwide, only 14 percent of parliamentarians are women (p. 10). These figures refer to some deficits in key institutions of democracy. The report continues that there is "the disturbing spread of ´illiberal´ democracies, as in Kyrgyzstan and Zimbabwe, where elected governments act the same as their authoritarian predecessors, depriving citizens of human rights and ignoring constitutional limits on power" (p. 63). In many countries, arrangements for public accountability of democratic institutions do not exist. Corruption, abuses of power, and intimidation by criminal elements weaken democratic accountability. In Bangladesh, for example, the nation's banking industry is so corrupted that people getting credit from the formal banking sector have to pay a direct bribe equal to 2–20% of the loan value (pp. 65–66). Electoral processes have been subverted by fraud, for example, in recent elections in Cameroon, Haiti, Chad, Zimbabwe, and Madagascar (pp. 66–67). In many countries, political parties

> are not yet able to fulfill their traditional functions of political education, mobilization and representation of diverse interests. In many African countries opposition parties disappear between elections, while ruling parties behave like they used to under single party systems (p. 69).

These are only some scattered examples of the many types of democratic deficits.

It is difficult to measure the variation in democratic deficits, but *Human Development Report 2002* (pp. 36–45) provides statistical data on several subjective indicators of governance, which can be regarded as measuring different aspects of democratic deficits. I use six of those indicators to test the hypothesis about the ultimate constraints upon democracy: Polity score 2000 (-10 to 10), press freedom 2000 (100 to 0), voice and accountability 2000–01 (-2.5 to 2.5), law and order 2001 (0 to 6), rule of law 2000–01 (-2.5 to 2.50), and seats in parliament held by women (as percent of total). These indicators are constructed in such a way that the Press freedom indicator should be positively correlated with MT and negatively correlated with national IQ and IPR. Polity score, voice and accountability, law and order, rule of law, and seats in parliament held by women indicators should be negatively correlated with MT and positively correlated with national IQ and IPR.

- **Polity score** reflects the presence of institutional factors necessary for democracy. Data on this variable are from the University of Maryland's Polity IV project.

- **Press freedom** is a Freedom House indicator, with a score between 0 and 30 having a free press, those with a score between 31 and 60 having a press that is partly free, and those with a score between 61 and 100 having a press that is not free.

- **Voice and accountability** is a World Bank indicator that combines several indicators of the political process (including selection of governments) with indicators of civil liberties, political rights and press freedom and independence. Estimates are subject to a large margin of error.

- **Law and order** measures a range from 0 to 6 (higher is better).

- **Rule of law** is a World Bank indicator. A score varies from -2.50 to 2.50 (higher is better).

- **Seats in parliament held by women** is an indicator of women's representation in political decision-making institutions. Where there are lower and upper houses, data refer to the weighted average of women's share of seats in both houses. These data are as of 18 March 2002.

All data on these variables are from *Human Development Report 2002* (UNDP 2002, pp. 36–45). They do not cover all 172 of the countries in this study. I think these indicators measure deficiencies in the quality of democracy from some perspectives. Correlations between these variables and MT, national IQ, and IPR are presented in Table 8.5.

In Table 8.5, all correlations are positive or negative as hypothesized, but nearly all are only moderate. In most cases, these variables are most strongly correlated with IPR. The weakest correlations in all cases are with MT. The press freedom indicator is moderately correlated with national IQ and MT and more strongly with IPR, which indicates that the causal roots of variation in press freedom can be traced to national IQ and MT via IPR, at least to some extent. The pattern is similar in most other cases.

The empirical evidence presented in Table 8.5 supports the central argument of this study. Democratic deficiencies tend to be more common and serious, the higher the annual mean temperature and the lower the value of national IQ and IPR. The relationships are not especially strong, but they are systematic and they seem to be strong enough to maintain significant qualitative differences in these key institutions of democracy.

I continue this analysis by comparing the means of the six variables in the seven national IQ categories. The means should increase or decrease systematically from national IQ level 1 to IQ level 7 (Table 8.6).

Table 8.6 is in many respects similar to Table 8.4. The means of variables rise or decrease (press freedom) from IQ level 1 to IQ level 7, but the rising (or decreasing) patterns are not fully regular. However, the means for IQ level 1 are in all cases much lower (or higher) than for IQ level 7, which indicates strong relationships between national IQ and the means of these six variables.

In the seven categories of national IQ, correlations between the mean of national IQ and the means of these six variables are much higher than the correlations based on single countries in Table 8.5. Correlations vary from 0.763 (women's representation) to 0.910 (Voice and accountability). The deficits in democratic governance are strongly dependent on the level of national IQ. These differences will most probably continue in the future because it is not reasonable to expect any drastic changes in national IQs. However, this conclusion concerns group averages. Large standard deviations indicate that

Table 8.5. Correlations between six indicators of governance measuring democratic deficits and MT, national IQ, and IPR in samples of 133–162 countries

Measures of democratic deficits	N	Mean temperature (MT)	National IQ	IPR
Polity score 2000	147	-0.360	0.426	0.631
Press freedom 2000	162	0.360	-0.459	-0.674
Voice and accountability 2000-01	162	-0.451	0.577	0.764
Law and order 2001	133	-0.505	0.555	0.535
Rule of law 2000-01	157	-0.418	0.605	0.686
Women (as % of total)	151	-0.380	0.341	0.448

single countries can deviate significantly from the group averages. This variation offers opportunities for human choices.

Conclusion

My purpose in this chapter was to deepen the analysis of the limits of democratization by showing that the quality of democracy rises systematically from the lowest to the highest level of national IQ. For this purpose, the 172 countries of this study were divided into seven national IQ categories and 13 indicators were selected to measure the quality of democracy and deficiencies in democratic governance from different perspectives. The arithmetic means of each of the 13 indicators were calculated for countries in each of the seven national IQ categories. According to the hypothesis, the means of variables were expected to rise (or decrease) systematically from national IQ category 1 to national IQ category 7.

The results of empirical analysis support the hypothesis. The means of each of the 13 indicators rise (or decrease) from IQ level 1 to IQ level 7, although there are some irregularities in the patterns of the means. Correlations between the means of national IQs and the means of 13 indicators in this comparison group of seven national IQ categories are much stronger than correlations based on single countries. These strong and systematic relationships support the hypothesis about the limits of democratization: The quality of democracy rises regularly with the level of national IQ, no matter what indicator is used to

Table 8.6. The arithmetic means of six variables indicating deficiencies in democratic governance in the seven categories of national IQ

Variable	Category of national IQ						
	1	2	3	4	5	6	7
	(59–69)	(70–79)	(80–84)	(85–89)	(90–94)	(95–99)	(100–108)
Polity score 2000, N = 147							
N	25	19	26	19	20	25	13
Mean	-0.1	1.4	0.2	1.7	5.4	8.6	7.6
Press freedom 2000, N = 162							
N	28	20	32	22	21	26	13
Mean	63.0	50.0	53.1	51.5	46.7	25.1	25.7
Voice and accountability 2000-01, N = 162							
N	28	20	32	22	21	26	13
Mean	-0.73	-0.17	-0.24	-0.14	0.13	1.04	1.04
Law and order 2001, N = 133							
N	20	14	27	16	17	26	13
Mean	2.7	3.3	3.5	3.1	4.2	4.8	5.4
Rule of law 2000-01, N = 157							
N	27	19	29	22	21	26	13
Mean	-0.75	-0.29	0.02	-0.33	0.14	0.85	1.33
Seats in parliament held by women 2002, N = 151							
N	27	18	27	20	20	26	13
Mean	9.4	13.0	8.0	14.0	12.0	19.5	19.6

measure the quality of democracy or deficits in democratic governance. The equalization of the quality of democracy in the world would presuppose the disappearance of this strong relationship. It does not seem possible for the reason that evolved differences in national IQs are nearly constant. An extensive biological mixing of racial groups would be needed to level out differences in national IQs. This process is already taking place, but it is an extremely slow process and may never reach all the geographical regions of the world. Besides, all people are not equally adapted to flourish and survive in all climatic and geographical circumstances.

PART II

Country Reviews and Conclusions

CHAPTER 9

Descriptive Country Reviews

T he results of statistical analyses carried out in previous chapters support the three hypotheses on both the causal roots and the limits of democratization. My central argument is that the level of democratization and the quality of democracy do not vary at random, that there are measurable regularities in this variation, and that the degree of resource distribution (IPR) explains a major part of this variation. In fact, IPR explains approximately 70 percent of the variation in the level of democratization (ID and GID). A problem was to explain the variation in IPR. Why does the degree of resource distribution vary so much in the world? I have tackled this question by assuming that differences in the mental abilities of populations (national IQ) are causally related to the variation in the degree of resource distribution and that differences in national IQs evolved when human populations adapted to greatly varying climatic and other environmental conditions. The results of this study show that these hypothesized ultimate causal factors are significantly correlated with IPR, and through it with ID. Because these two ultimate causal factors are outside conscious human control, I argue that they constitute ultimate limits to democratization, and that consequently they explain the persistence of significant differences in the measured level of democratization as well as in the quality of democracy.

My point is that the impact of these ultimate constraints is not limited to the measured level of democratization; their impact extends to the quality of democracy too. I selected seven indicators to measure differences in the quality of democracy from various perspectives, and six other indicators that show deficiencies in governance from the perspective of democracy. The results of statistical analyses presented and discussed in Chapter 8 demonstrate that the impact of ultimate constraints extends to different aspects of the quality of democracy, which tends to rise with the level of national IQ no matter what indicator is used to measure the quality of democracy or democratic deficits. The same pattern is repeated from one indicator to another. These observations led to the conclusion that the variation in the quality of democracy is principally a consequence of the impact of IPR and national IQ (and MT), but I want to emphasize that these constraints explain only a part of the variation. The quality of democracy and democratic deficits seem to vary significantly at all levels of national IQ. All countries have not been democracies even at the highest level of national IQ, and all countries are not nondemocracies even at the lowest level. The variation in the average quality of democracy can be causally traced to the level of national IQ, whereas the variation around the average at each level of national IQ must be due to other factors.

Statistical analyses clarified the existence and strength of hypothesized relationships, but what does it mean in political practice to have differences in the quality of democracy or in democratic governance (for the concept of "governance," see Greig et al. 2007, p. 237)? A considerable part of the political research literature describes and analyzes political practice, the adaptation of political behavior and institutions to varying environmental conditions and constraints. Political behavior and institutions are continually tested and modified by some kind of natural selection in politics. They become adapted to prevailing environmental conditions that constrain the scope of possible alternatives. This unconscious process of natural selection in politics produces a temporary and continually changing balance of competing strivings, which is reflected in the nature of political behavior and institutions and in the quality of democracy.

It was noted in Chapter 8 that the average level and quality of democracy vary systematically with the level of national IQ. In this chapter, my intention is to complement the results of statistical analyses by illustrating differences in the quality of democracy and in democratic deficits by descriptive country reviews. Each retrospective review of the level and quality of democracy in a country extends to the year 1950 or to a later year of independence. References will be made to the level of democratization (ID), the extent of political rights and civil liberties, the extent of press freedom, and the significance of corruption, and sometimes also to the rule of law (the judiciary), political violence, insurgencies, and the position of ethnic minorities. Brief descriptive reviews are sometimes complemented by examples which illustrate politics in practice, especially democratic deficits. The 172 countries are divided into the same seven categories by the level of national IQ as in Chapter 8. The purpose of brief country reviews is to illustrate significant differences in the quality of democratic governance between the seven national IQ categories and the variation in the quality of democracy at each level of national IQ. Note that the time period for these descriptive reviews is much longer than in the previous statistical analyses, which cover only recent years.

Special attention will be paid to countries which deviate clearly from their national IQ category's average level and quality of democracy. The group of large outliers comprises countries for which the actual value of ID-2006 deviates more than one standard deviation from the IQ category's mean (see tables 6.1 and 8.4). For example, the mean of ID-2006 for IQ category 1 (IQ 59–69) is 7.5 and one standard deviation is 5.1 (Table 8.4). Ethiopia's actual value of ID-2006 (Table 6.1) 11.8 is 4.3 index points higher than this IQ level's mean 7.5, which means that Ethiopia is not a large positive outlier, although its level of democratization is clearly higher than expected on the basis of this IQ category's mean value of ID-2006.

Country reviews are based on information derived from various sources, including Vanhanen's FSD1289 *Measures of Democracy 1810–2006*, various research literature, and especially Freedom House's *Freedom in the World* reports, *Keesing's Record of World Events*, Arthur S. Banks et al., *Political Handbook of the World 2007*, *The World Guide: Global Reference, Country by Country (2007)*, and *The Economist* journal. The documentation of sources is usually limited to direct quotations. Reviews start from the national IQ level 1. The present or present perfect tenses in these reviews refer to the situation at the end of 2006.

CHAPTER 10

Countries at National IQ Level 1 (IQ 59–69)

This IQ category includes the following 30 countries, whose estimated national IQs vary from 59 to 69: Angola, Burkina Faso, Burundi, Cameroon, the Central African Republic, Chad, the Democratic Republic of Congo, the Republic of Congo, Côte d'Ivoire, Djibouti, Equatorial Guinea, Eritrea, Ethiopia, Gabon, Gambia, Guinea, Guinea-Bissau, Haiti, Lesotho, Liberia, Malawi, Mali, Mozambique, Niger, Nigeria, Senegal, Sierra Leone, Somalia, Swaziland, and Zimbabwe. All these countries except Haiti are sub-Saharan African countries.

We can see from Table 8.4 that the mean of ID-2006 is only 7.5 for this IQ category; the mean of Freedom House's PR-2005 (political rights) is 4.9, and the mean of CL-2005 (civil liberties) 4.6. All these means are below the minimum criteria for democracy. Some countries deviated clearly from these averages. The level of democracy was more than one standard deviation (5.1) higher in Burundi, the Democratic Republic of Congo, Guinea-Bissau, Liberia, and Malawi, and, on the other hand, more than one standard deviation lower in Angola, Côte d'Ivoire, Eritrea, Somalia, and Swaziland (see Table 6.1). None of these 30 countries has been continually above the minimum threshold of democracy since 1950 or from the year of independence.

In sub-Saharan Africa, there has been fluctuation between autocracy and democracy in almost all countries during the period of independence. Ethnic clashes, civil wars, and military coups have ravaged most countries. Presidents have been unwilling to relinquish power through elections, party systems are fragmentary, and nearly all parties are without stable local organizations. Political activities have usually been limited to cities, principally to the capital city, and the level of effective participation in politics is low. Elections have often been tarnished by violence and irregularities. These and other democratic deficits in sub-Saharan Africa are approximately in balance with the two ultimate constraining factors, MT and national IQ (see Table 7.1). Residuals based on MT and national IQ are small or moderate for nearly all of these countries.

This means that we cannot expect a high level of democratization in any sub-Saharan African country. There is significant variation and fluctuation in the level of democratization within the group, but the average level of democratization has remained low because of the constraining factors (for the history and evolution of political systems in sub-Saharan Africa, see also Coleman and Rosberg 1964; Merle 1968; de Lusignan 1970; Doro and Stultz 1970; Ungar 1989; Clark and Gardinier 1997; Decalo 1990 and 1998; Esterhuysen 1998; Chazan et al. 1999; Randall and Svåsand 2002; van de Walle 2002; Joseph 2003; Lewis 2003; Lindberg 2006; Meredith 2006; Posner and Young 2007). In the following, I try to describe briefly the level and quality of democracy or the lack of democracy in single countries based on IQ category.

In *Angola*, beginning with the transition from Portuguese rule in 1975, rival nationalist factions competed for power, which transformed a colonial war into a bloody civil war. It claimed more than one million lives, displaced 4 million people, and sent hundreds of thousands fleeing to neighboring countries. Some 300,000 whites left Angola. Attempts to establish and stabilize democratic institutions after the 2002 ceasefire have not yet succeeded. John McMillan (2005, p.155) says that "Angola presents a horrifying case of squandered possibilities." Corruption and patronage are endemic in the government. Political debate is lively, but "opposition parties blame the MPLA for attacks on their members and offices, especially in the provinces of Huambo and Moxico where UNITA has traditionally claimed strong support" (*Freedom in the World 2005*, p. 33). Briefly stated, the quality of democratic politics is low, although the constitution guarantees freedom of assembly, and hundreds of nongovernmental organizations have emerged.

Burkina Faso has been continually below the threshold of democracy since its independence in 1960. Blaise Compare usurped power in a bloody coup in 1987 and installed himself as president. Since then he was elected to office in 1991, 1998, and 2005 without any effective opposition. Parliamentary elections were more competitive, especially the 2002 election, in which opposition parties won nearly half of the National Assembly seats. A very low level of electoral participation is characteristic of politics in Burkina Faso. A large majority of the population is practically excluded from national politics; and while there are many political parties, they are mainly small urban groups without any grass roots organizations. Freedom of speech and freedom of assembly are generally respected, but police forces routinely ignore prescribed limits on detention and seizure, and security forces "commit abuses with impunity, including torture and occasional extrajudicial killing" (*Freedom in the World 2005*, p. 110).

Burundi has suffered from serious ethnic violence and the lack of democracy since its independence in 1962, but in 2004 the Hutu and Tutsi groups finally made a compromise and agreed on new democratic institutions. Burundi crossed the threshold of democracy in the 2005 legislative elections. However, it should be noted that under the new 2005 constitution, 40 percent of the seats in the National Assembly are reserved for Tutsis, who make up only 14 percent of the population. Despite democratization, people are subjected to arbitrary violence, whether from the government or from guerrilla groups. Some rebel groups continue armed opposition to the government, and democratic institutions are fragile. Dave Peterson (2006, p. 128) concludes on the basis of democratic reconstruction in Burundi that "even the most violent and sorely divided societies can be restored, given sufficient political will and generous resources to support the process of negotiation and change" (cf. *The Economist*, September 16, 2006, pp. 51–52). The Hutu and Tutsi ethnic leaders were finally able to make a democratic compromise and to share power through a system of proportional representation (Banks et al. 2007, p. 183). It was a remarkable achievement.

Cameroon (independent 1960) has been ruled by the Cameroon People's Democratic Movement, which has won all presidential and legislative elections, and in 2006 the country was still slightly below the minimum threshold of democracy. President Biya had agreed to allow the formation of opposition parties in 1990, "but otherwise tried to crush opposition activity by repression, using the security forces and other means to intimidate activists" (Meredith 2006, p. 399). Presidential elections "have been devalued by rampant intimidation, manipulation, and fraud, and legislative elections have also been fraudulent" (*Freedom in the World* 2005, p. 126). A low level of electoral participation, extensive corruption, and repression of the media are other democratic deficits. However, the country was temporarily above the minimum threshold of democracy in 1992–96.

Central African Republic became a nondemocracy after its independence in 1960 to 1992. It crossed the threshold of democracy in the 1993 competitive legislative and presidential elections, but dropped again below the threshold by a military coup in 2003. General Francois Bozize deposed President Patasse after six months of fighting between government troops and soldiers loyal to Bozize. He legalized his power through legislative and presidential elections in 2005, and the country recrossed the threshold of democracy, but executive power remained in the hands of General Bozize, who was confirmed as president by 64 percent of the vote. Elections have been characterized by irregularities and fraud. Political violence continued in the northern areas of the Central African Republic where "rebels, bandits, and soldiers were fighting" (*Keesing's* 2006, p. 47024).

Chad was a nondemocracy from its independence in 1960 to the 2001 presidential election, in which President Deby's support dropped below 70 percent. The country used to be in a state of almost constant ethnic civil war, and power was usually acquired by violent means. Colonel Idriss Deby gained power by a military coup in 1990 and made himself president. He was elected president in 1996, 2001, and 2006, but elections were marred by irregularities and fraud. Coup plots and rebel insurgencies continued. Political and ethnic violence has been due to the population's deep racial and other ethnic cleavages. The fact that Chad has never experienced free and fair transfer of power through elections illustrates the low quality of democratic governance. "Civilian authorities do not maintain effective control of the security forces, which routinely ignore constitutional protections regarding search, seizure, and detention" (*Freedom in the World* 2006, p. 184).

Congo, Democratic Republic of, remained below the threshold of democracy from its independence in 1960 until the 2006 legislative and presidential elections. During Mobutu's long dictatorship, corruption permeated every level of society. For example, it was estimated "that two-thirds of the country's 400,000 civil servants who were paid regularly every month were in fact fictitious; their wages were merely pocketed by senior officials" (Meredith 2006, p. 301). After the collapse of Mobutu's regime in 1997, regional armed groups struggled for power, and the position of the central government was weak. It is estimated that the conflict claimed the lives of more than 3 million people. People had no opportunities to elect their rulers. In the 2006 elections, which were super-vised by UN peacekeepers, the country crossed the minimum threshold of democracy, but elections were marred by violence. Corruption is rampant as in most other sub-Saharan African countries, freedom of expression is limited, and independent journalists are frequently threat-ened, arrested, or attacked by both rebels and government officials. It is questionable whether the democratic institutions established in 2006 can survive the pressure of a violent struggle for power. According to Simon Robinson (2007): "Rebel militias continue to rape and murder, especially in the country's East. Government troops commit atrocities as well" (cf. *The Economist,* February 10, 2007, p. 44). The quality of democracy is very low.

Congo, Republic of (Brazzaville), has also suffered from intermit-tent civil war. It has been difficult to establish and maintain democratic institutions. The fact that the current (2006) President Denis Sassou-Nguesso seized power by a military coup in 1997 illustrates this lack of democracy. Originally General Sassou-Nguesso had seized power by a coup in 1979 and maintained one-party rule as head of the Congolese Workers' Party until a democratic compromise in 1992. The country was temporarily above the threshold of democracy in 1992–1996. General Sassou-Nguesso had lost the 1992 presidential election, but he returned to power in 1997 with the help of his private army. In 2002 he won the presidential election by 89 percent of the vote. His power is based more on the means of violence than on popular support. Meredith (2006, p. 678) notes that "Congo-Brazzaville was convulsed by tribal strife that brought an end to its experiment with multi-party politics and wrecked parts of the capital."

In Côte *d'Ivoire* an attempt at democratization led to ethnic civil war in 2000. The country had been a one-party state since independence in 1960 to 1999, when General Robert Guei seized power by a military coup. He wanted to legalize his position in the 2000 presidential election, but when initial results showed that he was losing to Laurent Gbagbo, he attempted to remain in power by violent means. However, Laurent Gbagbo's supporters were stronger, and he was declared the winner with 59 percent of the vote, compared with 33 percent for Guei. Côte d'Ivoire crossed the Competition threshold of democracy, but remained below the Participation threshold. Political violence accelerated into a civil war, in which Guei was killed in 2002. Meredith (2006) says about the consequences of that civil war that it set Christian southerners against Muslim northerners and "split the country apart" (p. 679; see also *The Economist*, July 21, 2007, p. 40). In the end of 2006, the country was ruled by a transitional government.

Djibouti achieved independence in 1977. It has never been above the threshold of democracy, although multiparty elections have been held since 1992. Power is in the hands of a party representing the Issa (Somali) majority of the population. Because of a very low level of electoral participation, the country has not yet been able to cross the minimum threshold of democracy. Power is highly concentrated in the hands of the government, and most people are practically excluded from national politics. To some extent, the ethnic Afar (minority) insurgency continued despite peace agreements. In the 2003 legislative elections, the Union for a Presidential Majority captured all 65 seats with a reported 62 percent of the vote. President Guelleh was reelected in 2005 as the sole candidate (Banks et al. 2007, pp. 339–345). These electoral facts illustrate a low quality of democracy in Djibouti.

Equatorial Guinea has been continually ruled by dictators (Francisco Macias Nguema and Theodoro Obiang Nguema) since its independence in 1968. Macias Nguema's dictatorship was extremely cruel and arbitrary from 1968 to 1979, when Obiang Nguema deposed and murdered his uncle and usurped power. Some elections have been organized, but political rights and freedoms are strictly limited. For example, the 1992 "press law authorizes government censorship of all publications, and nearly all print and broadcast media are state run and tightly controlled" (*Freedom in the World 2006*, p. 240). The country is autocratically ruled by President Obiang Nguema and his Democratic Party of Equatorial Guinea, which won 98 of the 100 seats in the 2004 legislative elections (Banks et al. 2007, pp. 374–380).

Eritrea has been ruled by President Isaias Afwerki and his party since independence in 1993. No legislative or presidential elections have been organized. The power of the rulers was derived from the victory in the long war of independence. Political rights and freedoms are very limited. For example, independent nongovernmental organizations are not allowed to function. Torture, arbitrary detentions, and political arrests are widespread. However, there has been some pressure for democratization. In 2001, for example, eleven ruling party officials were arrested, "charged with 'treason' for criticizing the Government and demanding democratic reform" (*The World Guide 2007*, p. 217).

Ethiopia started to democratize its political system in 1995 after the long imperial rule of Emperor Haile Selassie and the dictatorship of Colonel Mengistu. Power remained in the hands of the Ethiopian People's Revolutionary Democratic Front, which overthrew Colonel Mengistu's regime in 1991, but political opposition got rights to take part in elections. In the 2005 legislative elections, the support of opposition parties grew so much that Ethiopia crossed the minimum threshold of democracy, but political freedoms are still limited, and the ruling party controls the means of violence. According to a report, the security forces suppressed unarmed protesters in the aftermath of the May 2005 legislative elections. Further, "193 victims had been shot, beaten, and strangled to death in a ´massacre´ by the security forces" (*Keesing's 2006, p.* 47503). This kind of information indicates that the quality of democracy is quite low in Ethiopia (cf. Harbeson 2005).

Gabon (independent 1960) was slightly above or below the threshold of democracy in the period 1990–2006. President Omar Bongo usurped power in 1973, and he and his Gabonese Democratic Party have won all elections. There are opposition parties, but Gabon's citizens have never been able to change their government democratically. Meredith (2006) says about the elections: "Through a mixture of fraud, force and help from the French government, Bongo managed to maintain his grip on power" (p. 398). Some opposition parties have boycotted elections, which have been spoiled by irregularities. The judiciary suffers from political interference. Torture has sometimes been used to produce confessions. Arbitrary arrest and long periods of pretrial detention are common. Press freedom is restricted in practice. The same concerns apply to the rights of assembly and association (see *Freedom in the World 2006*, pp. 266–267). Power is in the hands of President Bongo.

The Gambia was a one-party-dominated country from independence in 1965 until the 1994 military coup, which deposed President Dawda Jawara and his People's Progressive Party. The coupmaker Yahua Jammeh was elected president in 1996. Since then, he and his party have won all elections. The country was slightly above the threshold of democracy in 1997–2001, but the quality of democracy remained low, and there were coup plots. After the 2001 presidential poll, "several opposition supporters, human rights workers, and journalists were detained.... Allegations surfaced after the vote that Jammeh's party had brought in members of his ethnic group living in neighboring Senegal and had issued them voter cards" (*Freedom in the World 2005, p. 41*). The citizens of The Gambia have not yet been able to change their government democratically.

Guinea (independent 1958) was a one-party state until a military coup in 1984, and then it was for several years under a military government. The coupmaker General Lansana Conte legalized his position by a presidential election in 1993. Since then he and his party have won all presidential and legislative elections. Guinea rose temporarily above the threshold of democracy in 1995–99, but it again dropped below the threshold when President Conte and his Progress and Unity Party consolidated their hegemony. Opposition parties have boycotted elections, and, in connection with the 2003 presidential election, "members of the opposition accused Conte of taking control of electoral commission and of using state funds to finance his campaign" (*Freedom in the World 2005*, p. 254).

Guinea-Bissau was a one-party state from its independence in 1974 until 1994, when the former coupmaker and president Vieira was elected president in a relatively free election. He was deposed by a military coup in 1998. Since then multiparty elections and military coups and rebellions have alternated. Guinea-Bissau recrossed the threshold of democracy through the highly competitive legislative and presidential elections in 2004–05. Opposition parties have enjoyed relatively extensive political rights and freedoms since 2004, but democratic institutions are still fragile.

Haiti is a Caribbean country, where sub-Saharan Africans constitute nearly 100 percent of its population. Haiti has traditionally been ruled by dictators, and it has been extremely difficult to stabilize democratic institutions in Haiti despite several U.S. military interventions. Paramilitary thugs have terrorized the population, and elections have been marred by irregularities and fraud. Haiti is one of the most corrupt countries in the world. The governments have not been able to maintain the rule of law. For example, according to a report, "an estimated 8,000 people had been murdered and some 35,000 women had been sexually assaulted during the 22-month period after the removal of Aristide from office" in 2004 in Haiti's capital Port-au-Prince (*Keesing's 2006*, p. 47456). However, in the 2006 presidential and legislative elections Haiti crossed slightly the minimum threshold of democracy (see *Keesing's 2006*, pp. 47091–47092). The transition to democracy took place under the protection of a UN Stabilization Mission, which had more than 7,000 troops and civilian police deployed in Haiti (Banks et al. 2007, p. 510).

Lesotho was above the threshold of democracy at the beginning of its independence in 1966–1969. It recrossed the threshold of democracy in the 2002 highly competitive legislative elections. The ruling Lesotho Congress for Democracy won a majority of votes and seats, but there is a strong opposition in the National Assembly. Opposition parties benefited from a mixed electoral system, which replaced the former first-past-the-post system in November 2001. Press freedom and freedom of assembly and association are more extensive than in most other sub-Saharan African countries. However, "government critics in the media are subject to extremely high libel penalties," and journalists are occasionally harassed or attacked (*Freedom in the World 2006*, p. 415).

Liberia was autocratically ruled by its small Americo-Liberian minority until a bloody military coup in 1980. A long period of political instability, atrocities, and civil war followed the coup. Finally, combatants agreed to make a democratic compromise and to end the civil war, which had "left some 250,000 of Liberia's 3m-odd people dead, forced many more to flee, and destabilized the whole region" (*The Economist*, December 16, 2006, p. 42). In the 2005 legislative and presidential elections, the country crossed the threshold of democracy, at least temporarily. Because the 2005 elections were organized under the protection of the UN peacekeeping forces, it is too early to know whether democratic institutions survive when the foreign peacekeepers leave the country. Anyway, Liberia had a functioning multiparty system in 2006.

Malawi (independent 1964) is a surprisingly successful democracy in sub-Saharan Africa. After the long period of President Hastings Kamuzu Banda's one-party regime, Malawi's political elite groups agreed in 1993 to introduce a multiparty system and competitive elections. Since 1994, legislative and presidential elections have been really competitive and Malawi crossed the threshold of democracy. Freedoms of speech and of the press are generally respected in practice, as well as freedom of assembly and association. However, there are serious deficiencies in the quality of democracy. After the 1999 legislative elections, violence erupted in opposition strongholds in northern Malawi. Supporters of an opposition party attacked mosques, shops, and homes of suspected supporters of the ruling party (*Freedom in the World 2005*, p. 393). In April 2006 Vice President Cassim Chilumpha was arrested and "charged with treason and conspiracy to murder in an alleged plot to assasinate President Bingu wa Mutharika" (*Keesing's 2006*, p. 47193). The measured level of democracy (ID) is probably significantly higher than the quality of democracy. The survival of democracy since 1994 indicates that Malawi's political leaders have learned to compromise and to share power through elections.

In *Mali* competitive elections have been held since 1992, but the country remained below the threshold of democracy because of a very low level of electoral participation. Most people are excluded from national politics. However, *Freedom in the World 2006* (pp. 454–457) classifies Mali as a free country (democracy) and emphasizes that since the end of military rule, Mali's domestic political debate has been open and extensive. Elections have been managed in the spirit of transparency, Mali's media are among Africa's most open, and many civil groups and nongovernmental organizations operate without interference. Thus the quality of democracy may be higher than its ID value indicates, but I cannot classify it as a democracy because only approximately 10 percent of the population has participated in elections.

In *Mozambique* (independent 1975), the transition from a one-party state to competitive multiparty elections and democracy took place in 1994, after a long civil war in which "more than 1 million people had died and 5 million others had been uprooted from their homes...." (Meredith 2006, p. 609). The ruling Frelimo party remained in power, but the main opposition party (Renamo) has strong support in northern and central provinces. Deep political divisions persist, with occasional violence. Pervasive corruption, which plagues the legal system, is among many deficits in democratic governance. The level of electoral participation decreased so much in the 2004 legislative and presidential elections that the country again dropped below the participation threshold of democracy.

Niger was a one-party state from its independence in 1960 to 1992, when the Africa-wide trend towards democratization reached the country and an all-party national conference decided to adopt a democratic constitution. Elections have been highly competitive since 1993, and Niger also crossed the participation threshold for democracy in the 2004 legislative and presidential elections. Political rights and freedoms are generally respected. Power is not evenly distributed among the country's ethnic groups. The Hausa and Djerma ethnic groups dominate in politics, and the nomadic Tuaregs especially have been underrepresented.

Nigeria has been devastated by violent ethnic conflicts since independence in 1960. Elected regimes have alternated with military coups and military governments. During the military regimes, corruption was rampant. For example, "Abacha's greed exceeded that of all his predecessors. It was estimated that he stole more than $4 billion...." (Meredith 2006, p. 581). Nigeria recrossed the threshold of democracy in 1999 when General Olusegun Obasanjo, who had led a military regime from 1976 to 1979, was elected president. Elections have been marred by serious irregularities and fraud and ethnic violence continues in several parts of the country, especially between Muslims and Christians. In the Niger Delta, which holds rich oil deposits, violence has been rampant, and people remain poor (see Sandbakken 2006; O'Neill 2007). According to *The Economist* (August 4, 2007), "The cause of all this is extravagant corruption and mismanagement, coupled with a political culture that owes more to the principles of gangsterism than to any textbook on democracy." The country was able to elect a new president and parliament in April 2007, but those "elections saw abuses worse than those which had debilitated previous regimes and precipitated military coups" (Suberu 2007, p. 101).The quality of democracy is low.

In *Senegal,* competitive elections have been held since the 1980s and the country avoided military coups, but Senegal in 2006 was still below the minimum threshold of democracy because of a very low level of electoral participation (cf. *Freedom in the World 2006*, p. 617). As in many other African countries, only a small minority of the population takes part in national politics. The fact that the Socialist Party, which had been the ruling party since independence, lost power through the 2000 presidential and 2001 legislative elections, indicates the strength of democratic strivings in Senegal. The people of Senegal have a real chances to change their government democratically, which was, and still is rare in sub-Saharan Africa. Thus the quality of democracy in Senegal seems to be higher than the measures of democratization indicate. In the 2007 presidential election, the degree of electoral participation increased significantly, and Senegal crossed the threshold of democracy (see *Keesing's 2007*, p. 47732).

Sierra Leone was above the threshold of democracy at the beginning of its independence from the 1960s to 1972, when two parties competed for power. One-party regimes and military governments ruled the country in the period 1973–2002. After a bloody civil war, Sierra Leone approached the threshold of democracy in the 2002 presidential and parliamentary elections, but these were held under the protection of UN peacekeeping troops. President Ahmed Tejan Kabbah's Sierra Leone People's Party won 74 percent of the seats in parliament, which makes it a dominant party. As in many other African countries, political rights and freedoms are restricted in practice. The civil war had been extremely cruel. For example, see the following description of the third battle for Freetown in January 1999: "In a period of four days the RUF captured the city centre and most of the suburbs. With terrifying violence they massacred some 6,000 civilians, amputating hands and feet at random, destroyed hundreds of buildings and thousands of homes…." (Meredith 2006, p. 570). Such a heritage of cruel violence does not provide a favorable environment for democratic politics. However, in the 2007 legislative and presidential elections, Sierra Leone crossed the threshold of democracy.

Somalia was above the threshold of democracy during the first years of its independence from 1960 to 1969. A military coup displaced democratic institutions in 1969. Somalia has been without an effective national government since 1991, when rebel forces deposed President Barre and his authoritarian government. Since then, competing clan militias and guerrilla movements have struggled for power. The United Nations, with the support of U.S.-troops, failed completely in its attempt to pacify Somalia: "After spending $4 billion in the hope of rebuilding Somalia,...the UN departed, handing Mogadishu over to its warring factions" (Meredith 2006, pp. 483–484). Finally, rival groups established a transitional government and National Assembly in 2000–2002, but these institutions have not been able to stop fighting and to take control over the country. In 2004, the Transitional National Assembly was replaced by the Transitional Federal Parliament, filled by clan and subclan appointees, but Somaliland remained divorced from the new institutions, and fighting between warlords continued in 2006 (Banks et al. 2007, pp. 1122–1124).

Swaziland is a traditional African monarchy in which power is in the hands of the king and his family. There is a National Assembly, but its powers are limited and its members are not democratically elected. Political parties are banned. Consequently, political rights and freedoms as well as the freedom of expression are severely restricted. For example, in January 2006 dozens of political activists were detained and accused of destabilizing the regime (*Keesing's 2006, p.* 47026). There "are regular reports of police brutality, including torture, beatings, and suspicious deaths of suspects in custody" (*Freedom in the World 2006, p.* 685). Pro-democracy protests indicate that there is some popular pressure for a more democratic system. The new constitution of 2006 does not legalize political parties, and the king retains ultimate authority (Banks et al. 2007, pp. 1185–1186).

Zimbabwe was, after it achieved independence in 1980, for some years (1980–1984) above the threshold of democracy, but when the ruling Zimbabwe African National Union–Patriotic Front (ZANU-PF) became a hegemonic party, the country dropped below the threshold of democracy. President Robert Mugabe's rule has been arbitrary and violent. Despite repression, some opposition groups still survive and continue their struggle for democracy. In the 2002 presidential election, Mugabe's support dropped to 56 percent, and Zimbabwe re-crossed the Competition threshold of democracy, but that election was not free and fair. The ruling party had unleashed a new round of violence and intimidation on the electorate. From militia bases across the country, youth squads were deployed to hunt down opposition supporters. "They raided shops, destroyed houses, and set up roadblocks, dragging people out of buses and cars, demanding party cards.... MDC officials were abducted, beaten, tortured and sometimes murdered...." (Meredith 2006, pp. 642–643). In the 2005 legislative elections, Zimbabwe crossed slightly also the participation threshold of democracy (20%). The quality of democracy in Zimbabwe is much lower than its ID value indicates, but my point is that the survival of opposition indicates the existence of some kind of rudimentary democracy. The government has not yet been able to suppress all opposition forces and may not ever be able to do this. According to Freedom House's political rights (PR) and civil liberties (CL) estimates, Zimbabwe was "not free" in 2005 (*Freedom in the World 2006*, p. 803).

This review of 30 countries at the national IQ level 1 illustrates the difficulties of establishing and maintaining democratic institutions in sub-Saharan Africa and a low quality of democracy (cf. Berg-Schlosser 2004). As noted earlier, none of these 30 countries have been continually above the threshold of democracy since 1950 or from the year of independence. In 2006, 13 of them were above the minimum threshold of democracy, and 17 others were more or less below the threshold.

The five countries (Burundi, Congo Democratic Republic, Guinea-Bissau, Liberia, and Malawi) for which the actual ID values in 2006 were more than one standard deviation above this IQ category's average of 7.5 constitute the group of the largest positive outliers. Malawi is the most stabilized democracy of these five countries. Four other countries are quite recent democracies. They crossed the threshold of democracy in 2005 or 2006. In the cases of Congo Democratic Republic and Liberia, this took place under the protection of foreign peacekeeping troops. In Burundi and Guinea-Bissau, civil war or coups preceded the transition to democracy. Democratic institutions are fragile in all these countries.

In addition to these five largest positive outliers, eight other countries were slightly above the threshold of democracy in 2006 (the Central African Republic, Chad, Ethiopia, Haiti, Lesotho, Niger, Nigeria, and Zimbabwe). All are recent democracies, and it is questionable how long they will be able to maintain democratic institutions. The quality of democracy was especially low in Chad, Haiti, and Zimbabwe. Any of these countries may again drop below the threshold of democracy in the near future.

It is characteristic of the five largest negative outliers (Angola, Côte d'Ivoire, Eritrea, Somalia, and Swaziland) that their actual ID values were zero in 2006. Most had suffered from civil wars, and Angola, Côte d'Ivoire, and Somalia were without an effective national government in 2006. However, their large negative residuals predicted pressure towards some kind of democratization. In addition to these large negative outliers, 12 other countries (Burkina Faso, Cameroon, Congo Republic, Djibouti, Equatorial Guinea, Gabon, Gambia, Guinea, Mali, Mozambique, Senegal, and Sierra Leone) were more or less below the threshold of democracy in 2006. Because they differ only slightly from the regression line, they may remain below the threshold or rise slightly above it. I want to emphasize that various local and accidental factors affect the fluctuation of ID values.

Deficiencies in democratic governance are most conspicuous in the countries which were below the minimum level of democracy in 2006, but they seem to be almost as significant in the countries which were only slightly above that threshold. According to Freedom House's classification, the quality of democracy in 2005 was best in Lesotho, Mali, and Senegal (Free) and worst in 12 countries (Angola, Cameroon, Chad, Congo Democratic Republic, Côte d'Ivoire, Equatorial Guinea, Eritrea, Guinea, Haiti, Somalia, Swaziland, and Zimbabwe), which were classified as Not Free (*Freedom in the World 2006*).

Authoritarian regimes prevail in sub-Saharan Africa, the use of violence is common in politics, most countries have experienced ethnic violence or civil wars, political rights and freedoms are severely restricted in practice, corruption is widespread, and democratic changes of governments have been extremely rare. Many democratic experiments in Africa have failed, in some countries several times. However, it is remarkable that despite these difficulties, people have striven to establish democratic institutions and to maintain them in practically all sub-Saharan African countries. Many researchers have analyzed problems of democratic politics in Africa from different perspectives. I will refer to some examples.

Samuel Decalo (1998, p. 274) notes that whatever "democratic advances have been attained in Africa to date have to be still seen as largely structural; they are certainly a strong breath of fresh air, but likely to end up in some countries as only cosmetic and/or temporary." He continues: "If progress is made toward developing democratic government, it is likely to be gradual, messy, fitful and slow, with many imperfections along the way" (p. 302). According to my interpretation, the ultimate constraints of democratization explain why the quality of democracy remains low in Africa. Decalo (1998, p. 288) refers to the World Bank's position, according to which "Africa has no chance of attaining meaningful economic growth and development unless it first moves squarely into modalities of governance that include political accountability, participatory politics and a free market-economy." From the perspective of the ultimate constraints of democratization discussed in this study, it is unrealistic to expect that African countries could fulfill such requirements (cf. Hamdock 2003).

George B. N. Ayittey's (1999) critical observations on politics in Africa illustrate the nature of democratic deficits in sub-Saharan Africa. In a chapter "The Vampire African State," he says that dishonesty, thievery, and peculation (embezzlement) pervade the public sector and that the chief bandit is the head of state himself. According to his harsh evaluation, the "African state has been reduced to a mafia-like bazaar, where anyone with an official designation can pillage at will" (p. 151). African government officials get rich by misusing their positions, and "as functional illiterates, they are incapable of using the skills and knowledge they acquired from education to get rich on their own, in the private sector" (p. 153). Decision-making is extremely concentrated: "Decisions are taken by the head of state and a tiny cabal of advisers, cronies, and trusted lieutenants," and where parliaments exist, "they simply rubber stamp decisions that have already been taken" (p. 164). Ayittey continues that to "facilitate the dispensing of patronage and reduce any threat to his power, the strongman usurps control over all key state institutions: the army, police, civil service, state media, parliament, judiciary, central bank, and educational system" (p. 166). When other tactics fail to work, African dictators resort to terror and intimidation.

Staffan I. Lindberg (2006) is not as pessimistic about the prospects of democracy in Africa as Decalo and Ayittey. Lindberg emphasizes the positive impact of repeated national elections. His argument is that elections improve the quality of democracy. Elections are not insignificant. According to his observations, "democracy tends to take root after a sequence of three electoral cycles." Empirical evidence testifies "that after third elections regime breakdowns occur only in very rare instances" (p. 3, 156). I tend to agree with his argument. Repeated elections support democratization. He also stresses that we should not measure "African politics by different standards than those applied to the rest of world." He does not share "the culturalist view that liberal democracy is an inherently misguided choice for African countries because of peculiarities in their societies and cultures" (pp. 159–160). This study is based on the same idea. The same measures and standards are applied to all countries of the world because we share the same human nature.

My country reviews support in many points the generalizations of Decalo and Ayittey on the quality of democracy in Africa. Because the generally low quality of democracy in sub-Saharan Africa is in harmony with the regional differences in the ultimate constraining variables MT and national IQ, it is not reasonable to expect any dramatic rise in the quality of democracy. However, the low quality of democracy is not fixed; it depends partly on conscious human choices. It would certainly be worthwhile to explore what kinds of political institutions and policies have improved the quality of democracy in Africa. I agree with Lindberg's argument about the democratizing power of elections. The number of democracies and semi-democracies has increased significantly with the introduction of multiparty elections.

CHAPTER 11

Countries at National IQ Level 2 (70–79)

The following 20 countries are at the national IQ level 2: Benin, Botswana, Cape Verde, Comoros, Ghana, Guatemala, Jamaica, Kenya, Mauritania, Namibia, Nepal, Qatar, Rwanda, South Africa, Sri Lanka, Sudan, Tanzania, Togo, Uganda, and Zambia. Most of these countries (15) are sub-Saharan African countries, but Guatemala is a Latin American country, Jamaica a Caribbean country, Qatar an Arab country, and Nepal and Sri Lanka South Asian countries.

The mean of ID-2006 is 10.5, the mean of PR-2005 (political rights) is 3.7, and the mean of CL-2005 (civil liberties) is 3.5 for the 20 countries in this IQ category (see Table 8.4). These means indicate a slightly higher level of democracy than the corresponding means of IQ level 1. On the average these countries were approximately at the minimum threshold of democracy. Some of them deviated more than one standard deviation (6.1 for ID-2006) from the group mean of ID-2006 (10.5). The level and probably also the quality of democracy were more than one standard deviation (6.1) better in Ghana, Nepal, and Sri Lanka, and more than one standard deviation worse in Qatar and Sudan. It would be interesting to find out what kind of local or accidental factors might explain these large deviations.

Because most of the 20 countries in this IQ category are sub-Saharan African countries, it is reasonable to expect that the nature of their political systems is more or less similar to that of the countries of the first IQ category. As in the previous section, I try to describe the level and quality of democracy as well as the lack of democracy in single countries.

Benin started its independence as a democracy in 1960, but it ended in a coup in 1963, after which the country was autocratically ruled until 1991. Benin transited from a one-party state to a multiparty democracy abruptly in 1991. President Kerekou, who had originally taken power through a military coup in 1972, agreed to convene a national conference, which established democratic institutions. Kerekou lost his job to Nicephore Soglo in the 1991 presidential election. Meredith (2006) says about the nature of Kerekou's military rule that he and "his cronies had looted the state-owned banking system so thoroughly that nothing was left to pay the salaries of teachers and civil servants...." (p. 387). Kerekou made a comeback in the 1996 presidential poll, and in the 2001 presidential election he consolidated his dominance. After the 2003 legislative elections, Benin dropped again below the Competition threshold of democracy. Despite the dominance of President Kerekou and his party, opposition parties had opportunities to function freely, and political rights and freedoms remained extensive and respected in practice (cf. Seely 2005). In the 2006 presidential election, Benin recrossed the threshold of democracy (*Keesing's 2006*, p. 47132). The quality of democracy in Benin seems to be among the best in sub-Saharan Africa.

Botswana is the most stabilized democracy in sub-Saharan Africa. The persistent dominance of the ruling Botswana Democratic Party characterizes its political system. Its dominance is based on the support of the largest tribal group (Tswana). Opposition parties can function freely, although the ruling party has enjoyed preferential access to state-run media. The following statement describes the good quality of democracy in Botswana: "A free and vigorous press thrives in cities and towns, and political debate is open and lively.... The government generally respects freedom of assembly and association...." (*Freedom in the World 2005*, p. 96). However, Botswana has not continually been above the threshold of democracy since its independence in 1966. It crossed both the competition and participation thresholds in 1984, but dropped temporarily below the participation threshold in 1994–1996.

Cape Verde started its independence in 1975 as a one-party-dominated country. It crossed the threshold of democracy in 1991 and has remained a democracy since then. Political rights and freedoms are extensive and respected in practice. The quality of democracy is relatively good. The exceptional success of democracy in Cape Verde may be related to the fact that Creoles (mulattos) constitute 71 percent of the population. There have not been any significant ethnic conflicts in Cape Verde.

Comoros was ruled by autocratic presidents and military governments from its independence in 1975 until 1990 when it crossed the threshold of democracy through a competitive presidential election. A military coup led by Colonel Assoumani Azali dropped it temporarily below the threshold in 1999. Politics in Comoros has been characterized by violent coups and a conflict with the separatist Mayotte Island. The rights of freedom of assembly and association are generally respected, but, occasionally, police violently disperse protesters. Comoros recrossed the threshold of democracy in the highly competitive presidential election in 2006 (*Keesing's 2006*, p. 47240).

In *Ghana* the nature of the political system has fluctuated greatly from multiparty democracy to one-party state and military regime since its independence in 1957. Jerry Rawlings usurped power by a military coup in 1981. He legalized his position through a competitive presidential election in November 1992, but opposition parties "claimed massive fraud and refused to participate in parliamentary elections the following month, leaving Rawlings and his allies with a clear run" (Meredith 2006, p. 394). According to my measures of democracy, Ghana crossed the threshold of democracy in the 1996 competitive presidential and legislative elections. Political rights and freedoms are extensive and generally respected, but democratic politics has been endangered by occasional ethnic violence. A strong multiparty system, based partly on major ethnic divisions, has supported competitive politics and raised electoral participation.

Guatemala is a racially deeply divided country. Political power has traditionally been in the hands of the country's white minority and allied mestizos. A long civil war between the government forces and guerrillas supported by the Maya Amerindians claimed the lives of more than 200,000 people and made it difficult to maintain democratic institutions. The Maya Amerindians do not have full political equality with the whites and mestizos. Competitive elections have been organized almost regularly since the 1960s, but the level of electoral participation remained below the participation threshold of democracy until 1985, when Guatemala temporarily crossed the threshold of democracy (1985–1989). In the period 1990–2006, the level of participation was again below the threshold value. Politics has been characterized by violence, corruption is widespread, and political rights and freedoms are restricted in practice. For example, "human rights groups are targets of frequent death threats and the victims of acts of violence" (*Freedom in the World 2005*, pp. 261–262). The quality of democracy remained poor in such circumstances. The Amerindian population is still almost completely excluded from national politics and elections.

Jamaica has been above the threshold of democracy nearly continually since its independence in 1962. Political rights and freedoms are generally respected in practice, but the quality of democracy suffers from police abuses and violent crime. The government has not been able to extend the rule of law over its police force. "Violence is the major cause of death in Jamaica, and the murder rate is one of the highest in the world" (*Freedom in the World 2005*, pp. 325–326). Two equally strong parties—the Jamaica Labor Party and the People's National Party—have competed for power since independence.

In *Kenya* it has been difficult for any ethnic or political group to reach and consolidate a hegemonic position. Opposition groups have continually challenged the position of the ruling party. Presidential and legislative elections have been competitive since 1992. Kenya was temporarily above the threshold of democracy in 1992–96 and crossed it again in 2005. The quality of democracy suffers from a low level of electoral participation, and suffers also from violence in politics and from the government's attempts to suppress opposition activities and to restrict political freedoms. Corruption is rampant. When President Daniel arap Moi was obliged to stand down at the end of 2002 after twenty-four years in power, "investigators estimated that he and his cronies had looted as much as $3 billion" (Meredith 2006, p. 687). Popular efforts to make a new constitution that would reduce the powers of the president failed in 2000–2005 (see Cottrell and Ghai 2007).

Mauritania is an ethnically deeply divided country in which 70 percent of all Mauritanians "are descendants of the Moors, nomadic shepherds of north-west Africa, a mixture of Arab, Berber, and African peoples" (*The World Guide 2007*, p. 357). The Arab-related Moors have had a hegemonic position since independence in 1960, and African tribal groups (30%) have had a subjugated position. A number of Africans are still enslaved. There has been some competition in elections since 1992. Freedom of the press is strictly restricted as well as freedoms of assembly and association. The failure of democratization in Mauritania is partly related to the fact that the population is racially deeply divided. The same factor has been behind civil wars in Chad and Sudan. The latest military coup took place in 2005, but the country started to return to civilian rule in 2006, and in the 2007 presidential election Mauritania crossed the threshold of democracy (see *Keesing's 2007*, p. 47788).

Namibia has maintained a competitive political system and democratic institutions since its independence in 1990, but the dominance of the ruling South West Africa People's Organization (SWAPO) is so overpowering that the country has never crossed my Competition threshold of democracy. The ruling party's strong position is based on the support of the country's largest ethnic group, the Ovambo (47%). Press freedom has been extensive. However, the opposition has accused the government of harassment and unequal access to media coverage and campaign financing. The rebel activities of Caprivi separatists indicate that all ethnic minorities are not satisfied with their position. The hegemony of SWAPO reduces the quality of democracy in Namibia. Some other researchers, however, regard Namibia as a stabilized democracy (see, for example, *Freedom in the World 2006*; van Cranenburgh 2006). It is true that democratic institutions have become stabilized in Namibia, but the country has not yet been able to cross the competition threshold; this may happen in the next elections.

Nepal was traditionally autocratically ruled and started its democratic experiment in 1991, when popular pressure forced the king to legalize political parties and to accept a democratic constitution. The Maoist insurgency, which escalated in 2001, led to the collapse of democratic institutions and ultimately to the king's coup d'etat in 2005. Democracy was finished, but when the king was not able to get control over the country, he had to allow the re-establishment of democratic institutions in 2006. The king was deprived of practically all of his powers. Violence has characterized politics in Nepal during the last years. The quality of democracy degenerated, and the rule of law nearly disappeared.

According to a report, the Maoist rebels, despite peace talks, continued their military activities, "were involved in clashes with local people who resisted them, carried out abductions and beatings, interfered with development projects, persisted in levying rural 'taxes,' and continued to operate their own courts" (*Keesing's 2006*, p. 47522). In 2006, Nepal was returning to democratic politics, but the actual level of democratization may be lower than ID-2006 indicates for the reason that the government was unable to organize new elections in 2006.

Qatar is an autocratically ruled Arab country in which democratic rights and freedoms are tightly restricted. For example, the leading newspapers are owned by royal family members and other notables. However, a new constitution accepted by a referendum in 2003 presupposes the establishment of a directly elected National Assembly. The new constitution does not provide for the formation of political parties (Banks et al. 2007, pp. 1005–1006). Immigrant workers, who constitute a majority of the population (80%), are without citizenship and any political rights, a factor which makes democratization highly improbable.

Rwanda has never been able to maintain a democratic political system, but it has suffered from cruel ethnic violence between the Hutu and Tutsi communities since independence in 1962. In the genocidal violence in 1994, some 800,000 people were slaughtered, mainly Tutsis, and at least two million people fled the country. Meredith (2006) notes that the genocide of 1994 "was slaughter on a scale not witnessed since the Nazi extermination programme against the Jews" (p. 487). Ultimately the Tutsi-dominated Rwandan Patriotic Front (RPF) deposed the Hutu regime in July 1994 and usurped power. A new constitution unveiled in 2003 permits political parties to exist, but the RPF government declared the largest opposition party, the Hutu-based Democratic Republican Movement, illegal before the 2003 parliamentary elections. The Tutsi-dominated RPF won 73 percent of the vote and retained its dominant position. Legal opposition is still weak in Rwanda, and political rights and freedoms are seriously restricted in practice (cf. *The Economist*, January 13, 2007, p. 35).

South Africa was ruled by the parties of the country's white minority until the first democratic elections in 1994. The African National Congress (ANC), which had struggled against the apartheid regime since the 1960s, won a clear majority and established a new government. The ANC government has respected democratic rights and freedoms. The racial tension between the black majority and the white minority continues. In the 2004 parliamentary elections, the white-dominated Democratic Alliance emerged as the main opposition party. South Africa is a kind of ethnic democracy without realistic chances to change the government. The combined support of opposition parties dropped to 30.3 percent in the 2004 elections, which means that if the same trend continues in the next elections, South Africa would drop below the competition threshold of democracy. However, the existence of political rights and freedoms supports the survival of opposition and democracy in South Africa.

Sri Lanka has exceptionally been a democracy since its independence in 1948. A cruel ethnic civil war has ravaged the country since the 1980s, but it has not suppressed the function of democratic institutions. Elections have been held regularly and power has remained in the hands of elected officials. This indicates the strength of democracy in Sri Lanka and a relatively high quality of democracy. Freedom of expression is extensive and freedom of assembly is generally respected, although the civil war restricts political rights and freedoms in practice. The Tamil Tiger separatist rebels do not permit free expression in the areas under their control, and they terrorize Tamil journalists and other critics. Of course, the quality of democracy suffers from the consequences of the ethnic civil war (cf. *The Economist*, December 26, 2006, pp. 56–57). The ethnic cleavage between the Sinhalese majority and the Tamil minority and deep ideological divisions within the Sinhalese majority maintain a fragmented multiparty system and intensify electoral competition. Sri Lanka's much higher than expected level of democratization is principally due to these local factors.

Sudan (independent 1956) has never reached the threshold of democracy. It is an ethnically deeply divided country. The major cleavage is between the Arabs in the north and the black Africans in the south, but there are also other significant ethnic divisions. Probably millions of people have been killed in ethnic civil wars, which have continued since independence. Political power is in the hands of Arab-based parties of the north. The rebel Sudanese People's Liberation Army (SPLA) controls southern provinces. There is little press freedom, nor other political rights and freedoms in such circumstances. For example,

"Government forces are said to have routinely raided villages, burning homes, killing residents, and abducting women and children to be used as slaves in the North" (*Freedom in the World 2005*, p. 600). Sudan's exceptionally low quality of democracy is due to deep racial cleavages and civil war just like in Chad and Mauritania. Following the peace agreement between the government and the SPLM, a transitional 30-member power-sharing cabinet was established in 2005, but it is not an elected government (Banks et al. 2007, pp. 1171–1178).

Tanzania has also remained below the threshold of democracy since its independence in 1961, but it does not suffer from serious ethnic problems. The same hegemonic ruling party has remained in power without military coups or other interruptions. Opposition parties were legalized in 1992. Political rights and freedoms as well as the freedom of the press are still to some extent restricted. Political activities are principally limited to urban areas. As in many other sub-Saharan African countries, the rural population is mostly excluded from national politics. Corruption remains a serious problem, as in most other sub-Saharan African countries.

Togo (independent 1960) started a process of democratization in 1994, but it has been a slow process, and the country was still below the Competition threshold of democracy in 2006. The old ruling party has retained its majority position in competitive elections, and President Eyadema won new presidential elections in 1998 and 2003. After his death in February 2005, his son Faure Gnassingbe was elected president by 60 percent of the vote in April 2005 (cf. Seely 2005). The dominance of Eyadema's party implies that political rights and freedoms are restricted in the country. For example, demonstrations are often banned or violently halted, and human rights groups are closely monitored and sometimes harassed. Extrajudicial killings, arbitrary arrests, and torture continue (*Freedom in the World 2005*, p. 636).

Uganda's political history has been turbulent and violent since its independence in 1962. Its political system has fluctuated between democratic experiments and military and other authoritarian regimes. During Idi Amin's brutal dictatorship from 1971 to 1979, hundreds of thousands of people were killed. The National Resistance Army led by General Museveni deposed General Okello's military government in January 1986 and established a new authoritarian regime. Later on, Museveni legalized his position through elections, but political parties remained banned. In the 2001 presidential election, Museveni's support decreased to 69 percent, and Uganda crossed the threshold of democracy slightly. However, the nature of Uganda's democracy remained questionable because political parties were still banned. A multiparty system was re-established by a referendum in 2005. Uganda remained above the threshold of democracy in the presidential and legislative elections in 2006, but "domestic and international observers noted a number of irregularities" in the elections (*Keesing's 2006*, p. 47080). Andrew M. Mwenda (2007) argues that Uganda "is sliding backward toward a system of one-man rule engineered by the recently reelected President Museveni" (p. 33). The quality of democracy in Uganda is probably significantly lower than my measures of democracy (ID) indicate.

Zambia was dominated by President Kaunda and his United National Independence Party (UNIP) from independence in 1964 until the transition to a multiparty system in 1991. Kaunda and UNIP lost power in the first multiparty elections in 1991, but the victory of Frederick Chiluba's Movement for Multiparty Democracy (MMD) was so overpowering that the country remained below the threshold of democracy. The support of the opposition increased drastically in the 2001 presidential and legislative elections, and Zambia crossed the Competition threshold of democracy, but still remained below the Participation threshold. Lise Rakner and Lars Svåsand (2005, p. 86) argue that, because of irregularities in elections, "Zambia falls short of both international and local expectations of a democratic process." Finally, Zambia crossed the threshold of democracy in the 2006 presidential and legislative elections. The quality of democracy suffers especially from extensive corruption, and this continues in elections.

The review of these 20 countries shows that Sri Lanka is the only country which has been above the threshold of democracy since its independence. On the other hand, six (Mauritania, Namibia, Qatar, Rwanda, Sudan, and Tanzania) have never reached the minimum threshold of democracy. In 2006, 12 of these countries were above the threshold of democracy (Benin, Botswana, Cape Verde, Comoros, Ghana, Jamaica, Kenya, Nepal, South Africa, Sri Lanka, Uganda, and Zambia), whereas eight others (Guatemala, Mauritania, Namibia, Qatar, Rwanda, Sudan, Tanzania, and Togo) were below the threshold. The increased number of democracies implies that the quality of democracy may also be slightly higher in this category than in the first national IQ category. The quality of democracy seems to have been relatively good in Benin, Botswana, Cape Verde, Ghana, Jamaica, Namibia, and South Africa, which Freedom House classified as "free" in 2005 (*Freedom in the World 2006*), although Namibia according to my measures was slightly below the Competition threshold of democracy. In the other 13 countries, including some democracies, the quality of democratic governance was clearly lower. Most of these countries were below the minimum threshold of democracy in 2006.

Various local factors seem to explain the great variation in the level and quality of democracy. Countries like Cape Verde, Botswana, and Jamaica have benefited from the relatively high ethnic homogeneity of their populations, whereas countries like Guatemala, Kenya, Mauritania, Rwanda, Sri Lanka, Sudan, and Uganda have suffered from deep racial or other ethnic cleavages, which led to ethnic violence and civil war. Qatar's autocratic political system is based on the concentration of oil resources in the hands of the rulers and on the need to control the non-citizen majority of the population. The nature of democratic deficits in these countries is similar to that in the countries of the first national IQ category. It was difficult for most countries to cross the Competition and Participation thresholds of democracy, and most of the contemporary democracies crossed the threshold only recently. Political rights and freedoms are restricted in practice, the rule of law is defective, corruption is widespread, and politics is often characterized by violence, insurgencies, and rebels.

It is characteristic of these countries that nearly all are tropical or semitropical, a factor related to their low level of national IQ. Because the level of democratization is moderately or strongly related to the level of national IQ, it would not be reasonable to expect any drastic changes in the average level of democratization, although significant changes in single countries are always possible. National IQ (and MT behind it) constrains chances to raise the level of democratization and to improve the quality of democracy in this category of countries.

CHAPTER 12

Countries at National IQ Level 3 (80–84)

This national IQ category includes more countries than any other of the seven IQ categories. National IQ varies from 80 to 84 in the following 33 countries: Afghanistan, Algeria, Bahamas, Bahrain, Bangladesh, Barbados, Belize, Bhutan, Colombia, Dominican Republic, Egypt, El Salvador, Honduras, India, Iran, Jordan, Lebanon, Libya, Madagascar, Maldives, Morocco, Nicaragua, Oman, Pakistan, Panama, Papua New Guinea, Paraguay, Saudi Arabia, Solomon Islands, Syria, Tunisia, United Arab Emirates, and Venezuela. Most of these countries are tropical or semitropical. The category includes nearly all of the Middle Eastern and North African countries (13), many Latin American and Caribbean countries (11), nearly all South Asian countries (6), two Oceanian countries, and Madagascar from sub-Saharan Africa.

The mean of ID-06 (11.2) is for this category of 33 countries clearly higher than for the two previous categories, whereas the means of PR (political rights) (4.2) and CL (civil liberties) (4.0) do not indicate any rise in the average quality of democracy (see Table 8.4). On average, these countries were slightly above the minimum threshold of democracy on the basis of ID-2006 and at the level of "partly free" on the basis of PR and CL variables in 2005. The standard deviations of the three variables show that the variation in the level and quality of democracy was in this group even greater than in the two first national IQ levels. The level of democratization in 2006 (see Table 6.1) was more than one standard deviation (9.0) better in India, Lebanon, Nicaragua, Panama, and Papua New Guinea, and more than one standard deviation worse in Bahrain, Bhutan, Jordan, Libya, Oman, Saudi Arabia, and the United Arab Emirates. The actual level of democratization (ID-2006) deviated less than one standard deviation from the group's mean (11.2) in 21 other countries. The number of highly deviating countries implies the impact of other factors on the level and quality of democracy.

The Middle Eastern and North African countries are the least democratized at this IQ level. Of these 13 countries, only Algeria and Lebanon were above the threshold of democracy in 2006, but on the basis of Freedom House ratings, Algeria was "not free" in 2005. All the other countries had more or less autocratic systems, although the process of democratization had started in most of them. The lack of effective representative institutions, free elections, and legal political parties characterizes most of these countries. Power is concentrated in the hands of the executive institutions, and the independence of the judicial branch is limited. Freedom of expression and of association are restricted. Political systems have adapted to the constraints based on Islamic culture, but it may be unfair to blame Islam for the lack of democracy in the Middle East and North Africa because Islamic culture has not prevented democratization in countries like Bangladesh, Indonesia, and Turkey (cf. Held 1994; Brynen et al. 1995; Korany et al. 1998; *The Middle East 2000*; Hinnebusch 2006). Brynen et al. (1998, p. 278) come to the conclusion that "the seeds of some kind of change are widely sown through the societies, economies, and even regimes of the Arab world." I agree. The Arab countries are not condemned to authoritarian systems merely because of their Islamic culture. The concentration of economic and military power resources in the hands of small ruling groups has supported the survival of autocratic systems longer than expected on the basis of IPR and national IQ. Brynen et al. (1995, p. 7) refer to this factor in their assumption that "Arabs may be deferential to authoritarian rule not because of some ingrained cultural disposition, but as a consequence of a quite rational response to authoritarian repression."

Historically, it has been very difficult to establish and maintain democratic institutions in Latin American countries. Political rights and liberties have been limited, and effective participation in national politics has been restricted to relatively small privileged groups. Dictatorships, *caudillismo*, military juntas, unconstitutional regime changes, and fraudulent elections have characterized the political history of most Latin American countries, but despite repeated failures, new attempts were made to establish democratic institutions and practices (for political history, see Williams 1930; Gunther 1941; Herring 1961; Johnson 1964; Kantor 1969; Lambert 1969). Politics used to be violent and human rights weak. Jacques Lambert (1969, pp. 158–160) described the nature of *caudillismo* in Latin America and said that in order to gain power, the *caudillo* has to pay lip service to the forms of representative democracy, but because his authority depends on the use of illegal means of coercion, *caudillismo* leads to despotism and often terror. The illegal "origin and the very nature of their power almost inevitably force *caudillos* to resort to even more violence in maintaining power than in obtaining it." It is clear that political rights and liberties were weak in such conditions.

Since the 1980s, democratic systems have become stabilized in most Latin American countries, elections are organized regularly, most changes of government take place constitutionally, party systems are stronger than previously, and electoral participation has increased significantly. Democracy has become a universally recognized ideal, although political practice is still far from ideal in many fields. Political parties tend to be based more on leaders than on local organizations, all sections of the population do not have their own interest associations, elections are not always free and fair, the independence of the judicial branch is questionable in many countries, and the civilian control of the military and other security forces is defective (see, for example, O'Donnell et al. 1986; Martz 1988; Anglade 1994; Linz and Stepan 1996; Wiarda and Kline 1996). Democratic deficits in Latin America are partly due to the ethnic heterogeneity of populations. Political power is concentrated in the hands of the descendants of conquistadores and later European migrants, whereas Amerindians, blacks, mulattoes, and poor mestizos tend to be underrepresented or excluded from political institutions. It has been very difficult to correct inequalities based on ethnic divisions.

Mary W. Williams (1930) paid attention to the impact of tropical climate on human beings in Latin America. She said that climate "has been far more influential upon the history of Latin America than any other part of physiography." The tropics is "a region of climatic monotony encouraging listlessness and lack of ambition, which are also

fostered by nature's generosity, especially in the matter of food supply."
She continued that the tropics contribute to nervousness and lack of
self-control and that in comparison with the temperate zones, "in these
regions human actions are likely to be dominated more by emotion and
less by reason." Tropical and subtropical regions are also infested with
diseases unfriendly to man (pp. 14–15). Her arguments on the impact
of climate reflect Montesquieu's ideas. It may be that because of the
tropical climate it is not realistic to expect the quality of democracy to
rise in Latin America and other tropical countries to the same level as in
the countries of the temperate zone.

The six South Asian countries in this IQ category constitute a
heterogeneous group. Afghanistan, Bangladesh, and India were above the
threshold of democracy in 2006, whereas Bhutan, Maldives, and Pakistan
were nondemocracies. In each South Asian country, political institutions
have adapted to local circumstances. Local power structures are reflected
in the function of political institutions, and because there are great inequalities in the distribution of power resources, inequalities characterize political
institutions. The struggle for power is sometimes violent. Poor people are
also more or less excluded from political institutions in the democracies
(for political history and institutions, see Kumar 1978; Phadnis et al. 1986;
Rao 1987; Parmanand 1988; Kaushik 1996; Ganguly 2002; Schaffer 2002;
DeVotta 2002; Drèze and Sen 2002; Kurian et al. 2004). Compared to the
values of our constraining variables (MT and national IQ), the level of
democratization in democratic South Asian countries is already somewhat
higher than expected, whereas there seems to be unused potential for
democratization in Bhutan, Maldives, and Pakistan.

In the following country reviews, I refer briefly to political conditions
in single countries and to factors describing the quality of democracy.

Afghanistan was traditionally an autocratically ruled country, but it
crossed the threshold of democracy in the 2005 legislative elections (cf.
Reynolds 2006). New democratic institutions had been introduced in
2002–2005 under the protection of foreign military troops. However,
the new national government controls only a part of the country, and
terrorist attacks have continued in different parts of the country. The
government has not been able to safeguard the security of the people.
In such circumstances, all kinds of political rights and freedoms are
restricted in practice. The quality of democracy seems to be lower than
my ID measure indicates.

Algeria's political history has been violent since independence in 1962, but the country crossed the threshold of democracy in 1995 when General Liamine Zeroual was elected president by competitive election. However, democracy in Algeria is seriously limited. All parties do not have equal opportunities to function, and violence has marred elections. The freedom of the press is restricted by the government, and the same concerns freedoms of assembly and association. Berber parties and some other opposition parties have boycotted elections, and some Islamist militants continue their violent struggle against the regime. The position of the president is based on the support of the army. Meredith (2006) says that Algeria was condemned "to live with a low-level conflict, year after year. Over a ten-year period more than 100,000 people died. Nor was there any end in sight" (p. 460). In the presidential election of 2004, the support of opposition candidates dropped to 15 percent. The quality of democracy seems to be considerably lower than the nominal level of democratization (ID). According to PR and CL-2005, Algeria was "not free." Frédéric Volpi (2006, pp. 445–446) notes that the "pseudo-democratic situation that prevails in the country since the mid-1990s is well controlled by the military establishment allied to the conservative nationalist political elite" (see also Sandbakken 2006). The existence of a strong multiparty system supports democratic institutions.

The Bahamas have been a democracy since independence in 1973. Two major parties compete for power in parliamentary elections. Political rights and freedoms are extensive and are respected in practice. The ethnic homogeneity of the population and prosperity as a tourist country seem to have supported the success of democracy in the Bahamas.

Bahrain (independent 1971) is a typical Arab country without significant democratic institutions. Political and economic power is in the hands of the ruling Al Khalifa family, which enjoys the support of the country's dominant Sunni minority. Political rights and freedoms are strictly limited. High-ranking officials suspected of corruption are rarely punished, and the judiciary is not independent of the executive branch of the government (see *Freedom in the World 2005*, pp. 60–61). Immigrant workers, who constitute almost 40 percent of the population, are without any political rights. However, the support of the Shiite opposition is growing. The main Shiite opposition group, Al Wefaq National Islamic Society, increased its support in the 2006 House of Representatives elections (*Keesing's 2006*, p. 47608;*The Economist*, November 25, 2006, p. 47). Political parties are proscribed.

In *Bangladesh*, the struggle for power and democracy has raged since independence in 1971. The country was above the threshold of democracy since 1991, but political parties were not able to agree on the rules of democratic politics. There have been many political deadlocks and violent conflicts between the major parties. Despite deep disagreements, democratic institutions survived, elections were organized, and parties alternated in power up to 2006. The governments have attempted to restrict basic political rights and freedoms. Corruption is endemic and the rule of law is weak, and tribal minorities are discriminated against, so the actual quality of democracy may have been lower than the nominal level of democratization (ID). The constitutional system collapsed, at least temporarily, in January 2007 when the president declared an army-backed state of emergency and cancelled the parliamentary elections due in January (*The Economist*, January 20, 2007, p. 61; *Keesing's 2007*, p. 47690).

Barbados is a similar case to the Bahamas. The small island state has been a democracy since independence in 1966. Parliamentary elections have been free and fair, and political rights and freedoms are respected. The judicial system is independent, but a high crime rate is a problem as in the Bahamas. The ethnic homogeneity of the population and relative prosperity based on tourism constitute local factors which have supported the success of democratic politics.

Belize has been a democracy since independence in 1981. It is an exceptionally well-functioning democracy despite the fact that its population is ethnically very diversified. The major parties represent different ethnic groups, but numerous interracial marriages have blurred ethnic borderlines and decreased the danger of violent ethnic conflict. Political rights and freedoms are extensive and respected in practice. The quality of democracy seems to be relatively high in Belize. However, tens of thousands of migrant workers and refugees are without political rights and are exploited.

Bhutan is a landlocked mountainous Himalayan country, which has traditionally been ruled by the king and Buddhist monks. There is a National Assembly, but its powers are limited and its members are not elected by direct popular election. Political rights, like freedom of expression and freedoms of assembly and association, are strictly restricted. Nepali speakers living in Bhutan are second-class citizens whose rights are even more limited. The country's national IQ presupposes a higher level and quality of democracy. In fact, the new constitution drafted in 2005 presupposes a more democratic system (see Banks et al. 2007, pp. 125–127).

Colombia has suffered from a long civil war, insurgency, and terrorism, but despite great difficulties the country has been able to maintain basic democratic institutions since 1958. The president and parliament have been elected by regular and competitive elections without military coups or other interruptions. However, because of decades-long civil strife and insurgencies, political rights and freedoms are restricted in practice. The government has not been able to safeguard peace and security of its citizens. Some parts of the country are outside effective control of the central government. Corruption affects all aspects of public life, including the justice system. Eduardo Posada-Carbó (2006) emphasizes that the situation has improved during the last years and that democratic institutions have proven themselves resilient despite the odds. The strong multiparty system maintains democratic institutions.

The Dominican Republic experienced long periods of dictatorship and authoritarian rule, but presidents have been elected by competitive elections since 1966. People have changed their government several times through elections, which indicates that competitive democracy functions. People are free to organize political parties, civil society organizations, and labor unions. Freedom of the press is extensive, whereas the judiciary is politicized and riddled with corruption. The quality of democracy seems to be in balance with the level of democratization in the Dominican Republic.

Egypt has never been a democracy, although there has been some competition in elections since the 1970s. The dominance of the ruling National Democratic Party and President Mubarak was nearly absolute in 2006 (see, for example, *The Economist*, December 2, 2006, p. 42). It is not possible to establish political parties freely, the government controls television and radio stations, and elections are not free and fair. Religious parties are entirely banned, and other opposition parties remain weak and ineffective. Freedom of the press is limited, and freedoms of assembly and association are heavily restricted. Egypt's low level of democratization (ID) reflects its low quality of democratic governance. Meredith (2006) notes that the targets of Egypt's Islamic insurgency "included government officials, intellectuals, journalists, and foreign tourists. They attacked and murdered Coptic Christians and burned Christian shops and churches" (p. 461). Ultimately the government crushed the Islamic insurgency. The country's national IQ presupposes a considerably higher level of democratization. Competition in elections has gradually increased, which indicates some progress in democratization.

El Salvador, as with so many other Latin American countries, was traditionally ruled by *caudillos* or military governments. Since 1984 those in power have been elected by regular and competitive elections. A long civil war between left-wing and right-wing groups ended in 1992. Political violence decreased after the 1992 peace agreement, but there are still deficits in the quality of democracy. Corruption and gang violence are serious problems. The judicial system "continues to be ineffective and corrupt, and a climate of impunity is pervasive, especially for those politically, economically, or institutionally well connected" (*Freedom in the World 2005*, p. 214). There is still violence in politics (see *Keesing's 2006*, p. 47033). Intensive party competition supports democratic politics.

In *Honduras*, the quality of democracy suffers from similar factors as in El Salvador. Honduras has continually been above the threshold of democracy since 1981, but it is a democracy overshadowed by the military's strong position. Freedoms of assembly and association as well as of expression are generally respected, whereas the judicial system is weak and open to corruption. The police are highly corrupt: "Extrajudicial killings, arbitrary detention, and torture by the police still take place" (*Freedom in the World 2005*, pp. 278–279). The military exerts considerable, although waning, influence over the government. The situation is more or less similar to that in many other Latin American countries.

India has remained above the threshold of democracy since 1952, which is a significant achievement. Its multiparty system functions and elections have been free and fair (cf. Ganguly 2007). The quality of democracy in India is relatively good, but of course it is easy to discern many deficiencies in the Indian democracy. The government has not been able to maintain law and order in all parts of the country. Occasional communal violence between Muslims and Hindus continues, there are separatist ethnic insurgencies in various parts of the country, and members of lower castes and religious and ethnic minorities face unofficial discrimination and violence. Besides, "effective and accountable rule continues to be undermined by political infighting, pervasive criminality in politics, decrepit state institutions, and widespread corruption." It is also claimed that police "routinely torture or otherwise ill-treat suspects to extract confessions or bribes" (*Freedom in the World 2005*, pp. 288–292). I think that the quality of democracy in India does not differ much from its level of democratization. India's much higher than expected level of democratization is partly due to its vital and fragmented party system, which reflects the ethnic and regional diversity of its population.

Iran has never crossed the threshold of democracy. Since the Islamic revolution in 1979, its president and parliament have been elected through universal adult suffrage, but political parties are not allowed to take part in elections, and hard-line clericals are empowered to approve candidates and control the decisions made by elected officials. Besides, the highest power is in the hands of a nonelected Supreme Leader. In such conditions, freedom of expression is strictly limited, as well as freedoms of assembly and association. The judiciary is not independent. Suspected dissidents are arbitrarily arrested. The quality of democracy is low, but there is popular pressure for a more democratic system. Ladan Boroumand (2007, p. 65) refers to civil rights movements and says that numerous "reports from Iran tell of brutal official efforts to crush forces for civil rights that are in fact displaying considerable dynamism."

Jordan has also remained below the threshold of democracy since its independence in 1946. Power is concentrated in the hands of the king, although there is an elected parliament. The position of political parties is ambivalent, and the electoral system is skewed toward the monarchy's traditional support base. Freedom of expression is restricted as well as freedom of assembly, and "citizens enjoy little protection from arbitrary arrest and detention" (*Freedom in the World 2005*, pp. 332–334). The many deficits in the quality of democratic governance are in harmony with Jordan's low ID value. However, its national IQ presupposes a considerably more democratic system (see also Lust-Okar 2006).

Lebanon is the only democracy in this category of Middle Eastern countries. It has maintained democratic institutions since independence in 1946, although they were paralyzed during the civil war in 1975–1991. Besides, Lebanon was below the Participation threshold of democracy in 1946–1952. The Syrian occupation (from 1976) limited democracy in Lebanon seriously until the withdrawal of Syrian troops in 2005. Freedom of expression and freedoms of assembly and association are more extensive in Lebanon than in other Arab countries. First of all, political parties are legal and they can take part in elections. The party system is principally based on communal cleavages (cf. Safa 2006).

In *Libya* (independent 1951) political rights and liberties are even more seriously restricted than in most other Arab countries. In 2006, Libya was still under the dictatorship of Colonel Moammar Gaddafy, who ruled by degree. There was no elected legislature, and people had no rights to establish political parties or other independent organizations. Consequently, the quality of democracy is extremely low. Camilla Sandbakken (2006, p. 144) regards Libya as "an extreme example of a rentier state, with government income composed almost entirely of petroleum rents." In such a state, oil wealth hampers democratization, but Libya's national IQ presupposes a more democratic system.

Madagascar (independent 1960) is the only sub-Saharan African country in this national IQ category. Malayo-Indonesian tribes constitute a significant part of its population. Madagascar has been above the threshold of democracy since the 1989 presidential election, in which President Ratsiraka's support decreased below 70 percent. Political parties can freely compete in elections, but freedom of assembly is to some extent restricted in practice. Sometimes political parties have had difficulties to accept the results of elections, which weakens the quality of democracy.

Maldives (independent 1965) is a small island state which has never reached democracy. In 2006, Maldives was ruled by President Maumoon Abdul Gayoom, who had been in power since 1979. There is a parliament (the Majlis), but political parties are not allowed to take part in elections. Freedoms of assembly and expression are strictly restricted. The limitation of basic freedoms characterizes Maldives' political system. According to a report, "the government was operating a secret extrajudicial detention centre on Feydhoo Finolhu island, off Male atoll, where currently some 270 people were held without access to lawyers and where allegedly some detainees were tortured during interrogation" (*Keesing's* 2006, p. 47375). There is opposition against the president, but opposition supporters are persecuted. They claim that Gayoom is an autocrat whose regime "has clung on to power through coercion, fear and torture" (*The Economist*, December 23, 2006, pp. 87–89).

Morocco has never crossed the threshold of democracy since its independence in 1956. Its political system is dominated by the king, but in contrast to Jordan, political parties are legal and can take part in elections and politics. This means that political rights and freedoms are more extensive than in Jordan, although they are in many points restricted. For example, "journalists are subject to prison sentences and fines for defamation and libel, especially regarding the royal family, Islam, and the Western Sahara" (*Freedom in the World 2005*, p. 435). Islamic extremists are persecuted and excluded from electoral politics. According to my variables, Morocco has been above the competition threshold of democracy since 1997, but because of the dominance of the king, the country is still below the participation threshold of democracy (cf. Maghraoui 2002; Cavatorta 2005).

Nicaragua has been above the threshold of democracy since 1984, when a civil war between the Sandinista Liberation Front and the Contras was ended by a democratic compromise. Political parties can function freely, and a president and members of a National Assembly are elected through free elections. Freedom of the press and freedoms of assembly and association are generally respected in practice. Political tension between the major parties continues, but parties have learned to accept the results of elections. Intensive competition between the two major parties has raised a degree of electoral participation.

Oman is another Arab country ruled by a royal dynasty and without legal political parties and a legislature elected by direct popular vote. Political rights and freedoms are strictly limited. The Consultative Council established in 1991 is an advisory body. Citizens are allowed to elect "members to the 83-member Consultative Council, which has no legislative powers and may only recommend changes to new laws" (*Freedom in the World 2006*, p. 539).

Pakistan's political system in 2006 alternated between periods of military regimes and shorter periods of democratic experiments. The country was above the threshold of democracy in 1973–1976 and only slightly below the Participation threshold in 1988–1998. General Pervez

Musharraf usurped power by a coup d'etat in 1999 and deposed Nawaz Sharif's government based on the support of the Pakistan Muslim League. New parliamentary elections were held in 2002, but they were not free and fair. All parties were not allowed to take part in elections, and Musharraf was the only candidate in the presidential election. Power remained in the hands of President Musharraf until 2008, when he resigned under pressure. Freedoms of assembly and association are seriously restricted. After the 2002 elections, "secular opposition parties and their leaders have continued to face intimidation and harassment from intelligence agencies and other government organs" (*Freedom in the World 2006*, p. 544). Corruption is pervasive. The quality of democratic governance seems to be even lower than ID indicates. Husain Haqqani (2006) claims that democracy was never given a chance after independence: "Almost every Pakistani head of state and government has been imprisoned, assassinated, executed, or removed from power in a military coup or a palace coup backed by the military" (p. 115). The struggle for democracy continued intensively in 2006.

Panama was temporarily above the threshold of democracy in 1948–1967 and 1980–1987 and has been continually above the threshold since 1989. Its level of democratization was quite high in 2006 (ID 26.7). Elections have been highly competitive. Political rights and freedoms are extensive and respected in practice. However, the judicial system remains inefficient, politicized, and prone to corruption, and darker-skinned Panamanians and other ethnic minorities are discriminated against. Panama's high level of democratization (ID) is principally due to its exceptionally high level of electoral participation (43–51% in 1989–2006) and to the intensive competition between parties.

Papua New Guinea has been a democracy since independence in 1975. Its level of democratization in 2006 was much higher than expected on the basis of national IQ. Australia's administrative and economic support has helped Papua New Guinea to maintain its democratic institutions. Political parties can function freely and compete in elections. There is no dominant party. However, "voter fraud and other electoral irregularities are not uncommon," and corruption is a serious problem (*Freedom in the World 2006*, p. 557). Violence between native tribes is still a serious problem, and Bougainville's separatist rebellion indicated that all sections of the population are not satisfied with their positions. According to a report, conditions are deplorable in Southern Highlands province, communities have been deprived of services, and there was "total disregard for the rule of law" (Keesing's 2006, p. 47527). The extreme fragmentation of the party system (see Banks et al. 2007, pp. 958–959) is a local factor which explains the country's exceptionally high ID value.

Paraguay was traditionally ruled by *caudillos* and autocratic presidents. It has been above the threshold of democracy only since 2000, but it is a democracy shadowed by the military's strong position and endemic corruption. Political rights and freedoms are not yet secure. The quality of democracy is low.

Saudi Arabia has been an absolute monarchy since its establishment in 1932. Let us see how *Freedom in the World 2005* (pp. 542–546) describes the state of political rights and civil liberties in Saudi Arabia. The report notes that citizens cannot change their government democratically. There are no elections, and political parties are illegal. Citizens enjoy little effective protection from arbitrary arrest, prolonged pretrial detention, or torture at the hands of security forces. The judiciary is subject to the influence of the royal family and its associates. Freedom of expression is severely restricted. Trade unions, collective bargaining, and strikes are prohibited. Foreign workers are not protected under labor law. Freedom of religion is virtually nonexistent, and women in Saudi Arabia are second-class citizens. The situation is more or less similar in other Arab countries, although democratic deficits are not as severe in all of them (Seznec 2002; Herb 2002; Schwedler 2002). The ultimate constraints of democratization explored in this study explain a part of democratic deficits in the Middle East, but only a part. There is human potential for more democratic systems in the Middle East on the basis of MT and national IQ.

The Solomon Islands have been a democracy since independence in 1978, just like Papua New Guinea. The party system is principally based on interest conflicts between the main islands. Political rights and freedoms are generally respected in practice, but democratic institutions have occasionally been paralyzed by ethnic violence. Corruption is also a problem, which damages the quality of democracy. Benjamin Reilly (2006) explains the success of democracy in Oceanian societies by "centripetalism," which is defined as a continual process of conflict management. The goal is not consensus but accommodation; "centripetalism advocates institutional designs which encourage opportunities for dialogue and negotiation between opposing political forces in the context of electoral competition" (pp. 7, 167). It may be that appropriate institutional selections have helped those countries to maintain a higher level of democratization than expected on the basis of my explanatory variables.

Syria has never been a democracy. In 2006, the country was ruled by President Bashar Assad, who had inherited the job from his father. The ruling National Progressive Front, which is composed of the Baath Party with its coalition partners, is the only legal political organization. Freedom of expression and other political rights and liberties are heavily restricted, but there are some more or less illegal opposition groups.

Tunisia is a similar authoritatively ruled Arab country which has never reached the threshold of democracy. However, some small opposition parties are allowed to take part in parliamentary elections, although they do not have any chances to challenge the hegemony of the ruling Constitutional Democratic Rally. Political rights and freedoms are severely restricted.

United Arab Emirates is an autocratically ruled federation of seven emirates. It is without any democratic institutions and without political parties. Political rights and freedoms are as severely restricted as in Saudi Arabia. Immigrant workers, who constitute a majority of the population (81%), are without any political rights.

Venezuela has been a democracy since 1958 when the two major parties ended their civil war and agreed to share power through elections. Political violence, coup attempts, corruption, and restrictions in political rights and freedoms have weakened the quality of democracy. The Chavez government since 1998 further tightened control over opposition newspapers and television and radio stations and restricted other political rights and freedoms. The three main opposition parties boycotted the 2005 legislative elections, and President Chavez's Fifth Republic Movement won 96 percent of the seats in the National Assembly. President Chavez won the presidential election in December 2006 by 62 percent of the vote, which indicates that there was still a strong opposition.

The country reviews show that 19 of the 33 countries were above the minimum threshold of democracy in 2006. Six of them (the Bahamas, Barbados, Belize, Lebanon, Papua New Guinea, and the Solomon Islands) had always been democracies, and 13 others (Afghanistan, Algeria, Bangladesh, Colombia, Dominican Republic, El Salvador, Honduras, India, Madagascar, Nicaragua, Panama, Paraguay, and Venezuela) had also experienced nondemocratic periods. Thus more than half of the countries were democracies in 2006, which indicates that the level of democratization tends to rise with the level of national IQ. Of the other 14 countries, 13 had never been above the threshold of democracy (Bahrain, Bhutan, Egypt, Iran, Jordan, Libya, Maldives, Morocco, Oman, Saudi Arabia, Syria, Tunisia, and the United Arab Emirates), and, in addition, Pakistan was also below the threshold in 2006. It is remarkable that all these nondemocracies, except Bhutan, are Muslim countries.

The quality of democracy varies greatly within this national IQ category. According to Freedom House ratings, seven countries were Free in 2005 (the Bahamas, Barbados, Belize, Dominican Republic, El Salvador, India, and Panama). The quality of democracy is relatively good in all of them. In 14 "partly free" countries, of which 11 were democracies according to my measures, the quality of democracy was less satisfactory, and it was lowest in 12 "not free" countries (Algeria, Bhutan, Egypt, Iran, Libya, Maldives, Oman, Pakistan, Saudi Arabia, Syria, Tunisia, and the United Arab Emirates). All except Algeria were below the threshold of democracy in 2006.

An interesting question concerns the nature of the other factors which affect the level of democratization. It is easy to note that cultural region matters. Nearly all Middle Eastern and North African countries were nondemocracies in 2006, whereas all Latin American and Caribbean countries were democracies. The concentration of oil resources in the hands of the governments and some characteristics of the Arab culture are local factors which may be connected with the lack of democracy in the Middle East and North Africa. On the basis of national IQ, we could expect a much higher level of democratization in these countries. The existence of democratic systems in all Latin American and Caribbean countries at this level of national IQ is not unexpected from the perspective of national IQ. The level of democratization is approximately in balance with the level of national IQ in nearly all Latin American countries.

Civil wars and ethnic violence have hampered democratization or decreased the quality of democracy, especially in the cases of Afghanistan, Algeria, Bhutan, Colombia, Lebanon, Pakistan, Papua New Guinea, and the Solomon Islands. In most ethnically divided countries, some ethnic groups are discriminated against, which worsens the quality of democratic governance.

In most cases, the quality of democracy is closely related to the level of democratization, but the reviews show that there are also exceptions. Most countries at this level of national IQ insufficiently fulfill various criteria of the quality of democracy, and 14 countries were still below the minimum threshold of democracy in 2006. Because of the strong relationship between national IQ and the level of democratization, it would be unrealistic to expect any drastic rise in the average level of democratization or quality of democracy. However, significant changes in particular cases are possible. In general, large negative residuals (see Table 7.1) predict a rise in the level and quality of democracy, whereas large positive residuals imply that a decline in the level of democracy is more probable than a rise.

CHAPTER 13

Countries at National IQ Level 4 (85–89)

National IQ varies from 85 to 89 in the following 26 countries: Azerbaijan, Bolivia, Brazil, Burma (Myanmar), Costa Rica, Cuba, East Timor, Ecuador, Fiji, Guyana, Indonesia, Iraq, Kuwait, Laos, Mauritius, Mexico, Montenegro, Peru, the Philippines, Serbia, Surinam, Tajikistan, Trinidad and Tobago, Turkmenistan, Uzbekistan, and Yemen. The number of tropical and semitropical countries is smaller than in the category of countries at national IQ level 3. Regionally this group is dominated by Latin American and Caribbean (10) and Central Asian and Southeast Asian countries (9). Azerbaijan, Montenegro, and Serbia are European countries; Iraq, Kuwait, and Yemen, Middle Eastern countries; and Mauritius, a sub-Saharan African country.

The mean of ID-2006 is for this IQ category of 26 countries clearly higher (14.2) than for the three previous categories, and the means of PR (political rights) (3.9) and CL (civil liberties) (3.7) have slightly decreased, which implies a small rise in the average level of democracy (see Table 8.4). More than half of these countries (15) were above the ID threshold of democracy in 2006, and nearly half (11) were free in 2005 on the basis of Freedom House ratings. The standard deviations of the three variables (Table 8.4) show that the variation in the level and quality of democracy was in this group approximately as large as in the previous national IQ category. The level of democratization was more than one standard deviation better in Brazil, Indonesia, and Serbia, and more than one standard deviation lower in Burma, Cuba, Fiji, Kuwait, Laos, Turkmenistan, and Uzbekistan (see Table 6.1).

In the previous section, I presented some general comments on the problems of the quality of democracy in Latin American countries. The same comments also apply to the Latin American countries of this national IQ category. Most people seem to support democracy in Latin America. Juan J. Linz and Alfred Stepan (1996, pp. 221–223) refer to the results of opinion surveys which indicate that most people in Uruguay (80%), Argentina (76%), and Chile (52%), and nearly half in Brazil (41%), agree with the statement that "democracy is preferable to any other form of government." More people also agree with the statement that "democracy allows the solution of problems" than with the opposite statement that "democracy does not solve problems." Marta Lagos (2003) notes on the basis of opinion surveys that cover all Latin American countries that from 1996 through 2002, there was little variation in the overall level of support for democracy. Regionwide, the support figure varied between 48 and 62 percent, which indicates that people support democracy in Latin America, although not unanimously (cf. Espíndola 2002). However, it should be noted that nearly all Latin American countries democratized quite recently and that democratic institutions are still unstable in many countries. Jennifer L. McCoy (2006) speaks of democratic crisis in the Americas in 1990–2005 when more than a dozen presidents were removed prematurely.

The process of democratization started in all Central Asian countries after the collapse of the Soviet Union in 1991, but they were not able to cross the threshold of democracy. Political institutions have become adapted to the concentration of economic power resources in the hands of the governments. The presidency overshadows legislative and judicial branches of government. Political rights and civil liberties are restricted. Opposition parties are banned or repressed (see, for example, Bremmer and Taras 1997; Karatnycky et al. 2001; Glenn 2003).

The group of Southeast Asian and Pacific countries includes both democracies (Indonesia and the Philippines) and nondemocracies (Burma, Fiji, and Laos). Benjamin Reilly (2006, p. 10) notes that the Pacific region stands out "as something of a democratic oasis not just in comparison to East Asia, but in the post-colonial world more generally."

Azerbaijan was below the minimum threshold of democracy during the first years of its independence (1991–2004), but rose slightly, perhaps temporarily, above the threshold in the 2005 parliamentary elections, which, according to Leila Alieva (2006), were fraudulent. The fact that President Ilham Aliyev received 78 percent of the vote in the 2003 presidential election may reflect the state of democracy in Azerbaijan better. For example, hundreds of opposition leaders and activists were detained by police in the connection with the 2003 presidential election. Freedom of expression as well as freedom of assembly are restricted in practice, and the judiciary is corrupt and inefficient. I think that the quality of democracy was considerably lower than the level of democratization (ID-2006) indicates. According to Freedom House's classification, Azerbaijan was a "not free" country in 2005 (*Freedom in the World 2006*, p. 57).

In *Bolivia,* periods of autocratic rule have alternated with attempts to establish democratic institutions. Since 1982 Bolivia has remained continually above the threshold of democracy. Presidential and legislative elections are highly competitive, and no party has achieved permanent dominance. Political rights and freedoms are generally respected in practice, but the quality of democracy suffers from political violence and also from corruption and inefficiency in the judiciary. The position of indigenous communities has improved. Evo Morales, who was elected president in 2005, is the first indigenous president of Bolivia (see *The Economist,* December 16, 2006, pp. 52–53).

Brazil has been above the threshold of democracy since 1988. Before that, democratic regimes alternated with military governments. Democratic institutions seem to have become stabilized in Brazil. Its multiparty system is highly competitive and the level of electoral participation is relatively high. There are, of course, deficiencies in the quality of democracy. For example, the judiciary is weak, and Brazil's "police are among the world's most violent and corrupt, and they systematically resort to torture to extract confessions from prisoners" (*Freedom in the World 2005*, pp. 100–101). The ethnic diversity of Brazil's population constitutes a local factor which has fragmented the party system and intensified party competition. The much higher than expected level of democratization (ID) is principally due to a high degree of electoral participation.

Burma (Myanmar) had democratic institutions in the 1950s and was above the threshold of democracy in 1960–61, but the 1962 military coup dropped it below the threshold. Since then the country has been ruled by military governments. Civil wars against separatist ethnic insurgencies in various parts of the country had strengthened the position of the military so much that the civilian government was no longer able to control it. Political parties were banned, there were no elections, political rights and freedoms, including press freedom, were strictly restricted, the judiciary was not independent, and the army continued its struggle against separatist ethnic minorities. Several million Burmese fled to neighboring countries. However, despite all restrictions, strong opposition groups demonstrated and demanded democratization of the system (cf. Thein 2006).

Costa Rica is probably the most stabilized democracy in Latin America. According to my measures, it has been a democracy continually since 1950, although it was slightly below the Participation threshold in 1950–52. The quality of democracy may be the best in Latin American countries. Deficits in the function of its democratic institutions have been relatively small, although corruption is still a major problem (*Freedom in the World 2006*, pp. 85–186). Whites constitute a large majority of the population, which may explain the success of democracy in Costa Rica.

Cuba is an exceptional authoritarian country in Latin America. It was above the threshold of democracy in 1940–51, but a military coup in 1952 ended its democratic experiment, and it has been under Fidel Castro's communist regime since 1959. The Cuban Communist Party is the only legal party in the country, and freedoms of the press and of assembly and association are strictly limited. On the basis of national IQ, we can expect a much more democratic system in Cuba. Its highly deviating position is due to the survival of its communist system.

East Timor achieved independence in 2002 under the protection of the United Nations after a long and bloody war of independence against Indonesian troops. Democratic institutions were established, but in the first elections the support of the independence movement (Freitlin) was so strong that the country remained slightly below the Competition threshold of democracy. The government generally respects freedom of assembly and association, but it has restricted freedom of the press. The police and the military have not been able to provide adequate security and order (*Freedom in the World 2006*, pp. 221–223). In 2006, violent demonstrations and clashes took place in the capital, and the government had to invite foreign peacekeeping contingents to restore order (Banks et al. 2007, p. 1229). In such circumstances, the quality of democratic governance suffered. However, East Timor crossed the threshold of democracy in the 2007 presidential and legislative elections (see *Keesing's 2007*, pp. 47933, 47981).

Ecuador is a similar case to Bolivia, and has been clearly above the threshold of democracy since 1984. Various irregularities in the function of democratic institutions and coup attempts indicate that democracy is still fragile and the quality of democracy low. Indigenous people are discriminated against and are "frequent victims of abuse by military officers working in league with large landowners during disputes over land" (*Freedom in the World 2005*, p. 206). Indigenous people have their own political organizations but are still underrepresented in the National Congress (Banks et al. 2007, pp. 356–358).

Fiji has been a democracy since independence in 1970, except during short periods of military rule. Democratic competition in Fiji is based on deep ethnic cleavage between indigenous Fijians and Indo-Fijians, but this same cleavage has caused several military coups and mutinies, "fuelled by indigenous Fijian fears that the country's minority ethnic Indians, who dominate the economy, would also dominate politically" (*Chronicle of Parliamentary Elections 2002*, p. 61). Democratic institutions were modeled to support the dominance of indigenous Fijians, which means that political rights and freedoms have been to some extent restricted. The latest military coup took place December 5, 2006, and Fiji dropped below the threshold of democracy (*Keesing's 2006*, pp. 47631–47632).

Guyana is an ethnically deeply divided country in which East Indians and blacks constitute the largest ethnic (racial) groups. Politics has been characterized by sometimes violent competition between the major ethnic groups, but democratic institutions have survived since independence in 1966, although the country has not always been above the Competition threshold of democracy. Political rights and freedoms are relatively well respected, but a very high crime rate and political murders weaken the quality of democracy. Tension between the major racial groups continues, as the following example shows: "Racial polarization has seriously eroded Guyana law enforcement: Many Indo-Guyanese say they are victims of Afro-Guyanese criminals at the same time that they are largely ignored by the predominantly Afro-Guyanese police; many Afro-Guyanese claim that the police are manipulated by the government for its own purposes" (*Freedom in the World 2005*, p.

272). Political parties are ethnically based, which intensifies political competition and raises the degree of electoral participation.

Indonesia has been a democracy for only a short period, having crossed the threshold of democracy in the competitive legislative elections in 1999 and more clearly in the first direct presidential election in 2004. These elections were free and fair, but there are other deficiencies in the quality of democracy. Press freedom is restricted in practice, corruption is endemic, including the judiciary, and civilian control over the military is only partial. Transparency International estimated that "during his 32-year rule Suharto and his family embezzled some US$35 billion from the state" (*Keesing's 2006*, p. 47256; see also Webber 2006, p. 408–409). These data illustrate the extent of corruption. Separatist insurgencies in various parts of the country continue. Meredith L. Weiss (2007, p. 36) argues that "the depth and scope of democratization remain uncertain" in Indonesia. I agree. Douglas Webber (2006) describes Indonesia as a patrimonial democracy, in which holders of public offices exploit their positions primarily for their personal rather than "universalistic" ends. However, the emergence of a strong multiparty system supports the survival of democratic institutions.

Iraq has never been a democracy. A military coup deposed the king in 1958, after which Iraq was ruled by military governments until the U.S. led its coalition's invasion in 2003, which deposed Saddam Hussein's regime. The emergence of strong democratic strivings and many competing parties in Iraq after the destruction of Saddam Hussein's repressive regime indicates that there is human potential for democratization, but unsolved ethnic conflicts between the major groups halted the process of democratization, and the country drifted to civil war. The American occupation forces were unable to suppress terrorism and to maintain peace. Consequently, the survival of established democratic institutions is uncertain (cf. Filali-Ansary 2003; Makiya 2003; Stepan and Robertson 2003; Mujani and Little 2004; Manning 2006). In 2006, Iraq was, according to my measures, only slightly below the threshold of democracy, but the struggle for power was so violent that democratic institutions could not function properly. The government did not control the whole country.

Kuwait has been ruled by a royal family since independence in

1961. The emir shares legislative power with a National Assembly, which is elected by a limited popular vote. The emir still has overriding power in Kuwait, political parties are banned, press freedom is limited, and immigrant workers, who constitute a majority of the population (60%), are without any political rights and freedoms. On the basis of national IQ, we could expect a more democratic system. The existence of several semi-legal political groupings indicates popular pressure for democratization (Banks et al. 2007, pp. 682–683).

Laos has been ruled by authoritarian regimes since its independence in 1953. The country suffered from a long civil war between the royalist government and the Communist Pathet Lao guerrillas, who finally seized power in 1975. The ruling Lao People's Revolutionary Party is the only legal party, all media are controlled by the state, corruption is widespread, and the courts are controlled by the ruling party. There is no democracy, but this does not necessarily disturb ordinary Laotians in their daily lives. It is remarkable that "none of the interviewees expressed their concern on corruption, human rights, and democracy" in the AsiaBarometer Survey of 2004 (Douangngeune 2006, p. 145). The lack of democracy in Laos is due to its communist system, just like in Cuba. The dominance of the Lao People's Revolutionary Party is complete; there is no organized political opposition.

Mauritius has been a democracy since independence in 1968. The racial and religious diversity of its population has supported democracy by providing a natural basis for a multiparty system. Indo-Mauritians constitute a clear majority (68%). Political rights and freedoms are respected in practice. Mauritius provides an example of the success of democracy and of the relatively high quality of democracy in an ethnically divided society. However, there is tension between ethnic groups.

In *Mexico* it was difficult to establish democracy despite its neighborhood with the United States. Historically, the country was ruled by *caudillos* and dictators since independence in 1821 and finally by the Institutional Revolutionary Party (PRI) until the democratic breakthrough in the 1988 presidential election, in which the support of the ruling party's presidential candidate dropped to 50.7 percent. Since then, political rights and freedoms have been extended, and a dominant party system was transformed into a multiparty system. The quality of democracy has improved significantly in Mexico, although corruption is still rampant, indigenous people are discriminated against in some parts of the country, and the military may not be completely under civilian control. The strong multiparty system supports democratic institutions.

Montenegro was a part of the former Yugoslavia and then a part of the state of Serbia and Montenegro in 2003–2005, which ceased to exist in 2006 when Montenegro selected independence (see Darmanovic 2007). In this study, data for Serbia and Montenegro are given separately since 2003. Montenegro has clearly been above the threshold of democracy since the beginning, and the quality of democracy is relatively good. The fragmented party system maintains a relatively high index of democratization (ID) value.

Peru is a typical Latin American country which was historically ruled by *caudillos*, military governments, and authoritarian presidents, and in which democratization took place only recently (1980). Political rights and freedoms are relatively extensive and respected in practice, but there are many deficits in the quality of democracy. It has been difficult for the government to maintain internal peace and the rule of law. Tens of thousands of people (mainly Amerindians) were killed in the struggle against the Maoist Shining Path guerrillas. More than 20 parties have participated in legislative elections, which indicates something about the extent of political rights and liberties.

The Philippines have been clearly above the threshold of democracy since the collapse of President Marcos' dictatorship in 1986. Political instability continues, but legislative and presidential elections have been held regularly. There have been many military coup attempts. Political rights and freedoms are extensive, but there are problems in the quality of democracy. Corruption is rife in business and government, and "a few dozen powerful families continue to play an overarching role in politics and hold an outsized share of land and corporate wealth" (*Freedom in the World 2005*, p. 503). For example, former President Estrada "was accused of plundering the proceeds of tobacco taxes whilst he was in office and of accepting large bribes from racketeers running illegal lotteries" (*Keesing's 2006*, p. 47417). Further, the rule of law has not been respected in many cases, and the Islamic insurgency continues in the southern provinces. However, according to the AsiaBarometer Survey of 2004, most respondents were very satisfied or somewhat satisfied with their political rights and freedoms (Yu-Jose 2006, p. 257).

The Philippines' higher than expected level of democratization (ID) is due institutionally to the country's extremely fragmented party system (see Banks et al. 2007, pp. 978–984).

Serbia, a part of the former Yugoslavia, has been a democracy since the establishment of the state of Serbia and Montenegro in 2003. There is a highly competitive multiparty system in Serbia, and political rights and freedoms are extensive. A major problem concerns the conflict with Albanian separatists in Kosovo, who demanded complete independence, which demand was unacceptable to Serbia. In April 2006, Montenegro's voters chose separation from Serbia, and both countries became independent states (Banks et al. 2007, p.1077).

Surinam is in many respects as deeply ethnically divided a democracy as Guyana. Surinam achieved independence in 1975 as a democracy, but a military coup led by Desi Boutersee occurred in 1980. Political opposition was brutally suppressed, but popular pressure forced Boutersee to accept democratic elections in 1991. Democratic institutions were re-established and have survived since then. Political parties are principally based on ethnic groups, and no party has achieved permanent dominance. Press freedom and other political rights and freedoms are extensive and generally respected in practice, but ethnic tension continues and characterizes politics in Surinam. One weakness in the quality of democracy concerns the position of indigenous and tribal peoples, which have been discriminated against. The ethnic diversity of the population is a local factor which has furthered the fragmentation of the party system and intense political competition.

Tajikistan is a former Soviet republic which achieved independence in 1991. In 2006, the country was still below the Competition threshold of democracy. There are some opposition parties, but President Imomali Rakhmonov and his Democratic People's Party dominate politics. The press is not permitted to criticize the president or his family. The media outlets of opposition groups are harassed. Freedom of assembly is limited by complicated requirements that restrict the right to hold political gatherings. The judiciary is subservient to the executive branch. Police frequently abuse detainees during arrest and interrogation. Corruption is rampant. However, there is human potential for a more democratic political systems. The inheritance of the Soviet economic and political structures seems to explain the persistence of an authoritarian system in Tajikistan, but national IQ presupposes a clearly more democratic system.

Trinidad and Tobago is the third deeply ethnically divided Caribbean country in this national IQ category. Trinidad and Tobago has continually been above the threshold of democracy, except in 1971–1975, since independence in 1962. The two major parties represent principally blacks (People's National Movement, PNM) and East Indians (United National Congress, UNC). The PNM has been in power more often than the UNC, but it did not achieve permanent dominance. Political rights and freedoms are extensive and respected in practice, but there is corruption in the police force and racial tension between the parties is high.

Turkmenistan is the least democratic of the five former Central Asian Soviet republics. President Suparmurat Niyazov's power was absolute, and his Democratic Party of Turkmenistan, the former Communist Party, was the country's only legal political party. Freedom of the press and other political rights and freedoms are severely restricted. The judicial system is subservient to the president, and corruption is widespread. Besides, the government "places significant restrictions on academic freedom, with schools increasingly being used to indoctrinate, rather than educate, students" (*Freedom in the World 2005*, p. 655). President Niyazov died in December 2006, but it did not change the country's autocratic political system (see *The Economist*, January 6, 2007, p. 45).

Uzbekistan has also remained below the threshold of democracy since its independence in 1991. The former Communist Party leader Ismail Karimov was elected president in 1991 and was still in power in 2006. There are hardly any opposition parties. Freedom of the press and other political rights and freedoms are strictly restricted. Corruption is widespread. In the AsiaBarometer Survey of 2003, most respondents (82.1%) supported the view "that ordinary people cannot influence political decisions or the actions of government" (Dadabaev 2005, p. 228; Dadabaev 2006). Uzbekistan's national IQ implies, as in the case of Turkmenistan, that there is human potential for a more democratic political system. The survival of socialist economic and administrative structures is a local factor which explains the lack of democracy in these Central Asian countries.

Yemen has never reached the threshold of democracy, although there have been elections since 1990. Power is concentrated in the hands of the ruling General People's Congress (GPC). There are some legal opposition parties, which is rare in Arab countries, but their chances of challenging the dominance of the GPC and President Saleh were quite limited. Yemenis enjoy some freedom of assembly and the right to form associations, but the state maintains a monopoly over the media, and journalists face threats of violence, death, and arbitrary arrest. There are some democratic characteristics in Yemen's political system, but the quality of democracy remains low.

The country reviews show that 15 of the 26 countries were above the minimum threshold of democracy in 2006. Four of them (Costa Rica, Mauritius, Montenegro, and Serbia) had always been democracies, and 11 others had sometimes been below the threshold (Azerbaijan, Bolivia, Brazil, Ecuador, Guyana, Indonesia, Mexico, Peru, the Philippines, Surinam, and Trinidad and Tobago). Eight countries had never been above the threshold of democracy (East Timor, Iraq, Kuwait, Laos, Tajikistan, Turkmenistan, Uzbekistan, and Yemen), and, in addition to them, Cuba, Fiji, and Burma were below the threshold in 2006. The average level of democratization continued its rise with the level of national IQ.

According to Freedom House ratings, 11 of these countries were free in 2005 (Bolivia, Brazil, Costa Rica, Indonesia, Mauritius, Mexico, Montenegro, Peru, Serbia, Surinam, and Trinidad and Tobago). According to my measures, all these countries were democracies in 2006, the quality of democracy seems to have done quite well in most of them. The other four democracies (Azerbaijan, Ecuador, Guyana, and the Philippines), experienced more problems in the quality of democracy.

The quality and level of democracy varied greatly from relatively highly democratic countries to autocratic dictatorships. It was possible to indicate some local factors which may explain at least part of this variation. Nearly all of the democracies with the highest ID values are ethnically divided countries. This shows that democracy is not impossible in ethnically divided countries and that ethnic cleavages can adapt to democratic politics. These countries have provided a natural social basis for competing politics and for a multiparty system. Political leaders in such countries have learned to compromise and agree on the rules of power sharing through elections. The group of nondemocracies also includes some deeply ethnically divided countries, but ethnic groups in these countries have not yet learned to compromise. Ethnic violence has characterized politics in Burma and Iraq. In Fiji, ethnic conflict led to a military coup in 2006. In Kuwait, the immigrant workers who constitute a majority of the population are without citizenship and any political rights. Besides, the concentration of oil resources in the hands of the traditional ruling family has hampered democratization.

The nature of an economic system seems to be another local explanatory factor. In the cases of socialist and former socialist countries (Cuba, Laos, Tajikistan, Turkmenistan, and Uzbekistan), the inheritance of socialist political and economic structures provides a satisfactory explanation for the lack of democracy. In the case of Yemen, the inheritance of traditional authoritarian structures has hampered democratization.

As in the countries in the first three national IQ categories, there are many deficiencies in the quality of of democratic governance. Deficits are, of course, most significant in nondemocracies, but there are also various deficits in democracies. There may be restrictions in freedom of the press as well as in freedoms of assembly and association. Corruption is a serious problem in many countries. Some deficits are related to political violence, separatist insurgencies, or discrimination against ethnic minorities.

CHAPTER 14

Countries at National IQ Level 5 (90–94)

National IQ varies from 90 to 94 in the following 22 countries: Albania, Argentina, Armenia, Bosnia and Herzegovina, Brunei, Bulgaria, Cambodia, Chile, Croatia, Cyprus, Georgia, Greece, Ireland, Kazakhstan, Kyrgyzstan, Lithuania, Macedonia, Malaysia, Romania, Thailand, Turkey, and Vietnam. The number of tropical and semitropical countries is limited to five Southeast Asian countries. Most of these countries (13) constitute a geographically continuous group of countries extending from the Balkans via Turkey to Central Asia. The five Southeast Asian countries constitute another geographically homogeneous group. Argentina and Chile are Latin American countries inhabited by descendants of European immigrants. Ireland and Lithuania are two European countries outside the Balkans. Their place in this category may be due to measurement errors in national IQs, which are several index points lower than in their neighboring countries. Of these 22 countries, 15 are European or European inhabited Latin American countries, 2 are Central Asian countries, and 5 are Southeast Asian countries.

The mean of the index of democratization (ID-2006) (19.3) for this category of 22 countries is much higher than for previous categories, and the means of political rights (PR-2005) (3.2) and civil liberties (CL-2005) (2.9) are clearly lower than for previous IQ categories (see Table 8.4). These changes in group means indicate the rising level of democratization. The standard deviations of the three variables (Table

8.4) show that the variation in the level and quality of democracy remained approximately as large as in the previous national IQ categories. The level of democratization was more than one standard deviation (12.6) above the mean of this IQ category (19.2) in Argentina, Cyprus, Greece, and Ireland, and more than one standard deviation below in Brunei, Cambodia, Georgia, Kazakhstan, Kyrgyzstan, Thailand, and Vietnam (see Table 6.1).

Albania has been above the threshold of democracy since 1991, when the communist system collapsed and Albania's political system was transformed into a multiparty democracy. There are weaknesses in the quality of democracy. For example, the 2005 People's Assembly elections "were judged to have complied only partially with international standards. Observers noted flawed procedures, including multiple voting and violations of secrecy" (*Freedom in the World 2006*, p. 23). The fact that 57 parties registered for the 2005 legislative elections indicates the fragmentation of the party system but also the existence of political freedom (Banks et al. 2007, pp. 16–20).

Argentina's political system has been democratic since 1983. Before that Argentina experienced only short periods of democracy between much longer periods of authoritarian regimes and military governments. Political rights and freedoms are generally respected, although it would be possible to indicate various deficiencies in the function of political institutions. For example, arbitrary arrests and abuse by police are rarely punished in civil courts owing to intimidation of witnesses and judges, and indigenous people are without full civil rights (*Freedom in the World 2005*, pp. 39–41).

Armenia has been above the threshold of democracy since independence in 1991, but there have been violent incidents in politics and irregularities in elections. However, opposition parties are able to function and to take part in elections. The quality of democracy suffers from various restrictions in political rights and liberties and from bribery and nepotism.

Bosnia and Herzegovina's (independent 1991) democratic system emerged as a consequence of the 1995 Dayton peace accord., which ended a brutal civil war. Political parties are nearly completely based on ethnic groups. Because of deep ethnic (religious) animosities, the survival of the combined state is not yet sure (cf. Manning 2006). Political rights and freedoms have been generally respected, but in practice there are various restrictions. For example, corruption "in the judiciary, police forces, and civil service forms a considerable obstacle to establishing the rule of law in Bosnia-Herzegovina" (*Freedom in the World* 2005, p. 94).

Brunei (independent 1984) is an autocratically ruled oil-producing country without any significant democratic institutions. Executive and legislative powers are in the hands of the sultan, who controls the country's oil resources. Political rights and freedoms are strictly limited, and ethnic Chinese people are without full citizenship status. Brunei is a highly deviant country, for its national IQ presupposes a fully democratic system. I think that the sultan's absolute control over the country's oil resources provides a local explanation for Brunei's lack of democracy. The government does not need tax revenues from the people. The fact that the AsiaBarometer 2004 had to "omit questions that touch upon the political environment and institutions of Brunei" (Sulaiman and Hotta 2006, pp. 261–262) illustrates the authoritarian nature of the country's political system.

Bulgaria and *Romania* have been multiparty democracies since 1990 when the communist system collapsed. Political parties learned to share power through democratic competition. Political rights and freedoms are extensive and respected in practice. However, the Roma population remains subjected to discrimination, police violence, and segregation in both countries.

Cambodia (independent 1953) has suffered from civil wars and various authoritarian regimes, especially the bloody rule of the Khmer Rouge in 1975–79. By the time their regime collapsed after a Vietnamese invasion in early 1979, "approximately 1.7 million Cambodians had died of starvation, overwork, and disease, or had been executed" (Un 2006, p. 156). The first free parliamentary elections were held in 1993 under the protection of the UN peacekeeping forces. There are serious deficits in the quality of democracy. The Cambodian People's Party (CPP) usurped hegemonic power by violent means in 1997. Kheang Un (2006) notes that the "conflict significantly affected the democratization of Cambodia, dealing a severe blow to its newfound democracy, and leaving many to fear that the country would regress back to authoritarianism" (p. 157). Since then elections have been marred by irregularities. Opposition parties are not fully free to function. Most political rights and freedoms are to some extent restricted in practice. Duncan McCargo (2005) comes to the conclusion that there "can be no liberalization of Cambodian politics until the CPP's formidable network of power and patronage unravels, which is unlikely to happen while Hun Sen is still on the scene" (p. 110). In 2006 Cambodia was still below the minimum threshold of democracy.

Chile has been a democracy since 1989, when Augusto Pinochet's military regime was deposed and the country re-established democratic institutions through elections. Since then democracy has become stabilized.

Croatia has been above the threshold of democracy since 1992, but the quality of democracy was poor during the ethnic civil war between the Croat and Serb communities in 1991–95. Since then the quality of democracy has improved, although Serbs are still discriminated against. According to a U.S. State Department report released in 2003, "severe discrimination continues against ethnic Serbs and, at times, other minorities in a wide number of areas, including the administration of justice, employment, housing, and freedom of movement" (*Freedom in the World 2005*, p. 175).

Cyprus has been an excellent democracy since independence in 1960, but the division of the island into Greek and Turkish sections is still an unsolved problem.

Georgia was a democracy since 1991 when it achieved independence from the Soviet Union, but it dropped below the Competition threshold of democracy, probably only temporarily, in the 2004 presidential election. The quality of democracy suffers from ethnic insurgencies in Abkhazia, Ajaria, and South Ossetia. Georgia has not been able to solve these separatist problems. Press freedom and freedoms of assembly and association are to some extent restricted in practice. Corruption is widespread. For example, "Students frequently pay bribes to receive high marks or pass entrance examinations" (*Freedom in the World 2005*, p. 247).

Greece has been a multiparty democracy since 1974, when the latest military regime was deposed. The quality of democracy is in most respects good, although "members of some minority religions face social discrimination and legal barriors," and the Roma community continues to face considerable discrimination (*Freedom in the World 2006*, pp. 285–286).

Ireland has been a democracy since independence in 1922, and the quality of democracy is among the best in the world.

Kazakhstan is a former Soviet republic which became independent in 1991. It adopted some democratic institutions, but the country remained below the threshold of democracy. Nursultan Nazarbayev, who was the first secretary of the Kazakh Communist Party at the end of the Soviet period, was elected president in 1991, 1995, 1999, and 2005 without serious competition. There are some opposition parties, but the government has restricted their functions. Press freedom and freedoms of assembly and association are also restricted. For example, the 2004 parliamentary elections were marred by irregularities (*Chronicle of Parliamentary Elections* 2004, p. 191). Ethnic minority groups, including Russians, have complained of discrimination in employment and education. Corruption is widespread at all levels of government and business. According to survey studies, more than half of the population prefer democracy over dictatorship (Rose 2002, p. 110; Dababaev 2006), but Kazakhstan seems to still have a long way to go to achieve democracy.

Kyrgyzstan is another former Central Asian Soviet republic. Askar Akayev ruled Kyrgyzstan as the president without serious opposition until violent demonstrations in March 2005 forced him to flee to Russia and to resign. However, the overthrow of Akayev's authoritarian regime did not transform Kyrgyzstan into a democracy. The former opposition leader Kurmanbek Bakiyev was elected president by 89.5 percent of the vote in July 2005. The country remained below the threshold of democracy, but it is plausible to expect that the quality of democracy will improve (cf. Radnitz 2006).

Lithuania has been a democracy since independence in 1991. The party system is not yet stabilized, but otherwise democratic institutions function well. The problem of ethnic minorities was solved by extending citizenship to all those born within Lithuania's borders.

Macedonia has been a democracy since independence in 1991. Ethnic conflict with the sizeable Albanian minority diminishes the quality of democracy. Political rights and freedoms are generally respected, but the judicial system is claimed to be corrupted and incompetent. According to a report on the 2006 legislative elections: "Whilst the campaign period had been marred by violence and ethnic tensions, the elections were largely incident free" (*Keesing's 2006*, p. 47378).

Malaysia is an ethnically deeply divided Southeast Asian country which has been above the threshold of democracy since 1959. Democracy's success is based on the dominance of the ruling cross-ethnic National Front. Other parties are allowed to compete in elections, but the British first-past-the-post electoral system supports the dominance of the ruling party. The government has limited freedom of expression as well as freedoms of assembly and association. For example, the police were used in recent years "to jail mainstream politicians, alleged Islamic militants, trade unionists, suspected Communist activists," and many others (*Freedom in the World 2005*, p. 399). According to the AsiaBarometer Survey 2004, 22–31 percent of respondents were dissatisfied with their political rights (Saravanamuttu 2006, p. 206). The quality of democracy is defective at several points. According to Meredith L. Weiss (2007, p. 30), Malaysia has a "competitive electoral authoritarian regime" (cf. Thirkell-White 2006). Thomas B. Pepinsky (2007, p. 126) says that without "true institutional reform, Malaysians must always fear that while repression and coercion may abate in the short term, they lie perennially ready to hand as the last arguments of threatened power-holders intent on saving an authoritarian status quo."

Thailand has been less successful from the perspective of democracy than Malaysia. Since 1932 civilian and military governments have alternated. Because of the overriding power of the king (and the military behind him), it was difficult for Thailand to reach my thresholds of democracy, although people were able to change their government through elections. Thailand was above the threshold of democracy in 1997–2004. Freedom of expression is limited. In particular, it is not allowed to say anything critical on the position or policies of the king. Official corruption is widespread, involving both bureaucrats and law enforcement officials (cf. Khamchoo and Stern 2006; Case 2007). After a military coup in September 2006, most political rights and freedoms were cancelled temporarily (see *The Economist*, September 23, 2006, pp. 27–28).

Turkey has been above the threshold of democracy nearly continuously since 1950. Only short periods of military rule have interrupted democratic politics. In 2006, the position of the military was still exceptionally strong in Turkey. There are some restrictions on freedom of the media as well as freedoms of assembly and association. For example, "fines, arrests, and imprisonment are regularly allotted to media and journalists who, for example, criticize the military or portray the Kurds in too positive of a light" (*Freedom in the World 2005*, p. 648). The greatest problem, from the perspective of democracy concerns the position of the Kurdish minority (see, for example, *The Economist*, December 16, 2006, pp. 39–40).

Vietnam is ruled by the hegemonic Communist Party of Vietnam, and the country has never reached the threshold of democracy. Opposition parties are not allowed to function, and all political rights and freedoms are strictly restricted. However, as a consequence of economic reforms started in the late 1980s, the economic freedom of people increased and the state control slackened. Political rights and freedoms also improved slightly. Do Manh Hong (2006) describes this change by pointing out "nowadays, people in Vietnam can demonstrate against a decision of the government (mainly at the local level but not at the central level), although the government does restrict some for their dissension" (p. 100). Vietnam's national IQ presupposes a fully democratic system, from which Vietnam is still far away.

The country reviews show that the number of democracies (15) has risen significantly at this national IQ level. Five countries (Armenia, Cyprus, Ireland, Lithuania, and Macedonia) have always been above the threshold of democracy, and ten others were above the threshold in 2006 (Albania, Argentina, Bosnia and Herzegovina, Bulgaria, Chile, Croatia, Greece, Malaysia, Romania, and Turkey). Five countries (Brunei, Cambodia, Kazakhstan, Kyrgyzstan, and Vietnam) have never been democracies, and two others (Georgia and Thailand) were below the threshold in 2006. The quality of democracy was relatively good at least in Argentina, Bulgaria, Chile, Croatia, Cyprus, Greece, Ireland, Lithuania, and Romania, which, according to Freedom House ratings, were "free" countries in 2005. On the other hand, the quality of democracy was certainly poor in Brunei, Cambodia, Kazakhstan, and Vietnam, which were "not free" countries on the basis of Freedom House ratings.

The quality of democracy varies greatly between democracies and nondemocracies, and especially between large positive and negative outliers. It was possible to indicate some local or temporary factors which may explain a part of these deviations. Argentina's large positive deviation was a temporary consequence of the 2003 presidential election, in which the degree of Competition rose exceptionally high (see Chapter 6). A high level of socioeconomic development and resource distribution (IPR) provide an explanation for the much higher than expected level of democratization in Cyprus, Greece, and Ireland. Of the seven large negative outliers, Brunei is a traditionally ruled oil-producing country, Georgia and Thailand are probably only temporarily negative outliers, and four other large negative outliers (Cambodia, Kazakhstan, Kyrgyzstan, and Vietnam) are former or contemporary communist/socialist countries.

CHAPTER 15

Countries at National IQ Level 6 (95–99)

National IQ varies from 95 to 99 in the following 26 countries: Australia, Belarus, Belgium, Canada, the Czech Republic, Denmark, Estonia, Finland, France, Germany, Hungary, Israel, Latvia, Malta, Moldova, New Zealand, Poland, Portugal, Russia, Slovakia, Slovenia, Spain, Sweden, Ukraine, the United States, and Uruguay. They constitute a geographically continuous northern group of countries. Australia, New Zealand, and Uruguay are in the temperate zone in the south. It is remarkable that all these countries, except Israel, are European or European offshoot countries.

The mean of the index of democratization (ID-2006) (30.3) is for this category of 26 countries approximately three times higher than for the first three national IQ categories, and the means of political rights (PR-2005)(1.6) and civil liberties (CL-2005) (1.5) are drastically lower than for previous IQ categories (see Table 8.4). All of these countries except Belarus were democracies in 2006. On the basis of Freedom House ratings, 23 of them were free, one partly free, and two not free in 2005. The rise in the level and quality of democracy seems to have accelerated when national IQ rises above 95. The standard deviations of the three variables (Table 8.4) show that the level and quality of democracy vary relatively less in this category of IQ than in five previous categories. The level of democratization (ID-2006) was more than one standard deviation higher than the average (30.3) in

Belgium, Denmark, and Sweden, and more than one standard deviation lower in Belarus, Poland, Russia, and Slovakia.

There are, of course, various deficits in all democracies, even in economically highly developed Western democracies, but previously deficits were much more serious than nowadays (for the historical evolution of democratic systems, see Sternberger et al. 1969). It would be possible to find various shortages in European democracies, although their shortcomings are relatively small compared to democratic deficits in other parts of the world. Some qualitative differences are due to electoral laws. The nature of democratic systems in Europe and European offshoot countries has been described and analyzed in innumerable studies. Such studies include references to various defects in the function of democratic institutions (see, for example, Dahl 1967; Daalder and Mair 1983; Grofman and Lijphart 1986; Kaase 1986; Mair 1990; Blondel 1995; Schmidt 2000; Karvonen and Kuhnle 2001).

In the 20th century, Europe experienced two extreme deviations from the regular pattern of democratization. The Bolsheviks usurped power in Russia in 1917 and established an autocratic communist system, which interrupted the process of democratization in Russia for 70 years. After World War II, the socialist experiment was extended to Eastern and Central European countries which belonged to the Soviet Union's sphere of interest. The seizure of power by Fascists in Italy in the 1920s and by Nazis in Germany in the 1930s interrupted democratic development in those countries and also in some other European countries until the end of the World War II. Communist, Fascist, and Nazi systems were based on the extensive use of violence, political rights and liberties were curtailed or completely abolished, opponents of the systems were terrorized, and millions of people were killed, especially in the Soviet Union and in the countries occupied by Nazi Germany (see Seton-Watson 1964; Aspaturian 1968; Chkhikvadze 1969; Polonsky 1975; Linz and Stepan 1978; Brown 1988; Berg-Schlosser and Mitchell 2000, 2002). These European aberrations into cruel autocracies contradict my theory of democratization and indicate that sometimes even highly intelligent nations may fall into lunatic behavior (cf. North Korea). However, ultimately they recovered from their delusions and returned to the normal pattern of democratization. In Germany and Italy, democratization took place immediately after World War II (Deutsch and Smith 1983; Pasquino 1986); in Russia and Eastern

Europe, after the collapse of the communist systems in 1989–91. The establishment of democratic systems in the post-Soviet nations and the former socialist countries of Eastern Europe has progressed unevenly, but in most of those countries democratic institutions are already fully stabilized (see Szabo 1996; Bremmer and Taras 1997; Nagle and Mahr 1999; Krastev 2002; Gel'man 2003; Puglisi 2003). Belarus failed to follow the example of others (see Potocki 2002). Popular support for established democratic institutions is strong in practically all countries of postcommunist Europe (see Samuels 2003).

Australia has been a stabilized democracy since 1901. Citizens can participate in free and fair multiparty elections and choose their representatives to the parliament. Australia is one of the least corrupt states in the world. The press is free and independent and freedom of religion is respected, as is academic freedom. The government respects the rights of assembly and association, the judiciary is independent, and prison conditions are generally good. Women enjoy equal rights and freedoms. The quality of democracy is high, although it would always be possible to find some deficiencies. A democratic shortage in the Australian case is related to the position of its aboriginal people, who are underrepresented at all levels of political leadership (*Freedom in the World 2005*, pp. 47–48).

The quality of democracy seems to be approximately similar, with local variations in details, in nearly all other European and European offshoot democracies. This group of high-quality democracies includes at least Belgium, Canada, Denmark, Estonia, Finland, France, Germany, Latvia, Malta, New Zealand, Slovakia, Slovenia, Sweden, and the United States. Various shortages in the quality of democracy are related to the discrimination and underrepresentation of the Roma people, especially in Slovakia; to the unequal position of noncitizen Russians in Estonia and Latvia; to problems with large non-European immigrant groups, especially in Belgium, France, Germany, and Sweden; to the position of indigenous Maori people in New Zealand; and to the position of blacks and millions of illegal immigrant workers in the United States.

Belarus (independent 1991) is the only country below my threshold of democracy at this level of national IQ. Because of President Lukashenka's dominant position, Belarus was not able to cross the competition threshold of democracy. There are opposition parties, but they cannot function freely, and elections are not free and fair (see also

Silitski 2005). The government systematically curtails press freedom, and freedoms of assembly and association are also severely restricted. The judiciary is subject to heavy government influence. For example, the 2006 presidential election was marred by irregularities and violent actions against the supporters of opposition candidates (see *Keesing's 2006*, p. 47165). After the election, opposition candidate Kazulin was sentenced to five-and-a-half years in prison (*Keesing's 2006* p. 47388). However, there was still opposition against Lukashenka's regime, and the country's national IQ clearly presupposes a more democratic system.

The Czech Republic has been a democracy since its establishment in 1992, but its predecessor Czechoslovakia was below the threshold of democracy until the collapse of the communist regime in 1989 and the first free elections in 1990. The Roma (Gypsy) continue to experience discrimination.

Hungary was below the threshold of democracy during the period of Communist dictatorship after the World War II. It has been a democracy since the collapse of the Communist regime and the first free elections in 1990. The quality of democracy is relatively good, elections are free, and freedoms of speech and association are respected, but the Roma (Gypsy) people are still discriminated against.

Israel has been a highly democratic country since the 1949 parliamentary elections. Its electoral system supports the survival of an extremely fragmented party system. Political rights and freedoms are extensive and respected in practice, but the rights of Arab citizens of Israel are to some extent restricted. Israel is an ethnic democracy of its dominant Jewish population (cf. McHenry and Mady 2006).

Moldova has sometimes been above and sometimes below the Competition threshold of democracy since independence in 1991. It again crossed the threshold of democracy in the 2005 legislative elections. The Communist Party of Moldova (PCM) and noncommunist parties struggle for power. Opposition parties are relatively free to function, although freedom of the press is restricted. The opposition has claimed that the PCM attempts to establish a dictatorship. The most serious problem concerns the status of Transdnestr. The separatists in Transdnestr demand independence; Moldova would be willing to give the region autonomous status (see Banks et al. 2007, pp. 816–817).

Poland, just like Hungary, was below the threshold of democracy during the period of Communist rule until the collapse of the socialist system in 1989. Since then Poland has been a democracy with a multiparty system and free elections.

Portugal was an autocracy until the 1974 military coup. It has been a democracy since the introduction of a multiparty system and the first free elections in 1976. The quality of democracy is approximately as good as in other Western European countries.

In *Russia* the collapse of the Soviet Union in 1991 led to democratization. The country has been above the threshold of democracy since the 1993 Duma elections, although it was only slightly above the Competition threshold after the 2004 presidential election. The state dominance of the media restricted press freedom. Opposition political parties criticized "the distorted and unbalanced coverage of their campaigns and the limits placed on their ability to reach voters through the airways" (*Freedom in the World 2005*, p. 520). Freedoms of assembly and association are relatively extensive with some restrictions. Corruption is a serious problem that is widespread throughout the government and business world. The quality of democracy seems to have been lower than the level of democratization (ID-2006) indicates, but I do not agree with Freedom House's evaluation that Russia was a "not free" country in 2005 (cf. Gill 2006).

Spain had been temporarily above the threshold of democracy in 1933–1938, but its democratic institutions were destroyed in the civil war, which ended in 1939 with the victory of General Franco. The country was below the threshold of democracy during Franco's dictatorship. After Franco's death in 1975, the process of democratization started, and Spain crossed the threshold of democracy through the first free elections in 1977. The quality of democracy has suffered from the unsolved problem of Basque terrorism and separatism.

Ukraine's democracy has suffered from the bitter struggle for power between political parties. It has been difficult for parties to share power through elections, but Ukraine has been above the threshold of democracy since its independence in 1991. Political rights and freedoms are extensive and generally respected. Freedom of the press seems to be more extensive than in Russia. The quality of democracy may be lower than the level of democratization (ID) indicates. According to Freedom House's classification, Ukraine is a "free" country, but the report refers to various shortcomings in the country's democratic process (*Freedom in the World 2006*, pp. 747–753).

Uruguay was a stabilized democracy in 1950–1972, but a military coup interrupted democratic politics in 1973. Uruguay returned to democracy in 1984 and has been a democracy since then. Uruguay's quality of democracy is among the best in Latin America.

The country reviews show that 25 of the 26 countries were above the minimum threshold of democracy in 2006 and that 17 had been democracies throughout the period of analysis. In most cases, the actual level of democratization (ID-2006) deviated only a little or moderately from the mean of this IQ category (30.3). It is remarkable that all former socialist countries and Soviet republics except Belarus had become democratized and achieved approximately the same level of democratization as the other European countries at this level of national IQ. Israel is a special case in the sense that there are significant differences in the political rights of the country's Jewish and Arab citizens. These observations support my argument about the causal link between national IQ and the level of democratization.

CHAPTER 16

Countries at National IQ Level 7 (100–108)

National IQ varies from 100 to 108 in the following 15 countries: Austria, China, Iceland, Italy, Japan, North Korea, South Korea, Luxembourg, Mongolia, the Netherlands, Norway, Singapore, Switzerland, Taiwan, and the United Kingdom. The group includes eight European countries and seven East Asian countries. All these countries, except Taiwan and Singapore, are situated in temperate or cold climatic zones.

The mean of the index of democratization (ID-2006) (27.1) is a little lower for this category of 15 countries than for the previous national IQ category, and the means of political rights (PR-2005) (2.1) and civil liberties (CL-2005) (2.1) are slightly higher than for the previous IQ category (see Table 8.4). On the basis of ID-2006, 13 of these countries were democracies in 2005 and China and North Korea were nondemocracies. According to Freedom House ratings, 12 countries were free in 2005, Singapore partly free, and China and North Korea not free. The level of democratization was more than one standard deviation higher than average only in the Netherlands and Switzerland on the basis of ID-2006, and more than one standard deviation lower in China and North Korea.

Some Southeast Asian political leaders have argued that liberal democracy is merely a Western European concept that is incompatible with "Asian values." I think that it would be difficult to use "Asian values" to explain the variation in the level of democratization among the group of East Asian countries. Because all these countries have more or less similar cultural values, these values cannot explain extreme differences in the level of democratization within the group of East Asian countries, of which Japan, South Korea, Mongolia, Singapore, and Taiwan are democracies and only China and North Korea nondemocracies (for Asian values, see Blondel et al. 1999; Khong Cho-oon 1999, Inoguchi 2006). Clear differences in socioeconomic systems (IPR) better explain differences in the level and quality of democracy.

Eight European countries in this category (Austria, Iceland, Italy, Luxembourg, the Netherlands, Norway, Switzerland, and the United Kingdom) are old and stabilized democracies, as well as Japan in East Asia. All have been above the threshold of democracy throughout the period of comparison since 1950. What was said about European democracies in the previous section applies to these countries as well. They are multiparty democracies in which political rights and freedoms are extensive and respected in practice. The nature of political institutions varies significantly, but essentially those in power have been elected through competitive and free elections. Democratic institutions are more recent in the other East Asian countries, or they are still nondemocracies

China is an extremely deviating country. It contradicts the hypothesis about the causal relationship between the level of national IQ and democratization, but it contradicts less the hypothesis about the connection between resource distribution (IPR) and democratization (cf. Rowen 2007). Economic power resources are highly concentrated in the hands of the government and, after a partial transition to a market economy, also in the hands of big domestic and foreign corporations. This explains China's low IPR value. The ID value has been zero throughout the period of analysis. There are no legal opposition parties and no competitive elections. Press freedom is severely limited, and freedoms of assembly and association are also severely restricted. However, the control of the Chinese Communist Party (CCP) is no longer as complete as it was earlier: "The gradual implementation of reforms over the past several decades has freed millions of Chinese from CCP control of their day-to-day lives" (*Freedom in the World 2005*, p. 147). Andrew J. Nathan (2003) notes that China's authoritarian system has proven resilient. Under "conditions that elsewhere have led to democratic transition, China has made a transition instead from totalitarianism to a classic authoritarian regime, and one that appears increasingly stable" (cf. An Chen 2003). My argument is that China's very high national IQ predicts not only economic growth and modernization, but also democratization (cf. Guo 2006a, 2006b).

Korea, North, is an equally deviating case as China on the basis of national IQ, whereas it is not a negative outlier on the basis of IPR. The extreme concentration of economic and other power resources is in balance with the extreme concentration of political power. North Korea has not yet started to reform its economic system. Political rights and freedoms are even more severely restricted than in China. For example, press freedom does not exist in any sense. Individuals are under absolute state control: "Reports of arbitrary detentions, disappearances, and extrajudicial killings are common; torture is widespread and severe" (*Freedom in the World 2005*, p. 471). There are tens of thousands of political prisoners (see Sung-Chul Choi 1997). Just now democratization seems to be impossible in North Korea, but its population's high intelligence means that there is human potential for drastic reforms in political and economic systems.

Korea, South, provides an excellent comparison point for North Korea. South Korea adopted a different sociopolitical system in 1948 when Korea was divided into two independent states. At first it was difficult to stabilize democratic institutions in South Korea. Military coups and military governments alternated with democratic governments, but since 1980 South Korea has been continuously above the threshold of democracy. Its level of democratization is in balance with both national IQ and IPR. The quality of democracy is relatively good in South Korea; political rights and freedoms are extensive. The great differences between the two Koreas can be traced to different political choices, not to differences in national IQ or climatic conditions (cf. Hyun 2006).

Mongolia transitioned from a one-party Communist system to a multiparty democracy in 1990 and has remained a democracy since then. Its level of democratization (ID) in 2006 was only moderately lower than expected on the basis of national IQ, and socioeconomic reforms had raised its IPR value. Elections have been fairly free. Political rights and freedoms are respected in practice. The transformation of Mongolia's political and economic system may provide an example for North Korea. Anyway, it indicates that the emergence of democracy is not impossible in East Asia.

Singapore has sometimes been above the threshold of democracy and sometimes slightly below since its independence in 1965. It dropped below the competition threshold in the 2001 parliamentary elections, but rose slightly above in the 2006 elections. Opposition political parties are legal, but they have remained weak because of the dominance of the ruling multiethnic People's Action Party (PAP). Elections have not been fair. The government restricts in many ways the opportunities of opposition parties to compete in elections. Freedoms of assembly and association are restricted in practice, and consequently people do not dare to express their political opinions. The AsiaBarometer Survey 2004 noted "especially those who belong to the low-income class, do not dare to reveal their personal opinions or ideas on politically sensitive issues that may challenge the legitimacy of the government" (Sonoda 2006, p. 223). The quality of democracy may be lower than the measured level of democratization (ID). It should be noted that the PAP won 82 of the 84 seats in the parliament, although its share of the vote was not more than 65 percent (see *Keesing's 2006*, p. 47258). Because of Singapore's extremely high national IQ, I expect further democratization of its political system.

Taiwan's transition from an authoritarian system dominated by the Kuomintang Party to democracy took place gradually from 1990 to 1996, when President Lee Teng-hui was elected by direct popular vote. Since then, competing political parties have functioned freely. Freedom of the press is respected in practice as well as freedoms of assembly and association. Taiwan's level of democratization is in balance with its very high national IQ. The democratization which took place in Taiwan indicates that "Asian values" do not bind East Asian countries to authoritarian systems.

The country reviews show that 13 of the 15 countries were highly developed democracies in 2006. Nine had been democracies throughout the period of analysis, whereas four others (South Korea, Mongolia, Singapore, and Taiwan) had had authoritarian regimes before democratization. Only two (China and North Korea) had never been democracies; they contradict the hypothesis. The lack of democracy in China and North Korea can be traced to political choices made in these countries. Their autocratic systems are based on the persistence of the socialist concentration of political, economic, and military power resources. Democratic deficits are extensive. Citizens cannot change their government through elections, and opposition parties are illegal. The government controls the judiciary, and the rights and liberties of ordinary citizens are limited. Officials can jail people without trial. The government controls the media, and the freedoms of expression and association are tightly restricted. Different political choices in South Korea, Mongolia, and Taiwan led to the emergence of quite different political and economic systems.

Contrary to the hypothesis, the average level of democratization (ID-2006) in this category was somewhat lower (27.1) than in national IQ category 6, but it was much higher than in IQ category 5. The decline in the average level and quality of democracy is due to the zero value of ID for China and North Korea.

CHAPTER 17

Summation

The statistical analyses carried out in Chapter 8 showed that the average level of democratization and of the quality of democracy rises systematically with the level of national IQ, although many single countries deviate from the average pattern at all levels of national IQ. The descriptive country reviews in this chapter illustrate the quality of democracy in single countries and its variation at the same level of national IQ and among the seven national IQ categories.

Differences in the quality of democracy, no matter how they are measured, are great between the countries of the two lowest and of the two highest national IQ categories. Those differences are reflected not only in the relative number of democracies and nondemocracies, but also in several other aspects of democratic governance. For example, political violence, coups d'etat, other illegal political interventions, irregularities in elections, deficits in the rule of law, restrictions in the freedoms of expression, assembly, and association, corruption, and insecurity of individual people seem to be much more common in the countries with low levels of national IQ than in the countries with high levels. Unfortunately, systematic statistical data on most of these differences are not available.

However, we do have statistical data on some characteristics of political systems, as discussed in the country reviews. We have data on the existence and persistence of democracy over the period of analysis from 1950, or from the year of independence, to the year 2006. Some countries were above the threshold of democracy (competition 30 and participation 20) throughout the period of analysis (always democracy), and some others were never above the threshold (never democracy). Further, we have data on democracies in 2006 (Democracy 2006) and on the countries which were below the threshold of democracy in 2006 (Below threshold 2006). Freedom House's classification of countries into "free," "partly free," and "not free" categories reflect differences in the quality of democracy from the perspective of political rights and civil liberties. Data on these variables by national IQ level are summarized in Table 17.1.

The data summarized in Table 17.1 imply that, to some extent, the limits of democratization can be traced to differences in national IQ (and annual mean temperature, MT). There are great differences in the relative frequency of countries between the two first and the two last IQ levels.

The relative frequency of countries which were above the threshold of democracy throughout the period of analysis increases almost regularly from the first level of national IQ (59–69) to the highest level (100–108), from zero to 60 percent. In the case of the "Never democracy" variable, the relative frequency of countries decreases from 30.0 percent at national level 1 to 13.3 percent at national IQ level 7. "Never democracies" are much more frequent than "always democracies" at the first four IQ levels, whereas the frequencies turn opposite at the three highest IQ levels.

The contrast between IQ levels is not as strong in the relative frequency of democracies in 2006, but the percentage of democracies increases from 46.7 percent at national IQ level 1 to 86.7 percent at national IQ level 7. The relative number of democracies rises sharply at national IQ level 5 (90–94). The difference between IQ levels is opposite in the case of nondemocracies in 2006. Their relative frequency decreases from 53.3 percent at IQ level 1 to 13.3 percent at IQ level 7.

The differences between national IQ levels are similar, although not completely regular, in the cases of the three Freedom House categories, which reflect differences in the quality of democracy. The relative frequency of "free" countries increases from 10.0 percent at national IQ level 1 to 80.0 percent at national IQ level 7, the relative frequency of "partly free" countries decreases from 50.0 percent to 6.7 percent and the frequency of "not free" countries from 49.0 percent to 13.3 percent.

The variation in the nature of political systems between national IQ

Table 17.1 Some variables on the existence and persistence of democracy and on the quality of democracy (number and percentage of countries) by the level of national IQ in the group of 172 countries

Level of national IQ	N	Always democracy	Never democracy	Democracy in 2006	Below threshold in 2006	Freedom House 2005		
						Free	Partly Free	Not Free
IQ level 1	30	0	8	14	16	3	15	12
%		0	26.7	46.7	53.3	10.0	50.0	49.0
IQ level 2	20	1	6	12	8	7	8	5
%		5.0	30.0	60.0	40.0	35.0	40.0	25.0
IQ level 3	33	6	13	19	14	7	14	12
%		18.2	39.4	57.6	42.4	21.2	42.4	36.4
IQ level 4	26	4	8	15	11	11	7	8
%		15.4	30.8	57.7	42.3	42.3	26.9	30.8
IQ level 5	22	5	5	15	7	9	9	4
%		22.7	22.7	68.2	31.8	40.9	40.9	18.2
IQ level 6	26	17	1	25	1	23	1	2
%		65.4	3.8	96.2	3.8	88.5	3.8	7.7
IQ level 7	15	9	2	13	2	12	1	2
%		60.0	13.3	86.7	13.3	80.0	6.7	13.3
Total	172	42	43	113	59	72	55	45
%		24.4	25.0	65.7	34.3	41.9	32.0	26.2

levels is so great and persistent that it is probably impossible to equalize the level or quality of democracy. Differences in national IQ and annual mean temperature are background factors which affect the degree of resource distribution (IPR) and constrain democratization as well as maintain great differences in the quality of democracy.

However, the results of country reviews also illustrate that the hypothesized relationship between national IQ and the quality of democracy is not complete. Many single countries deviate more or less from the average pattern. Some countries at low levels of national IQ have established relatively well functioning democratic systems in which political rights and liberties are respected, and, on the other hand, some countries at high levels of national IQ are still non-democracies in which people's political rights and liberties are severely restricted. These observations refer to the impact of specific local factors and of conscious human choices. It would be worthwhile to explore what kind of other factors have tended to further or hamper democratization (cf. Reilly 2006, pp. 21–24). In the country reviews, I referred to several local, institutional, temporary, and other specific factors which seem to have caused some countries to deviate significantly from the average relationship between national IQ and measures of democracy.

CHAPTER 18

Conclusions

The results of this study show that the variation in political systems from the perspective of democracy can be partly traced not only to the degree of resource distribution (IPR), but also to some background factors which partly explain the uneven distribution of politically relevant economic, intellectual, and other power resources. Montesquieu's arguments on the significance of climatic and geographical conditions led me to the idea that we should seek ultimate limits of democratization from climatic conditions which have affected human nature through the process of natural selection. Richard Lynn and some others have argued that the observed differences in the average intelligence of populations emerged as a consequence of the adaptation of human populations to colder climatic conditions outside Africa, in particular during the last Ice Age. Thus I got the idea that the annual mean temperature (MT) of a country should be causally related to the average intelligence of a nation (national IQ), and that differences in national IQ may provide the best causal explanation for the extensive variation in the index of power resources (IPR), which provides a more proximate explanation for the variation in the level of democratization. On the basis of these ideas, I formulated three hypotheses on the relationships between annual mean temperature (MT), national IQ, IPR, and an index of democratization (ID) (see Chapter 1).

Empirical variables needed to test the three hypotheses were defined in Chapter 2, and the three hypotheses were transformed into research hypotheses. The three hypotheses were tested by correlation and regression analyses in Chapter 3. Empirical evidence supports all hypotheses. MT explains 43 percent of the variation in national IQ, and national IQ explains 57 percent of the variation in IPR, which explains 67 percent of the variation in the gender-weighted index of democratization (GID-2006) and 66 percent of the variation in the index of democratization (ID-2006). Thus the causal path was traced back from IPR to national IQ and further to MT. Besides, ID and GID are directly related not only to IPR but also to national IQ and MT, although their impact on ID and GID takes place through IPR (see Chapter 3).

The relationship between MT and national IQ (first hypothesis) was analyzed at the level of single countries in Chapter 4. It was noted that the original relationship between MT and national IQ was probably considerably stronger than 43 percent for the reason that relatively recent migrations of people between different climatic zones have weakened this relationship. When the 26 countries most affected by ancient and recent migrations of people were excluded from the comparison group, the negative correlation between MT and national IQ rose to -0.805 and the explained part of variation to 65 percent in the remaining group of 146 countries.

The impact of MT and national IQ on IPR (first and second hypotheses) was analyzed at the level of single countries in Chapter 5. Because of their moderate intercorrelation (-0.659), the explanations provided by these two ultimate explanatory variables overlap at most points. Taken together they explain 67 percent of the variation in IPR, which represents a quite high level of explanation. The results of regression analyses disclosed the countries which deviate clearly from the hypothesized relationships between the explanatory variables (MT and national IQ) and the dependent variable (IPR). It was possible to indicate some specific local factors which seem to explain large deviations from the regression lines.

The impact of IPR on the level of democratization (third hypothesis) was examined at the level of single countries in Chapter 6. The correlation between IPR and ID-2006 rises to 0.813 and the explained part of variation to 66 percent. Only 34 percent of the variation in ID remained unexplained. Attention was paid on large positive and negative outliers.

Each of the large outliers was discussed separately in order to see what specific factors might explain its divergent position.

Direct relationships between the two ultimate explanatory variables (MT and national IQ) and the level of democratization (ID-2006) were analyzed at the level of single countries in Chapter 7. It is true that the impact of MT and national IQ on the measures of democratization takes place nearly completely through IPR, but it was interesting to see to what extent the explanations provided by MT and national IQ over-lapped with the explanation provided by IPR. The results of the three regression analyses do indeed overlap at most points. The same countries tend to cluster around the regression line or to deviate clearly from it in a positive or negative direction according to all three regressions. It was found that residuals are smaller than one standard deviation for 81 countries and larger than one standard deviation for 22 countries according to all three regressions. These observations show that the explanation of the variation in the level of democratization based on the degree of resource distribution (IPR) can be partly traced to the two ultimate explanatory factors (MT and national IQ). My conclu-sion is that because MT and national IQ are nearly completely outside conscious human control, it would be extremely difficult and most probably impossible to equalize the level and quality of democracy in all countries of the world.

In Chapter 8, the results of statistical analyses were checked by comparing the average level and quality of democracy between seven national IQ categories. It was hypothesized that the average quality of democracy would systematically rise with the level of national IQ. In this analysis, 13 variables were used to measure the level and quality of democracy from different perspectives. The results confirmed the hypothesis. The average level and quality of democracy rose system-atically with the level of national IQ in all cases, and thus the results support the basic argument on the constraining power of national IQ. The quality of democracy tends to rise with the level of national IQ no matter which indicator is used to measure the quality of democracy. However, it was also noted that many countries deviate significantly from the average pattern at all levels of national IQ.

Finally, in Chapters 9–17, descriptive country reviews were used to illustrate the variation in the level and quality of democracy between the seven national IQ categories. The nature of each country's political system was described briefly from the perspective of democratic governance. Country reviews show great differences in the level and quality of democracy between the countries of the two lowest and two highest national IQ categories. Political systems tend to be less democratic and more violent and corrupted at low levels of national IQ than at high levels. Similar systematic differences emerge in political rights and liberties, the rule of law, and the security of people between the low and high levels of national IQ, but country reviews also show that many countries deviate more or less from these average patterns. This implies that there is room for human choices and that the quality of democratic governance is not strictly tied to the average intelligence of the population.

Briefly stated, the results of empirical analyses support the central hypothesis of this study. Differences in the annual mean temperature and in the average intelligence of the population constrain the variation in the degree of resource distribution and through it the variation in the level and quality of democracy to a significant extent. However, because the observed relationships are only moderately strong, many countries deviate more or less from the average patterns. This means that, at all levels of national IQ, there seems to be room for human choices which affect the quality of democratic governance. On the other hand, because of the ultimate constraints indicated in this study, it is probably never possible to achieve the same level and quality of democracy in all countries and regions of the world. This is the central message of this study. We should learn to accept the fact that because of evolved human diversity we are bound to live in the world in which political systems will always differ significantly from each other from the perspective of democratic governance. Such differences as well as many other global inequalities in human conditions (cf. Lynn and Vanhanen 2006) reflect the evolved diversity of life.

Because the level and also the quality of democratization varies extensively at all levels of MT and national IQ, it would be useful to explore what kinds of local factors have been connected with considerably higher than expected and considerably lower than expected levels of democratization. A part of such variation may be due to measurement errors and temporary or accidental factors (cf. Taleb 2007), but certainly there are also more systematic and persistent local and other factors. I have referred to some of those factors in previous chapters.

They explain existent deviations but also provide hints about the means by which it has been possible to affect the level and quality of democracy. In the following sections, the findings on such factors are summarized and discussed by regional groups.

Europe and European offshoots

Nearly all European and European offshoot countries (48) are at the three highest national IQ categories (90–108). They were hypothesized to be democracies and nearly all of them were democracies in 2006. It was noted that the countries for which ID-2006 values are much higher than expected on the basis of MT and national IQ are economically highly developed market economies, whereas large negative outliers tend to be former socialist countries (see Table 7.2). It was concluded that the nature of the economic system matters independently from MT and national IQ. Economic and intellectual power resources are widely distributed in economically highly developed market economies, whereas in some former socialist countries (especially in Belarus and Russia), the institutional and structural characteristics of the socialist command economies had not yet lost their importance, and consequently economic power resources remained heavily concentrated in the hands of the government. In such countries, it would be useful to continue structural reforms intended to establish and stabilize a market economy, including the establishment of efficient family farms. Such reforms would distribute economic and intellectual power resources more widely within the society and thus strengthen the social basis of competitive politics.

A problem is that the choice of appropriate reform policies depends on the government, which may not be willing to introduce policies which might benefit opposition groups. However, the introduction of institutional and other reforms depends also on the abilities and choices of opposition parties. They can pressure the government to introduce appropriate reforms. My point is that a low quality of democracy is not inevitable in any European country, and that this factor is not in harmony with the constraining factors discussed in this study, although it may be in harmony with the present degree of resource distribution. Serious democratic deficits are principally due to unfavorable historical legacies, which retard the introduction of necessary reforms but, of course present leaders and their supporters are also responsible for policy choices that affect the course of development.

Latin America and the Caribbean

Nearly all Latin American and Caribbean countries (27) are at the medium level of national IQ (80–89). On the basis of their national IQ values, they are expected to be above the minimum threshold of democracy, and nearly all were in 2006. However, the level of democratization is not expected to be as high as in the regional group of European and European offshoot countries, and indeed it is not. Because of the effect of constraining factors, it is quite probable that the average level and also the quality of democracy remain clearly lower in tropical Latin American and Caribbean countries than in Europe and North America, but deviating cases imply that, to some extent, it has been possible to break these constraints in both directions. Residuals based on MT and national IQ are relatively small for most countries in this regional group. However, positive residuals were large especially for Argentina, Brazil, Nicaragua, Panama, Trinidad and Tobago, and Uruguay in 2006. Negative residuals were large only for Cuba.

It was not possible to indicate any common factor which could explain the better than expected success of democracy in the countries with large positive residuals. Their deviations are related to such specific local factors as electoral and party systems. Some deviations seem be due to temporary and accidental factors. For example, Argentina's exceptionally high ID for 2006 is a consequence of the 2003 presidential election. In 2002, Argentina was not a highly deviating country. Nicaragua's large positive residual is a consequence of the exceptionally highly competitive presidential election in 2006; it was not a large positive outlier in 2005. Panama and Uruguay have been positive outliers over longer periods. The multiparty systems of Brazil and Trinidad and Tobago reflect the ethnic diversity of their populations, which has increased electoral participation and competition. Juan J. Linz and Alfred Stepan (1996, pp. 187–188) emphasize that Brazil is still an unconsolidated democracy and that there are serious problems concerning extreme social inequality, a fragmented party system, and the rule of law in particular. In Guyana, Surinam, and Trinidad and Tobago, party systems have become adapted to the ethnic heterogeneity of their populations, which has furthered the survival of democracy.

Cuba's lack of democracy is due to its socialist system. The country would need a system change, and this is highly probable because of its large negative residuals. In Guatemala, the deep ethnic conflict between Amerindians and the ruling white-mestizo group has decreased the level and quality of democracy. Guatemala would need a power-sharing arrangement between the conflicting ethnic groups.

The ethnic heterogeneity of populations is a permanent problem in nearly all Latin American countries, which have traditionally been ethnic hegemonies in which power was concentrated in the hands of the whites and mestizos. The concentration of landownership supported hegemonic political systems. It was difficult to share power between ethnic groups and, consequently, to establish democracies based on equal political rights and liberties. Extreme economic inequalities, which tended to coincide with ethnic divisions, made it even more difficult. It may not be possible to solve these problems satisfactorily, and therefore it is not reasonable to expect the disappearance of democratic deficits in Latin America. However, it is possible to strengthen the social basis of existing democratic institutions by appropriate social reforms and to raise the quality of democracy by institutional improvements. From this perspective, it would be useful to examine what kinds of institutional and structural differences separate relatively well functioning democracies from more defective democracies in Latin America.

Marta Lagos (2003, pp. 172–173) says that "consolidated Latin American democracies will most likely continue to differ from consolidated Western democracies to the degree that the people of the two sets of countries continue to differ, for it is people who shape institutions and not the other way around." I agree with this statement.

Sub-Saharan Africa

National IQs vary between 59 and 79 in all 46 sub-Saharan African countries except Madagascar and Mauritius, whose populations are only partly African. Consequently, the constraining variables predict a low level of democratization for all sub-Saharan African countries. Some may cross the minimum threshold of democracy successfully, but many others will probably fluctuate below and above the threshold. Because the residuals of ID-2006 based on national IQ and MT are small or moderate for nearly all sub-Saharan African countries, it is not justified to expect any drastic changes in the level or quality of democracy. However, the level of democratization varies in sub-Saharan Africa. Some countries have been more successful than expected in their striving for democracy and some others less successful than expected on the basis of MT and national IQ. It would be useful to know what kinds of institutions and policies are best suited to support democratization in sub-Saharan Africa (cf. Lindberg 2006).

The countries with large positive residuals provide hints about appropriate institutional strategies. Ghana and Malawi are the only large positive outliers on the basis of national IQ. Multiparty systems have become stabilized in these two countries, but the survival of their highly competitive political systems is not yet sure. Malawi has been a large positive outlier since 1994, but Ghana only since 2004. Angola, Lesotho, and Swaziland are the only large negative outliers on the basis of annual mean temperature (MT). Their outlying position is due to the fact that MT is somewhat lower for southern African countries than for tropical sub-Saharan African countries. It should be noted that these three countries are not large negative outliers on the basis of national IQ.

Botswana is the only sub-Saharan African country which has con-tinually been above or only slightly below the threshold of democracy since its independence in 1966. What could we learn from its institu-tions and experiences? It is remarkable that Botswana has been contin-ually ruled by the same dominant party (Botswana Democratic Party). It seems to me that the ethnic structure of Botswana's society makes this kind of dominant party system possible. The Tswana tribal group comprises approximately 90 percent of the population, and the ruling party represents principally this dominant tribal group. The party system has adapted to the tribal system and has stabilized a democratic system which is dominated by one party (cf. Holm 1988). Could other sub-Saharan African countries follow Botswana's example? Unfortunately it seems to me that very few if any of the other countries could copy Botswana's model of democracy for the simple reason that almost all of them are ethnically much more heterogeneous than Botswana. The lack of numerically dominant tribal group makes it difficult to establish a similar dominant party system.

Uganda provides an example of a restricted democracy in an ethnically very heterogeneous country. The largest tribal group, the

Baganda, does not comprise more than 17 percent of the population. Because of the fierce tribal competition, it was not possible to stabilize democratic institutions and a party system adapted to tribal divisions during the first decades of independence. Finally, Yoweri Museveni's National Resistance Movement routed other military forces in 1986 and restored peace based on the hegemony of his military and political movement (cf. Kokole and Mazrui 1988). In 1996, Museveni legalized his power position through a competitive presidential election, and in the 2001 presidential election Uganda crossed the threshold of democracy. Political parties were still banned, but presidential elections were competitive. This kind of restricted democracy might be better adapted to some African countries than a full democracy allowing party competition along ethnic lines. However, Uganda's system may be less stable than Botswana's dominant party system for the reason that Uganda's system is crucially based on Museveni's personality. By a referendum in 2005, the establishment of political parties became legal, and a multiparty system emerged in Uganda (see Banks et al. 2007, pp. 1272–1276).

Senegal provides an example of a successful path to democratization through a dominant party system. The Socialist Party established by Leopold Senghor ruled without opposition until the 1978 elections when some opposition parties were allowed to take part in elections (cf. Coulon 1988). Since the 1993 election, Senegal was only slightly below the participation threshold of democracy, and finally in the 2000 presidential election the opposition's candidate won the presidency. The fact that the largest tribe (Wolof) comprises nearly half of the population supported the survival of the dominant party system, but ultimately it was not enough to stabilize it. Ghana and Nigeria are examples of countries in which it has been very difficult to adapt political institutions and party systems to the requirements of the ethnic heterogeneity of their populations (cf. Chazan 1988; Diamond 1988).

From the perspective of democracy, a parliamentary system of government and a multiparty system adapted to the ethnic divisions of the population might be best suited to the plural societies of sub-Saharan Africa, but in practice these institutions may not function as expected. The experience shows that African ethnic parties have quite often been unable to agree on the democratic sharing of power and on the basic rules of the game in democratic politics. Disagreements have led to violent clashes and breakdowns of democratic institutions. It is worthwhile to experiment with fully democratic political institutions, but if they repeatedly fail in practice, it might be useful to consider how to establish a less democratic but more functional political system. Perhaps it would be possible to establish a political system that combines dominance by one group and some kind of representation of various tribal and regional interest groups. From the perspective of such a compromise, a strong presidency based on the support of the dominant ethnic or regional group, on the support of a dominant party, or on the support of the military might be a more practicable governmental system than a fully parliamentary system presupposing cooperation between ethnically based parties. Political rights and civil liberties would be more restricted in such dominance systems than in full democracies, but they might be able to guarantee civil peace and legal order.

The Middle East and North Africa

Nearly all 18 countries in this regional group are in national IQ categories 3 and 4 (80–89), just like most Latin American countries. However, there is a big difference between these two regions in the level of democratization. Nearly all Latin American countries are already democracies, whereas nearly all Middle Eastern and North African countries are nondemocracies. National IQ does not explain this difference. It is evident that the lack of democracy in the Middle East must be based on different local factors.

The results of this study offer an important message to the people of the Middle East autocracies: they are not condemned to stay under autocratic rule forever. Both ultimate constraints of democratization, MT and national IQ, predict a breakthrough of democracy in the Middle East. The present hegemonic systems are based on the concentration of crucial economic power resources (oil) as well as of the means of violence in the hands of the governments and on the control of intellectual power resources. Consequently, negative residuals based on IPR are small or only moderate for nearly all of these countries, but their low IPR values are not in harmony with their much higher national IQs. I do not know by what means democratization is going to take place, but because residuals based on MT and/or national IQ are highly negative for most of these countries (Bahrain, Egypt, Iran, Iraq, Jordan, Kuwait, Libya, Morocco, Oman, Qatar, Saudi Arabia, the United Arab Emirates, and

Yemen), I have to predict democratization. There is sufficient intellectual potential for democratization in the Middle East. In principle, democratization could take place through constitutional reforms, but more abrupt breakthroughs are also possible. I do not think that Islamic culture could permanently prevent democratization in the Arab world (cf. Brynen et al. 1995), although it seems to have hampered it.

East Asia

The six East Asian countries in the study are at the highest national IQ category (100–108). They are hypothesized to be highly democratic countries on the basis of national IQ, but in fact two (China and North Korea) are nondemocracies. Recent democratization in South Korea, Taiwan, and Mongolia was in harmony with my hypothesis, but China and North Korea still contradict the hypothesis. My argument is that special local factors, principally their socialist economic and political system, explain the lack of democracy in these countries. However, because the national IQs of these countries are the highest in the world, they have human potential for democratization, and I expect them to democratize in the future. But this presupposes a fundamental transformation of their political and economic systems; such a transformation is already taking place in China.

Other Asian and Oceanian countries

Nearly all 27 Central Asian, South Asian, Southeast Asian, and Oceanian countries are in national IQ categories 3, 4, and 5 (80–94). On the basis of national IQ, these countries could be above the minimum threshold of democracy, and the countries at national IQ level 5 (90–94) should be well-functioning democracies. Yet in fact, only 11 of these 27 countries (Afghanistan, Bangladesh, India, Indonesia, Malaysia, Nepal, Papua New Guinea, the Philippines, Singapore, the Solomon Islands, and Sri Lanka) were above the threshold of democracy in 2006. Of these 11 democracies, Afghanistan, Nepal, and Singapore had been above the threshold for only one or two years. Bangladesh dropped below the threshold in 2007, whereas Fiji and Thailand had been democracies one or two years earlier. Political systems fluctuated in some countries and varied from democracies to autocracies. This great variation emphasizes the significance of specific local conditions.

Positive residuals based on MT and national IQ were large for India, Indonesia, Papua New Guinea, and Sri Lanka, indicating that their measured level of democratization was significantly higher than expected. These four countries are all ethnically very heterogeneous, and their political systems have more or less adapted to ethnic heterogeneity. Such countries indicate that "it is possible to achieve democratic sustainability even in highly diverse societies" (Reilly 2006, p. 5). Singapore was a large negative outlier on the basis of national IQ. Its level of democratization should be much higher. For the five other democracies, residuals were smaller than one standard deviation in 2006.

Of the 16 nondemocracies, 14 were large negative outliers in 2006 (Bhutan, Brunei, Burma, Cambodia, Fiji, Kazakhstan, Kyrgyzstan, Laos, Maldives, Pakistan, Thailand, Turkmenistan, Uzbekistan, and Vietnam). How do we explain why so many countries contradict the hypothesis? Specific local factors may explain part of these deviations. Seven of the 14 large negative outliers are socialist or former socialist countries, and some of the other seven have suffered from civil wars or serious ethnic violence (Bhutan, Burma, Fiji, and Pakistan). Brunei is an autocratic oil-producing country in which economic power resources are highly concentrated in the hands of the government. Thailand is probably a large negative outlier only temporarily. I do not have any special explanation for the Maldives.

The message of this study for the autocratically ruled contemporary and former socialist countries of Asia is that all have intellectual potential to establish and stabilize more democratic political systems. The socialist concentration of economic power resources and striving to control intellectual resources has held back democratization by depriving potential opposition groups of independent economic power resources. It would be possible to improve environmental conditions for democratization by economic reforms intended to further a market economy and by guaranteeing rights to private property. Some of these countries have already established democratic institutions, but there are serious deficits in their functioning. Their future depends on the ability of political leaders to make appropriate choices, but also on popular pressure from below. As in the case of the Middle East autocracies, the residuals based on IPR are for these countries small or only moderate, whereas negative residuals based on national IQ are large. I have to predict democratization because the constraining factors presuppose a much higher level of democracy in all these countries. They are latecomers to the global pattern of democratization (cf. Friedman 1994; Marsh et al. 1999).

The significance of constraining factors

The central message of this study is that we are bound to live in the world in which the nature of political systems varies considerably and in which it is not possible to establish and maintain equally democratic political systems in all countries. Significant differences in the quality of democracy will persist. If democratization were based only on the degree of resource distribution, as argued in my previous studies, it might in principle, be possible to achieve the same level of democratization in all countries because the components of the index of power Resources (IPR) seem to be under human control. By appropriate policies it would be possible modify the values of all components of IPR.

Now, however, the results of this study imply that human chances to change the relative differences in the degree of resource distribution between countries are significantly limited by the more fundamental factors which explain a considerable part of the present variation in IPR. As noted above, the differences in the average intelligence of populations (national IQ) explain nearly 60 percent of the variation in IPR. Human possibilities to equalize national IQs throughout the world are quite limited for the reason that differences in IQs are partly based on small genetic differences between individuals and populations. The evolved genetic diversity of individuals is outside conscious human control. Therefore, I have to conclude that the variation in IPR seems to depend to a significant extent on a causal factor which is not under conscious human control.

Further, the results of this study show that the variation in national IQ is strongly related (43%) to the variation in the annual mean temperature (MT). This relationship is causal. Significant differences in climatic conditions seem to have caused the evolution of intelligence differences between human populations. Climatic conditions are even more outside human control than intelligence differences between populations. The present intelligence differences between populations (national IQ) emerged probably thousands and tens of thousands of years ago when modern humans migrated from Africa to other parts of the world (cf. Kanazawa 2007). We should understand that it is not possible to revoke evolved human diversity and its consequences.

My point is that because the contemporary variation in the level and quality of democracy can be partly traced back through the degree of resource distribution to the differences in national intelligence and further to the differences in climatic conditions, it is highly improbable that we could ever achieve a similar level and quality of democracy throughout the world. We have to accept that because of human diversity, we live in a world of many kinds of disparities and inequalities, including inequalities in the quality of democracy and in the possibilities to enjoy similar political rights and civil liberties (cf. Lynn and Vanhanen 2006). Political systems adapt to environmental constraints in the continual process of natural selection in politics, and this process of adaptation produces different institutional arrangements and behavior patterns. People in countries with low national IQs are not as able to organize themselves, to take part in national politics, and to defend their interests and rights against those in power as people in countries with higher national IQs. This difference is reflected in the quality of democracy.

However, because the observed relationship between the level of democracy and explanatory and constraining variables is incomplete, there is always plenty of room for human choices that affect social conditions, political institutions, governance, and the quality of democracy. It is worthwhile to explore how to adapt political institutions to environmental constraints and to further democratization within such constraints. The present variation in the level of democratization at the same level of IPR and constraining variables indicates that human choices matter. In the previous chapters, I referred to various factors that seem to explain some variation in the level of democratization independently from my explanatory variables. The enormous research literature tackling these problems includes plenty of material which illustrates the significance of policy choices and individual political leaders. In other words, I do not argue that human choices are unimportant and that the constraining variables automatically determine the nature of political systems and the extent of democratic deficits without human choices to affect the results. Human choices matter, but my argument is that constraining factors limit the range of feasible choices.

According to the Inter-Parliamentary Union's Universal Declaration on Democracy, democracy "is a political system that enables people to freely choose an effective, honest, transparent and accountable government" (UNDP's *Human Development Report 2002*, p. 55). It is evident, on the basis of the results of this study, that there is and will be significant variation between countries in the extent to which these noble democratic aims have been achieved and can be achieved in practice.

There is enormous variation in the extent to which a political system "enables people" to choose a government. My participation threshold of democracy for contemporary elections presupposes that at least 20 percent of the total population votes in elections. In many countries the percentage of people who have taken part in elections is much smaller. I have excluded such countries from the category of democracies. The percentage of participation varies also above the 20 percent threshold and can in extreme cases rise above 60 percent.

Political systems vary greatly in the extent to which people can "freely choose" a government. In extreme cases there is no opportunity to choose freely because there are no alternatives, sometimes not even an alternative to abstain from election. In the countries in which there are alternatives in elections, the possibilities to choose freely may still vary in many important respects. The nature of an electoral system may discriminate against some parties or social groups and favor some others, for example, by effectively preventing minority parties from getting their candidates elected. The party system of a country may be regulated in such a way that certain types of parties are prohibited, which takes away from many people the opportunity to choose freely. I think that "freely choose" presupposes the freedom to establish parties and competition between candidates and parties. Therefore my competition threshold of democracy presupposes that the share of the largest party or of the winning candidate in executive elections should not rise to 70 percent or higher, because a higher percentage implies that opportunities to choose freely between alternatives have been seriously restricted.

Political systems vary greatly in the extent to which people can choose an "effective" government. Democracy presupposes that those in power, or most of them, are elected, or that they are responsible to elected political institutions. In this respect political systems vary greatly, and it is often difficult to measure to what extent the most powerful ones are really elected. There are systems in which elections concern institutions that are without effective power. In such systems power centers are outside elected institutions, but even among democracies the relative importance of elected institutions and rulers varies greatly.

There is variation also in the extent to which people can choose an "honest" government. The honesty of governments varies from relatively honest to extremely corrupt and dishonest. In democracies people are expected to trust their governments and the actions and promises of their governments. At the opposite end of the honesty dimension are extremely dishonest and corrupted governments that deceive people. In practice there may be deficiencies in the honesty of all governments, but the extent of dishonesty varies. It is difficult to measure the honesty of governments. Transparency International's corruption perception index 2007 is a variable that measures one aspect of the honesty of governments.

The variation among governments extends to "transparency" of governments, which varies from relatively open to highly secretive governments. The actions and policies of open governments are clearly stated and open for examination and discussion, whereas highly secretive governments conceal their actions and their reasons from people. Democracy presupposes a relatively transparent government, but the actual transparency of governments may vary considerably among democracies too. In democracies the media check the transparency of government actions day by day. In autocracies the chances of the press to check the transparency of government actions are strictly limited.

Finally, the "accountability" of governments varies from constitutionally accountable democratic governments to autocratic and dictatorial governments which are not accountable to anybody, or only to the closed group of their supporters. In democracies, governments are accountable to citizens in elections, and also, if necessary, to judicial bodies, which can examine the legality of particular governmental actions and decisions made by ministers or other executive officers. In practice the accountability of democratic governments varies considerably. Disagreements on the accountability of governments may lead to illegal actions and unconstitutional changes of governments. In nondemocracies the lack of accountability may lead to arbitrary actions against people, highly irrational policies, nepotism, and large-scale theft of state funds.

All the criteria of democracy stated in the Inter-Parliamentary Union's declaration can be regarded as measuring the quality of democracy, and as noted above, there can be considerable variation from country to country. Each criterion constitutes a continuum, from countries in which political practice is in harmony with the criterion to countries in which political practice does not satisfy the criterion. So the continuum extends from highly democratic to less democratic and nondemocratic countries. Depending on the extent to which a country satisfies these criteria, the quality of democracy also varies greatly within the group of countries above the minimum threshold of democracy.

Because the level of democratization as measured by the index of democratization (ID) and the gender-weighted index of democratization (GID) is moderately or strongly correlated with the ultimate constraints of democratization (national IQ and annual mean temperature, MT), I hypothesize that *the extent to which countries fulfill those criteria of democracy would be moderately or strongly correlated with national IQ and MT.* In principle, all these criteria for democracy are measurable, although the indicators used in this study measure only some aspects of those criteria. By appropriate indicators it would be possible to test the hypothesis with empirical evidence covering all criteria for democracy. My argument is that the quality of democracy remains uneven in the world because the variation in the quality of democracy is constrained by the differences in the average intelligence of populations and in the annual mean temperature. Because these ultimate constraining factors remain outside human control, it does not seem possible to equalize the quality of democracy in the world. We should learn to live with the consequences and all the problems caused by this inequality, but at the same time we should think over how to mitigate the consequences of democratic deficits and how to improve the quality of democracy, especially in countries in which it is lower than expected on the basis of the ultimate limiting variables.

I fully agree with the argument of the United Nations Development Program's *Human Development Report 2002*, p. 51) that many persistent development problems reflect failures of governance and that good governance is democratic governance. The report describes the meaning and practical consequences of democratic governance very well. I only have to point out on the basis of the results of this study that good democratic governance as described in the report seems to be unattainable for most developing countries for the reason that the variation in the quality of democracy is to a significant extent constrained by the ultimate explanatory factors discussed in this study. Therefore it is not reasonable to expect that tropical developing countries could attain the targets of democratic governance and then become able to solve many persistent development problems. It would be useful to think over how to further development despite persistent failures of governance.

The limits of democratization discussed in this study reflect the evolved diversity of life. This means that all nations do not have equal chances to establish and maintain democratic systems. Therefore it would be immoderate to blame people for failures of democratic governance in countries for which the constraining factors do not predict a high level and quality of democracy. It would be more justified to blame people for failures of democratic governance in countries with large negative residuals. In such countries the failures and defects of democracy depend more on political choices than on the ultimate constraining factors discussed in this study. From the perspective of democracy, it is encouraging to note that people strive to establish democracy and to improve the quality of democratic governance everywhere in the world, even in countries for which MT and national IQ do not predict a democratic system or only a low level of democratization. We should understand that in such countries it is enormously more difficult to establish democracy and to maintain a high quality of democracy than in countries for which MT and national IQ predict a high level of democratization.

Appendix 1

The measures of annual mean temperature for 172 countries

	Country	Mean temperature stations	Number of stations	Years	Mean temp. TYN CY 1.1	MT
1	Afghanistan	14.5	21	1961–1990	12.6	13.6
2	Albania[1]	16.2	3	1931–1960	11.4	13.8
3	Algeria	19.8	24	1961–1990	22.5	21.2
4	Angola	23.6	2	1961–1990	21.5	22.6
5	Argentina	16.3	62	1961–1990	14.8	15.6
6	Armenia	12.1	1	1961–1990	7.1	9.6
7	Australia[1]	20.0	26	1931–1960	21.6	20.8
8	Austria	6.8	7	1961–1990	6.3	6.6
9	Azerbaijan	12.6	18	1961–1990	11.9	12.6
10	Bahamas	24.6	1	1961–1990	24.8	24.7
11	Bahrain	26.5	1	1961–1990	27.1	26.8
12	Bangladesh[1]	25.5	7	1931–1960	25.0	25.3
13	Barbados[1]	26.3	1	1931–1960	26.0	26.2
14	Belarus	6.1	6	1961–1990	6.2	6.2
15	Belgium	9.7	1	1961–1990	9.6	9.7
16	Belize[1]	26.6	1	1931–1960	25.3	26.0
17	Benin	27.3	6	1961–1990	27.5	27.4
18	Bhutan[2]	13.3	1	1931–1960	7.4	10.4
19	Bolivia[1]	21.7	18	1931–1960	21.5	21.6
20	Bosnia and Herzegovina	9.6	1	1961–1990	9.8	9.7
21	Botswana[3]	18.0	8	1941–1970	21.5	19.8
22	Brazil	23.1	205	1961–1990	24.9	24.0

	Country	Mean temperature stations	Number of stations	Years	Mean temp. TYN CY 1.1	MT
23	Brunei	26.8	1	1961–1990	26.9	26.9
24	Bulgaria	11.9	7	1961–1990	10.5	11.2
25	Burkina Faso[1]	27.9	6	1931–1960	28.2	28.1
26	Burma (Myanmar)[1]	26.3	5	1931–1960	23.0	24.7
27	Burundi[1]	23.2	1	1931–1960	19.7	21.5
28	Cambodia[1]	27.0	5	1931–1960	26.8	26.9
29	Cameroon	24.8	10	1961–1990	24.6	24.7
30	Canada	1.3	225	1961–1990	3.9	2.6
31	Cape Verde	23.5	1	1961–1990	23.3	23.4
32	Central African Rep.[1]	25.5	13	1931–1960	24.9	25.2
33	Chad[1]	28.1	11	1931–1960	26.5	27.3
34	Chile	12.3	30	1961–1990	8.5	10.4
35	China	12.3	37	1961–1990	6.9	9.6
36	Colombia	24.3	17	1961–1990	24.5	24.4
37	Comoros[1]	25.4	2	1931–1960	25.5	25.5
38	Congo, Dem. Rep.[3]	24.0	23	1941–1963	24.0	24.0
39	Congo, Republic of[1]	24.3	11	1931–1960	24.5	24.4
40	Costa Rica	24.8	3	1961–1990	24.8	24.8
41	Côte d'Ivoire[1]	26.3	3	1931–1960	26.4	26.4
42	Croatia	13.6	2	1961–1990	10.9	12.3
43	Cuba	25.2	1	1961–1990	25.2	25.2
44	Cyprus	19.0	1	1961–1990	18.4	18.7
45	Czech Republic	8.0	4	1961–1990	7.5	7.8
46	Denmark	7.9	15	1961–1990	7.5	7.7

	Country	Mean temperature stations	Number of stations	Years	Mean temp. TYN CY 1.1	MT
47	Djibouti	29.9	1	1961–1990	28.0	29.0
48	Dominican Republic	25.4	20	1961–1990	24.5	25.0
49	East Timor[10]	26.6	–	–	25.8	26.2
50	Ecuador	19.0	14	1961–1990	21.8	20.4
51	Egypt	21.9	30	1961–1990	22.1	22.0
52	El Salvador	22.1	3	1961–1990	24.4	23.3
53	Equatorial Guinea[3]	25.1	2	–	24.5	24.8
54	Eritrea	25.0	3	1961–1990	25.5	25.3
55	Estonia	5.4	3	1961–1990	5.1	5.3
56	Ethiopia[4]	20.4	11	1971–1980	22.2	21.3
57	Fiji	25.5	2	1961–1990	24.4	25.0
58	Finland	2.5	12	1961–1990	1.7	2.1
59	France	12.1	16	1961–1990	10.7	11.4
60	Gabon	25.3	12	1961–1990	25.0	25.2
61	Gambia[4]	27.5	3	1971–1980	27.5	27.5
62	Georgia	13.0	1	1961–1990	5.8	9.4
63	Germany	7.7	19	1961–1990	8.4	8.1
64	Ghana[1]	26.2	4	1931–1960	27.2	26.7
65	Greece	17.2	22	1961–1990	15.4	16.3
66	Guatemala[1]	18.0	1	1931–1960	23.4	20.7
67	Guinea	25.1	11	1961–1990	25.7	25.4
68	Guinea–Bissau[1]	26.3	1	1931–1960	26.7	26.5
69	Guyana	26.1	2	1961–1990	26.0	26.0
70	Haiti[5]	25.4	–	–	24.9	25.2

	Country	Mean temperature stations	Number of stations	Years	Mean temp. TYN CY 1.1	MT
71	Honduras	25.2	8	1961–1990	23.5	24.4
72	Hungary	10.1	7	1961–1990	9.8	10.0
73	Iceland	3.7	7	1961–1990	1.7	2.7
74	India	25.3	39	1961–1990	23.7	24.5
75	Indonesia[1]	26.6	8	1931–1960	25.8	26.2
76	Iran	17.2	28	1961–1990	17.2	17.2
77	Iraq	22.4	10	1931–1960	21.4	21.9
78	Ireland	9.6	11	1961–1990	9.3	9.5
79	Israel	19.9	3	1961–1990	19.2	19.6
80	Italy[1]	15.2	17	1931–1960	13.4	14.3
81	Jamaica[1]	27.1	1	1931–1960	24.9	26.0
82	Japan	13.7	158	1961–1990	11.1	12.4
83	Jordan	18.9	4	1961–1990	18.3	18.6
84	Kazakhstan	5.8	29	1961–1990	6.4	6.1
85	Kenya	24.2	5	1961–1990	24.7	24.5
86	Korea, North	7.8	7	1961–1990	5.7	6.8
87	Korea, South	12.7	12	1961–1990	11.5	12.1
88	Kuwait	25.7	1	1961–1990	25.3	25.5
89	Kyrgyzstan	7.1	2	1961–1990	1.6	4.4
90	Laos	25.6	4	1961–1990	22.8	24.2
91	Latvia	5.7	5	1961–1990	5.6	5.7
92	Lebanon	19.9	1	1961–1990	16.4	18.2
93	Lesotho[4]	13.7	3	1971–1980	11.8	12.8
94	Liberia[4]	26.4	2	1971–1980	25.3	25.9

	Country	Mean temperature stations	Number of stations	Years	Mean temp. TYN CY 1.1	MT
95	Libya[1]	20.4	7	1931–1960	21.8	21.1
96	Lithuania	6.2	14	1961–1990	6.2	6.2
97	Luxembourg	8.3	1	1961–1990	8.7	8.5
98	Macedonia	10.1	4	1961–1990	9.8	10.2
99	Madagascar	23.6	14	1961–1990	22.6	23.1
100	Malawi	21.4	15	1961–1990	21.9	21.7
101	Malaysia	26.6	14	1961–1990	25.4	26.0
102	Maldives	28.0	1	1961–1990	27.6	27.8
103	Mali	28.3	15	1961–1990	28.2	28.3
104	Malta	18.6	1	1961–1990	19.2	18.9
105	Mauritania[4]	27.1	11	1971–1980	27.6	27.4
106	Mauritius	25.0	1	1961–1990	22.4	23.7
107	Mexico	22.1	10	1961–1990	21.0	21.6
108	Moldova	9.6	1	1961–1990	9.4	9.5
109	Mongolia	-0.8	40	1961–1990	-0.7	-0.8
110	Montenegro[11]	13.6	2	1961–1990	9.9	11.8
111	Morocco	17.1	15	1961–1990	17.1	17.1
112	Mozambique[1]	23.2	7	1931–1960	23.8	23.5
113	Namibia[4]	19.3	4	1971–1980	19.9	19.6
114	Nepal[6]	17.8	1	1971–1980	8.1	13.0
115	Netherlands	9.4	5	1961–1990	9.2	9.3
116	New Zealand	12.1	178	1961–1990	10.5	11.3
117	Nicaragua	25.3	22	1961–1990	24.8	25.1
118	Niger[1]	28.0	10	1931–1960	27.1	27.6

	Country	Mean temperature stations	Number of stations	Years	Mean temp. TYN CY 1.1	MT
119	Nigeria	26.8	4	1961–1990	26.8	26.8
120	Norway	2.1	13	1961–1990	1.5	1.8
121	Oman[6]	26.1	2	1971–1980	25.6	25.9
122	Pakistan	22.1	33	1961–1990	20.2	21.2
123	Panama[7]	25.6	8	1971–1980	25.4	25.5
124	Papua New Guinea[8]	27.0	4	1971–1980	25.2	26.1
125	Paraguay	22.6	9	1961–1990	23.5	23.1
126	Peru	25.5	18	1961–1990	19.6	22.6
127	Philippines	27.3	10	1961–1990	25.8	26.6
128	Poland	6.8	18	1961–1990	7.8	7.3
129	Portugal	15.4	12	1961–1990	15.1	15.3
130	Qatar	26.7	1	1961–1990	27.1	26.9
131	Romania	8.8	11	1961–1990	8.8	8.8
132	Russia (USSR)	-1.2	174	1961–1990	3.6	2.4
133	Rwanda[3]	21.1	1	–	17.9	19.5
134	Saudi Arabia	26.0	5	1961–1990	24.6	25.3
135	Senegal[1]	26.4	5	1931–1960	27.9	27.2
136	Serbia[11]	13.6	2	1961–1990	9.9	11.8
137	Sierra Leone	26.2	6	1961–1990	26.0	26.1
138	Singapore	26.7	1	1961–1990	26.4	26.6
139	Slovakia	7.9	3	1961–1990	6.8	7.4
140	Slovenia	9.8	1	1961–1990	8.9	9.4
141	Solomon Islands	27.0	1	1961–1990	25.6	26.3
142	Somalia[1]	27.3	1	1931–1960	27.0	27.2

	Country	Mean temperature stations	Number of stations	Years	Mean temp. TYN CY 1.1	MT
143	South Africa	16.3	13	1961–1990	17.8	17.1
144	Spain	15.2	30	1961–1990	13.5	14.4
145	Sri Lanka	25.7	6	1961–1990	26.9	26.3
146	Sudan	28.2	42	1961–1990	26.8	27.5
147	Surinam	26.7	3	1961–1990	25.7	26.2
148	Swaziland[3]	18.3	2	–	21.4	19.9
149	Sweden	4.1	16	1961–1990	2.1	3.1
150	Switzerland	7.0	4	1961–1990	5.5	6.3
151	Syria	18.4	11	1961–1990	17.7	18.1
152	Taiwan	22.0	1	1931–1960	22.0	22.0
153	Tajikistan	14.7	1	1961–1990	2.0	8.4
154	Tanzania[1]	23.3	1	1931–1960	22.3	22.8
155	Thailand	26.9	47	1961–1990	26.3	26.6
156	Togo	27.1	4	1961–1990	27.1	27.1
157	Trinidad and Tobago	26.0	1	1961–1990	25.7	25.9
158	Tunisia	18.9	7	1961–1990	19.1	19.0
159	Turkey	15.2	35	1961–1990	11.1	13.2
160	Turkmenistan	16.2	12	1961–1990	15.1	15.7
161	Uganda[1]	22.3	2	1931–1960	22.8	22.6
162	Ukraine	8.3	47	1961–1990	8.3	8.3
163	United Arab Emirates	26.8	5	1961–1990	27.0	26.9
164	United Kingdom	9.0	20	1961–1990	8.4	8.7
165	United States	11.6	285	1961–1990	8.5	10.1
166	Uruguay	17.2	11	1961–1990	17.5	17.4

	Country	Mean temperature stations	Number of stations	Years	Mean temp. TYN CY 1.1	MT
167	Uzbekistan	12.9	6	1961–1990	12.1	12.5
168	Venezuela	25.5	20	1961–1990	25.3	25.5
169	Vietnam[1]	26.5	4	1931–1960	24.4	25.5
170	Yemen[9]	26.1	–	–	23.8	25.0
171	Zambia	20.4	27	1961–1990	21.4	20.9
172	Zimbabwe	18.8	6	1961–1990	21.0	19.9

Sources:

Mean temperature, stations

If not otherwise noted, World Meteorological Organization, *Climatological Normals (CLIN0) for the period 1961–1990*, Geneva: WMO No. 847. This source gives the mean temperature of each month over the period of 1961–1990 for each meteorological observation station as well as the means of 12 months. The data given in this column are arithmetic means of the means of observation stations.

1. World Meteorological Organization, *Climatological Normals (CLINO) for Climat and Climat Ship Stations for the Period 1931–1960*. Edition 1971. Geveva: WMO/OMM, No. 117. TP.52.

2. Data concern Darjeeling observation station in India. See CLINO 1971, p. 42071. There was no observation station in Bhutan.

3. Meteorological Office, *Tables of temperature, relative humidity, precipitation and sunshine for the world. Part IV. Africa, the Atlantic Ocean South of 35°N and the Indian Ocean*. 1983. This source gives average monthly maximum and minimum temperatures. Data in this table are means of yearly maximum and minimum temperatures.

4. U.S. Department of Commerce, National Oceanic and Atmospheric Administration, National Environmental Satellite, Data, and Information Service, National Climatic Data Center, *World Weather Records 1971–1980, Volume 5, Africa*. 1993.

5. Estimation. The same as in Dominican Republic. There is no observation station in Haiti.

6. *World Weather Records 1971–1980, Volume 4, Asia*. 1992.

7. *World Weather Records 1971–1980, Volume 3, West Indies, South and Centraö America*. August 1991.

8. *World Weather Records 1971–1980, Volume 6, Islands of the World*. April 1994.

9. Estimation. The same as for Oman. There are no observation

stations in Yemen.

10. Data for East Timor are the same as for Indonesia.

11. Data for Montenegro and Serbia are the same as for the previous combined Serbia and Montenegro.

Mean temperature, TYN CY 1.1

TYN CY 1.1. Online: <http://www.cru.uea.ac.uk/~timm/cty/obs/ TYN_CY_1_1_cty-table.html>.

Appendix 2

IR, ER, IPR

Data on tertiary gross enrollment ratio, adult literacy, the Index of Intellectual Power Resources (IR), the Index of Economic Power Resources (ER), the Index of Power Resources (IPR), and the mean of the four basic variables (Mean) in 172 countries

	Country	Tertiary enrollment ratio %	Adult literacy %	IR	ER	IPR	Mean
1	Afghanistan	1	281	14.5	49.4	7.1	27.7
2	Albania	16	99	57.5	75.4	43.3	66.0
3	Algeria	20	79	45.0	44.5	20.0	45.5
4	Angola	1	67	34.0	35.5	12.1	29.5
5	Argentina	61	97	79.0	47.9	37.8	58.5
6	Armenia	26	99	62.5	52.9	33.1	58.5
7	Australia	74	99	86.5	70.6	61.1	76.0
8	Austria	49	99	74.0	79.6	58.9	74.0
9	Azerbaijan	15	99	57.0	40.5	23.1	51.0
10	Bahamas	304	95	62.5	71.2	44.5	54.5
11	Bahrain	353	86	60.5	15.0	9.1	39.0
12	Bangladesh	7	41	24.0	54.6	13.1	36.7
13	Barbados	373	99	68.0	55.9	38.0	53.7
14	Belarus	61	99	80.0	29.9	23.9	49.7
15	Belgium	61	99	80.0	80.1	64.1	81.7
16	Belize	23	75	38.5	43.6	16.8	39.0
17	Benin	41	35	19.5	43.2	8.4	31.2
18	Bhutan	64	47	26.5	43.0	11.4	35.2
19	Bolivia	41	87	64.0	33.9	21.6	49.5
20	Bosnia and Herzegovina	151	97	56.0	69.6	39.0	61.6
21	Botswana	6	81	43.5	30.6	13.3	37.7
22	Brazil	20	89	54.5	44.2	24.1	46.5

	Country	Tertiary enrollment ratio %	Adult literacy %	IR	ER	IPR	Mean
23	Brunei	143	93	53.5	15.6	8.3	40.0
24	Bulgaria	41	98	69.5	66.4	46.1	62.0
25	Burkina Faso	1	22	11.5	38.6	4.4	22.2
26	Burma (Myanmar)	11	90	50.5	36.5	18.4	43.0
27	Burundi	2	59	30.5	42.8	13.0	30.2
28	Cambodia	3	74	38.5	30.0	11.5	34.2
29	Cameroon	5	68	36.5	38.2	13.9	36.7
30	Canada	57	99	78.0	76.7	59.8	73.7
31	Cape Verde	63	76	41.0	55.6	22.8	54.0
32	Central African Republic	21	49	25.5	34.6	8.8	25.2
33	Chad	11	26	13.5	38.2	5.2	20.7
34	Chile	43	96	69.5	46.7	32.5	52.5
35	China	15	91	53.0	40.8	21.6	43.7
36	Colombia	27	93	60.0	33.6	20.2	48.2
37	Comoros	23	56	29.0	28.0	8.1	27.0
38	Congo, Democratic Rep.	21	67	34.5	45.4	15.7	38.2
39	Congo, Republic of	4	83	43.5	36.3	15.8	40.5
40	Costa Rica	19	95	57.0	54.6	31.1	51.7
41	Côte d'Ivoire	31	49	26.0	39.2	10.2	33.7
42	Croatia	39	98	68.5	75.2	51.5	73.7
43	Cuba	54	99	76.5	20.0	15.3	48.2
44	Cyprus	363	97	66.5	74.7	49.7	69.7
45	Czech Republic	37	99	68.0	80.2	54.5	57.7
46	Denmark	67	99	83.0	82.3	68.2	77.2
47	Djibouti	13	65	33.0	45.0	14.8	35.5
48	Dominican Republic	33	87	60.0	41.8	25.1	45.0
49	East Timor	103	59	34.5	25.4	8.8	31.7
50	Ecuador	201	91	55.5	36.2	20.1	46.5
51	Egypt	29	71	50.0	46.3	23.1	51.5
52	El Salvador	18	80	49.0	36.0	17.6	42.5
53	Equatorial Guinea	13	87	44.0	30.6	13.5	35.7
54	Eritrea	1	57	29.0	41.6	12.1	32.7
55	Estonia	64	99	81.5	69.8	56.9	70.0

	Country	Tertiary enrollment ratio %	Adult literacy %	IR	ER	IPR	Mean
56	Ethiopia	2	42	22.0	47.4	10.4	33.2
57	Fiji	153	93	54.0	49.5	26.7	53.3
58	Finland	87	99	93.0	82.4	76.6	90.2
59	France	55	99	77.0	77.1	59.4	72.0
60	Gabon	82	71	39.5	39.0	15.4	38.5
61	Gambia	1	38	19.5	35.2	6.9	22.5
62	Georgia	41	99	70.0	51.6	36.1	62.2
63	Germany	50	99	74.5	77.4	57.7	71.2
64	Ghana	3	58	30.5	37.2	11.3	33.5
65	Greece	72	96	84.0	70.2	59.0	79.0
66	Guatemala	10	69	39.5	22.0	8.7	30.7
67	Guinea	2	29	15.5	44.1	6.8	28.2
68	Guinea–Bissau	01	40	20.0	40.5	8.1	26.2
69	Guyana	93	96	52.5	34.2	18.0	42.7
70	Haiti	11	52	26.5	41.3	10.9	29.5
71	Honduras	16	80	48.0	23.1	11.1	36.2
72	Hungary	52	99	75.5	78.9	59.6	69.7
73	Iceland	613	99	80.0	84.3	67.4	79.5
74	India	11	61	35.0	68.2	24.6	50–0
75	Indonesia	16	90	53.0	70.3	37.3	62.7
76	Iran	22	77	49.5	59.6	26.0	55.2
77	Iraq	15	741	44.5	39.7	17.7	47.0
78	Ireland	55	99	77.0	71.1	54.7	77.0
79	Israel	57	97	77.0	61.8	47.6	66.5
80	Italy	59	98	78.5	59.6	54.6	72.2
81	Jamaica	19	80	49.5	64.1	31.7	53.2
82	Japan	52	99	75.5	76.1	57.5	76.9
83	Jordan	35	90	62.5	44.1	27.6	58.7
84	Kazakhstan	48	99	73.5	40.0	29.4	53.0
85	Kenya	41	74	39.0	41.7	16.3	38.2
86	Korea, North	204	99	59.5	5.0	3.0	32.2
87	Korea, South	89	98	93.5	81.4	76.1	89.0
88	Kuwait	22	93	57.5	25.1	14.4	44.5
89	Kyrgyzstan	40	99	69.5	42.2	29.3	55.5
90	Laos	6	69	37.5	42.6	16.0	34.5
91	Latvia	71	99	85.0	65.2	55.4	74.0
92	Lebanon	48	86	67.0	53.3	35.7	64.0
93	Lesotho	3	82	42.5	41.1	17.5	36.7
94	Liberia	31	571	30.0	34.0	10.2	30.0
95	Libya	56	82	69.0	29.2	20.1	53.2

	Country	Tertiary enrollment ratio %	Adult literacy %	IR	ER	IPR	Mean
96	Lithuania	69	99	84.0	73.1	61.4	77.5
97	Luxembourg	604	99	79.5	79.9	63.5	77.5
98	Macedonia	27	96	61.5	65.3	40.2	64.2
99	Madagascar	3	71	37.0	36.4	13.5	32.5
100	Malawi	0	64	32.0	37.0	11.8	28.5
101	Malaysia	29	89	59.0	63.4	37.4	59.2
102	Maldives	03	96	48.0	32.2	15.5	41.5
103	Mali	2	19	10.5	37.0	3.9	17.7
104	Malta	263	88	57.0	75.1	42.8	67.2
105	Mauritania	3	51	27.0	38.5	10.4	32.7
106	Mauritius	17	84	50.5	64.0	32.3	49.5
107	Mexico	22	91	56.5	46.0	26.0	48.5
108	Moldova	32	98	65.0	44.1	28.7	54.2
109	Mongolia	39	98	68.5	56.8	38.9	66.0
110	Montenegro*	361	961	66.0	58.1	44.9	68.7
111	Morocco	11	52	31.5	52.0	16.4	43.0
112	Mozambique	1	46	23.5	34.9	8.2	25.0
113	Namibia	6	85	45.5	14.3	6.5	30.2
114	Nepal	6	49	27.5	66.2	18.2	41.0
115	Netherlands	58	99	78.5	78.2	61.3	80.2
116	New Zealand	72	99	85.5	69.9	59.8	73.5
117	Nicaragua	18	77	47.5	25.6	12.2	39.2
118	Niger	1	29	15.0	41.3	6.2	20.7
119	Nigeria	10	67	38.5	34.5	13.3	33.0
120	Norway	80	99	89.5	82.5	73.8	88.7
121	Oman	13	81	47.0	27.6	13.0	38.5
122	Pakistan	3	50	26.5	51.7	13.7	39.5
123	Panama	46	92	69.0	40.7	28.1	53.2
124	Papua New Guinea	31	57	30.0	55.0	16.5	38.0
125	Paraguay	26	93	59.5	27.7	16.5	43.0
126	Peru	301	88	59.0	31.8	18.8	47.2
127	Philippines	29	93	61.0	54.6	33.3	61.7
128	Poland	59	99	79.0	71.3	56.3	75.5
129	Portugal	56	92	74.0	68.5	50.7	68.2
130	Qatar	223	89	55.5	15.2	8.4	38.2
131	Romania	36	97	66.5	66.3	44.1	66.7
132	Russia	65	99	82.0	36.7	30.1	53.5
133	Rwanda	3	65	34.0	42.8	14.6	34.0
134	Saudi Arabia	28	79	53.5	21.6	11.6	41.7

	Country	Tertiary enrollment ratio %	Adult literacy %	IR	ER	IPR	Mean
135	Senegal	5	39	22.0	38.4	8.4	29.2
136	Serbia*	361	961	66.0	61.0	40.3	65.5
137	Sierra Leone	2	35	18.5	30.9	5.7	36.7
138	Singapore	191	92	55.5	57.0	31.6	54.5
139	Slovakia	34	99	66.5	76.2	50.7	60.7
140	Slovenia	70	99	84.5	81.2	68.6	84.2
141	Solomon Islands	34	77	40.0	43.7	17.5	41.2
142	Somalia	31	381	20.5	37.1	7.6	27.7
143	South Africa	15	82	48.5	29.1	14.1	37.4
144	Spain	64	98	81.0	68.4	55.4	67.5
145	Sri Lanka	51	91	48.0	61.9	29.7	56.7
146	Sudan	31	61	32.0	38.0	12.2	33.5
147	Surinam	123	90	51.0	43.0	21.9	41.7
148	Swaziland	4	80	42.0	13.0	5.5	29.2
149	Sweden	82	99	90.5	82.8	74.9	85.0
150	Switzerland	45	99	72.0	77.1	55.5	79.7
151	Syriia	181	80	49.0	48.5	23.8	49.0
152	Taiwan	604	98	79.0	65.3	51.6	78.0
153	Tajikistan	16	99	57.5	26.6	15.3	43.7
154	Tanzania	1	69	35.0	37.8	13.2	34.7
155	Thailand	41	93	67.0	60.5	40.5	63.7
156	Togo	41	53	28.5	46.0	13.1	37.5
157	Trinidad and Tobago	12	98	55.0	46.8	25.7	50.2
158	Tunisia	26	74	50.0	57.5	38.7	53.5
159	Turkey	28	87	57.5	61.1	35.1	65.5
160	Turkmenistan	221	99	60.5	15.2	9.2	37.7
161	Uganda	3	67	35.0	40.9	14.3	38.7
162	Ukraine	66	99	82.5	60.7	50.1	66.5
163	United Arab Emirates	22	77	49.5	11.4	5.6	34.7
164	United Kingdom	63	99	81.0	66.6	53.9	65.0
165	United States	83	99	91.0	65.8	59.9	74.0
166	Uruguay	38	98	68.0	61.4	41.8	61.5
167	Uzbekistan	15	99	57.0	25.6	14.6	40.5
168	Venezuela	39	93	66.0	45.0	29.7	51.2
169	Vietnam	10	90	50.0	31.7	15.8	41.0
170	Yemen	9	49	29.0	46.0	13.3	37.5
171	Zambia	21	68	35.0	34.7	12.1	28.7
172	Zimbabwe	4	90	47.0	22.2	10.4	32.7

Sources

* Data concern the former state of Serbia and Montenegro.
Tertiary gross enrollment ratio
If not otherwise noted, The World Bank, *World Development Indicators 2006,* Table 2.11. Data refers to the year 2004.

1. The World Bank, *World Development Indicators 2004,* Table 2.11. Data refers to the years 1990–91 or 2000–2001.

2. The World Bank, *World Development Indicators 2003,* Table 2.12.

3. UNDP, *Human Development Report 2006,* Table 26. Gross tertiary enrolment ratios are estimated on the basis of female ratios.

4. Estimation. Tertiary enrollment rations were estimated for Bahamas, Bhutan, North Korea, Luxembourg, Solomon Islands, and Taiwan on the basis of comparable neighboring countries.

Adult literacy

If not otherwise noted, UNDP, *Human Development Report 2006,* Table 1. Adult literacy rate (% ages 15 and above) 2004. Cf. The World Bank, *World Development Indicators 2006,* Tables 1.6 and 2.13.
1. CIA, *The World Factbook 2007.*
IR (Index of Intellectual Power resources)
The arithmetic mean of Tertiary enrollment ratio% and Adult literacy%.
ER (Index of economic power resources)
It is calculated by the formula ER = (FF x AP) + (DD x NAP). Data on FF (family farms) and AP (labor force in agriculture are given in Appendix 3 and data on DD (Index of the degree of decentralization of economic power resources) are given in Appendix 4.
IPR (Index of Power Resources)
It is calculated by the formula IPR = (IR x ER)/100.
Mean
The arithmetic mean of the four basic indicators (Tertiary enrollment ratio%, Adult literacy%, FF, and DD).

Appendix 3

The percentage of Family Farms of the total area of agricultural holdings in 172 countries (1980–2005) and the percentage of the agricultural population in 2000–2005

	Country	Year	Criterion of family farms	Family farms %	AP %
1	**Afghanistan**	2005	20 ha	55	80
	Estimation. Maletta 2007. Cf. Wiley 2003; Kurian 1992: 9; World Atlas 1970 Vol. 2: 34–35.				
2	**Albania**	2005	Private family farms	80	58
	Estimation. Sallaku and Shehu 2007. Cf. Stanfield 1998; Eastern Europe 1999: 114; FAO 2007.				
3	**Algeria**	2001	20 ha	48	14
	FAO 2007. Cf. Kurian 1992: 27; LTC 1979: 1.				
4	**Angola**	1998	50% of the land under customary tenure (80%)	40	85
	Estimation. Bruce 1998: 205, 209–212. Cf. Kurian 1992: 46.				
5	**Argentina**	1988	1,000 ha	25	12*
	FAO 1990 World Census: 147. Cf. FAO 2007.				
6	**Armenia**	2005	Private family farms	70	45
	Estimation.Vardanyan and Grigoryan 2007; Lerman 1996; FAO Corporate Document Repository, III. CIS Countries 2007. Cf. Eastern Europe 1999: 139.				
7	**Australia**	1990	Percentage of the number of holdings below 500 ha	60	4
	FAO 2007. Cf. FAO 1990 World Census: 219.				
8	**Austria**	2000	100 ha	68	3
	FAO 2007. Cf. FAO 1990 World Census: 69, 183.				
9	**Azerbaijan**	2005	Family farms	70	41
	Estimation. FAO Corporate Document Repository, III. CIS Countries 2007. Cf. Eastern Europe 1999: 160; Karatnycky et al. 2001: 96.				
10	**Bahamas**	1994	20 ha	19	5
	FAO 2007. Cf. FAO 1990 World Census: 66, 115.				

	Country	Year	Criterion of family farms	Family farms %	AP %
11	Bahrain	2005	Family farms	20	1
	Estimation. "Bahrain Agriculture and Fishing" 2006. Cf. Kurian 1992: 103–104; LTC 1979: 189.				
12	Bangladesh	1996	2 ha	69	63
	FAO 2007. Cf. Kurian 1992: 121–122; LTC 1979: 67; FAO 1980 World Census, Census Bulletin No. 5, 1983.				
13	Barbados	1989	20 ha	19	10
	FAO 2007. Cf. FAO 1990 World Census: 117.				
14	Belarus	2005	Private farms	5	14
	Estimation. FAO Corporate Document Repository. Belarus, 2007. Cf. Europa 2005: 742; Eastern Europe 1999: 188; Karatnycky et al. 2001: 110.				
15	Belgium	2000	100 ha	87	1
	FAO 2007. Cf. FAO 1990 World Census: 69, 185.				
16	Belize	1973	80 ha	32	23
	LTC 1979: 127; Kurian 1992: 149.				
17	Benin	2005	50% of area under indigenous community	45	56[1]
	Estimation. Bruce 1998: 6, 19–23, based tenure (90%)				
18	Bhutan	2005	Family farms	40	63
	Estimation. Wangchuk 2006; Kurian 1992: 185. Cf. Haaland 1986.				
19	Bolivia	1996	Small farmers	45	451
	Chávez 2006. Cf. Kurian 1992: 193; Eckstein et al. 1978: 21–23; LTC 1979: 128–129.				
20	Bosnia and Herzegovina		1980; Family-owned farms	64	6[1]
	Karatnycky et al. 2001: 127. Family-owned farms covered 64 percent of arable area. Cf. Bojnec 2005; FAO 1980 World Census, Census Bulletin No. 24, 1986.				
21	Botswana	2005	50% of area under customary tenure (90%)	45	45[1]
	Estimation. Bruce 1998: 205, 211–217. Cf. FAO 2005; Kurian 1992: 211; FAO 1970 World Census, Census Bulletin No. 21, 1978.				
22	Brazil	1996	200 ha	29	20
	FAO 2007. Cf. Kurian 1992: 131–132; FAO 1980 World Census, Census Bulletin No. 22, 1986.				
23	Brunei	1964	8 ha (63%), owned or in ownerlike possession	38	3
	LTC 1979: 69. Cf. Kurian 1992: 252–253.				
24	Bulgaria	2005	Family farms	40	9

	Country	Year	Criterion of family farms	Family farms %	AP %
	Estimation. See "Bulgaria. Natural conditions, farming traditions and agricultural structures" 2006. Cf. Eastern Europe 1999: 247; Karatnycky et al. 2001: 142.				
25	Burkina Faso	2005	50% of area under community-based tenure (80%)	40	90
	Estimation. Bruce 1998: 6, 24–30; FAO 1990 World Census: 85.				
26	Burma	2003	50 % of the area of holdings under 8 ha	38	70
	FAO 2007; Hudson-Rodd 2004. Cf. Kurian 1992: 1354–1355; FAO 1990 World Census: 169. The state owns all land and property in Burma (Hudson-Rodd 2004: 5).				
27	Burundi	2005	50% of area under indigenous community-based tenure (90%)	45	93
	Estimation. Bruce 1998: 141, 149–154. Cf. Kurian 1992: 280.				
28	Cambodia	2001	Family farms	30	75
	Estimation. Boreak 2006; Ballard 2007; Childress 2001. Cf. Kurian 1992: 297–298;*The Far East and Australasia* 1999: 209.				
29	Cameroon	2005	50% of area under community-based tenure (80%)	40	70
	Estimation. Bruce 1998: 6, 31–37. Cf. Kurian 1992: 314–315.				
30	Canada	2001	Area of holdings owned	62	2
	FAO 2007. Cf. FAO 1990 World Census: 119.				
31	Cape Verde	2004	2 ha	89	24[1]
	FAO 2007. Cf. FAO 1980 World Census, Census Bulletin No. 23, 1986; Bruce 1998: 6, 38–40.				
32	Central African Republic	2005	50% of area under indigenous community-based tenure (90%)	45	741
	Estimation. Bruce 1998: 6, 41–45. Cf. Kurian 1992: 342; FAO 1970 World Census, Census Bulletin No. 21, 1978.				
33	Chad	2005	50% of area under indigenous community-based tenure (90%)	45	80
	Estimation. Bruce 1998: 6, 46–51. Cf. Kurian 1992: 358; FAO 1970 World Census, Census Bulletin No. 21, 1978.				
34	Chile	1997	200 ha	20	14
	FAO 2007. Cf. Kurian 1992: 376-377.				

	Country	Year	Criterion of family farms	Family farms %	AP %
35	China	2005	30% of the area of household responsibility system	30	45
	Estimation. Lohmar and Somwaru 2002; Lohmar 2002; Chai 1998: 11–31. Cf. FAO 2007.				
36	Colombia	2001	100 ha	42	23
	FAO 2007. Cf. Kurian 1992: 402–403; FAO 1990 World Census: 149; LTC 1979: 137.				
37	Comoros	2005	50% of area under indigenous community-based tenure (60%)	30	80
	Estimation. Bruce 1998: 141, 155–159; Kurian 1992: 422.				
38	Congo, D.R.	1990	Area owned and 50% of the area under communal tenure	54	64[1]
	FAO 2007; Bruce 1998: 7, 131–136. Cf. Kurian 1992: 2143; LTC 1979: 62–63.				
39	Congo, Rep.	2005	50% of area under indigenous community-based tenure (90%)	45	42[1]
	Estimation. Bruce 1998: 6, 52–57. Cf. Kurian 1992: 436; FAO 1970 World Census, Census Bulletin No. 21, 1978.				
40	Costa Rica	1973	100 ha	33	20
	LTC 1979: 139; Kurian 1987: 502 (90% of the farms are owner-cultivated).				
41	Côte d'Ivoire	2005	50% of area under indigenous community-based tenure (70%)	35	68
	Estimation. Bruce 1998: 7, 78–82; Kurian 1992: 924. Cf. FAO 1970 World Census, Census Bulletin No. 24, 1978.				
42	Croatia	2003	20 ha	83	3
	FAO 2007.				
43	Cuba	2000	Private farms	20	20
	Sheak 2002. Cf. Puerta and Alvarez 2006; Kurian 1992: 476–477.				
44	Cyprus	1994	20 ha	71	7
	FAO 2007. Cf. FAO 1990 World Census: 159.				
45	Czech Republic	2000	100 ha	12	4
	FAO 2007. Cf. Trnka and Pivcova 2007.				
46	Denmark	2000	100 ha	60	3
	FAO 2007. Cf. FAO 1990 World Census: 69, 189.				

	Country	Year	Criterion of family farms	Family farms %	AP %
47	Djibouti	2005	50 % of area under indigenous tenure system	50	75*
	Estimation. Bruce 1998: 141, 160–163. Cf. FAO 2007.				
48	Dominican Republic	1981	20 ha	12	17
	"Dominican Republic. Land Tenure and Land Policies" 2006. Cf. Kurian 1992: 518; FAO 1970 World Census, Census Bulletin No. 22; LTC 1979: 143.				
49	East Timor	2005	Family farms	20	70
	Estimation. Fitzpatric 2001.				
50	Ecuador	2000	50 ha	39	8
	FAO 2007. Cf. LTC 1979: 144; Kurian 1992: 536–537.				
51	Egypt	2000	4.2 ha	71	32
	FAO 2007. Cf. Kurian 1992: 561–562; LTC 1979: 7–8.				
52	El Salvador	1971	20 ha	36	17
	LTC 1979: 147; Kurian 1992: 586–587. Cf. "El Salvador—The Land Tenure System" 2006; FAO 1970 World Census: 53.				
53	Equatorial Guinea	2005	Area of family-size holdings owned by the holder	35	711
	Estimation. Kurian 1987: 656; *Africa South of the Sahara* 2000: 438.				
54	Eritrea	2005	50% of area under usufructuary rights	45	80
	Estimation. Bruce 1998: 141, 164–168. Cf. Castellani 2000; *Africa South of the Sahara* 2000: 449–450.				
55	Estonia	2001	50 ha	44	11
	FAO 2007. Cf. Eastern Europe 1999: 338.				
56	Ethiopia	2005	50 % of area under community-based tenure systems	50	80
	Estimation. Bruce 1998: 141, 169–174. Cf. FAO 2007; FAO 1990 World Census: 93; "UN Report Calls for Land Ownership," 2002; Kurian 1992: 621				
57	Fiji	1991	20 ha	45	70
	FAO 1990 World Census: 223. Cf. Boydell and Shah 2003; Nawaikula 2006.				
58	Finland	2000	100 ha	93	4
	FAO 2007. Cf. FAO 1990 World Census: 191.				
59	France	2000	100 ha	56	4
	FAO 2007. Cf. FAO 1990 World Census: 193.				

	Country	Year	Criterion of family farms	Family farms %	AP %
60	Gabon	2005	50% of area under indigenous community-based tenure (90%)	45	60
	Estimation. Bruce 1998: 6, 58–62. Cf. Kurian 1992: 651; LTC 1979: 13.				
61	Gambia	2005	50% of area under indigenous community-based tenure (90%)	45	75
	Estimation. Bruce 1998: 6, 63–67.				
62	Georgia	2004	20 ha	69	40
	FAO 2007. Cf. FAO Corporate Document Repository: III. CIC Counties, 2006; Eastern Europe 1999: 366; Karatnycky et al. 2001: 193.				
63	Germany	2000	100 ha	58	3
	FAO 2007.				
64	Ghana	2005	50% of area under community-based tenure (80%)	40	60
	Estimation. Bruce 1998: 6, 68–73. Cf. Asumadu 2003; Larbi et al. 2006.				
65	Greece	2000	30 ha	79	12
	FAO 2007. Cf. FAO 1970 World Census: 511–513.				
66	Guatemala	2000	Small farms	19	50
	Amnesty International 2006. Cf. Viscidi 2004; Kurian 1992: 715; FAO 1980 World Census, Census Bulletin No. 17, 1985; LTC 1979: 152–3.				
67	Guinea	2005	50% of area under community-based tenure (95%)	47	76
	Estimation. FAO 2007; FAO 1990 World Census: 95. Cf. Kurian 1992: 736.				
68	Guinea-Bissau	2005	50% of area under community-based tenure (90%)	45	82
	Estimation. Bruce 1998: 7, 74–77. Cf. FAO 2005; Kurian 1992: 750; LTC 1979: 15.				
69	Guyana	2005	Family farms	30	30*
	Estimation. National Development Strategy, 1997; Kurian 1992: 763–764.				
70	Haiti	2005	5 ha	60	66

	Country	Year	Criterion of family farms	Family farms %	AP %
	Estimation. Bethell 2002; Smucker et al. 2000; Kurian 1992: 780; LTC 1979: 154.				
71	Honduras	1993	20 ha	29	34
	FAO 2007; FAO 1990 World Census: 127. Cf. Kurian 1992: 797; LTC 1979: 155.				
72	Hungary	2005	Small holders—private farmers	47	6
	Osskó and Sebestyén 2005. Cf. Eastern Europe 1999: 392; *Central and South-Eastern Europe* 2000: 394				
73	Iceland	1994	Owner-occupied agricultural holdings	73	5
	Thorheirsson 2006.				
74	India	1996	10 ha	85	60
	FAO 2007. Cf. FAO 1990 World Census: 161.				
75	Indonesia	1993	5 ha	88	43
	FAO 2007. Cf. Kurian 1992: 852–853; LTC 1979: 95; FAO 1960 World Census Vol. 1/c: 72–73.				
76	Iran	2003	50 ha	82	30
	FAO 2007. Cf. FAO 1990 World Census: 163. Cf.*The Middle East and North Africa* 1998: 464.				
77	Iraq	1971	50 ha	74	30*
	LTC 1979: 192. Cf. FAO 1970 World Census: 100–102; Kurian 1987: 972.				
78	Ireland	2000	100 ha	84	8
	FAO 2007; Kurian 1992: 902. Cf. FAO 1990 World Census: 195.				
79	Israel	2005	Family farms and 50% of the area of collective farms	50	2
	Estimation. LTC 1979: 193–5. Cf. "Israel Lands: Privatization or National Ownership?" 2006; FAO 1980 World Census, Census Bulletin No. 24, 1986.				
80	Italy	2000	100 ha	62	5
	FAO 2007. Cf. FAO 1990 World Census: 197.				
81	Jamaica	1996	20 ha	46	18
	FAO 2007. Cf. "Jamaica—Profile in Agriculture" 2006; Kurian 1992: 942; LTC 1979: 157; FAO 1980 World Census, Census Bulletin No. 15, 1985.				
82	Japan	1995	10 ha	78	5
	FAO 2007. Cf. FAO 1980 World Census, Census Bulletin No. 12, 1984.				
83	Jordan	1997	50 ha	67	5

	Country	Year	Criterion of family farms	Family farms %	AP %
	FAO 2007. Cf. Kurian 1992: 958–959; FAO 1980 World Census, Census Bulletin No. 26, 1989; LTC 1979: 196.				
84	Kazakhstan	2005	Family farms	20	20
	Estimation. Schoenian 2006; USAID/Kazakhstan 2005, Cf. Eastern Europe 1999: 428; Karatnycky et al. 2001: 218.				
85	Kenya	1980	Small holdings below 8 ha	46	75
	FAO 1980 World Census, Census Bulletin No. 25, 1986. Cf. Bruce 1998: 141, 175–180; Kurian 1992: 978–979; FAO 1970 World Census: 52; LTC 1979: 17–21.				
86	Korea, North	2005	Private small plots	5	36
	Estimation. Reed 2001; Kurian 1992: 1009–1010.				
87	Korea, South	1990	3 ha	88	6
	FAO 1990 World Census: 167. Cf. Kurian 1992: 1030–1031; FAO 1980 World Census, Census Bulletin No. 15, 1985.				
88	Kuwait	1970	20 ha, owned or in ownerlike possession	38	1
	LTC 1979: 197; FAO 1970 World Census, Census Bulletin No. 12, 1975. Cf. Kurian 1992: 1057.				
89	Kyrgyzstan	2002	20 ha	49	55
	FAO 2007. Cf. "Information on implementation of land and agrarian reform in the Kyrgyz Republic" 2000; Hodous 2006; Eastern Europe 1999: 451.				
90	Laos	1999	50 % of area under customary tenures	50	80
	Estimation. Kurian 1992: 1075; *The Far East and Australia* 1999: 601. Cf. FAO 2007.				
91	Latvia	2001	50 ha	60	13
	FAO 2007. Cf. Eastern Europe 1999: 474; *Central and South-Eastern Europe* 2000: 425.				
92	Lebanon	1998	10 ha	70	7*
	FAO 2007. Cf.Kurian 1992: 1095; FAO 1970 World Census: 51–3.				
93	Lesotho	2005	50% of area under customary tenure (90%)	45	86
	Estimation. Ambrogetti 1997; Bruce 1998: 205, 218–219; Kurian 1992: 1113.				
94	Liberia	2005	50% of area under customary law	40	70
	Estimation. "Liberia Country Study" 2006. Cf. LTC 1979: 24; Bruce 1998: 83–87; Kurian 1992: 1130.				

	Country	Year	Criterion of family farms	Family farms %	AP %
95	Libya	2005	Family farms	50	17
	Estimation. "Libya—Land Use and Irrigation" 2006. Cf. Kurian 1992: 1149–1150; LTC 1979: 26.				
96	Lithuania	2003	50 ha	68	16
	Stanaits 2006. Cf. "Lithuania—Economic Reforms" 2006; Eastern Europe 1999: 499.				
97	Luxembourg	2000	100 ha	71	1
	FAO 2007. Cf. FAO 1990 World Census: 199.				
98	Macedonia	1998	Private family farms	70	22
	Melmed-Sanjak et al. 1998. Cf. "Macedonia—Agriculture" 2006; FAO 1980 World Census, Census Bulletin No. 24, 1986.				
99	Madagascar	2005	50% of area under customary tenure	45	75[1]
	Estimation. "Madagascar: the debate on the land ownership policy document" 2005; Bruce 1998: 223–227; Kurian 1992: 1169–1170.				
100	Malawi	2005	50% of area under customary tenure	40	90
	Estimation. Nothale 2006; Bruce 1998: 205, 230–237. Cf. FAO 2007; Kurian 1992: 1186–1187.				
101	Malaysia	1960	20 ha, owned or in ownerlike possession	55	13
	FAO 1960 World Census Vol. 1/b. Cf. Kurian 1992: 1207–1208; LTC 1979: 109.				
102	Maldives	2005	40% of area under state ownership	40	22
	Estimation. "Maldives," 2006; Kurian 1992: 1225.				
103	Mali	2005	50% of area under communal tenure	45	80
	Estimation. "Land tenure in Mali today" 2006; Bruce 1998: 7, 88–93; Kurian 1992: 1238–1239.				
104	Malta	1980	5 ha	80	3
	FAO 1980 World Census, Census Bulletin No. 6, 1983. Cf. World Atlas 1969 Vol. 1: 271.				
105	Mauritania	2005	Family farms	40	50
	Estimation. Bruce 1998: 7, 95–101. Cf. Kurian 1992: 1255; FAO 1980 World Census, Census Bulletin No. 26, 1989.				
106	Mauritius	1971	Area of small farms	27	14
	Nohlen and Nuscheler 1982 Vol. 5: 264. Cf. Kurian 1992: 1270–1271.				

	Country	Year	Criterion of family farms	Family farms %	AP %
107	Mexico	1970	100 ha for private properties and 50% of the area of Ejidos and Communidades Agrarias	32	18
	LTC 1979: 159–160. Cf. Kurian 1992: 1291; FAO 1970 World Census: 52, 100; Nohlen and Nuscheler 1982 Vol. 3: 126–130.				
108	Moldova	2005	Peasant farms	40	41
	Estimation. Stratan 2007. Cf. Europa 2005: 3976; Schoenian 2001; Eastern Europe 1999: 550–552.				
109	Mongolia	2005	Private livestock ownership	97	40
	Estimation. Animal husbandry is more important than agriculture in Mongolia. See Nasanjargal 2002; Tserendash 2006. Cf.*The Far East and Australia* 1999: 695–696.				
110	Montenegro	2005	20 ha	75	2
	Estimation. FAO 1980 World Census, Census Bulletin No. 24, 1986. Cf. Karatnycky et al. 2001: 430.				
111	Morocco	1996	20 ha	67	40
	FAO 2007. Cf. Kurian 1992: 1316-1317; LTC 1979: 30.				
112	Mozambique	2005	40% of area of state-owned land	40	81
	Estimation. Bruce 1998: 205, 238–246; Kurian 1992: 1336–1337.				
113	Namibia	2005	50% of area under communal land tenure	25	47
	Estimation. FAO 2007; Bruce 1998: 205, 247–252; "Online NewsHour—Land Redistribution in Southern Africa: Namibia Programs" 2006. The large farms of 4,000 white farmers cover approximately half of the arable area. Cf. LTC 1979: 36; Kurian 1992: 1370.				
114	Nepal	2002	5 ha, owned or in ownerlike possession	77	76
	FAO 2007. Cf. Kurian 1992: 1390; FAO 1990 World Census: 171.				
115	Netherlands	2000	100 ha	86	2
	FAO 2007. Cf. FAO 1980 World Census, Census Bulletin No. 19, 1985.				
116	New Zealand	1980	2,000 ha	51	10
	FAO 1980 World Census, Census Bulletin No. 27, 1989.				
117	Nicaragua	2001	70 ha	44	29
	FAO 2007. Cf. Kurian 1992: 1408; LTC 1979: 168-9.				
118	Niger	2005	50% of area under community based tenure	45	90

	Country	Year	Criterion of family farms	Family farms %	AP %
	Estimation. FAO 1980 World Census, Census Bulletin No. 16, 1985; Bruce 1998: 7, 102–109.				
119	Nigeria	2005	50% of area under community based tenure	45	70
	Estimation. Owoeye 2006; "Nigeria: Land Use, Soils, and Land Tenure" 2006; Bruce 1998: 7, 110–115. Cf. LTC 1979: 38–41.				
120	Norway	1999	100 ha	94	4
	FAO 2005. Cf. FAO 1990 World Census: 203.				
121	Oman	2005	Family farms	40	38[1]
	Estimation. Kurian 1992: 1461; *The Middle East and North Africa* 1998: 850.				
122	Pakistan	2000	20 ha, owned	57	42
	FAO 2007. Cf.Kurian 1992: 1479; FAO 1990 World Census: 173.				
123	Panama	2001	Owned area of hoödings	32	21
	FAO 2007. Cf. FAO 1990 World Census: 133; Kurian 1992: 1501; FAO 1980 World Census, Census Bulletin No. 11, 1984.				
124	Papua New Guinea	2005	60% of the land under customary tenure	59	85
	Estimation. Armitage 2006. Cf.Kurian 1992: 1519; Nohlen and Nuscheler 1983 Vol. 8: 289–292.				
125	Paraguay	1991	200 ha	14	45
	FAO 1990 World Census: 153. Cf. Kurian 1992: 1537–1538; LTC 1979: 173–175; FAO 1980 World Census, Census Bulletin No. 24, 1986.				
126	Peru	1994	100 ha	40	9
	Estimation. FAO 1990 World Census: 155. Cf. Kurian 1992: 1559–1560; LTC 1979: 176–177; FAO 1970 World Census: 100–102.				
127	Philippines	2002	10 ha	79	36
	FAO 2007. Cf. FAO 1990 World Census: 175; Kurian 1992: 1586-1587; FAO 1980 World Census, Census Bulletin No. 23, 1986.				
128	Poland	2002	50 ha	73	16
	FAO 2007. Cf. Karatnycky et al. 2001: 293.				
129	Portugal	1999	100 ha	55	10
	FAO 2007. Cf. FAO 1990 World Census: 207.				
130	Qatar	2000	50 ha	27	2[1]
	FAO 2007. Cf. "Qatar – Agriculture and Fishing" 2006; *The Middle East and North Africa* 1998: 873; Kurian 1992: 1603.				
131	Romania	2005	Private holdings	69	32
	Rusu and Pamfil 2007; "FAO project tcp/rom2801." 2006. Cf. Eastern Europe 1999: 615–616; *Central and South-Eastern Europe* 2000: 548.				

	Country	Year	Criterion of family farms	Family farms %	AP %
132	Russia	2005	Peasant private farms	10	11
	Estimation. "Russia: Yeltsin's Agricultural Policies" 2007; Praust 2006; "Russian official outlines plans for first farms census in 80 years" 2006. Cf. Eastern Europe 1999: 658–659; Karatnycky et al. 2001: 328.				
133	Rwanda	2005	50 % of area under indigenous community based tenure	45	90
	Estimation. "Aquaculture Development in Rwanda" 2006; Bruce 1998: 141, 181–186. Cf. Kurian 1992: 1517–1518; FAO 1980 World Census, Census Bulletin 26, 1986.				
134	Saudi Arabia	2005	Family farms	40	12
	Estimation. "Saudi Arabia – Modern Agriculture in Saudi Arabia" 2006; Kurian 1992: 1669; FAO 1980 World Census, Census Bulletin No. 17, 1985.				
135	Senegal	2005	50% of area under indigenous community based tenure	40	77
	Estimation. Niang 2004; Bruce 1998: 7, 116–121; Kurian 1992: 1691; LTC 1979: 47.				
136	Serbia	2005	20 ha	75	30
	Estimation. FAO 1980 World Census, Census Bulletin No. 24, 1986. Cf. Karatnycky et al. 2001: 430.				
137	Sierra Leone	2005	50% of area under indigenous community based tenure	45	65*
	Estimation. Bruce 1998: 7, 122–125; Kurian 1992: 1721.				
138	Singapore	2005	Family farms	50	0
	Estimation. *The Far East and Australasia* 1999: 1062; Kurian 1987: 1773; FAO 1970 World Census, Census Bulletin No. 29, 1980.				
139	Slovakia	2002	Private farms and 50% of agricultural co-operatives	31	6
	Bandlerova and Morisova 2003; Blaas 2006; "Slovakia," 2006. Cf. Eastern Europe 1999: 758.				
140	Slovenia	2000	Family farms	87	5
	Estimation. FAO 2007. Cf. Slovenian National Committee of ICID (SINDIC), 2006; FAO 1990 World Census: 209.				
141	Solomon Isl.	2005	50% of customarily owned land	45	75
	Estimation. "Solomon Islands Logging" 2006. Cf. Kurian 1992: 1753–1754; World Atlas 1973 Vol. 2: 664.				

	Country	Year	Criterion of family farms	Family farms %	AP %
142	Somalia	2005	50% of area under traditional tenure	40	71
	Estimation. Bruce 1998: 141, 187–191; Kurian 1992: 1768–1769.				
143	South Africa	2005	Family farms	20	30
	Estimation. "Land Redistribution in Southern Africa" 2006; Lehohla 2004; Bruce 1998: 205, 253–260. Cf. FAO 1960 World Census Vol. 1/b: 232–3.				
144	Spain	1989	100 ha, total area	38	5
	FAO 1990 World Census: 211. Cf. FAO 1980 World Census, Census Bulletin No. 21, 1986.				
145	Sri Lanka	2002	Small holdings, 8 ha	76	34
	"Data based on census of agriculture – 2002," 2006. Cf. FAO 2005.				
146	Sudan	2005	Family farms	40	80
	Estimation. "Sudan – Agriculture" 2006; Bruce 1998: 141, 192–196; Kurian 1992: 1806–1807.				
147	Surinam	2005	Owner-operated farms	20	8
	Estimation. Kurian 1992: 1822.				
148	Swaziland	2005	50% of Swazi Nation Land (63%)	28	35[1]
	Estimation. Magagula 2006; Bruce 1998: 205, 261–265; Kurian 1992: 1835.				
149	Sweden	2000	100 ha	76	2
	FAO 2007. Cf. FAO 1980 World Census, Census Bulletin No. 21, 1986.				
150	Switzerland	1990	100 ha, productive area	99	5
	FAO 1990 World Census: 213.				
151	Syria		50 ha	50	26
	Estimation. "Syria – Agriculture" 2006; Kurian 1992: 1852–1853; FAO 1970 World Census: 53.				
152	Taiwan	2005	5 ha	90	5
	Estimation. LTC 1979: 119.				
153	Tajikistan	1996	Lifelong inheritable holdings	20	67
	Estimation. FAO, Land Reform in Tajikistan, 2007; Foroughi 2006. Cf. Europa 2005; Karatnycky et al. 2001: 372.				
154	Tanzania	2005	50% of area under alternative community based tenures	40	80
	Estimation. Tulahi and Hingi 2006; Bruce 1998: 141, 205, 266–269; Kurian 1992: 1873-1875.				
155	Thailand	2003	10 ha, owned area of holdings	60	49

	Country	Year	Criterion of family farms	Family farms %	AP %
	Estimation. FAO 2007. Cf. FAO 1990 World Census: 177; Kurian 1992: 1897.				
156	Togo	2005	50% of area under community based tenure	45	65
	Estimation. Bruce 1998: 7, 126–130; Kurian 1992: 1918.				
157	Trinidad and Tobago	2004	10 ha	44	9
	FAO 2007. Cf. Kurian 1992: 1943; FAO 1980 World Census, Census Bulletin No. 16, 1985; LTC 1979: 183.				
158	Tunisia	1995	50 ha	63	55
	FAO 2007. Cf. Kurian 1992: 1959–1960; LTC 1979: 58–59; *The Middle East and North Africa* 1998: 992–993.				
159	Turkey	2001	50 ha	88	35
	FAO 2007. Cf. FAO 1990 World Census: 179; Kurian 1992: 1982-1983.				
160	Turkmenistan	2005	Family farms	10	48
	Estimation. "Turkmenistan - Privatization" 2006; Eastern Europe 1999: 836; Karatnycky et al. 2001: 387.				
161	Uganda	2005	50% of area under community based tenure	40	82
	Estimation. Bruce 1998: 141, 197–200; Kurian 1992: 2010; FAO 1990 World Census: 111.				
162	Ukraine	2005	Family farms	30	25
	Estimation. Bondnar and Lile 2002; USAID Europe and Eurasia, 2005; Woronowycz 1997. Cf. Eastern Europe 1999: 859; Karatnycky et al. 2001: 402.				
163	United Arab Emirates	2005	Family farms	30	7
	Estimation. Kurian 1992: 2024–2025; World Atlas 1970 Vol. 2: 143; Bowen-Jones 1980: 59–62.				
164	United Kingdom	2000	100 ha	31	1
	FAO 2007. Cf. FAO 1990 World Census: 215.				
165	United States	2002	809 ha, total area	48	1
	FAO 2007. Cf. FAO 1990 World Census: 143.				
166	Uruguay	2000	1000 ha	46	14
	FAO 2007. Cf. Kurian 1992: 2041; FAO 1980 World Census, Census Bulletin No. 8, 1984.				
167	Uzbekistan	2005	Family farms	10	44

	Country	Year	Criterion of family farms	Family farms %	AP %
	Estimation. Törhönen 2002; Eastern Europe 1999: 892.				
168	Venezuela	1997	200 ha	25	13
	FAO 2007. Cf. Kurian 1992: 2071–2072; FAO 1970 World Census: 53, 56.				
169	Vietnam	2001	30% of the area of the production contract system	30	57
	Estimation. FAO 2007; *The Far East and Australia* 1999: 1183; Kurian1992: 2092–2093.				
170	Yemen	1980	10 ha, owned or in ownerlike possession	46	53[1]
	Estimation. FAO 1980 World Census, Census Bulletin No. 10, 1984. Cf. Kurian 1992: 2122–2123.				
171	Zambia	2005	50% of area under customary tenure	40	85
	Estimation. Bruce 1998: 205, 270–275; Kurian 1992: 2164.				
172	Zimbabwe	2005	50% of the area under African customary tenure	30	66
	Estimation. Green 2006; Chitiyo 2000; Bruce 1998: 205, 276–282. Cf. Kurian 1992: 2183–2184.				

Variables:

Year = The year of census or other source of data. Estimations concern the situation in 2005.

Criterion of Family Farms = The upper hectare limit of family farms, or other criteria described. The other criteria may limit the category of family farms to the area owned or in ownerlike possession, or to a certain percentage (usually 50) of the area under indigenous community-based tenure. In several cases, the estimated percentage share of the land under community-based tenure of the total area is indicated in brackets.

Family Farms% = The percentage share of family farms of the total area of holdings or of agricultural land.

AP% = The percentage of agricultural population usually in 2000–2005. Labor force by occupation.

Abbreviations:

Eastern Europe 1999 = *Eastern Europe and the Commonwealth of Independent States 1999*
FAO 2007 = FAO, *World Census of Agriculture – Results by country*
LTC 1979 = Land Tenure Center, *Land Concentration in the Third World: Statistics on Number and Area of Farms Classified by Size of Farms*
World Atlas = *World Atlas of Agriculture*, Volumes 1–4

AP = Agricultural population (Labor force by occupation)
If not otherwise noted, CIA, *The World Factbook 2007*. Most data are from the period 1995–2006.
* CIA, *The World Factbook 2000*.
1. FAO, *Production Yearbook 1998*.

Appendix 4

Data on the estimated degree of economic power resources (DD) and on its components in 172 countries

	Country	Population below poverty line %	Richest 10% minus 10% %	Inverse total %	DD
1	Afghanistan	53	20*	27	27
2	Albania	19	12	69	69
3	Algeria	17	17	66	44[1]
4	Angola	70	20*	90	10
5	Argentina	21	28	51	51
6	Armenia	38	23	39	39
7	Australia	14	15	71	71
8	Austria	7	13	80	80
9	Azerbaijan	49	11	40	20[1]
10	Bahamas	9	17	74	74
11	Bahrain	-	-	-	15[2]
12	Bangladesh	52	18	30	30
13	Barbados	20*	20*	60	60
14	Belarus	34	12	54	34[3]
15	Belgium	6	14	80	80
16	Belize	33	20*	47	47
17	Benin	41	18	41	41
18	Bhutan	32	20*	48	48
19	Bolivia	43	32	25	25
20	Bosnia and Herzegovina	19	11	70	70
21	Botswana	35	46	19	19
22	Brazil	22	30	48	48
23	Brunei	-	-	-	15[2]
24	Bulgaria	17	14	69	69
25	Burkina Faso	47	27	26	26

	Country	Population below poverty line	Richest 10% minus 10%	Inverse total	DD
26	Burma (Myanmar)	25	22	53	33[1]
27	Burundi	62	23	15	15
28	Cambodia	46	24	30	30
29	Cameroon	40	26	34	34
30	Canada	8	15	77	77
31	Cape Verde	30	25*	45	45
32	Central African Republic	75	38	0	54
33	Chad	69	20*	11	11
34	Chile	12	37	51	51
35	China	18	23	59	39[3]
36	Colombia	36	33	31	31
37	Comoros	60	20*	20	20
38	Congo, Dem. Republic	50*	20*	30	30
39	Congo, Republic of	50*	20*	30	30
40	Costa Rica	13	27	60	60
41	Côte d'Ivoire	30	22	48	48
42	Croatia	11	14	75	75
43	Cuba	-	-	-	20[2]
44	Cyprus	10*	15*	75	75
45	Czech Republic	5	12	83	83
46	Denmark	5*	12	83	83
47	Djibouti	50	20*	30	30
48	Dominican Republic	22	30	48	48
49	East Timor	42	20*	38	38
50	Ecuador	35	29	36	36
51	Egypt	27	18	55	35[1]
52	El Salvador	35	29	36	36
53	Equatorial Guinea	50*	30*	20	20
54	Eritrea	52	20*	28	28
55	Estonia	9	18	73	73
56	Ethiopia	45	18	37	37
57	Fiji	25	15*	60	60
58	Finland	5	13	82	82
59	France	7	15	78	78
60	Gabon	50*	20*	30	30
61	Gambia	67	27	6	6
62	Georgia	41	19	40	40
63	Germany	9	13	78	78
64	Ghana	47	20	33	33
65	Greece	14	17	69	69
66	Guatemala	41	34	25	25

	Country	Population below poverty line	Richest 10% minus 10%	Inverse total	DD
67	Guinea	43	22	35	35
68	Guinea-Bissau	50*	30	20	20
69	Guyana	40*	241	36	36
70	Haiti	70	38	0	54
71	Honduras	43	32	20	20
72	Hungary	7	12	81	81
73	Iceland	5*	10*	85	85
74	India	37	20	43	43
75	Indonesia	25	18	57	57
76	Iran	16	24	60	40[1]
77	Iraq	-	-	-	25[2]
78	Ireland	13	17	70	70
79	Israel	19	19	62	62
80	Italy	13	17	70	70
81	Jamaica	12	20	68	68
82	Japan	12	12	76	76
83	Jordan	16	21	63	43[1]
84	Kazakhstan	18	16	65	45[3]
85	Kenya	46	25	29	29
86	Korea, North	-	-	-	5[2]
87	Korea, South	6	13	81	81
88	Kuwait	-	-	-	25[2]
89	Kyrgyzstan	32	14	54	34[3]
90	Laos	48	19	33	13[3]
91	Latvia	16	18	66	66
92	Lebanon	28	20*	52	52
93	Lesotho	47	36	17	17
94	Liberia	60*	20*	20	20
95	Libya	-	-	-	25[2]
96	Lithuania	9	17	74	74
97	Luxembourg	6	141	80	80
98	Macedonia	16	20	64	64
99	Madagascar	65	24	11	11
100	Malawi	58	32	10	10
101	Malaysia	8	28	64	64
102	Maldives	40*	30*	30	30
103	Mali	72	30	0	54
104	Malta	10*	15*	75	75
105	Mauritania	43	20	37	37
106	Mauritius	10	20*	70	70
107	Mexico	23	28	49	49

	Country	Population below poverty line	Richest 10% minus 10%	Inverse total	DD
108	Moldova	37	16	47	47
109	Mongolia	43	27	30	30
110	Montenegro	12	20*	68	68
111	Morocco	17	21	62	42[1]
112	Mozambique	65	22	13	13
113	Namibia	45	54	1	54
114	Nepal	38	30	32	32
115	Netherlands	9	13	78	78
116	New Zealand	10*	18	72	72
117	Nicaragua	54	28	18	18
118	Niger	67	25	8	8
119	Nigeria	64	26	10	10
120	Norway	5	13	82	82
121	Oman	-	-	-	20[2]
122	Pakistan	35	17	48	48
123	Panama	26	31	43	43
124	Papaua New Guinea	37	30	33	33
125	Paraguay	26	35	39	39
126	Peru	38	31	31	31
127	Philippines	35	24	41	41
128	Poland	12	17	71	71
129	Portugal	10*	20	70	70
130	Qatar	-	-	-	15[2]
131	Romania	20	15	65	65
132	Russia	16	24	60	40[3]
133	Rwanda	63	14	23	23
134	Saudi Arabia	-	-	-	20[2]
135	Senegal	44	23	33	33
136	Serbia	30	15	55	55
137	Sierra Leone	68	34	0	54
138	Singapore	10*	23	77	77
139	Slovakia	10	11	79	79
140	Slovenia	8	11	81	81
141	Solomon Islands	40*	20*	40	40
142	Somalia	50*	20*	30	30
143	South Africa	32	35	33	33
144	Spain	14	16	70	70
145	Sri Lanka	23	22	55	55
146	Sudan	40	30*	30	30
147	Surinam	40*	15*	45	45
148	Swaziland	69	40	0	54

	Country	Population below poverty line	Richest 10% minus 10%	Inverse total	DD
149	Sweden	6	11	83	83
150	Switzerland	8	16	76	76
151	Syria	12	20*	68	
152	Taiwan	5*	31	64	64
153	Tajikistan	44	16	40	40
154	Tanzania	53	18	29	29
155	Thailand	16	23	61	61
156	Togo	32	20*	48	48
157	Trinidad and Tobago	23	20	47	47
158	Tunisia	7	22	71	51[1]
159	Turkey	18	23	59	59
160	Turkmenistan	58	22	20	20
161	Uganda	35	20	45	45
162	Ukraine	15	14	71	71
163	United Arab Emirates	-	-	-	10[2]
164	United Kingdom	15	18	67	67
165	United States	14	20	66	66
166	Uruguay	15	21	64	64
167	Uzbekistan	30	12	58	38[3]
168	Venezuela	28	24	48	48
169	Vietnam	26	20	54	34[3]
170	Yemen	38	16	46	46
171	Zambia	83	26	0	5[4]
172	Zimbabwe	63	30	7	7

Sources

Population below poverty line

If not otherwise noted, *World Development Indicators 2006*, Table 2.7; *Human Development Report 2006*, Tables 3 and 4, and CIA, *The World Factbook 2007*. Data are arithmetic means of various data on population below poverty line given in these three sources or in one or two sources.

* Estimation. Due to the lack of data, Population below poverty line% was estimated for Barbados, the Democratic Republic of Congo, the Republic of Congo, Cyprus, Denmark, Equatorial Guinea, Gabon, Guinea-Bissau,

Guyana, Iceland, Malta, New Zealand, Portugal, Singapore, the Solomon Islands, Somalia, and Surinam principally on the basis of data for comparable neighboring countries.

Richest 10 percent minus 10 percent

If not otherwise noted, *World Development Indicators 2006*, Table 2.8; *Human Development Report 2006*, Table 15, and CIA, *The World Factbook 2007*. Data are arithmetic means of the percentage share of income or consumption of the richest 10 percent of the population given in three or two sources. In some cases, data are based on only one source. In each case, 10 percentage points is subtracted from the share of the richest 10 %.

1. (UNDP) *Human Development Report 2004*, Table 14.

* Estimation. Due to the lack of data, Richest 10% minus 10% was estimated for Afghanistan, Angola, Barbados, Belize, Bhutan, Cape Verde, Chad, Comoros, the Democratic Republic of Congo, the Republic of Congo, Cyprus, Djibouti, East Timor, Equatorial Guinea, Eritrea, Fiji, Gabon, Iceland, Lebanon, Liberia, Maldives, Malta, Mauritius, Montenegro, the Solomon Islands, Somalia, Sudan, Surinam, Syria, and Togo. The actual values of neighboring countries were taken into account in these estimations, which vary from 5 to 30.

Inverse total percent

This is calculated by adding the percentages of the first two columns (Population below poverty line % and Richest 10 % minus 10 %). and then subtracting the sum from 100 percent.

DD (the degree of decentralization of economic power resources)

If not otherwise noted, DD is the same as the inverse total %.

1. DD value was reduced by 20 points in the cases of Algeria, Azerbaijan, Burma, Egypt, Iran, Jordan, Morocco, Syria, and Tunisia. The government controls crucial economic power resources based on oil production in Algeria, Azerbaijan,

and Iran. In the other countries, most important economic power resources are also concentrated in the hands of the government.

2. In the lack of data, DD values are completely estimated for 11 countries. Bahrain, Brunei, Iraq, Kuwait, Libya, Oman, Qatar, Saudi Arabia, and the United Arab Emirates are oil-producing countries, in which the government controls the crucial oil resources, and Cuba and North Korea are socialist countries, in which the government controls all important economic power resources.

3. DD value was reduced by 20 points in the cases of some contemporary socialist and former socialist countries (Belarus, China, Kazakhstan, Kyrgyzstan, Laos, Russia, Uzbekistan, and Vietnam). The most important economic power resources are controlled by the government in all these countries.

4. DD value was raised to 5 points in seven countries for which Inverse total% is less than 5 points (the Central African Republic, Haiti, Mali, Namibia, Sierra Leone, Swaziland, and Zambia).

APPENDIX 5

Abbreviations Used

DD   Degree of decentralization of economic power resources
ER   Index of economic power resources
FF   Family farms
GID   Gender-weighted index of democratization
ID   Index of democratization
IQ   Intelligence quotient
IPR   Index of power resources
IR   Index of intellectual power resources
MT   Annual mean temperature

References

Africa A–Z. See Esterhuysen, 1998.

Africa South of the Sahara 2000. 2000. London: Europa Publications.

Alieva, Leila. 2006. "Azerbaijan's Frustrating Elections," *Journal of Democracy* 17, 2: 147–160.

Allen, John L. 2003. *Student Atlas of World Geography.* Third Edition. NYC McGraw-Hill.

Altman, David, and Aníbal Pérez-Liñán. 2002. "Assessing the Quality of Democracy: Freedom, Competitiveness and Participation in Eighteen Latin American Countries," *Democratization* 9, 2: 85–100.

Ambrogetti, Agostino. 1997. "Communal systems of land tenure and fair access to the land: The case of Lesotho." FAO, Sustainable Development Department, http://www.fao.org/sd/LTdirect/LTan0019.htm.

Amnesti International. 2006. "Guatemala. Land of injustice?" http://web.amnesti.org/library/index/ENGAMR340032006.

Anglade, Christian. 1994. "Democracy and the Rule of Law in Latin America," in Ian Budge and David McKay, eds. *Developing Democracy: Comparative research in honour of J. F. P. Blondel.* London: Sage Publications.

"Aquaculture Development in Rwanda." 2006. http://www.fao.org/docrep/006/p3718e/p3718e03.htm.

Arden, Rosalind. 2003. "The Arthurian Romance," in Helmuth Nyborg, ed., *The Scientific Study of General Intelligence: Tribute to Arthur R. Jensen.* Amsterdam: Pergamon.

Aristotle, The Politics of or a Treatise on Government. 1952. Translated by William Ellis. London: J.M. Dent & Sons.

Armitage, Lynne. 2006. "Customary land tenure in Papua New Guinea: Status and prospects," http://dlc.dlib.indiana.edu/archive/00001043/00/armitage.pdf.

Aspaturian, Vernon V. 1968. "The Soviet Union," in Roy C. Macridis and Robert E. Ward, eds., *Modern Political Systems: Europe.* Englewood Cliffs, New Jersey: Prentice-Hall.

Asumadu, Kwame. 2003. "Reform of Ghana's Land Tenure System," http://www.ghanaweb.com/GhanaHomePage/features/artikel.php?ID=36246.

Ayittey, George B. N. 1999. *Africa in Chaos.* New York: St. Martin's Griffin.

"Bahrain Agriculture and Fishing." 2006. http://www.photius.com/countries/bahrain/economy/bahrain_economy_agriculture_and_fish~87.html.

Ballard, B. 2007. "Land tenure database development in Cambodia." Phnom Penh: Cambodia Development Resource Institute. http://www.fao.org/docrep/009/a0306t/A0306T08.htm.

Ballington, Julie, and Azza Karam. 2005. *Women in Parliament: Beyond Numbers.* A Revised Edition. Stockholm: International Institute for Democracy and Electoral Assistance.

Bandlerova, A., and E. Morisova. 2003. "Importance of ownership and lease of agricultural land in Slovakia in the pre-accession period." http://www.cazv.cz/2003/AE5_03/3-Bandlerova-Morisova.pdf.

Banks, Arthur S., Thomas C. Muller and William R. Overstreet. 2007. *The Political Handbook of the World: 2007.* Washington, D.C.: CQ Press.

Beetham, David. 2003. "Democratic Quality: Freedom and Rights." Center on Democracy, Development, and the Rule of Law, Stanford Institute on International Studies. http://iis-db.stanford.edu/pubs/20433/Freedom_and_Rights.pdf.

Bendix, Reinhard and Seymour Martin Lipset, eds. 1967. *Class, Status and Power: Social Stratification in Comparative Perspective.* London: Routledge & Kegan Paul.

Berg-Schlosser, Dirk. 2004. "Indicators of Democracy and Good Governance as Measures of the Quality of Democracy in Africa: A Critical Appraisal," *Acta Politica* 39: 249–278.

Berg-Schlosser, Dirk. 2005. "Conclusions: Successful democratisation across cultures," in Ursula J. van Beek, ed., *Democracy Under Construction: Patterns From Four Continents.* Bloomfield Hills & Opladen: Barbara Budrich Publishers.

Berg-Schlosser, Dirk, ed. 2004. *Democratization: The State of the Art*. Wiesbaden: VS Verlag für Sozialwissenschaften.

Berg-Schlosser, Dirk, and Jeremy Mitchell, eds. 2000. *Conditions of Democracy in Europe, 1919–39: Systematic Case Studies*. New York: St. Martin's Press.

Berg-Schlosser, Dirk, and Jeremy Mitchell, eds. 2002. *Authoritarianism and Democracy in Europe, 1919–39: Comparative Analyses*. Houndmills, Basingstoke: Palgrave Macmillan.

Bethell, Amber. 2002. "Land Tenure and Reform in Haiti." http://www.spatial.maine.edu/~onsrud/Landtenure/CountryReport/Haiti.pdf

Blaas, Gejza. 2006. "Agricultural Reform in Slovakia: Changing Institutions and Structures." http://src-h.slav.hokudai.ac.jp/kaken/ieda2001/pdf/blaas.pdf.

Blondel, Jean. 1995. *Comparative Government: An Introduction*. Second edition. London: Prentice Hall/Harvester Wheatsheaf.

Blondel, Jean, Takashi Inoguchi, and Ian Marsh. 1999. "Economic development v. political democracy," in Ian Marsh, Jean Blondel, and Takashi Inoguchi, eds., *Democracy, Governance, and Economic Performance: East and Southeast Asia*. Tokyo: United Nations University Press.

Bogaards, Matthijs. 2000a. "Elections, Election Outcomes, and Democracy in Southern Africa," *Democratization* 14, 1: 73–91.

Bogaards, Matthijs. 2000b. "Measuring Democracy through Election Outcomes: A Critique with African Data," *Comparative Political Studies* 40, 10: 1211–1237.

Bojnec, Stefan. 2005. "Agriculture in post-war Bosnia and Herzegovina: Social buffer vs. development." Paper presented at the XIth EAAE (European Association of Agricultural Economists) Congress, Copenhagen, Denmark, August 24–27. http://www.eaae2005/dk/.

Bondnar, Anatolly, and Boo Lile. 2002. "Land Privatization in Ukraine." http://www.fig.net/pub/fig_2002/ts7-6/ts7_6_bondar_lilje.pdf.

Boreak, Sik. 2006. "Land Ownership, Sales and Concentration in Cambodia." Working Paper 16. Phnom Penh: Cambodia Development Resource Institute. http://www.cdri.org.kh/webdata/download/wp/wp16e.pdf

Boroumand, Ladan. 2007. "Iran's Resilient Civil Society: The Untold Story of the Fight for Human Rights," *Journal of Democracy* 18, 4: 64–79.

Bowen-Jones, H. 1980. "Agriculture in Bahrain, Kuwait, Qatar, and UAE," in M. Ziwar-Dalfari, ed., *Issues in Development: The Arab Gulf States*. London: MD Research and Sciences Ltd.

Boydell, Spike, and Krishn Shah. 2003. "An inquiry into the nature of land ownership in Fiji." The International Association for the Study of Common Property, Second Pacific Regional Meeting, Brisbane, 7–9 September. http://

dlc.dlib.indiana.edu/archive/00001208/00/Boydell_&_Shah_inquiry_into_land.pdf

Bremmer, Ian, and Ray Taras, eds. 1997. *New States, New Politics: Building the Post-Soviet Nations.* Cambridge: Cambridge University Press.

Brody, Nathan. 2003. "Jensen's Genetic Interpretation of Racial Differences in Intelligence: Critical Evaluation," in Helmuth Nyborg, ed., *The Scientific Study of General Intelligence: Tribute to Arthur R. Jensen.* Amsterdam: Pergamon.

Brown, J. F. 1988. *Eastern Europe and Communist Rule.* Durham and London: Duke University Press.

Bruce, J. W. 1998. *Country Profiles of Land Tenure: Africa, 1996.* LTC Research Paper 130. Madison: Land Tenure Center, University of Madison. http://pdf.wri.org/ref/elbow_98_synthesis.pdf

Brynen, Rex, Bahgat Korany, and Paul Noble, eds. 1995. *Political Liberalization and Democratization in the Arab World. Volume 1, Theoretical Perspectives.* Boulder: Lynne Rienner Publishers.

Brynen, Rex, Bahgat Korany, and Paul Noble. 1998. "Conclusion: Liberalization, Democratization, and Arab Experiences," in Bahgat Korany, Rex Brynen, and Paul Noble, eds. *Political Liberalization and Democratization in the Arab World. Volume 2, Comparative Perspectives.* Boulder: Lynne Rienner Publishers.

"Bulgaria. Natural conditions, farming traditions and agricultural structures." 2006. http://www.fao.org/regional/seur/Review/Bulgaria.htm.

Carroll, John B. 2003. "The Higher-Stratum Structure of Cognitive Abilities: Current Evidence Supports *g* and About Ten Broad Factors," in Helmuth Nyborg, ed., *The Scientific Study of General Intelligence: Tribute to Arthur R. Jensen.* Amsterdam: Pergamon.

Case, William. 2007. "Democracy's Quality and Breakdown: New Lessons from Thailand," *Democratization* 14, 4: 622–642.

Castellani, L. G. 2000. *Recent Developments in Land Tenure Law in Eritrea, Horn of Africa.* Land Tenure Center, University of Wisconsin-Madison. http://www.terrafirma.co.mz/downloads/Eritrean%20Land%20Law.pdf

Cavalli-Sforza, Luigi Luca, and Francesco Cavalli-Sforza. 1995. *The Great Human Diasporas. The History of Diversity and Evolution.* Reading, Massachusetts: Helix Books.

Cavalli-Sforza, L. Luca, Paolo Menozzi, and Alberto Piazza. 1996. *The History and Geography of Human Genes.* Abridged Paperback Edition. Princeton, New Jersey: Princeton University Press.

Cavatorta, Francesco. 2005. "The International Context of Morocco's Stalled Democratization," *Democratization* 12, 4: 548–566.

Central Intelligence Agency (CIA). 2000. *The World Factbook 2000.* Washington, D.C.: Brassey's.

Central Intelligence Agency (CIA). 2005–2007. *The World Factbook. http://* www.cia.gov/cia/publications/factbook/.

Central and South-Eastern Europe 2000. 2000. London: Europa Publications https://www.cia.gov/library/publications/the-world-factbook/

Chai, J. C. 1998. *China's Transition to a Market Economy.* Oxford: Clarendon Press.

Chávez, Franz. 2006. "Bolivia: Government Takes Up Challenge of Land Reform," http://ipsnews.net/news.asp?idnews=32429.

Chazan, Naomi. 1988. "Ghana: Problems of Governance and the Emergence of Civil Society," in Larry Diamond, Juan J. Linz, and Seymour Martin Lipset, eds., *Democracy in Developing Countries. Vol. 2. Africa.* Boulder: Lynne Rienner Publishers.

Chazan, Naomi, Peter Lewis, Robert A. Mortimer, Donald Rotchild, and Stephen John Stedman. 1999. *Politics and Society in Contemporary Africa.* 3rd edition. Boulder: Lynne Rienner Publishers.

Chen, An. 2003. "Rising Class Politics and Its Impact on China's Path to Democracy," *Democratization* 10, 2: 141–162.

Childress, M. 2001. "Cambodia Maps its Land Tenure Future." *Land Tenure Center Newsletter,* No. 82, Fall: 1–8. http://www.ies.wisc.edu/ltc/news82a1. html.

Chitiyo, Tapera Knox. 2000. "Land Violence and Compensation: Reconceptualizing Zimbabwe's Land and War Veterans' Debate." *TrackTwo,* Vol. 9, No. 1. May. http://www.ccr.uct.ac.za/archive/two/9_1/ximbabwe.html.

Chkhikvadze, V. M. 1969. *The Soviet State and Law.* Moscow: Progress Publishers.

Chol, Sung-Chui. 1997. *Understanding Human Rights in North Korea.* Seoul: The Institute of Unification Policy, Hanyang University.

Chronicle of Parliamentary Elections. See Inter-Parliamentary Union.

Clark, John F., and David E. Gardinier, eds. 1997. *Political Reform in Francophone Africa.* Boulder: Westview Press.

Coleman, James S., and Carl G. Rosberg, eds. 1964. *Political Parties and National Integration in Tropical Africa.* Berkeley: University of California Press.

Coppedge, Michael. 2004. "Quality of Democracy and Its Measurement," in Guillermo O'Donnell, Jorge Vargas Cullell, and Osvaldo M. Iazzetta, eds, *The Quality of Democracy: Theory and Applications.* Notre Dame,

Indiana: University of Notre Dame Press.

Cottrell, Jill, and Yash Ghai. 2007. "Constitution Making and Democratization in Kenya (2000–2005)," *Democratization* 14, 1: 1–25.

Coulon, Christian. 1988. "Senegal: The Developement and Fragility of Semidemocracy," in Larry Diamond, Juan J. Linz, and Seymour Martin Lipset, eds., *Democracy in Developing Countries. Vol. 2 Africa.* Boulder: Lynne Rienner Publishers.

Cullell, Jorge Vargas. 2004. "Democracy and Quality of Democracy: Empirical Findings and Methodological and Theoretical Issues Drawn from the Citizen Audit of the Quality of Democracy in Costa Rica," in Guillermo O'Donnell, Jorge Vargas Cullell, and Osvaldo M. Iazzetta, eds. *The Quality of Democracy: Theory and Applications.* Notre Dame, Indiana: University of Notre Dame Press.

Daalder, Hans, and Peter Mair, eds. 1983. *Western European Party Systems: Continuity and Change.* Beverly Hills, California: Sage Publications.

Dadabaev, Timur. 2005. "Uzbekistan: Post-Soviet Realities," in Takashi Inoguchi, Miguel Basáñez, Akihiko Tanaka, and Timur Dadabaev, eds., *Values and Life Styles in Urban Asia.* Mexico City: SIGLO XXI Editores.

Dadabaev, Timur. 2006. "Political Cultures, Development Strategies and Public Support in Post-socialist Central Asian Societies: Analysis of Public Polls in Uzbekistan and Kazakhstan," *Political Science in Asia (PSA)* 2, 1: 71–100.

Dahl, Robert A. 1967. *Pluralist Democracy in the United States: Conflict and Consent.* Chicago: Rand McNally & Company.

Dahl, Robert A. 1971. *Polyarchy: Participation and Opposition.* New Haven and London: Yale University Press.

Dahl, Robert A. 1989. *Democracy and Its Critics.* New Haven and London: Yale University Press.

Darmanovic, Srdjan. 2007. "Montenegro: A Miracle in the Balkans?" *Journal of Democracy* 18, 2: 152–159.

"Data based on census of agriculture – 2002." 2006. http://www.statistics.gov.lk/agriculture/CENSUSDATA2002.pdf.

Decalo, Samuel. 1990. *Coups and Army Rule in Africa.* New Haven and London: Yale University Press.

Decalo, Samuel. 1998. *The Stable Minority: Civilian Rule in Africa.* Gainesville: Florida Academic Press.

De Lusignan, Guy. 1970. *L'Afrique Noire depuis l'Indépendance: L'évolution des états francophones.* Paris: Fayard.

Deutsch, Karl W., and D. Brent Smith. 1983. "The German Federal Republic:

Western Germany," in Roy C. Macridis, ed., *Modern Political Systems: Europe*. Englewood Cliffs, New Jersey: Prentice-Hall.

DeVotta, Neil. 2002. "Illiberalism and Ethnic Conflict in Sri Lanka," *Journal of Democracy* 13, 1: 84–98.

Diamond, Jared. 1998. *Guns, Germs and Steel: A Short History of Everybody for the Last 13,000 Years*. London: Vintage.

Diamond, Larry. 1988. "Introduction: Roots of Failure, Seeds of Hope," in Larry Diamond, Juan J. Lunz, and Seymour Martin Lipset, eds., *Democracy in Developing Countries. Vol. 2 Africa*. Boulder: Lynne Rienner Publishers.

Diamond, Larry. 1999. *Developing Democracy Toward Consolidation*. Baltimore and London: Johns Hopkins University Press.

Diamond, Larry. 2002. "Thinking About Hybrid Regimes," *Journal of Democracy* 13, 2: 21–35. http://psweb.sbs.ohio-state.edu/faculty/mcooper/ps744readings/diamond.pdf

Diamond, Larry, Juan J. Linz, and Seymour Martin Lipset, eds. 1995. *Politics in Developing Countries: Comparing Experiences with Democracy*. Second edition. Boulder: Lynne Rienner Publishers.

Diamond, Larry, and Leonardo Morlino. 2004. "The Quality of Democracy." *CDDRL Working Papers*, No. 20, 21 September. Center on Democracy, Development, and the Rule of Law, Stanford Institute on International Studies. http://cddrl.stanford.edu.

"Dominican Republic: Land Tenure and Land Policy." 2006. http://www.country-data.com/cgi-bin/query/r-3826.html

Doro, Marion E., and Newell M. Stultz, eds. 1970. *Governing in Black Africa: Perspectives on New States*. Englewood Cliffs, New Jersey: Prentice-Hall.

Douangngeune, Bounlouane. 2006. "Laos: Lao Society as It Is," in Takashi Inoguchi, Akihito Tanaka, Shigeto Sonoda, and Timur Dadabaev, eds, *Human Beliefs and Values in Striding Asia*. Japan: Akashi Shoten.

Drèze, Jean, and Amartya Sen. 2002. *India: Development and Participation*. Oxford: Oxford University Press.

D'Souza, Dinesh. 1995. *The End of Racism. Principles for a Multiracial Society*. New York: The Free Press.

Eastern Europe and the Commonwealth of Independent States. 1999. 1998. London: Europa Publications Limited.

Eckstein, S., G. Donald, D. Horton, and T. Carroll. 1978. *Land Reform in Latin America: Bolivia, Chile, Mexico, Peru, and Venezuela*. Staff Working Paper No. 275. Washington, D.C.: World Bank. http://www.wds.worldbank.org/external/default/WDSContentServer/WDSP/IB/2003/07/22/000178830_

98101903400124/Rendered/PDF/multi0page.pdf

Economist. 2004–2007.

"El Salvador – The Land Tenure System." http://countrystudies.us/el-salvador/54.htm.

Encyclopedia International, Vol. 11. 1964. New York: Crolier Incorporated.

Espíndola, Roberto. 2002. "Political Parties and Democratization in the Southern Cone of Latin America," *Democratization* 9, 3: 109–130.

Esterhuysen, Pieter, ed. 1998. *Africa A–Z: Continental and Country Profiles.* Pretoria: Africa Institute of South Africa.

Europa World Yearbook. 2003–2006. London: Europa Publications.

FAO. 1966–70. *Report on the 1960 World Census of Agriculture,* Vol. 1: a–c. Rome (Food and Agriculture Organization of the United Nations).

FAO. 1973–80. *Report on the 1970 World Census of Agriculture,* Census bulletins 1–29. Rome: Food and Agriculture Organisation of the United Nations.

FAO. 1981. *1970 World Census of Agriculture.* Analyses and International Comparison of the Results. Rome: Food and Agriculture Organization of the United Nations.

FAO. 1983–89. *Report on the 1980 World Census of Agriculture. Results by Countries.* Rome: Food and Agriculture Organization of the United Nations.

FAO. 1997. *Report on the 1990 World Census of Agriculture. International comparison and primary results by country (1986–1995).* Rome: Food and Agriculture Organization of the United Nations.

FAO. 1999. *Production Yearbook 1998.* Vol. 53, Rome: Food and Agriculture Organization of the United Nations.

FAO. Corporate Document Repository. 2007. "Belarus." http://www.fao.org/DOCREP/.

FAO. Corporate Document Repository. 2007. "III.CIS Countries: Transcaucasus States (Georgia, Armenia, Azerbaijan)." http://www.fao.org/DOCREP/.

FAO. Land Reform in Tajikistan, 2007. "Land Reform and Land Tenure in Tajikistan (Status as of January 1, 2007)." http://www.landreform-tajikistan.tj/.

FAO. Statistics Division. 2007. *World Census of Agriculture – Results by Country.* http://www.fao.org./ES/ess/census/.

"FAO project tcp/rom/2801." 2006. http://www.fao.org/sd/2002/TCPROM2801/fao_tcp_document.htm.

The Far East and Australia 1999. 1999. London: Europa Publications.

Filali-Ansary, Abdou. 2003. "The Sources of Enlightened Muslim Thought," *Journal of Democracy* 14, 2: 19–33.

Finnish Social Science Data Archive. 2007. *FSD1289 Measures of Democracy 1810–2006*. http://www.fsd.uta.fi/english/data/catalogue/FSD1289/

Finnish Social Science Data Archive *(FSD1289), Measures of Democracy 1810–2006*. University of Tampere. http://www.fsd.uta.fi.

Finnish Social Science Data Archive *(FSD2140)*, University *Gender-Weighted Index of Democratization 1995–2006*. *University* of Tampere. http://www.fsd.uta.fi.

Finnish Social Science Data Archive *(FSD2183)*, *Women's Representation in National Parliaments 1970–2006*. University of Tampere. http://www.fsd.uta.fi.

Fitzpatrick, Daniel. 2001. "Land Issues in a Newly Independent East Timor." Australia: Information and Research Services. Research Paper No. 21 2000–01.

Foroughi, Payam. 2006. "Food Security in Tajikistan; Private Farming Shows Promise." http://www.isar.org/pubs/ST/TJfarming49.html.

Freedom House. 2001. *Freedom in the World. Annual Survey of Political Rights and Civil Liberties 2000–2001*, Adrian Karatnycky, General Editor. New York: Freedom House.

Freedom House. 2003. *Annual Survey of Freedom Country Scores 1972–73 to 1999–00*. www.freedomhouse.org.

Freedom House. 2004. *Freedom in the World 2004. Annual Survey of Political Rights and Civil Liberties*. Aili Piano and Arch Puddington, eds. New York: Rowman & Littlefield Publishers.

Freedom House. 2005. *Freedom in the World 2005. The Annual Survey of Political Rights and Civil Liberties*. New York: Rowman & Littlefield Publishers.

Freedom House. 2006. *Freedom in the World 2006. Annual Survey of Political Rights and Civil Liberties*. New York: Rowman & Littlefield Publishers.

Freedom in the World. See Freedom House.

Friedman, Edward, ed. 1994. *The Politics of Democratization: Generalizing East Asian Experience*. Boulder: Westview Press.

Ganguly, Sumit. 2002. "India's Multiple Revolutions," *Journal of Democracy* 13, 1: 38–51.

Ganguly, Sumit. 2007. "Six Decades of Independence," *Journal of Democracy* 18, 2: 30–40.

Ganji, Akbar. 2005. "The Struggle Against Sultanism," *Journal of Democracy* 16, 4: 38–51.

Gardner, Stephen H. 1998. *Comparative Economic Systems*. Second edition. Orlando, Florida: Harcourt Brace College Publishers.

Gel'man, Vladimir. 2003. "Post-Soviet Transitions and Democratization: Towards Theory Building," *Democratization* 10, 2: 87–104.

Giddens, Anthony. 1995. *Sociology*. Second Edition, Fully revised and updated. Cambridge: Polity Press.

Gill, Graeme. 2006. "A New Turn to Authoritarian Rule in Russia?" *Democratization* 13, 1: 58–77.

Glenn, John. 2003. "The Economic Transition in Central Asia: Implications for Democracy," *Democratization* 10, 3: 124–147.

Gottfredson, L. S. 1997. "Editorial: Mainstream science on intelligence," *Intelligence* 24: 13–24.

Gould, Stephen Jay. 1984(1981). *The Mismeasure of Man*. Harmondsworth, England: Penguin Books.

Green, Samantha. 2006. "Zimbabwe Land Conflict." ICE Case Studies. http://www.american.edu/TED/ice/zimbabwe.htm.

Greig, Alistair, David Hulme and Mark Turner. 2007. *Challenging Global Inequality. Development Theory and Practice in the 21st Century*. Houndmills, Hampshire: Palgrave Macmillan.

Grofman, Bernard, and Arend Lijphart, eds. 1986. *Electoral Laws and Their Political Consequences*. New York: Agathon Press.

Grusky, David P., ed. 1994. *Social Stratification: Class, Race and Gender in Sociological Perspective*. Boulder: Westview Press.

Gunther, John. 1941. *Inside Latin America*. New York and London: Harper & Brothers.

Guo, Dingping. 2006a. "China: The Evaluation of the Material and Mental Foundations for a Harmonious Society," in Takashi Inoguchi, Akihiko Tanaka, Shigeto Sonoda, and Timur Dadabaev, eds., *Human Beliefs and Values in Striding Asia*. Japan: Akashi Shoten.

Guo, Dingping. 2006b. "Political Culture and Political Developement in China: An Interpretation of Three Surveys," *Political Science in Asia (PSA)* 2, 1: 11–47.

Gurr, Ted Robert, Keith Jaggers, and Will H. Moore. 1990. "The Transformation of the Western State: The Growth of Democracy, Autocracy, and State Power Since 1800." *Studies in Comparative International Development* 25, 1: 73–108.

Haaland, G. 1986. "Farming Systems, Land Tenure and Ecological Balance in Bhutan." Paper presented at the Ninth European Conference on Modern

South Asian Studies, Heidelberg, July.

Hamdok, Abdalla. 2003. "Governance and policy in Africa: Recent experiences," in Steve Kayizzi-Mugerwa, ed., *Reforming Africa's Institutions: Ownership, Incentives, and Capabilities*. Tokyo: United Nations University Press.

Haqqani, Husain. 2006. "History Repeats Itself in Pakistan," *Journal of Democracy* 17, 4: 110–124.

Harbeson, John W. 2005. "Ethiopia's Extended Transition," *Journal of Democracy* 16, 4: 144–158.

Held, Colbert C. 1994. *Middle East Patterns: Places, Peoples, and Politics*. Boulder: Westview Press.

Herb, Michael. 2002. "Emirs and Parliaments in the Gulf," *Journal of Democracy* 13, 4: 41–47.

Herring, Hubert. 1961. *A History of Latin America*. Newly revised third edition. London: Jonathan Cape.

Herrnstein, R. J., and C. Murray. 1994. *The Bell Curve: Intelligence and Class Structure in American Life*. New York: The Free Press.

Hinnebusch, Raymond. 2006. "Authoritarian Persistence, Democratization Theory and the Middle East: An Overview and Critique," *Democratization* 13, 3: 373–395.

Hodous, Florence. 2006. "Agriculture in Uzbekistan and Kyrgyzstan: Towards a Different Social Order?" http://www.thinking-east.net/site/index.php?option=com_contend&task=vie&id=139.

Holm, Johan D. 1988. "Botswana: A Paternalistic Democracy," in Larry Diamond, Juan J. Linz, and Seymour Martin Lipset, eds., *Democracy in Developing Countries. Vol. 2. Africa*. Boulder: Lynne Rienner Publishers.

Hong, Do Manh. 2006. "Vietnam: Economic Development and Improvement of Living Standard," in Takashi Inoguchi, Akihito Tanaka, Shigeto Sonoda, and Timur Dadabaev, eds., *Human Beliefs and Values in Striding Asia*. Japan: Akashi Shoten.

Howells, W. W. 1992. "The dispersion of modern humans," in Steve Jones, Robert Martin, and David Pilbeam, eds., *The Cambridge Encyclopedia of Human Evolution*. Cambridge: University Press.

Hudson-Rodd, Nancy. 2004. "Housing, Land, and Property Rights in Burma." Center for Housing, Rights, and Evictions (COHRE), COHRE Asia and Pacific Programme, Collingwood, Victoria, Australia.

Human Development Report. See UNDP.

Huntington, Samuel P. 1996. *The Clash of Civilizations: Remaking of World Order*. New York: Touchstone.

Hyun, Daesong. 2006. "Korea: Lives and Civic Virtue in Transition," in Takashi Inoguchi, Akihito Tanaka, Shigeto Sonoda, and Timur Dadabaev, eds. *Human Beliefs and Values in Striding Asia*. Japan: Akashi Shoten.

IDEA (International Institute for Democracy and Electoral Assistance). 2006. *Global Database of Quotas for Women*. http://www.quotaproject.org/displayCountry.cfm?CountryCode.

"Information on implementation of land and agrarian reform in the Kyrgyz Republic." 2000. Kyrgyzstan Land Reform Project, *Land Reform Newsletter*, Issue 8, November.

Inglehart, Ronald. 2000. "Culture and Democracy," in Laurence E. Harrison and Samuel P. Huntington, eds. *Culture Matters: How Values Shape Human Progress*. New York: Basic Books.

Inglehart, Ronald, and Christian Welzel. 2005. *Modernization, Cultural Change, and Democracy: The Human Development Sequence*. Cambridge: Cambridge University Press.

Inoguchi, Takashi. 2006. "Forward: Comparative Asian Political Culture," *Political Science in Asia* 2, 1: 5–10.

Inter-Parliamentary Union. 2000–2006. *Chronicle of Parliamentary Elections*, Geneva.

Ippolito, Gabriela. 2004. "In Search of a New Paradigm: Quality of Democracy," in Guillermo O'Donnell, Jorge Vargas Cullell, and Osvaldo M. Iazzetta, eds. *The Quality of Democracy: Theory and Applications*. Notre Dame, Indiana: University of Notre Dame Press.

"Israel Lands: Privatization or National Ownership?" 2006. Jewish Virtual Library. A Division of The American-Israeli Cooperative Enterprise. http://www.jewishvirtuallibrary.org/jsource/Society_&_Culture/land.html.

Itzkoff, Seymour W. 2000. *The Inevitable Domination by Man: An Evolutionary Detective Story*. Ashfield, Massachusetts: Paideia Publishers.

Jacoby, Russell, and Naomi Glauberman, 1995. *The Bell Curve Debate*. New York: Random House.

Jaggers, K., and T.R. Gurr. 1995. "Tracking Democracy's Third Wave with Polity III Data." *Journal of Peace Research* 32: 469–482.

"Jamaica—Profile in Agriculture." 2006. Jamaica Sustainable Development Network. http://www.jsdnp.org.jm/susAgriculture-agricJA.htm.

Jensen, Arthur R. 1998. *The g Factor: The Science of Mental Ability*. Westport, Connecticut: Praeger.

Johnson, John J. 1964. *The Military and Society in Latin America*. Stanford, California: Stanford University Press.

Jones, Steve. 1992a. "Genetic diversity in humans," in Steve Jones, Robert Martin, and David Pilbeam, eds, *The Cambridge Encyclopedia of Human Evolution.* Cambridge: Cambridge University Press.

Jones, Steve. 1992b. "Natural selection in humans," in Steve Jones, Robert Martin and David Pilbeam, eds, *The Cambridge Encyclopedia of Human Evolution.* Cambridge: Cambridge University Press.

Joseph, Richard. 2003. "Africa: States in Crisis," *Journal of Democracy* 14, 3: 159–170.

Kaase, Max, ed. 1986. *Politische Wissenschaft und politische Ordnung: Analysen zu Theorie und Empirie demokratischer Regierungsweise.* Opladen: Westdeutscher Verlag.

Kanazawa, Satoshi. 2007. "Temperature and evolutionary novelty as forces behind the the evolution of general intelligence," *Intelligence,* article in press. Available online at http://www.sciencedirect.com.

Kantor, Harry. 1969. *Patterns of Politics and Political Systems in Latin America.* Chicago: Rand McNally & Company.

Karatnycky, A., A. Motyl, and A. Schnetzer, eds. 2001. *Nations in Transit 2001.* New Brunswick. N.J.: Transaction Publishers.

Karatnycky, Adrian, Aili Piano, and Arch Puddington, eds. 2003. *Freedom in the World: The Annual Survey of Political Rights and Civil Liberties 2002.* New York: Freedom House.

Karl, Terry Lynn. 2004. "Latin America: Virtuous or Perverse Cycle," in Guillermo O'Donnell, Jorge Vargas Cullell, and Osvaldo M. Iazzetta, eds. *The Quality of Democracy: Theory and Applications.* Notre Dame, Indiana: University of Notre Dame Press.

Karvonen, Lauri, and Carsten Anckar. 2002. "Party Systems and Democratization: A Comparative Study of the Third World," *Democratization* 9, 3: 11–29.

Karvonen, Lauri, and Stein Kuhnle, eds. 2001. *Party Systems and Voter Alignments Revisited.* London and New York: Routledge.

Kaushik, P. D. 1996. *New Dimensions of Government and Politics of Nepal.* New Delhi: South Asian Publishers. *Keesing's Record of World Events.* 2000–2007.

Keman, Hans. 2004. "Polyarchy and Defected Democracy Around the World: A Research Note," *Acta Politica* 39: 297–313.

Khamchoo, Chaiwat, and Aaron Stern. 2006. "Thailand: Democracy and the Power of Popular Leader," in Takashi Inoguchi, Akihito Tanaka, Shigeto Sonoda, and Timur Dadabaev, eds. *Human Beliefs and Values in Striding Asia.* Japan: Akashi Shoten.

Khong, Cho-oon. 1999. "Singapore," in Ian Marsh, Jean Blondel, and Takashi Inoguchi, eds., *Democracy, Governance, and Economic Performance: East and Southeast Asia*. Tokyo: United Nations University Press.

Kokole, Omari H., and Ali A. Mazrui. 1988. "Uganda: The Dual Policy and the Plural Society," in Larry Diamond, Juan J. Linz, and Seymour Martin Lipset, eds., *Democracy in Developing Countries. Vol. 2. Africa*. Boulder: Lynne Rienner Publishers.

Korany, Bahgat, Rex Brynen, and Paul Noble, eds. 1998. *Political Liberalization and Democratization in the Arab World. Volume 2, Comparative Experiences*. Boulder: Lynne Rienner Publishers.

Krastev, Ivan. 2002. "The Balkans: Democracy without Choices," *Journal of Democracy* 13, 3: 39–53.

Kumar, Satish. 1978. *The New Pakistan*. New Delhi: Vikas Publishing House.

Kurian, G. T. 1987. *Encyclopedia of the Third World*, Volumes 1–3, 3rd edition. New York: Facts on File.

Kurian, G. T. 1992. *Encyclopedia of the Third World*, Volumes 1–3, 4th edition. New York: Facts on File.

Kurian, Rency. 2004. *Antecedents and Correlates of Elite: A Socio-Political Analysis*. Delhi: Devika Publications.

Lagos, Marta. 2003. "A Road with No Return?" *Journal of Democracy* 14, 2:163–173.

Lambert, Jacques. 1969. *Latin America: Social Structures and Political Institutions*. Berkeley: University of California Press.

"Land Redistribution in Southern Africa: South Africa Programs." 2006. OnlineNewsHour. http://www.pbs.org/newshour/bb/africa/land/gp_safrica.htm.

Land Tenure Center (LTC). 1979. *Land Concentration in the Third World: Statistics on Number and Area of Farms Classified by Size of Farms*. No. 28, Training and Methods Series. Madison: University of Wisconsin.

"Land tenure in Mali today." 2006. Spot helps resolve land tenure issues. http://ceos.fr:8100/cdrom-00b/ceos1/casestud/mali/mali.htm.

Larbi, W. O., E. Odoi-Yemo, and L. Darko. 2006. "Developing a Geographic Information System for Land Management in Ghana." http://www.gtz.de/orboden/capetown/cape41.htm.

Lehohla, Pali. 2004. "Agricultural census ends data drought." http://www.statssa.gov.za/news_archive/16sep2004_1.asp.

Lerman, Zwi. 1996. "Land Reform and Private Farms in Armenia: 1996 Status." EC4NR Agriculture Policy Note No. 8. World Bank, Washington,

D.C., November.

Levitsky, Steven, and Lucan A. Way. 2002. "The Rise of Competitive Authoritarianism," *Journal of Democracy* 13, 2: 51–65.

Lewis, Peter M. 2003. "Nigeria: Elections in a Fragile Regime," *Journal of Democracy* 14, 3: 131–144.

"Liberia Country Study. Land Tenure." GlobalSecurity.org. http://www.globalsecurity.org/military/library/report/1985/liberia_3_landtenure.htm.

"Libya – Land Use and Irrigation." 2006. http://countrystudies.us/libya/63.htm.

Lindberg, Staffan I. 2006. *Democracy and Elections in Africa.* Baltimore: Johns Hopkins University Press.

Lindberg, Staffan I. 2006. "The Surprising Significance of African Elections," *Journal of Democracy* 17, 1: 139–151.

Lijphart, Arend. 1999. *Patterns of Democracy: Government Forms and Performance in Thirty-Six Countries.* New Haven and London: Yale University Press.

Linz, Juan J., and Alfred Stepan, eds. 1978. *The Breakdown of Democratic Regimes: Europe.* Baltimore: Johns Hopkins University Press.

Linz, Juan J., and Alfred Stepan. 1996. *Problems of Democratic Transition and Consolidation: Southern Europe, South America, and Post-Communist Europe.* Baltimore and London: Hopkins University Press.

Lipset, Seynour Martin, and Jason M. Lakin. 2004. *The Democratic Century.* Norman: University of Oklahoma Press.

"Lithuania – Economic Reforms." 2006. http://www.country-data.co,/cgi-bin/quert/r-8292.html.

Lohmar, Bryan. 2002. "The Ongoing Reform of Land Tenure Policies in China." *Agricultural Outlook,* September. Economic Research Service/USDA. http://www.ers.usda.gov/publications/agoutlook/sep2002/ao294f.pdf.

Lohmar, Bryan, and Afapi Somwaru. 2002. "Does China's Land-Tenure System Discourage Structural Adjustment?" *China's Food and Agriculture: Issues for the 21st Century/AIB-775.* http://www.ers.usda.gov/publications/aib775/aib775n.pdf.

LTC 1979. See Land Tenure Center.

Lust-Okar, Ellen. 2006. "Elections under Authoritarianism: Preliminary Lessons from Jordan," *Democratization* 13, 3: 456–471.

Lynn, Richard. 1991a. "Race differences in intelligence," *Mankind Quarterly* 31, 3: 254–296.

Lynn, Richard. 1991b. "The evolution of racial differences in intelligence," *Mankind Quarterly* 32, 1–2: 99–121.

Lynn, Richard. 1997. "Geographical variation in intelligence," in H. Nyborg, ed., *The Scientific Study of Human Nature*. Oxford: Pergamon.

Lynn, Richard. 2003. "The Geography of Intelligence," in Helmuth Nyborg, ed., *The Scientific Study of General Intelligence: Tribute to Arthur R. Jensen*. Amsterdam: Pergamon.

Lynn, Richard. 2006. *Race Differences in Intelligence: An Evolutionary Analysis*. Augusta, Georgia: Washington Summit Publishers.

Lynn, Richard. 2007. "The Evolutionary Biology of National Differences in Intelligence," *European Journal of Personality* 21: 733–734.

Lynn, Richard. 2008. *The Global Bell Curve: Race, IQ, and Inequality Worldwide*. Augusta, Georgia.: Washington Summit Publishers.

Lynn, Richard, and Tatu Vanhanen. 2002. *IQ and the Wealth of Nations*. Westport, Connecticut.: Praeger.

Lynn, Richard, and Tatu Vanhanen. 2006. *IQ and Global Inequality*. Augusta, Georgia: Washington Summit Publishers.

"Macedonia – Agriculture." 2006. Encyclopedia of the Nations, Europe. http://www.nationsencyclopedia.com/Europe/Macedonia-AGRICULTURE.html.

"Madagascar: The Debate on the Land Ownership Policy Document." 2005. http://www.cirad.fr/en/actualite/communique.php?annee=2005&id=199.

Magagula, G. T. 2006. "Land reform and agricultural production in Swaziland," http://www.unu.edu/unupress/unupbooks/80604e/80604E0i.htm.

Maghraoui, Abdeslam M. 2002. "Depolitization in Morocco," *Journal of Democracy* 13, 4: 24–32.

Mair, Peter, ed., 1990. *The West European Party System*. Oxford: OxfordUniversity Press.

Makiya, Kanan. 2003. "A Model for Post-Saddam Iraq," *Journal of Democracy* 14, 3: 5–12.

"Maldives." 2006. http://www.fao.org/docrep/003/x6900e0i.htm.

Maletta, Hector E. 2007. "Arable Land Tenure in Afghanistan in the Post-Taliban Era." *African and Asian Studies,* Vol. 6. http://ssrn.com/abstract=906669.

Mannheim, J. B., and R. C. Rich. 1986. *Empirical Political Analysis: Research Methods in Political Science*. 2nd edition. New York and London: Longman.

Manning, Carrie. 2006. "Political Elites and Democratic State-building Efforts in Bosnia and Iraq," *Democratization* 13, 5: 724–738.

Marsh, Ian, Jean Blondel, and Takashi Inoguchi, eds. 1999. *Democracy, Governance, and Economic Performance: East and Southeast Asia*. Tokyo:

United Nations University Press.

Marshall, Monty G., and Keith Jaggers. 2003. *Polity IV Project. Political Regime Characteristics and Transitions, 1800–2002.* http://www.cidcm. umd.edu/inscr/polity/.

Martz, John D. 1988. "Latin America and the Caribbean," in Robert Wesson, ed., *Democracy World Survey 1987.* Boulder: Lynne Rienner Publishers.

McCargo, Duncan, 2005. "Cambodia: Getting Away with Authoritarianism?" *Journal of Democracy* 16, 4: 98–112.

McCoy, Jennifer. 2006. "International Response to Democratic Crisis in the Americas, 1990–2005," *Democratization* 13, 5: 756–775.

McHenry, Dean, and Abdel-Fattah Mady. 2006. "A Critique of Quantitative Measures of the Degree of Democracy in Israel," *Democratization* 13, 2: 256–282.

McMillan, John. 2005. "Promoting Transparency in Angola," *Journal of Democracy* 16, 3: 155–169.

Melmed-Sanjak, Jolyne, Peter Bloch, and Robert Hanson. 1998. "Project for the analysis of land tenure and agricultural productivity in the Republic of Macedonia." Land Tenure Center Working paper 19 abstract. http://www. ies.wisc.edu/ltc/wp19.html.

Mendez, Juan E. 2004. "Fundamental Rights as a Limitation to the Democratic Principle of Majority," in Guillermo O'Donnell, Jorge Vargas Cullell, and Osvaldo M. Iazzetta, eds., *The Quality of Democracy: Theory and Applications.* Notre Dame, Indiana: University of Notre Dame Press.

Meredith, Martin. 2006. *The State of Africa: A History of Fifty Years of Independence.* London: Free Press.

Merle, Marcel, ed. 1968. *L'Afrique Noire Contemporaine.* Paris: Librairie Armand Colin.

Meteorological Office. 1983. *Tables of temperature, relative humidity, precipitation and sunshine for the world. Part IV. Africa, the Atlantic Ocean South of 35°N and the Indian Ocean.* London: Her Majesty's Stationery Office, UDC 551.582.2.

The Middle East. 2000. Ninth edition. Washington, D.C.: CQ Press, A Division of Congressional Quarterly Inc.

The Middle East and North Africa 1998. 1998. London: Europa Publications.

Mitchell, Timothy D., Mike Hulme, and Mark New. 2001. "Climate data for political areas," *Area* 34: 109–112.

Mitchell, T. D., Mike Hulme, and Mark New. 2003. "A comprehensive set of climate scenarios for Europe and the globe." http://www.cru.uea.ac.uk/-timm/cty/obs

Montesquieu. 1961 (1748). *De l'Esprit des Lois*. Texte établi avec introduction, notes et relevé de variantes par Gonzague Truc. Paris: Garnier Frères.

Montesquieu. 1989. *The Spirit of Laws*. Translated and edited by Anne M. Cohler, Basia Carolyn Miller, and Harold Samuel Stone. Cambridge: Cambridge University Press.

Mujani, Saiful, and R. William Liddle. 2004. "Politics, Islam, and Public Opinion," *Journal of Democracy* 15, 1: 109–123.

Mwenda, Andrew M. 2007. "Personalizing Power in Uganda," *Journal of Democracy* 18, 3: 23–37.

Nafziger, E. W. 1997. *The Economics of Developing Countries*. 3rd ed. Upper Saddle River, New Jersey: Prentice-Hall.

Nagle, John D., and Alison Mahr. 1999. *Democracy and Democratization: Post-Communist Europe in Comparative Perspective*. London: Sage Publications.

Nasanjargal, Darjaa. 2002. "Mongolia." World Food Summit: Five years later. http://www.fao.org/docrep/005/y4172m/rep2/mongolia.htm.

Nathan, Andrew J. 2003. "Authoritarian Resilience," *Journal of Democracy* 14, 1: 6–17.

National Development Strategy (Guyana). 1997. "Chapter 22: Land," and "Chapter 29: Agricultural Land Policy." http://www.sdnp.org.gy/nds/chapter22.html and www.guyana.org/NDS/chap29.htm.

Nawaikula, Niko. 2006. "Land Rights in Fiji – A Sad Irony," http://www.nltb.com.fj/commentary/00_05_02.html.

Niang, Thiendou. 2004. "Land tenure and family farming in Africa: With special reference to Senegal," http://www.poptel.org.uk/iied/docs/aboutiied/Key_Notes_Thiendou_Niang_Senegal.pdf.

"Nigeria: Land Use, Soils, and Land Tenure." 2006. AllRefer.com. http://reference.allrefer.com/country-guide-study/nigeria/nigeria 90.htm.

Nohlen, D,. and F. Nuscheler, eds. 1982–83. *Handbuch der Dritten Welt*. Vols 2–8. Hamburg: Hoffmann und Campe.

North Korea – Higher Education." AllRefer.com. http://reference.allrefer.com/country-guide-study/north-korea59.html.

Nothale, D. W. 2006. "Land tenure systems and agricultural production in Malawi." http://www.unu.edu/unupress/unupbooks/80604EOh.htm.

Nyborg, Helmuth. 2003a. "General Introduction: Arthur Jensen - The Man, His Friends and This Book," in Helmuth Nyborg, ed., *The Scientific Study of General Intelligence: Tribute to Arthur R. Jensen*. Amsterdam: Pergamon.

Nyborg, Helmuth, ed. 2003b. *The Scientific Study of General Intelligence: Tribute to Arthur R. Jensen*. Amsterdam: Pergamon.

O'Donnell, Guillermo. 2004. "Human Development, Human Rights, and Democracy," in Guillermo O'Donnell, Jorge Vargas Cullell, and Osvaldo M. Iazzetta, eds., *The Quality of Democracy: Theory and Applications*. Notre Dame, Indiana: University of Notre Dame Press.

O'Donnell, Guillermo, Jorge Vargas Cullell, and Osvaldo M. Iazzetta, eds. 2004. *The Quality of Democracy: Theory and Applications*. Notre Dame, Indiana: University of Notre Dame Press.

O'Donnell, Guillermo, Philippe C. Schmitter, and Laurence Whitehead, eds. 1986. *Transitions from Authoritarian Rule: Latin America*. Baltimore and London: Johns Hopkins University Press.

Olson, Steve. 2002. *Mapping Human History: Discovering the Past through our Genes*. London: Bloomsbury Publishing.

O'Neill, Tom. 2007. "Curse of the Black Gold," *National Geographic*, Vol. 211, February 2007: 88–117.

"Online News Hour—Land Redistribution in Southern Africa: Namibia Programs." 2006. http://www.pbs.org/newshour/bb/africa/land/gp_namibia.html.

Oppenheimer, Stephen. 2003. *Out of Eden: The Peopling of the World*. London: Constable.

Osskó, András, and Robert Sebestyén. 2005. "Land Consolidation in Hungary." Regional Workshop, "Land consolidation and territorial organization," 7–10 March, Prague/Czech Republic. http://www.fao.org/Regional/seur/events/landcons/docs/Hungary.

Owoeye, Yinka. 2006. "Land ownership in Nigeria," http://www.redmaf.com/pdf/landownership.pdf.

Parker, Philip. 2000. *Physioeconomics: The Basis for Long-Run Economic Growth*. Cambridge, Massachusetts: The MIT Press.

Parmanand. 1988. *Political Development in South Asia*. New Delhi: Sterling Publishers.

Pasquino, Gianfranco. 1986. "The Demise of the First Fascist Regime and Italy's Transition to Democracy," in Guillermo O'Donnell, Philippe C. Schmitter, and Laurence Whitehead, eds., *Transitions from Authoritarian Rule: Southern Europe*. Baltimore and London: Johns Hopkins University Press.

Pasquino, Gianfranco. 2005. "The Quality of Democracy," Lectures One and Two. Centre for the Study of Democratic Government, University of Oxford. government.politics.ox.ac.uk.

Pepinsky, Thomas B. 2007. "Malaysia: Turnover without Change," *Journal of Democracy* 18, 1: 113–127.

Peterson, Dave. 2006. "Burundi's Transitions: A Beacon for Central Africa," *Journal of Democracy* 17, 1: 125–131.

Phadnis, Urmila, S. D. Muni, and Kalim Bahadur, eds. 1986. *Domestic Conflicts in South Asia*. New Delhi: South Asian Publishers.

Philip's Encyclopedic World Atlas. 2000. Comprehensive edition, in association with the Royal Geographical Society. London: George Philip Limited.

Plomin, Robert. 2003. "Molecular Genetics and *g*," in Helmuth Nyborg, ed., *The Scientific Study of General Intelligence: Tribute to Arthur R. Jensen*. Amsterdam: Pergamon.

Polity IV Project. See Marshall and Jaggers.

Polonsky, Antony. 1975. *The Little Dictators: The History of Eastern Europe since 1918*. London and Boston: Routledge & Kegan Paul.

Posada-Carbó, Eduardo. 2006. "Colombia Hews to the Path of Change," *Journal of Democracy* 17, 4: 8–94.

Posner, Daniel N., and Daniel J. Young. 2007. "The Institutionalization of Political Power in Africa," *Jourbal of Democracy* 18, 3: 126–140.

Potocki, Rodger. 2002. "Dark Days in Belarus," *Journal of Democracy* 13, 4: 142–156.

Powell, G. Bingham. 2003. "On Democratic Responsiveness." Center on Democracy, Development, and the Rule of Law, Stanford Institute on International Studies. cddrl.stanford.edu/events/quality_of_democracy/.

Praust, R. E. 2006. "Family Farms and Shadow Economy of the Russian Agrarian Sector." www.ies.wisc.edu/ltc/live/basgolsem_ch3.pdf.

Przeworski, Adam, Michael E. Alvarez, José Antonio Cheibub, and Fernando Limongi. 2000. *Democracy and Development: Political Institutions and Well-Being in the World, 1950–1990*. Cambridge: Cambridge University Press.

Puerta, Ricardo A., and José Alvarez. 2006. "Organization and Performance of Cuban Agriculture at Different Levels of State Intervention." *Cuba in Transition*, Vol. 3. lanic.utexas.edu/la/cb/cuba/acse/cuba3/puerta1.html.

Puglisi, Rosario. 2003. "The Rise of the Ukrainian Oligarchs," *Democratization* 10, 3: 99–123.

"Qatar—Agriculture and Fishing." 2006. countrystudies.us/persian-gulf-states/76.htm.

Radnitz, Scott. 2006. "What Really Happened in Kyrgyzstan?" *Journal of Democracy* 17, 2: 132–146.

Rakner, Lise, and Lars Svåsand. 2005. "Stuck in Transition: Electoral Processes in Zambia 1991–2001," *Democratization* 12, 1: 85–105.

Randall, Vicky, and Lars Svåsand. 2002. "Political Parties and Democratic

Consolidation in Africa," *Democratization* 9, 3: 30–52.

Rao, V. Bhaskara, and V. Venkateswarlu. 1987. *Parliamentary Democracy in India*. New Delhi: Mittal Publications.

Reilly, Benjamin. 2006. *Democracy and Diversity: Political Engineering in Asia-Pacific*. Oxford: Oxford University Press.

Reynolds, Andrew. 2006. "The Curious Case of Afghanistan," *Journal of Democracy* 17, 2: 104–117.

Rindermann, Heiner. 2007. "The *g*-Factor of International Cognitive Ability Comparisons: The Homogeneity of Results in PISA, TIMSS, PIRLS and IQ-Tests Across Nations," *European Journal of Personality* 21: 667–706. Published online in Wiley InterScience (http://www.interscience.wiley.com).

Ritter, Horst. 1981. *Humangenetik*. Basel: Herder Freiburg.

Robinson, Simon. 2007. "Inside Congo," *Time*, January 29: 26–31.

Rose, Richard. 2002. "How Muslims View Democracy: Evidence from Central Asia," *Journal of Democracy* 13, 4: 102–111.

Rose, Steven, Leon J. Kamin, and R. C. Lewontin. 1984. *Not in Our Genes: Biology, Ideology and Human Nature*. Harmondsworth, England: Penguin Books.

Rowen, Henry S. 2007. "When Will the Chinese People Be Free?" *Journal of Democracy* 18, 3: 38–52.

Rueschemeyer, Dietrich. 2003. "On Democratic Equality." Center on Democracy, Development, and the Rule of Law, Stanford Institute on International Studies. http://www.cddrl.stanford.edu/events/quality_of_democracy/.

Rushton, J. Philippe. 1995. *Race, Evolution, and Behavior: A Life History Perspective*. New Brunswick, New Jersey: Transaction Publishers.

Rushton, J. Philippe. 2000. *Race, Evolution, and Behavior: A Life History Perspective*. 2nd Special Abridged Edition. Port Huron, Michigan: Charles Darwin Research Institute.

Rushton, J. Philippe. 2003. "Race Differences in *g* and the 'Jensen Effect'," in Helmuth Nyborg, ed., *The Scientific Study of General Intelligence: Tribute to Arthur R. Jensen*. Amsterdam: Pergamon.

"Russia: Yeltsin's Agricultural Policies." 2007. http://www.country-data.com/cgi-bin/query/r-11451.html.

"Russian officials outline plans for first farms census in 80 years." 2006. Johnson's Russia List. http://www.cdi.org/russia/johnson/7224-8.cfm.

Rusu, Marioara, and Virgil Pamfil. 2007. "Romania cses study: Agricultural land reform and land consolidation in Romania." http://www.fao.org/REGIONAL/Seur/events/landscons/.

Safa, Oussama. 2006. "Lebanon Springs Forward," *Journal of Democracy* 17, 1: 22–37.

Sallaku, Fathardt, and Agim E. Shehu. 2007. "Land fragmentation and land consolidation in Albania," http://www.fao.org/REGIONAL/SEUR/events/landcons/.

Samuels, Richard. 2003. "Comparing Theories of Democratic Support: Lessons from Post-Communist Europe," *Democratization* 10, 2: 105–120.

Sandbakken, Camilla. 2006. "The Limits to Democracy Posed by Oil Rentier States: The Cases of Algeria, Nigeria and Libya," *Democratization* 13, 1: 135–152.

Saravanamuttu, Johan. 2006. "Malaysia: High Satisfaction and Political Conservatism," in Takashi Inoguchi, Akihito Tanaka, Shigeto Sonoda, and Timur Dadabaev, eds, *Human Beliefs and Values in Striding Asia*. Japan: Akashi Shoten.

"Saudi Arabia – Modern Agriculture in Saudi Arabia." 2006. AllRefer.com. http://reference.allrefer.com/country-guide-study/saudi-arabia/saudi-arabia76.htm.

Sazegara, Mohsen. 2005. "What Should 'We' Do Now?" *Journal of Democracy* 16, 4: 64–73.

Schaffer, Howard B. 2002. "Back and Forth in Bangladesh," *Journal of Democracy* 13, 4: 6–14.

Schmidt, Manfred G. 2000. *Demokratietheorien*. 3. Auflage. Opladen: Leske + Budrich.

Schmitter, Philippe. 2003. "Quality of Democracy: The Ambiguous Virtues of Accountability." Center on Democracy, Development, and the Rule of Law, Stanford Institute on International Studies. http://cddrl.stanford.edu/events/quality_of_democracy/.

Schoenian, Susan. 2001. "A Forgotten Country: Moldova," http://sheepandgoat.com/articles/Moldova.html.

Schoenian, Susan. 2006. "Raising Sheep in South Kazakhstan," http://www.sheepandgoat.com/articles/kazakh.html.

Schwedler, Jillian. 2002. "Yemen's Aborted Opening," *Journal of Democracy* 13, 4: 48–55.

Seely, Jennifer C. 2005. "The Legacies of Transition Governments: Post-transition Dynamics in Benin and Togo," *Democratization* 12, 3: 357–377.

Seton-Watson, Hugh. 1964 (1956). *The East European Revolution*. Third edition. New York: Frederick A. Praeger.

Seznec, Jean-Francois. 2002. "Srirrings in Saudi Arabia," *Journal of Democracy*

13, 4: 33–40.

Sheak, Bob. 2002. "The 'Greening of Cuba' continued." *Rural Action,* January. http://www.ruralaction.org/read2jan2002.html.

Silitski, Vitali. 2005. "Preempting Democracy: The Case of Belarus," *Journal of Democracy* 16, 4: 83–97.

"Slovakia." 2006. http://www.fao.org//docrep/005/y2722e/y2722e12.htm.

Slovenian National Committee of ICID (SINDIC). 2006. "Slovenia," www.icid.org/v_slovenia.pdf.

Smucker, Glenn R., T. Anderson White, and Michael Bannister. 2000. "Land Tenure and the Adoption of Agricultural Technology in Haiti." Capri Working Paper No. 6. Washington, D.C.: International Food Policy Research Institute.

"Solomon Islands Logging." 2006. http://www.hartford-hwp.com/archives/24/005. htm.

Somit, Albert, and Steven A. Peterson. 2005. *The Failure of Democratic Nation Building: Ideology Meets Evolution.* New York: Palgrave Macmillan.

Sonoda, Shigeto. 2006. "Singapore: A Globalized Social Life under Soft Authoritarian Rule," in Takashi Inoguchi, Akihito Tanaka, Shigeto Sonoda and Timur Dadabaev, eds., *Human Beliefs and Values in Striding Asia.* Japan: Akashi Shoten.

Stanaits, Saulius. 2006. "Social, economic and demographic changes of rural areas in Lithuania," http://www.igipz.pan.pl/zpz/banski/Tom2/ERDN-t2-part03.pdf.

Stanfield, J. D. 1998. "Albania's Privatization Pause." *Land Tenure Center Newsletter* No 76. Spring: 2–7.

Stepan, Alfred. 2001. *Arguing Comparative Politics.* Oxford: Oxford University Press.

Stepan, Alfred, and Graeme B. Robertson. 2003. "An 'Arab' More Than a 'Muslim' Democracy Gap," *Journal of Democracy* 14, 3: 30–44.

Sternberger, Dolf, and Bernhard Vogel, eds., 1969. *Die Wahl der Parlamente, Band I: Europa.* Redaktion von Dieter Nohlen. Berlin: Walter de Gruyter.

Stratan, Alexandru. 2007. "Efficient functioning of the agricultural sector of Moldova: Major achievements and problems." State Agrarian University of Moldova. http://departments.agri.huji.ae.il/economics/stratan.pdf.

Stringer, Chris. 2003. "Out of Ethiopia." *Nature,* Vol. 423, 12 June: 692–694.

Suberu, Rotimi T. 2007. "Nigeria's Muddled Elections," *Journal of Democracy* 18. 4: 95–110.

"Sudan – Agriculture." 2006. http://countrystudies.us/sudan/55.htm.

Sulaiman, Hj Hamzah, and Zen-U Lucian Hotta. 2006. "Brunei: The Living Conditions, Preferences, and Concerns," in Takashi Inoguchi, Akihito Tanaka, Shigeto Sonoda, and Timur Dadabaev, eds, *Human Beliefs and Values in Striding Asia*. Japan: Akashi Shoten.

"Syria – Agriculture." 2006. http://countrystudies.us/syria/43.htm.

Szabo, Máté, ed., 1996. *The Challenge of Europeanization in the Region: East Central Europe*. Budapest: Hungarian Political Science Association.

Taleb, Nassim Nicholas. 2007. *The Black Swan: The Impact of the Highly Improbable*. New York: Random House.

Tessler, Mark, and Eleanor Gao. 2005. "Gauging Arab Support for Democracy," *Journal of Democracy* 16, 3: 83–97.

Thorheirsson, Sigurgeir. 2006. "Agriculture in Iceland," http://www.landbuna-tur.is/wgbi.nsf/key2/mhhr5ajd7s.html.

Thein, Myat. 2006. "Myanmar: Life and Well-Being from a Comparative Sociocultural Perspective," in Takashi Inoguchi, Akihito Tanaka, Shigeto Sonoda, and Timur Dadabaev, eds., *Human Beliefs and Values in Striding Asia*. Japan: Akashi Shoten.

Thirkell-White, Ben. 2006. "Political Islam and Malaysian Democracy," *Democratization* 13, 3: 421–441.

Tilly, Charles. 2007. *Democracy*. New York: Cambidge University Press.

Törhönen, Mika-Petteri. 2002. "Land Tenure in Transition: Case Uzbekistan." FIG XXII International Congress, Washington D.C., April 19–26. http://www.fig.net/pub/fig_2002/Ts7-6/TS7_6_torhonen.pdf.

Transparency International. 2007. Corruption Perception Index. http://www.transparency.orf.

Trnka, Jiri, and Jana Pivcova. 2007. "The situation of land management and reparcelling in the Czech Republic," http://www.fao.org/regional/seur/events/landcons/.

Tserendash. 2006. "Livestock and natural pasture interaction in Mongolia," http://www.cirtualcentre.org/ru/workshop/ws_01/download/Mongolia_Liv_Eng.doc.

Tulahi, Charles L., and Perpetua M. Hingi. 2006. "Agrarian reform and rural development in Tanzania." Presented at the International Conference of Agrarian Reform and Rural Development, Porto Alegre, Brazil, 7–10 Match.

"Turkmenistan—Privatization." 2006. http://www.country-data.com/cgi-bin/query/r-13870.html.

Tyndell Center for Climate Change Research (TYN CY 1.1). 2003. Data for each of the 289 countries and territories. http://www.cru.uea.ac.uk/-timm/cty/obs/TYN_CY_1_1_cty-table.html.

UNDP (United Nations Development Programme). 1999. *Human Development Report 1999*. New York: Oxford University Press.

UNDP. 2000. *Human Development Report 2000*. New York: Oxford University Press.

UNDP. 2002. *Human Development Report 2002: Deepening Democracy in a Fragmented World*. New York: Oxford University Press.

UNDP. 2004. *Human Development Report 2004: Cultural Liberty in Today's Diverse World*. New York. Oxford University Press.

UNDP. 2006. *Human Development Report 2006. Beyond scarcity: Power, Poverty and the Global Water Crisis*. New York: Palgrave Macmillan.

UNESCO. 1999. *Statistical Yearbook 1999*. 1999. Paris: Unesco Publishing and Bernan Press.

Ungar, Sanford J. 1989. *Africa: The People and Politics of an Emerging Continent*. New York: Simon & Schuster, Inc.

Un, Kheang. 2006. "Cambodia: Beliefs and Perceptions in a Postconflict Society," in Takashi Inoguchi, Akihito Tanaka, Shigeto Sonoda, and Timur Dadabaev, eds., *Human Beliefs and Values in Striding Asia*. Japan: Akashi Shoten.

"UN Report Calls for Land Ownership." 2002. http://www.uneca.org/era2002kit/era–irin.htm.

USAID, Europe and Eurasia. 2005. "Ukraine Land Titling Initiative Boosts Private Property Ownership," http://www.usaid.gov(locations/europe_eurasia/press/success/ukraine/_land_titling_initiative.html.

USAID/Kazakhstan. 2005. "Kazakhstan land administration report," http://pdf.dec.org/pdf_docs/PANDC696,pdf.

U.S. Department of Commerce, National Oceanic and Atmospheric Administration, National Environmental Satellite, Data, and Information Service, National Climatic Data Center. 1991–94. *World Weather Records 1971–1980, Volumes 3–6*. Peter M. Steurer.

Van'Beek, Ursula J., ed. 2005. *Democracy under construction: Patterns from four continents*. Bloomfield Hillas & Opladen: Barbara Budrich Publishers.

Van Cranenburgh, Oda. 2006. "Namibia: Consensus Institutions and Majoritarian Politics," *Democratization* 13, 4: 584–604. https://library.uncg.edu/depts/ref/bibs/psc/PSC350_namibia.pdf

Van de Walle, Nicholas. 2002. "Africa's Range of Regimes," *Journal of Democracy* 13, 2: 66–80.

Vanhanen, Tatu. 1971. *Dependence of Power on Resources: A Comparative*

Study of 114 States in the 1960s. Publications 11. Jyväskylä: University of Jyväskylä, Institute of Social Sciences.

Vanhanen, Tatu. 1979. *Power and the Means of Power: A Study of 119 Asian, European, American, and African States, 1850–1975.* Ann Arbor: Published for Center for the Study of Developing Societies, Delhi, by University Microfils International.

Vanhanen, Tatu. 1984. *The Emergence of Democracy: A Comparative Study of 119 States, 1850–1979.* Commentationes Scientiarum Socialum 24. Helsinki: The Finnish Society of Sciences and Letters.

Vanhanen, Tatu. 1990. *A Process of Democratization: A Comparative Study of 147 States, 1980–88.* New York: Crane Russak.

Vanhanen, Tatu. 1997. *Prospects of Democracy. A Study of 172 Countries.* London and New York: Routledge.

Vanhanen, Tatu. 2003. *Democratization: A Comparative Analysis of 170 Countries.* London and New York: Routledge.

Vardanyan, Manuk, and Vahagn Grigoryan. 2007. "Rural Land Market in Armenia: Formation Peculiarities and Development Trends." Food and Agriculture Organization of the United Nations and Slovak University of Agriculture, Nitra.

Viscidi, Lisa. 2004. "Land Reform and Conflict in Guatemala," http://www.counterpunch.org/viscidi09082004.htm.

Volpi, Frédéric. 2006. "Algeria's Pseudo-Democratic Politics: Lessons for Democratization in the Middle East," *Democratization* 13, 3: 442–455.

Volpi, Frédéric, and Francesco Cavatorta. 2006. "Forgetting Democratization? Recasting Power and Authority in a Plural Muslim World," *Democratization* 13, 3: 363–372.

Wade, Nicholas. 2006. *Before the Dawn. Recovering the Lost History of Our Ancestors.* New York: Penguin Press.

Wangchuk, Tashi. 2006. "Change in the land use system in Bhutan: Ecology, history, culture, and power." Department of Forestry Services, Ministry of Agriculture. http://www.thdl.org/texts/reprints/.

Webber, Douglas. 2006. "A Consolidated Patrimonial Democracy? Democratization in Post-Suharto Indonesia," *Democratization* 13, 3: 396–420.

Weiss, Meredith L. 2007. "What a Little Democracy Can Do: Comparing Trajectories of Reform in Malaysia and Indonesia," *Democratization* 14, 1: 26–43.

Wells, Spencer. 2003. *The Journey of Man: A Genetic Odyssey.* London: Penguin Books.

Welzel, Christian. 2007. "Are Levels of Democracy Affected by Mass Attitudes? Testing Attainment and Sustainment Effects on Democracy," *International Political Science Review* 28, 4: 397–424.

Wiarda, Howard J. and Harvey G. Kline, eds., 1996. *Latin American Politics and Development.* Boulder: Westview Press.

Wiley, Liz Alden. 2003. "Land rights in crisis: Restoring tenure security in Afghanistan."AfghanistanResearchandEvaluationUnit.http://www.reliefweb. int/rw/rwb.nsf/AllDocsByUNID/4accf9d78aaba09cc1256d270042cf16.

Williams, Mary Wilhelmine. 1930. *The People and Politics of Latin America.* Boston: Ginn and Company.

WMO No. 847. See World Meteorological Organization.

World Atlas of Agriculture. 1969–1976. Volume 1. Europe, USSR, Asia Minor (1969); Volume 2. Asia and Oceania (1970); Volume 3. Americas (1970); Volume 4. Africa (1976). Committee for the World Atlas of Agriculture. Novara: Instituto Geografico De Agostini.

World Bank. 2002–2006. *World Development Report.* New York: Oxford University Press.

World Bank. 2004–2006. *World Development Indicators.* Washington, D.C.: World Bank.

World Directory of Minorities. 1997. Edited by Minority Rights Group. London: Minority Rights Group International.

World Factbook. See Central Intelligence Agency.

World Guide: Global Reference, Country by Country. 2007. 11th edition. Oxford: New Internationalist Publications.

World Meteorological Organization. (WMO) 1971. *Climatological Normals (CLINO) for Climate and Climate Ship Stations for the Period 1931–1960.* Geneva: WMO/OMM, No. 117.TP.52.

World Meteorological Organization. (WMO) (no date). *Climatological Normals (CLINO) for the period 1961–1990.* Geneva: WMO No. 847.

World Weather Records, 1971–1980. See U.S. Department of Commerce.

Woronowycz, Roman. 1997. "With state-owned collective farms now gone, Ukraine seeks to complete privatization of land." *The Ukrainian Weekly,* Vol. LXV, No. 49, December 7. http://www.ukrweekly.com/ Archive/1997/499702.shtml.

Yu-Jose, Lydia N. 2006. "Philippines: Political Mood and Socioeconomic Timbre," in Takashi Inoguchi, Akihito Tanaka, Shigeto Sonoda, and Timur Dadabaev, eds., *Human Beliefs and Values in Striding Asia.* Japan: Akashi Shoten.

Name Index

Subject Index

Biographical Information

Tatu Vanhanen is Emeritus Professor of Political Science of the University of Tampere, Finland, and a visiting researcher at the department of Political Science, University of Helsinki. He studied at the University of Tampere and became Doctor of Social Sciences in 1968. Before his academic career he worked in the 1960s as the chief of information and research department of the Agrarian/Center Party, Helsinki. He has held positions at the University of Jyväskylä (1969–72), the Academy on Finland (1972–74), and the University of Tampere (Associated Professor of Political Science) in 1974–92. His main works have been on the comparative study of democratization, on ethnic conflict and violence, and on the application of evolutionary ideas to the study of politics and human conditions. His latest books include *Prospects of Democracy: A study of 172 countries* (1997), *Ethnic Conflicts Explained by Ethnic Nepotism* (1999), (jointly with Yrjö Agmavaara) *Geenien tulo yhteiskuntatieteisiin* (=the coming of genes to social sciences) (2001), (jointly with Richard Lynn) *IQ and the Wealth of Nations* (2002), *Democratization: A comparative analysis of 170 countries* (2003), (jointly with Richard Lynn) *IQ and Global Inequality* (2006), and *Globaalit ongelmat* (=global problems) (2008).